Community in the
Digital Age

Community in the Digital Age

Philosophy and Practice

Edited by
Andrew Feenberg and Darin Barney

ROWMAN & LITTLEFIELD PUBLISHERS, INC.
Lanham • *Boulder* • *New York* • *Toronto* • *Oxford*

ROWMAN & LITTLEFIELD PUBLISHERS, INC.

Published in the United States of America
by Rowman & Littlefield Publishers, Inc.
A wholly owned subsidary of The Rowman & Littlefield Publishing Group, Inc.
4501 Forbes Boulevard, Suite 200, Lanham, Maryland 20706
www.rowmanlittlefield.com

PO Box 317
Oxford
OX2 9RU, UK

British Library Cataloguing in Publication Information Available

Library of Congress Cataloging-in-Publication Data

Community in the digital age: philosophy and practice/edited by Andrew Feenberg
and Darin Barney.
        p. cm.
Includes bibliographical references and index.
    ISBN 0-7425-2958-4 (cloth: alk. paper) — ISBN 0-7425-2959-2 (pbk.: alk. paper)
    1. Electronic villages (Computer networks) 2. Cyberspace. 3. Internet—Social
aspects. I. Feenberg, Andrew. II. Barney, Darin David, 1966-
    TK5105.83.C658 2004
    303.48'33—dc22

                                                                2004006821

Printed in the United States of America

♾™ The paper used in this publication meets the minimum requirements of
American National Standard for Information Sciences—Permanence of Paper
for Printed Library Materials, ANSI/NISO Z39.48-1992.

Contents

Preface

Which way the Internet? The virtual world has undergone so many changes in its brief existence no one can predict its future with confidence. The first electronic communitarians were mainly computer hobbyists. For a brief moment, role-playing games looked like the wave of the future. "Pushing" information and advertising on users had its innings, followed by the excitement over online auctioning, pornography, and music file swapping. With each transformation, the Internet grows more complex: with new applications add new practices, often hybridizing, but seldom eclipsing established ones. Meanwhile, against the noisy background of commercialization, tens of millions of users quietly exchange e-mail and participate in something they call "online communities." The possibilities appear endless, from political discussion groups to self-help forums for medical patients, from countercultural fan clubs to antiglobalization movements, from college courses to extended family forums.

What do these diverse possibilities mean for human communities and political practices? The unfolding Internet and related technologies have provided fertile ground for serious research and intense philosophical argument, but the evidence is hard to interpret, the arguments are complex, and the experts disagree. Some compare the Internet with early television and see it falling under commercial control as a new kind of broadcast medium. Others are impressed by the vitality of online community and argue that the Internet will fundamentally alter our social and public life. For better or for worse? This too is in question as debate swirls around the consequences for human relations of a powerful virtual supplement to face-to-face encounter.

These debates form the substance of *Community in the Digital Age: Philosophy and Practice*. In the chapters that follow, we set out to provide a forum for disagreement amongst some of the leading North American social scientists and philosophers concerned with the social and political implications of this new technology. We have tried to avoid proselytizing for a single point of view. The result is a display of provocative argument on all sides of the question of the Internet, community, and democracy by a collection of scholars whose approaches to these questions are as varied as they are engaged.

Philosophers argue over whether the Internet will enhance or diminish public life. Most agree that television has been bad for democracy. Is the Internet the antidote to broadcasting that can reinvigorate public life? Or will it fragment society by enabling citizens to associate only with like-minded others? Social researchers look to the practice of online community for insight into our evolving social life. As suburbanization and the breakdown of the extended family and neighborhood isolate individuals more and more, the Internet appears as a possible corrective. Are virtual communities "real" enough to support the kind of personal commitment and growth we associate with community life, or are they fragile and ultimately unsatisfying substitutes for human interaction?

We invite you to examine these questions, informed by both philosophy and practice, with the thinkers we have gathered here. The genesis of this book was a lively conference held in 2002 at Harvey Mudd College, where we shared the Hixon/Riggs Visiting Professorship in Science Technology and Society. Most of the chapters that follow were debated at this forum; others were solicited for the purposes of this volume. Many people at Harvey Mudd contributed to the stimulating and supportive environment from which this book emerged. In particular, we would like to thank Tad Beckman, Richard Olson, Sheldon Wettack, Jeff Groves, Holly Hauck, Hank Riggs, and Adelaide Hixon for their support of this endeavor. We would also like to thank Brenda Hadenfeldt, Pamela Anderson, Sami Asiri, Sandra Parris, Jenn Nemec, and Carrie Obry for their assistance in the preparation of the manuscript. Finally, we would like to acknowledge the remarkable science and engineering students of Harvey Mudd College—this book is dedicated to the humanist in all of them.

Andrew Feenberg, Vancouver, British Columbia
Darin Barney, Ottawa, Ontario
November 2003

1

Consumers or Citizens?
The Online Community Debate

Andrew Feenberg and Maria Bakardjieva

INTRODUCTION

Unlike broadcast media, computer networks are not merely additional voices heard in everyday life. Computers construct a virtual social world with remarkable similarities to the world of face-to-face communication. Users establish social relations in this virtual world and undergo experiences that are significant to their personal development. Two models for this virtual world have emerged since the mid 1980s when networking first reached a moderately large user base. We will label them "the consumption model" and "the community model."

The consumption model is the one that is in the news. It originated in early efforts to put research centers, libraries, and other informational resources online. These applications offer a limited set of options to users who interact individually with the software for a narrow and well-defined purpose: searching and retrieving information. As more and more middle-class users went online, it dawned on businesses that techniques for handling information could be adapted to sales. The conceptual step from information retrieval to retrieval of goods and services was easy to make. High speeds of transmission and point-and-click interfaces made the Internet a success as a global electronic mall. The population visiting this "space" consists of free, active consumers viewing, picking, and clicking their way to goods. Users scarcely talk to each other (as in traditional brick-and-mortar commercial spaces), and never see or sense each other's presence. Privacy, anonymity, reliability, speed, and visual appeal are desired properties of this virtual space, mobilizing armies of designers in search of competitive technical solutions.

1

Despite the excitement generated by these commercial applications, the ancient practice of human communication occupies more users of computer networks more of the time. In the early days of networking, communication was in fact the main reason to go online. Rhetoric specific to the online community emerged from these early experiences and still shapes our image of the Internet. As a result, we expect more of the medium than only a consumer experience.

Community, the scene in which a large share of human development occurs, is a fundamental human value. Amitai Etzioni offers the following definition: "Communities are social entities that have two elements. One, a web of affect-laden relationships among a group of individuals, relationships that often crisscross and reinforce one another. . . . The other, a measure of commitment to a set of shared values, norms, and meanings, and a shared history and identity—in short, to a particular culture."[1] Of course community, even in this strong sense, is not exclusive. Individuals can belong to more than one, but each will have an inner life of some sort in which conversation proceeds on the basis of many shared assumptions.

By "online community" we mean relatively stable, long-term online group associations mediated by the Internet or a similar network. Because the concept of community is so morally charged, the community model of the Internet holds a promise with profound ethical implications. But there is no consensus about whether or not the technology can actually support community. Unlike the consumption model of the Internet, the success or failure of online community has no easy measure, no dollars and cents return and there is no NASDAQ quote to still doubts and settle debates. Whether the Internet contributes to community or undermines it remains an open question. This book addresses the controversies that surround claims about online community. It stages the debate through contributions by philosophers and social scientists with widely different perspectives and arguments. This introductory chapter frames the debate and at the same time intervenes in it.

There is a connection between the ideal of community and traditional themes of American political philosophy, so the debate over online community is fraught with political significance. Our hopes for the Internet reflect the intellectual heritage of John Dewey, who saw community as connected to participation, commonness, and shared beliefs, and hence as inherently democratic: "Regarded as an idea, democracy is not an alternative to other principles of associated life. It is the idea of community life itself."[2] Dewey believed democracy was threatened by technology to the extent that public issues were no longer easily localized in face-to-face contexts such as towns or villages. He called for a "great community" that would be equal to the challenge of modern technology.[3]

In recent years we have in fact seen increasing public debate about new issues involving technology in relation to the environment, medicine, and education, as well as the familiar problems of food purity, automation, job security, and worker health and safety. To the extent that the demands of lay actors gain influence in these domains, the scope of democratic public life expands to include technology. We call this process "democratic rationalization" in a sense defined below. The Internet opens new struggles between contesting visions of the future. In this chapter, we explore dimensions of virtual community that relate to these broader questions of human agency and democratic process in the technical sphere. We argue that imposing the community model of the Internet is a political intervention in a society such as ours in which technology builds the scaffolding of social life. Part III of this book contains a number of contributions to the debate on the democratic potential of the Internet.[4]

Why, it may be asked, does it matter which model of the Internet prevails? Won't the Internet continue to serve a variety of different interests in any case? It should become clear in the course of the discussion how we answer this question. Briefly, the issue concerns the emergence of a socially accepted definition of the technology. Technologies are often created with no single clear and stable meaning in the public eye. Television, for example, began as many things, a surveillance system, an educational medium, an entertainment medium, a source of political information and propaganda. By the mid 1950s, it was defined by its entertainment function with momentous consequences for regulation and technical design. It is not that the other applications disappeared, but they no longer determined public perception and the main emphasis of the technical evolution of the mature technology. Something similar seems likely to happen to the Internet in the years to come. The question thus concerns whether the constraints that shape its design as it matures will favor commercial or community applications.

We start our inquiry with a brief excursion into the theoretical debate on virtual community. This debate has centered on the possibility of true community online, a possibility that inspired the creators of the new medium but is viewed with skepticism by many critical observers today. We argue that the participants in this debate generalize from particular features of systems and software prevalent at different stages in the development of computer networking to conclusions assumed applicable to computer-mediated communication as such. The debate so far has not taken into account the results of empirical studies that show the importance of user agency in the shaping of online community. Constructivist technology studies provide a theoretical framework for generalizing from these empirical studies and open larger questions of democratic intervention into the evolution of the Internet.[5] We conclude that its current design and use are not the last word on computer networking. Rather, we are dealing with an unfinished and flexible technology still far from stabilization and maturity. Instead of emitting final judgments on the Internet, we should be reshaping it to better support community activities and values.

Rather than debating the possibility of online community, research should focus instead on how to design community-friendly networks. In the concluding sections of this chapter, we review several important terrains of online community activity and research where we believe the future of the Internet is being decided.

THE ETHICS OF ONLINE COMMUNITY

As noted above, the concept of community is normatively charged. Its usual formulations appear to confound prescription and description. The researcher's impulse is to flee the confusion in the search for well-ordered empirical concepts. Nevertheless, there is such a thing as community and it is no illusion that people relate to it on normative terms. One cannot be an observer only; one is also always a participant in some community and as such engaged at the ethical level. It ought to be possible to learn more about such engagements and their technical conditions in the online world.

How do users appropriate the virtual space of the computer network as an environment for community life? What software features facilitate or obstruct this process? These are the questions that must be addressed in validating the notion of online community. We do not want to bend the concept of community drastically to embrace any and all virtual sociability, as some Internet enthusiasts do. Rather, we will use the word in its customary sense to refer to fairly stable groups with a shared identity of some sort. Not all nor even most online interaction conforms to our concept of community, but we will argue that where groups seek community, they find the means to create it and use the technology to their purposes despite the various obstacles identified by critics of networking.

To make our case, we apply both sociological and ethical concepts of community that can be tested against the experiences of groups interacting online. Earlier work on MUDs (Multiple-User Domains) has illustrated that ethical conflict in these virtual worlds can precipitate design changes intended to silence or banish disruptive users and uses of the system.[6] We hope to identify a variety of relationships between ethical norms on one hand and system features on the other.

The pioneers of the early public networks back in the 1980s faced a very different virtual world from the one we encounter on the Internet today. Its structure and purpose were not given in advance. It was not ready-made for users to enter as they do a room in a building, which bears evidence of its purpose in the design of the space, furniture, walls, and lighting. Instead, users shared a blank screen with no signposts to guide them. They had to work together to define the online world they inhabited by imposing a *communication model* on the emptiness of cyberspace. They might define their online world as a meeting, a conference, a work team, a class, an information exchange among hobbyists or medical patients, and so on. But they could only do so by consensus, by declaring their shared space to be the receptacle of their intentions.

The performative establishment of such communication models continues today in online settings such as newsgroups and computer conferences. It is a generically new type of social act in which users creatively invent the computer as a medium, not necessarily confined to the functions embodied in the technology by its designers, nor simply reproducing practices originating in their face-to-face experience.[7] Online communities form through the establishment of a communication model adapted from face-to-face community, transforming computer networks into an environment within which a way of life can be elaborated. What is the quality of those communities and their way of life?

Sociology and philosophy propose five attributes of community with parallels in the online world. They are: 1) identification with symbols and ritual practices; 2) acceptance of common rules; 3) mutual aid; 4) mutual respect; 5) authentic communication. Each of these attributes has a long history in the study of community and few would deny that they are useful starting points for reflection and research. The emphasis on symbols and rituals in much anthropology is complemented by the theory of rule-governed behavior in Peter Winch's influential Wittgensteinian reading of community.[8] Marcel Mauss gave an early account of mutual aid through nonmarket exchanges and gift giving, an approach that continues in the work of Pierre Bourdieu.[9] Mutual respect is a common sense attribute of community. There is some relevant theory in Goffman.[10] Habermas's communication theory offers yet another perspective that highlights the pursuit of mutual understanding in the lifeworld, as opposed to strategic manipulation of the other.[11]

Each of these sociological attributes of community is associated with specific virtues, ethical commitments that sustain community. The identification with symbols requires *loyalty* and *respect* from community members. Obedience to common rules requires *self-control*. Mutual aid implies a world in which generosity is justified by a basic commitment to *fairness* on all sides. Mutual respect requires *civility*. And authentic communication can only take place where a certain degree of *sincerity, truthfulness*, and *tolerance* for others is present. We might call these eight ethical attributes "the virtues of community." Of course they are not universally practiced in real communities, but they must have sufficient weight to sustain the long-term commitments and sacrifices community life demands. Sanctions generally play a role in maintaining an acceptable level of community behavior.

How realistic is it to expect these virtues to manifest themselves in cyberspace to the extent they do in the "real" world? In chapter 9, Yumiko Nara and Tetsuji Iseda report here on their suggestive study of online ethical behavior.[12]

They conducted survey research in Singapore, Japan, and the United States, asking their respondents to compare their own online and offline ethics. One might suppose that the enormous difference in the structure of the two environments would have a corresponding impact on ethical attitudes and choices, but in fact the study found relatively small differences. The authors conclude that personality is a far more powerful determinant of ethical behavior than technology. If Nara and Iseda are right, then insofar as community is possible at all, it should be possible online, sustained by the virtues of community identified here.

Despite this reassuring conclusion, the virtues of community do not flourish equally in all environments. Without yielding to technological determinism, one can certainly observe differences in the effects of technical conditions on the ethical potential of groups of individuals. This shows up to some degree in Nara and Iseda's discovery of the negative effect of anonymity on behavior. Although the individual effect is small, the socially disruptive consequences of anonymity are obvious on the Internet. Other technical conditions for the widespread commitment to the virtues of community can be identified, such as access to the group's past. We will discuss these in more detail in the next section.

THE DEBATE OVER VIRTUAL COMMUNITY

In this section, we review the different visions of online communication of early enthusiasts, critics, and postmodern theorists. These are the visions that shape public discourse on the Internet. We do not hold these positions ourselves, but attempt to go beyond them to a new and more empirically based appreciation of the wide-ranging potentialities of the Internet. By contrast, these commentators base their judgment on features of the virtual world defined largely by the prevailing groupware. Changes in software and users account for the radically different conclusions they reach.

The Conditions of Virtual Community

Some of the earliest writing on computer networking promised universal interconnectedness in a "network nation."[13] The structure of the technology was presumed to determine its social impact. That impact would be revolutionary because computer networking not only connects computers, but also the people who use them. (Some of us can recall when this was a revolutionary insight!) These commentators expected computer-mediated communication to be as socially transforming as other forms of electronic mediation. Their predictions followed a simple logic: The telephone mediates one-to-one interaction and radio and television broadcasting mediates one-to-many interaction;

not until the computer network was it possible to mediate small group activity, the many-to-many communications in which so much of social life consists.

The early online enthusiasts believed that mediated group interaction would improve the quality of life, revivify public discourse, and favor class, race, and gender equality and participatory forms of social organization. These were the hopes of the generation of engineers and computer hobbyists who created bulletin boards, computer-conferencing systems, and the Internet. Eventually, similar notions were taken up in public discourse and, for good or ill, gave birth to a persistent metaphor: the Internet as a community technology. Because the technology was still in its infancy, this popular metaphor influenced design with results we see today.

The first publicly accessible virtual communities organized themselves not on the Internet but on independent computer conferencing systems such as EIES (Electronic Information Exchange System) and the Well.[14] Although few people had heard of computer conferencing in those early days, the success of these communities had a significant impact on the evolving image of the computer. That success in turn owed a great deal to the skill with which software designers anticipated the needs of participants in these new forums. Early designers such as Murray Turoff and Jacques Vallée developed software that met what we consider the four minimum technical conditions for effective online community. These conditions support the five attributes of community described above and facilitate the transposition of community-oriented virtues from the face-to-face environment to the network.

1. Bounding: forming closed online groups;
2. Tracking: listing how far each participant has read in community discussions;
3. Archiving: maintaining accessible records of community discussions;
4. Warranting: ensuring stable and (most of the time) genuine participant identities.

Clearly, a closed group in which members' presence is visible to each other, their common past accessible, and their true identity secured offers a favorable environment in which to display such moral qualities as loyalty, civility, and the other virtues of community. No doubt other conditions must be met depending on the interests and tasks of specific online groups. We return to the problem of the conditions of community in a later section of this chapter.

There were also many community-oriented visionaries among the creators of the Internet. Although they had much less control over the shape of their evolving system than the designers of computer conferencing systems, they too saw in it the promise of renewed community life. They introduced newsgroups and mailing lists as the equivalent in their technical environment of proprietary conferencing systems such as EIES. But as the Internet became the dominant medium of computer communication, the early vision of online community ran into trouble. Internet groupware does not support the basic technical conditions of community. As time went on, it became more and more obvious that the friendly, supportive interaction of early online communities was not determined by the nature of the technology alone, but that the users' social profile was also a factor. Without software appropriate to a more heterogeneous public, online community proved difficult to sustain.

The paradigmatic group communication applications found on the Internet were and still are mailing lists and newsgroups. The design of newsgroups supports the values of free speech, universal participation, mutual aid, and information sharing. However, important defining attributes of community life are missing. Because newsgroups are completely open, the acceptance of common rules, mutual respect, stable identity, and authentic communication are not easily ensured. Hence the notorious frequency of flaming and lack of trust in these forums.[15] Passive participants, known as "lurkers," leave no traces on the system. This can be discouraging for posters who may feel isolated and ignored in the midst of their community. Many Internet users are turned away by commercial advertising and outright hoaxes such as pyramid schemes. Netiquettes encode social practices for regulating behavior in newsgroups, but they are voluntary and have had limited success.

Mailing lists at least restrict participation through technological solutions such as closed and moderated groups. One usually knows who is sending messages. Yet they too suffer many of the problems of newsgroups. It is just as difficult to trace passive participation on mailing lists as it is in newsgroups. Furthermore, until recently, there was little or no continuity in the exchanges because the database could not be accessed thematically and past messages were difficult to review. Control of flaming is possible in mailing lists, but at a price: vesting extraordinary power in the gatekeepers, the persons acting as list owners or moderators. Depending on the type of mailing list, these gatekeepers can preview and censor contributions, let members in, or force them out.

Trouble in Cyberspace

Because mailing lists and newsgroups were first used by researchers, computer scientists, and hobbyists and drew on existing professional solidarities and shared values, their lack of community-oriented software features did not pose a grave problem. Those cozy beginnings are a thing of the past. Dutton referred to the new state of online affairs exemplified by the difficulties in building community on Santa Monica's public system: "Much is said about the strong norms within the Internet community, forgetting how homogeneous a community it serves. With the growth of commercial use, the expansion of its user base and the diminishing influence of old timers on this network, these norms are likely to be increasingly challenged."[16] In the face of deteriorating online morals, Dutton called for new rules and regulations for public electronic networks. If left normless, he argued, key participants would be chased away and online community undermined.

Not everyone thinks these problems can be solved. Observing the difficulty of community-building on the publicly accessible Internet, a number of commentators have concluded that this nascent social space is socially disruptive. This is Albert Borgmann's view. In chapter 3, Borgmann distinguishes between three different types of community—instrumental, final, and commodified. Instrumental communities serve extrinsic ends. They proliferate on the Internet where individuals gather to discuss politics or hobbies or to work in teams. Commodification is not simply economic but, more profoundly, refers to experience repackaged in a more convenient—commodious—form. This, too, the Internet accomplishes with ease. Where the Internet fails is in its promise to offer us such easy access to final communities, those ultimate associations in which one finds the meaning and purpose of life. Family and friendships exemplify this type of final community, which no repackaging can effectively commodify. "Final communities require the fullness of reality, the bodily presence of persons, and the commanding presence of things. Any attempt to secure the fulfillment of one's deepest capacities and aspirations in and through cyberspace will founder on the shoals of commodification."[17]

Darin Barney is no more hopeful than Borgmann regarding the prospects of online community. In chapter 2, he takes up Borgmann's concept of "focal things" and argues that in replacing them with virtual entities, the Internet blocks our access to real community. Focal things gather people in a coherent "world," an order of experience in which connections to others are mediated by shared objectivity. It is of course not the things per se that are important, but the practices that surround them and through which the community is formed. What worries Barney is the disappearance of these practices along with the things at which they are directed. The seminar table vanishes to be replaced by a search engine that is unable to sustain the promise of community the table evoked. Barney concludes, "It is certain that community is impossible without communication; it may also be the case that communication is meaningless without a world."[18]

In chapter 4, "Nihilism on the Information Highway," Hubert Dreyfus carries the argument against online community still further. He agrees that the commodious form of virtual community is a poor substitute for the arduous reality. But this is only a symptom of a deeper problem. Dreyfus applies Kierkegaard's analysis of the press to the Internet, which he sees as generalizing a type of subjectivity incapable of the ethical commitment implied in a serious relation to life's possibilities. This is the detached spectator, the denizen of the modern public sphere. The Internet supports an enlarged public sphere in which such empty subjects can express themselves freely. "In news groups anyone, anywhere, anytime can have an opinion on anything."[19] What we have been discussing as "online communities" Dreyfus dismisses as a playground of irresponsible and uninformed chatter. The Internet thus not only fails to promote community; it undermines the only kind of self that could have a community.

Strangely, many of these apparently negative traits of online communication are evaluated positively by postmodern theorists who see in the Internet a paradigm of desirable social transformations.[20] Liberation from the body and the unlimited freedom to join and leave virtual groups that the critics fault look like a virtue to these theorists. They see a new culture emerging in the practices of multiple identities made possible by the users' disembodiment. Invisible, the user can encounter others on his or her own terms, practice virtual "crossdressing," adopt fantasy personas, and unleash repressed dimensions of the self. As Sherry Turkle puts it, online interaction "brings postmodernism down to earth. . . . Multiple viewpoints call forth a new moral discourse. . . . The culture of simulation may help us achieve a vision of a multiple but integrated identity whose flexibility, resilience, and capacity for joy comes from having access to our many selves."[21] In chapter 6, Turkle explains the source of this transformation of the self in the practice of "cycling through" windows on the personal computer. Users cast themselves in one or another role—writer, seeker of information, purchaser of goods—at megahertz speed simply by switching from one window to another. The model of the distributed self arises at the computer interface.[22]

Mark Poster's chapter analyzes the consequences of this development for working people in a globalized economy. Poster presents us with a nuanced view of the computer, neither utopian nor dystopian. True, the computer can dehumanize its users, but it also transforms what it means to be human so profoundly no one-sided critique can encompass the full range of its effects. As Poster writes, "Sensitivity to new patterns of exploitation must be accompanied, as in Marx's analysis of early industrial capitalism, by an awareness of new possibilities for democratization."[23] The hybridization of human and machine in the new computerized economy shatters the unified identity of the modern subject and opens new possibilities for "multiple, dispersed, machine-linked subjectivities" capable of innovating new and unforeseen forms of resistance.[24]

Deterministic Assumptions

Although the authors discussed here follow different lines of argumentation, they all share the implicit assumption that the technical structure of the computer network determines how we communicate online. Technical feasibility will privilege some practices and bring them into greater prominence or, more radically, transform prevailing practice, overriding the cultural ethos handed down from the past. Four features of online communication are emphasized in support of this view.

1. As noted above, computer communications mediates small group activity. Communities can assemble online despite the obstacles of time and space. This feature of the new systems was the basis for the optimism of the early enthusiasts. But other features appear decisive to the critics and postmodern theorists.
2. They agree that the major difference between the "virtual" and the "real" world is the narrow bandwidth of online communication. The social contexts within which the acting subjects are situated in cyberspace are as thin and ephemeral as the flow of electronic signals set into motion by the fingers hitting the keyboard. The critics see in this a diminishing of experience itself; the postmoderns see it as an opportunity to unleash fantasy.
3. Universal interconnectedness and the stripping away of context blur human values and choices in a universal relativism. Every piece of information is equally valuable and every communication partner is equally present. The critics conclude that nothing is really valuable and no one is really present. The postmoderns seize on the liberation promised in a relativistic universe without Cartesian subjects and coordinates. Postmodern individualism can thrive in the new virtual environment where mobility between communities weakens conformist pressures, leaving everyone responsible for their own values.
4. The anonymity of computer interaction undermines moral responsibility for one's own acts and for other persons. The critics charge that under these conditions morality is impossible, while the postmoderns find in anonymity the opportunity for creating a new, more tolerant, and more self-conscious morality.

The various authors differ in the degree to which they share deterministic premises. The early enthusiasts made overly daring predictions based on their analysis of the technology, but then they had little else to go on at a time when the population of cyberspace numbered in the hundreds. The critics also tacitly assume that certain obvious technical features of computer networks govern the type of social relations they mediate. These are the very same features that support online commerce, the ability to switch rapidly from one concern or interlocutor to the next unfettered by the dense stuff of physical reality. A world in which people can be turned on and off like a water faucet is certainly not one in which community will thrive. The postmodern theorists draw on these same intuitions about the nature of cyberspace, but they appreciate the role of user practices and appropriations a bit more than the others. However, the users who interest them are precisely the ones who appropriate the very features of the technology the critics deplore. They ignore the variety of outcomes that result from users appropriating the network for different purposes. Thus neither critics nor postmoderns take online community seriously. They fail to appreciate the significance of stable, predictable online environments and personal identities, supporting the committed exchanges we usually associate with the idea of community. Banal it may be, but not for that matter less important than the exotic problems and possibilities on which they focus.

The Social Construction of Online Communities

Advocates of online community, critics of networking, and postmoderns are all preoccupied with the benefits and dangers of the features or limitations of network technology. In contrast, sociologists and cultural analysts of cyberspace provide empirical accounts of what actually occurs in online social groups.

Maria Bakardjieva's chapter on "Virtual Togetherness" offers a framework for just such empirical study. She dismisses the general question of the possibility of online community on the grounds that our evaluation of the Internet should be guided not by the distinction between the real and the virtual but by that between human interaction and commerce. The human significance of the Internet lies in its ability to support "a cultural trend of 'immobile socialization,' or in other words, socialization of private experience through the invention of new forms of intersubjectivity and social organization online."[25] Human beings engage with each other in many different ways, producing many different kinds of value in their own and each others' lives on the Internet as in the real world. Some of these interactions have the affective and moral qualities we associate with community, others have different communicative purposes such as obtaining information, and still others are strictly commercial and minimize human connection. Empirical study should review the whole gamut of types of interaction rather than privileging a specific type.

Bakardjieva's chapter belongs to a large body of research that reaches completely different conclusions from the arguments we have considered so far. These researchers attempt to show that the online social space is not governed exclusively by the technical characteristics of the network but is socially constructed by user appropriation of the technology.

Their empirical studies have shown that:

1. Participants are often able to overcome the narrowness of the communication channel and find ways to create personal images of each other despite it.[26]
2. Rather than obeying the constraints of the technical structure of the network, participants actively appropriate what is available, at times

using features of the system and preexisting cultural resources in un-expected ways.[27]

3. Participants are able to create dynamic and rich communities by in-venting new forms of expression and through interactive negotiation of meanings, norms, and values.[28]

4. Different online communities demonstrate distinctive normative orien-tations established and maintained through written ethical codes (neti-quettes) and through "metacommunication."[29]

It is interesting to contrast this sociological literature with the critical ap-proaches outlined in the previous section. The social research does not deny the existence of the problems the critics identify, but it blames them for the way users appropriate the technology rather than on technical fea-tures of computer networking. For example, an online hooligan showing blatant disregard for group norms takes advantage of certain technical af-fordances (e.g., free and often anonymous access to the discussions of a group), but these might be blocked or altered by a different social organi-zation. Extraordinary users can reproduce bounded communities even on the most challenging terrain of the Internet. In our own empirical research we observed a case where a completely open group patrolled its bound-aries effectively by strictly ignoring offensive behavior by "outsiders." From this nondeterministic standpoint, the online environment embodies both obstacles and opportunities for community. Along with obvious features, it contains "dormant affordances" that await discovery and incorporation in new community-building practices.

FROM DETERMINISM TO AGENCY

The Politics of Technology

Early enthusiasts, critics, and postmodern theorists emphasize a few gen-eral affordances of computer networking and pay less attention to the dis-tinctive characteristics of the various user populations. Empirical studies show that in practice, interacting users appropriate the technology as mem-bers of particular social groups with particular goals in mind. In that context, they discover and enact new affordances not always deducible from obvious technical features.

To these sociological observations we add the further historically grounded proposition that technical design itself is subject to change under many influences. In our example above, social control of uncivil behavior re-quired a social solution due to the open design of Internet software. A soft-ware solution, bounded groups, was already in place in the early systems that preceded the Internet, but was not available there until recently for reasons connected with the nature of the underlying technology.

The different evaluations of the Internet's community-building potential correspond roughly to Langdon Winner's distinction between technologies that are "inherently political" and technologies that acquire political implications through contingent features.[30] Does the Internet contain insuperable technical obstacles to community, or is its impact a matter of user initiatives and design? We believe the latter position is correct. But that opens up important questions concerning agency in technological development.

The Social Construction of New Communication Technologies

Social constructivists (Pinch and Bijker, Law, Latour, Hughes, and others) and social historians (Marvin, Schivelbusch) have shown us that the design of new technological systems emerges from a process of negotiation and struggle among "relevant social groups."[31] Technologies may end up clearly defined but they do not start out that way. All technological artifacts exhibit "interpretative flexibility," that is to say, they can be differently understood by different participants in the design process. This is especially true in the early stages when actors' interpretations of the artifact lead to conflicting notions of how to improve its design. Historians study how specific sets of social practices, relations, and organizational forms are anchored to a new technology as a dominant interpretation emerges in the course of its development.

Thus human agency is central to the process of technological advance, contrary to technological determinism.[32] But note that this constructivist position is also different from the common sense claim that technology is "neutral" and can be used for a variety of purposes. Of course, within certain limits that is true too, but the issue here is not merely how the technology is used but *what it becomes* as a result of the different possible uses that are imagined for it. Different designs correspond to each of those possible uses. In the early stages of development, the role of human agents in this process is obvious. This is the case with the Internet today. Later, as a technology is stabilized, its design tends to dictate users' behavior more successfully and agency recedes into the background, at least until new demands emerge to challenge the established design. Not one-sided determinism, but reciprocity best describes the human-technology relation.

Latour explains these reversals of agency as the "delegation" of moral obligations to technical artifacts.[33] Even though Latour's examples (the door closer, the speed bump) sound a bit too mechanistic to qualify as substitutes for moral self-control, devices are indeed fraught with intricate "programs for action," "scripts," which specify what behavior is considered right and wrong by a particular community. Artifacts "scaffold" human behavior in compliance with customary and ethical standards. This raises important questions for our understanding of the Internet. How much and what type of "ethical guidance" do we find in the online environment? Is it possible to anchor human relations in the technical structure of virtual worlds? Concretely, can design reinforce the "community model" as a democratic alternative for the development of this medium?

It is important not to underestimate the significance of the issues involved. The Internet resembles radio and television in the early stage of development. It is still unclear what it will become, but predictably, like these earlier communications technologies, it will reshape our culture once it settles into a stable form. Just as we say that radio and television are entertainment media, and in the process lump together our expectations and practice of listening and viewing with certain technical characteristics, so we will someday have a widely accepted definition of computer networking. What will it be? As with radio and television, the answer to that question will depend on the emergence of standard technical affordances, practices, and legal, organizational, and cultural forms associated with the technology and determining its social meaning. That is in part a political process in both the narrowest and the broadest sense of the term.[34]

Democratic Rationalization

Social constructivism analyzes the influence of "relevant social groups" when studying the development of an artifact. Early constructivist research focused on scientists, designers, engineers, administrators, and businessmen, leaving the users of technology out of the picture. But in the case of the computer, this is an oversight in obvious need of correction. Turkle, for example, found a lot of what constructivists call interpretative flexibility in her study of user communities.[35] The openness of the device allows users to draw their own conclusions about its nature and purpose independent of the intentions of computer designers or deterministic technical constraints. The history of such innovations as e-mail and the World Wide Web testifies to the impact of outsiders and the users who adopt their innovations.

Constructivism frees technology studies from the dogmatic assumption that efficiency and efficiency alone determine which of the various possible designs of an artifact will end up gaining general acceptance. Where determinists assume that political "interference" in technical decisions reduces efficiency, constructivism argues that there can be many possible interpretations and configurations, each leading to a successful outcome according to a variety of criteria. These alternatives are not comparable in some simple quantitative sense, as they accomplish different goals and are embedded differently in social institutions. We thus need an account that emphasizes the inventiveness with which users engage with such products as computers.

To this end, Feenberg has introduced the concept of "democratic rationalization."[36] This concept gives constructivism a critical edge by bringing out the political implications of user agency for technical design. "Rationalization" in this context means a technically and economically coherent realization of a basic technological idea. (Obviously, there may also be "irrational" alternatives—alternatives that make little or no technical sense, but that is another story, irrelevant to our considerations of the Internet.) Some rationalizations may be heavily influenced by lay actors and so could be called "democratic" insofar as that they involve citizen agency.[37] Environmentalism has accustomed us to recognizing such lay interventions as expressions of democratic public opinion. We propose to extend a similar recognition to user involvement in the information revolution.

Democratic rationalizations challenge harmful consequences, undemocratic power structures, and barriers to communication rooted in technological design. In some cases, lay actors dissatisfied with the technical solutions preferred by experts, corporations, or government agencies force design changes through initiating public controversies that lead to lawsuits, boycotts, and regulation. In other cases, expert and lay actors collaborate in creating a product. This is called "participatory design." The type of democratic rationalization that has played the biggest role on the Internet is "creative appropriation," the process in which users innovate new functionalities for already existing technologies.[38] Creative appropriation has shaped the Internet from the very beginning. The system was originally designed for information-sharing among military researchers, but users exploited its potential as a medium for human communication.[39] The new interpretation of the purpose of the Internet was incorporated into its structure and now it belongs to its accepted social definition. New functions were "layered" on top of an existing technology.[40]

Layering in this sense involves reappropriating the network in unexpected ways as participants innovate or actualize new or dormant affordances.[41] As participants, they see the technology from a different angle than its designers. This is why they are able to perceive and actualize overlooked potentialities not envisioned in the technical, economic, and political rationality already inscribed in the network. They give it a new meaning on the basis of a "situated knowledge" rooted in their unique relation to the technology.

Political Implications: From Consumers to Citizens

The theory of democratic rationalization is intertwined with the emerging democratic applications of the Internet. Cyberconsumers become global citizens as they innovate new political practices, social forms, and technical designs. The early speculations on this process were unrealistically optimistic. Some of the more enthusiastic prophets of the information highway expected electronic town hall meetings to institute direct democracy on a national scale. While it is true that deliberation in online forums is a remarkable and widespread phenomenon, the flaws in this scheme are obvious. Who would want to live under thousands of laws made on the spur of the moment by voters, most of whom have no time to become acquainted with the issues let alone the details of the legislation on which they would be asked to vote? Even if referenda were confined to major issues, it is not clear that this would be an improvement on representative government. Consider the example of California, where money sways both types of elections with equal success! The real problem of democracy today does not lie in the form of voting, which these reform schemes target, but in the structure and financing of political campaigns and the media of communication, especially television.

Yet the early hope that online communication would enhance democracy was not misplaced. As a one-way, top-down medium of communication, television is not the ideal basis for a lively public sphere. Democracy can only benefit from the Internet's availability for free, reciprocal communication, which allows a far wider variety of opinions to be heard. In fact, this is what can now be observed as Internet-based groups intervene with increasing frequency and effectiveness in political life.

Amitai Etzioni's contribution to this book highlights the significance of such deliberation and its potential under the rather utopian conditions of universal consultation. Richard Kahn and Douglas Kellner describe the impact of these interventions today in chapter 10. They concede that commercial interests are busy colonizing the Internet, but this is not the whole picture. The Internet also opens a space for "new form of agency in the ongoing struggle for social justice and a more participatory democracy."[42] They discuss a number of political breakthroughs such as the antiglobalization movements that have established the democratic relevance of the Internet. Online communities play a role in these movements as the organizational backbone of mass mobilizations. Software innovations such as wikis and blogs support these communities with technical features suited to the growth of a democratic culture online.

Chapters by Philip Agre, Diane Johnson, and Bruce Bimber converge on a social capital analysis of the democratic impact of the Internet. They argue that the Internet serves ideological agents who lack conventional social capital, such as leadership in traditional organizations or access to wealth. Agre concludes that the main contribution of the Internet to democracy is not its ability to support deliberation, but rather its usefulness to "issue entrepreneurs" who build movements around their ideas and commitments.[43] Johnson and Bimber observe that "the threshold for entry into politics and community organizations appears to be falling."[44] The result is the emergence of a "postbureaucratic" politics in an increasingly pluralistic society. The movements cited by Kahn and Kellner are explained by the development of this enhanced pluralism, in which small, untested groups with organizing skill but little or no money succeed in altering the terms of public debate.

Democratic rationalization of the Internet and the democratic application of its powers go hand-in-hand with the evolution of the technology. As the Internet is appropriated for human interaction and online community, activists seize on its potential for informing and mobilizing a democratic public. The outcome promises deep transformations in political life.

GROUPWARE FOR COMMUNITY

Several contributors to this volume are skeptical about the chances of what we have called a "democratic rationalization" of the Internet. The consumption model is supported by powerful commercial interests. With these interests driving development, what hope is there for the creative, participatory, community-building potential of network technology? But the social shaping of the Internet is still in process. The technology and its social institution have not reached the point of stabilization. As computer networks penetrate the everyday lives of ever more diverse social groups and restructure a broad range of organizations, new interpretations, meanings, problems, conflicts, struggles, and designs proliferate. There is evidence of this in the survival and growth of early experiments in online community.[45] In addition, community-oriented commercial applications of computer networking have emerged in the last few years. In the next section, we review several of these terrains that will be important in the years to come for both researchers and activists.

Computer Supported Collaborative Work

Groupware, also known as computer supported cooperative work (CSCW), has suggestive implications for online community. CSCW represents a prominent strand in mainstream computer network research and application. Software to enable group collaboration aims at improving group productivity, reducing so-called process losses, overcoming time and space constraints, and increasing the range and speed of access to information.[46] The increasing number of long-distance collaborations in multinational companies intensified interest in CSCW and made it a force in the business world by the mid 1980s.[47]

Designers started out by focusing on the "rationalization" of the collective work process. This they accomplished through tight, deterministic structuring of group activities. As Lea and Giordano note, CSCW research and development still aim to support small, short-lived, interactive, task-oriented groups that would normally meet face to face.[48] This orientation reflects the fact that CSCW applications are designed in a business context where the paradigmatic group is a work team tackling a task set by management.

But the focus of the field has gradually opened up, in many cases thanks to the contribution of social scientists who have established the importance of informal interactions in highly structured organizations.[49] As a consequence, the concept of community has begun to attract interest within the CSCW field.

For example, Elizabeth Mynatt and her coauthors consider "network communities" to be an emergent "genre of collaboration." Their article defines these new social forms as computationally based environments that provide access to a persistent online world possessing technical and social affordances for nurturing community.[50] They see systems such as "Media Spaces" and MUDs as exemplary. This article is notable for drawing on social anthropology, rather than social psychology alone, in generating guidelines for the technical support of group interaction. The authors argue that "Network communities emerge from the intertwining of sociality and technology. It is the appropriation, and re-appropriation, of technology to accomplish the daily workings of social life that influences the character of a network community, including its eventual failure or success. Affordances suggest and support this appropriation."[51]

The five affordances that Mynatt and her colleagues identify in various network community technologies include:

1. Persistence: durability across time of both users and particular uses;
2. Periodicity: rhythms and patterns through which activity is structured over time in a meaningful way;
3. Boundaries: metaphorical spatial divisions that make possible different social groupings;
4. Engagement: the ability of participants to establish diverse forms and modes of communication;
5. Authoring: the ability of participants to change the configuration of their space.

Mynatt's article maps out a software structure conducive to community life online. The authors propose such things as facilities for linking members' offline and online identities, providing means for members to monitor each others' background presence online, incorporating techniques and features for acculturating new members, and enabling redesign, so that the community can rebuild the software to suit its evolving needs. These suggestions seem keyed directly to the objections of the critics of online community who argue that identity and commitment are impossible in cyberspace. Mynatt and her collaborators have instead studied the practice of actual participants in online communities and attempted to generalize from the empirically

identifiable procedures they employ to get around the very real but not insurmountable obstacles to success.

As in our earlier list of minimum (software) conditions for online community, the emphasis here is on features that enable groups to define themselves through control of membership and access to a collective memory
(points one and three on both lists). The authors also suggest the usefulness
of some sort of tracking feature (our point 2) and call for linking online and
offline identity as a way of achieving the goal of our point 4, which we call
"warranting." Thus, the conclusions are quite similar up to this point. The additional notions of "periodicity," "engagement," and "authoring" could be
added to a common list. Periodicity is generally achieved through moderat-
ing practices that skillfully open and close phases in online discussion, giving a sense of progress to what might easily degenerate into a collection of
random monologues. Engagement in Mynatt's sense of the term is now
commonplace on Web portals, which we discuss below. Authoring concerns
the ability of users to innovate features, precisely the sort of thing we refer
to more generally with the concept of democratic rationalization.

Given the influence of CSCW in the business world, this new focus on online community must be taken seriously as a possible source of significant innovation.

Web-Based Community Applications

In addition to work-oriented groupware, the relatively young Internet service industry is another source of experimentation and development. Community is interpreted by this industry as a commodity and as a scene on
which to sell commodities. Commercially supported web communities became a big business in little more than a year and are now a well-established
fact of life on the Internet. Here is a typical ad for one of them: "A virtual
community is a group of people with a common interest who are connected
through the Internet. People with a common interest can create their own
virtual community, and it can all be done using the ICQ tools and services.
The easiest way you can form a virtual community is by creating an ICQ Interest Group. The ICQ Interest Groups are located on the ICQ server."[52]

The simple-minded philosophy of the early Internet newsgroups can be
found in this statement: All you need to create a community is a common interest and a communication medium. In fact, the software tools offered by
the contemporary "community services" such as ICQ and Yahoo! are fairly
sophisticated and fulfill most of the conditions of community we have so far
identified. They enable participants to create both listed (visible to everyone
through the WWW) and unlisted invitation-only "clubs," "groups," or "communities." Not only can clearly defined and recognizable group boundaries
be established, boundary drawing is prompted by the software itself so even

beginners can understand it. The systems automatically present useful information on community membership, how many pages have been viewed each day, times of posting, and other similar parameters. Thus some form of participation tracking is available. Users are prompted to provide "profiles," e-mail addresses, and home page URLs. By these means the anchoring of online personae in real identities is possible and encouraged. Mynatt's "engagement" is supported as well. Some services allow the creation of shared online "photo albums" as visual complements to message text. And in addition to asynchronous discussion, participants can engage in a synchronous chat, or exchange e-mail by clicking a single button. The records of the asynchronous discussions are typically available for future reference, thus constituting a form of community memory.

As with moderated mailing lists, the power structure of the resultant social groups is again centered on one person or gatekeeper, the so-called founder or administrator who created the club. However, the software allows administrators to delegate some of their powers to other members of the group. For example, some members can be empowered to invite new members to the group, others can create new folders, or prune the archive, and so on. This makes it possible to innovate various structures of rights and responsibilities and to engage in a weak form of authoring.

These services must balance simplicity of use against sophistication of features. Specialists complain that designing computer conferencing software to run in a web browser is technically tricky. Thus, some features familiar from the early systems are missing from these new ones. But the features that are typically in place do satisfy the minimum conditions for community-building. And unlike early conferencing, which was available only to a select few, these services are in principle open to everybody with Internet access. They cater to a technically literate but nonexpert user population enthralled by the accessible point-and-click interface of the World Wide Web.

Of course, the commercialization of community raises red flags. Critics' fears of abusive forms of sociability and postmoderns' hopes for multiple and disengaged identities can all be verified in some of the public clubs; however, given the enormous variety, this is so far more a matter of participants' choice than an essential consequence of networking. Nevertheless, commercial interest in online community may be in the process of changing that, transforming successful communities formed for noncommercial purposes into marketing tools. Leslie Shade's chapter explores this transformation in the case of several communities of women and girls. In one case, the originators attracted a growing audience with feminist content and style. That, in turn, interested a buyer eager to capture the attention of female consumers. Here the commodification of community takes on the outrageous form of actual purchase. Shade writes, "What were once burgeoning feminist communities have since been transmogrified into female-oriented spaces where empowerment is often equated with consumer sovereignty."[53] There is a deeply disturbing tension in such cases between the gift-giving logic of community and commercial exchange.

Also worrisome are the problems resulting from private ownership of the hardware infrastructure of online community. The services are free but the companies reserve the right to impose fees in the future. At this stage, users "pay" by exposing themselves to advertising disseminated by the company hosting the community. These commercial intrusions certainly affect the atmosphere. What is more, the service provider can, at its sole discretion, terminate a club and discard its content for any reason (see for example Yahoo! Clubs Terms of Service, section 13). That could have dire consequences for an established community relying on the provider.[54] Their collective product, the archive of their interactions, could be simply erased as a result of a change in ownership or policy. Marginal groups advocating unpopular political views or lifestyles would seem to be particularly vulnerable.

In addition to these concerns are privacy and intellectual property issues typical of online communication in general. Under Yahoo! Clubs terms of service (section 8), Yahoo claims ownership of all nongraphical content that participants post in publicly accessible areas of the service; they automatically grant Yahoo! the "royalty-free, perpetual, irrevocable, non-exclusive and fully sublicensable right and license to use, reproduce, modify, adapt, publish, translate, create derivative works from, distribute, perform and display such Content (in whole or part) worldwide and/or to incorporate it in other works in any form, media, or technology now known or later developed." It is a little as though the YMCA claimed ownership of everything said at public meetings held on its premises; this policy does not foster trust and free expression. Despite these problems, the rapid growth of these portal-based online communities offers a rich terrain for experimentation and research.

Community Networks

Community networks have been around for over twenty years, longer than CSCW and much longer than portals. They attempt to use computer networking to advance the goals of existing local communities. Their focus has been on enhancing civic life, education, and economic development.[55] They employ political, organizational, and technical innovations emerging out of the joint efforts of civic activists, computer professionals, schools, universities, local governmental agencies, libraries, and nonprofit organizations.[56]

Community networks provide such basic services as forums (both moderated and unmoderated), access to documents and files, e-mail, and file download-upload capabilities.[57] Other services offered by community networks include chat, remote login, search capabilities, WWW access, and database facilities. Community networks have used a whole range of technologies to deliver these services, gradually evolving from dial-up bulletin board systems to Internet resources and, more recently, to WWW-based applications. These networks have served as a test bed for a huge number of different designs. As one would expect, the various conditions of community we have identified can be found fulfilled in many of these experiments, and it is here that authoring is most fully supported.

Computer professionals, academic researchers, and hobbyists associated with such projects have developed a number of software packages tailored to the needs of local community networks. FreePort, written by Case Western Reserve University (CWRU) for the Cleveland Free-Net (CFN) has been the software of choice of the majority of the Free-Nets in the United States. The university and the local hobbyist community in Halifax, Canada, collaborated on an original software package. "Csuite," as it was called, was initially developed for the needs of the local Chebucto Community Net, but subsequently adopted throughout the country and abroad.[58]

This spontaneous creativity represents an important instance of democratic rationalization. It deserves the attention of theorists, researchers, and perhaps even business as well. Douglas Schuler has argued that the field of Computer Supported Cooperative Work, narrowly perceived as a branch of office automation, should be expanded to include Computer Supported Community Work.[59] Presumably, groupware systems specially tailored to support broad participation in community affairs would thus be drawn into commercial R & D.

Schuler's chapter 14 focuses on the role of community networks in the mobilization of society's intellectual resources. He argues that we have a vital need to enhance "civic intelligence," and that this can be accomplished through the application of new communication technologies. The question is "in what ways can connecting a huge and potentially unruly and fractious group of people from a multitude of cultures and life circumstances, help society as a whole deal more effectively and equitably with [its] problems."[60] Schuler details several examples of the activities of community networks that use the Internet to gather and disseminate politically significant knowledge.

MYTH AND REALITY

This discussion shows that community-building groupware is proliferating in the context of different structures of ownership and control. Future developments in these three areas of networking hold the answer to a series of crucial questions: Will the Internet become the ultimate entertainment and/or information medium, a seamless environment for business transactions of all kinds? Or will the Internet emerge as a community technology, enlarging human contact both globally and locally in accordance with the early visions and the subsequent practice of community-building? Will "network communities" be accepted as a technical response to the human need for meaningful, reliable, and consequential relationships with others, or will they remain in the category of those technical possibilities that emerge for a short historical instant and fall into oblivion? What strategy can "liberate" online communities from the narrow confines of the corporate rationality within which they are increasingly emerging? Can systems originally conceived to enhance work–team performance or to generate revenue for Internet service providers be subverted by their creators and users so as to take on a new life in the public sphere? A multitude of social contexts and actions have to be aligned for a democratic appropriation of community technology to take place.

Critics of online community are thus right to dampen naive enthusiasm for the Internet. They are right to criticize the rhetoric of the Information Highway, including its easy praise of online togetherness and oblivion to the commercialization of the Internet. The idea of virtual community is indeed a powerful myth playing on the genuine desire we have to control our lives and be a part of a larger social whole that provides emotional and intellectual support.[61] But in the realm of technology, myth is sometimes future reality; this is one domain in which dreams (including nightmares) can come true. In this evaluation of the significance of myth, our constructivist view of technology contrasts most sharply with determinism. We argue for a discriminating approach to the possible realization of the myth of community in the evolving technology of computer networking.

The consumption model of the Internet is a plausible version of its future given the structural realities of the world in which we live. The alternative community model would take much more conceptual work, design efforts, and political mobilization. Yet, as we have tried to show, there are technical formats that could potentially pave the way to a more community-friendly Internet. It is the human actors, putting their competencies and resources to work, fighting for their beliefs and desires, who will determine which of the emergent structures prevail. From this perspective, it is not naive or futile to demand the dedication of resources to the development of online community. A political process oriented toward this goal can be seen as a logical extension of the right to free assembly. The demand for actual opportunities for free assembly in the online world is a vital moment of its democratization. The struggle for online community places technical democratization in the service of democracy itself.

NOTES

An earlier version of this chapter was published as "Community, Technology, and Democratic Rationalization" in *The Information Society* 18: (2000), 181–92. The chapter was written under National Science Foundation Award 9818724.

1. Amitai Etzioni, chapter 12 of this book.

2. John Dewey, *The Public and Its Problems* (Denver: Swallow, 1927).

3. For a discussion of Dewey's position, see Andrew Feenberg, *Questioning Technology* (New York and London: Routledge, 1999), chap. 6.

4. For an early critical discussion of the Internet and democracy, see Nancy Kurland and Terri Egan, "Engendering Democratic Participation via the Net: Access, Voice, and Dialogue," *The Information Society* 12, no. 4 (1996): 387–406.

5. For an example of an application of constructivist method to the study of on-line communication, see Andrew Feenberg, *Alternative Modernity: The Technical Turn in Philosophy and Social Theory* (Los Angeles: University of California Press, 1995), chap. 7.

6. Elizabeth Reid, "Hierarchy and Power: Social Control in Cyberspace," in *Communities in Cyberspace*, ed. M. A. Smith and P. Killock (London and New York: Routledge, 1999), 107–33.

7. Andrew Feenberg, "A User's Guide to the Pragmatics of Computer Mediated Communication," *Semiotica* 75, nos. 3/4 (1989): 266ff.

8. Peter Winch, *The Idea of a Social Science* (London and Henley: Routledge & Kegan Paul, 1958).

9. Marcel Mauss, *The Gift: Forms and Functions of Exchange in Archaic Societies,* trans. Ian Cunninson (New York: W.W. Norton, 1967); Pierre Bourdieu, *Esquisse d'une Théorie de la Pratique* (Geneva and Paris: Librairie Droz, 1972).

10. Erving Goffman, *Behavior in Public Places: Notes on the Social Organization of Gatherings* (New York: The Free Press, 1963).

11. Jürgen Habermas, *The Theory of Communicative Action: Lifeworld and System: A Critique of Functionalist Reason,* trans. T. McCarthy (Boston: Beacon, 1984, 1987).

12. Nara and Iseda, chapter 9 in this volume.

13. J. C. R. Licklider, and R. W. Taylor, "The Computer as a Communication Device," *Science & Technology* 76 (1968): 21–31; Starr Roxanne Hiltz and Murray Turoff, *The Network Nation: Human Communication via Computer* (Reading, Mass.: Addison-Wesley Publishing Group, 1978).

14. Hiltz and Turoff, *The Network Nation*; Howard Rheingold, *The Virtual Community: Homesteading on the Electronic Frontier* (Reading, Mass.: Addison-Wesley, 1993).

15. Lee Sproul and Sara Kiesler, *Connections: New Ways of Working in the Networked Organization* (Cambridge: MIT Press, 1991), 49ff.

16. William H. Dutton, "Network Rules of Order: Regulating Speech in Public Electronic Fora," *Media Culture and Society* 18 (1996): 285.

17. Borgmann, chapter 3. See also Albert Borgmann, *Crossing the Postmodern Divide* (Chicago: University of Chicago Press, 1992).

18. Barney, chapter 2. See also Darin Barney, *Prometheus Wired* (Chicago: University of Chicago Press, 2000).

19. Dreyfus, chapter 4.

20. Sherry Turkle, *Life on the Screen: Identity in the Age of the Internet* (New York: Simon and Schuster, 1995). See also Allurque Rosanne Stone, *The War of Desire and Technology at the Close of the Mechanical Age* (Cambridge: MIT Press, 1995).

21. Turkle, *Life on the Screen,* 268.

22. Turkle, chapter 6.

23. Poster, chapter 5.

24. Poster, chapter 5.

25. Bakardjieva, chapter 7.

26. Josph B. Walther, J. F. Anderson, D. W. Park, "Interpersonal Effects in Computer-Mediated Interaction: A Meta-Analysis of Social and Antisocial Communication," *Communication Research* 21 (1994): 460–87; Joseph B. Walther and J. K. Borgoon, "Relational Communication in Computer-Mediated Interaction," *Human Communication Research* 19, no. 1 (1992): 50–88.

27. Noshir S. Contractor and D. R. Siebold, "Theoretical Frameworks for the Study of Structuring Processes in Group Decision Support Systems: Adaptive Structuration Theory and Self-Organizing Systems Theory," *Human Communication Research* (1994): 528–63; Noshir S. Contractor and E. M. Eisenberg, "Communication Networks and New Media in Organizations," in *Organizations and Communication Technology*, ed. Janet Fulk and C. W. Steinfield (Newbury Park, Calif.: Sage, 1990), 143–72.

28. Elizabeth M. Reid, *Electropolis: Communication and Community on Internet Relay Chat*, unpublished master's thesis (Melbourne: University of Melbourne, 1991); Elizabeth M. Reid, "Virtual Worlds: Culture and Imagination," in *Cybersociety: Computer-Mediated Communication and Community*, ed. Steven G. Jones (Thousand Oaks, Calif.: Sage, 1995), 164–83; Nancy K. Baym, "The Emergence of Community in Computer-Mediated Communication," in *Cybersociety: Computer-Mediated Communication and Community*, ed. Steven G. Jones (Thousand Oaks, Calif.: Sage, 1995), 138–63; Nessim Watson, "Why We Argue about Virtual Community: A Case Study of the Phish.Net Fan Community," in *Virtual Culture: Identity and Communication in Cybersociety*, ed. Steve Jones (Thousand Oaks, Calif.: Sage, 1997), 102–32.

29. Baym, "The Emergence of Community," 138–63; Susan Herring, "Gender and Democracy in Computer-Mediated Communication," in *Communication Institute for Online Scholarship*, 1993; Andrew Feenberg, "A User's Guide to the Pragmatics of Computer Mediated Communication," *Semiotica* 75, nos. 3/4 (1989); William H. Dutton, "Network Rules of Order: Regulating Speech in Public Electronic Fora," *Media Culture and Society* 18 (1996): 269–90.

30. Langdon Winner, "Do Artifacts Have Politics," in Langdon Winner, *The Whale and the Reactor* (Chicago: University of Chicago Press, 1986).

31. Trevor Pinch, Thomas Hughes, and Wiebe Bijker, *The Social Construction of Technological Systems* (Cambridge: MIT Press, 1989).

32. See Raymond Williams, *Television: Technology and Cultural Form* (London: Fontana, 1974), for an insightful discussion of the case of television.

33. Bruno Latour, "Where Are the Missing Masses? The Sociology of a Few Mundane Artifacts," in *Shaping Technology/Building Society: Studies in Sociotechnical Change*, ed. Wiebe Bijker and John Law (Cambridge: MIT Press, 1992).

34. For an illuminating discussion of the struggle over the early development of radio, see Robert McChesney, *Rich Media, Poor Democracy: Communication Politics in Dubious Times* (Chicago: University of Illinois Press, 1999), chap. 5.

35. Sherry Turkle, *The Second Self* (New York: Simon and Schuster, 1984).

36. Feenberg, *Questioning Technology*.

37. Agency is of course only one of several important features of democracy; however, if its importance is overlooked, citizen action by concerned minorities may be trivialized or even treated as undemocratic. This issue is discussed at length in Feenberg, *Questioning Technology*, chap. 6).

38. Feenberg, *Questioning Technology*.

39. Rheingold, *The Virtual Community*; Abbate, *From Arpanet to Internet*; Feenberg, *Alternative Modernity*, chap. 7.

40. On layering, see Andrew Feenberg, "Technology in a Global World," in *Science and Other Cultures: Issues in Philosophies of Science and Technology*, ed. Robert Figueroa and Sandra Harding (New York and London: Routledge, 2003).

41. Feenberg, *Questioning Technology*, 219.

42. Kellner and Kahn, chapter 10.

43. Agre, chapter 11.

44. Johnson and Bimber, chapter 13.

45. Philip Agre and Douglas Schuler, *Reinventing Technology, Rediscovering Community: Critical Explorations of Technology as a Social Practice* (Greenwich, Conn.: Ablex, 1997).

46. Jolene Galegher and R. E. Kraut, "Technology for Intellectual Teamwork: Perspectives on Research and Design," in *Intellectual Teamwork: Social and Technological Foundations of Cooperative Work*, ed. Jolene Galegher and R. E. Kraut (Hillsdale, N.J., Hove and London: Laurence Erlbaum Associates, 1990), 1–20; Joseph E. McGrath and Andrea B. Hollingshead, *Groups Interacting with Technology: Ideas, Evidence, Issues, and an Agenda* (Thousand Oaks, Calif.: Sage, 1994).

47. C. Holtham, "Groupware: Its Past and Future," in *Groupware in the Twenty-First Century: Computer Supported Collaborative Working Toward the Millennium*, ed. P. Lloyd (Westport, Conn.: Praeger, 1994), 3–14.

48. Martin Lea and R. Giordano, "Representations of the Group and Group Processes in CSCW Research: A Case of Premature Closure?" in *Social Science, Technical Systems, and Cooperative Work*, ed. Geoffrey C. Bowker, Susan Leigh Star, W. Turner, L. Gasser (Mahwah, N.J. and London: Lawrence Erlbaum Associates, 1997), 5–26.

49. McGrath and Hollingshead, *Groups Interacting with Technology*; Bowker, Star, and Gasser, "Introduction," in *Social Science, Technical Systems, and Cooperative Work*.

50. Elizabeth Mynatt, Vicky O'Day, A. Adler, and Mizuko Ito, "Network Communities: Something Old, Something New, Something Borrowed . . . ," *Computer Supported Cooperative Work: The Journal of Cooperative Computing* 7 (1998): 123–56.

51. Mynatt, O'Day, Adler, and Ito, "Network Communities," 130.

52. www.icq.com/cybercommunities.html.

53. Shade, chapter 8.

54. Ito describes an incident that occurred with a university-hosted MUD community that fell victim to a system failure and a subsequent ban on "mudding" imposed by the university. Ito emphasizes the importance of machine materiality that virtual communities depend on. Mizuko Ito, "Virtually Embodied: The Reality of Fantasy in a Multi-User Dungeon," in *Internet Culture*, ed. D. Porter (New York and London: Routledge, 1997), 87–110.

55. Agre and Schuler, *Reinventing Technology, Rediscovering Community*.

56. See Douglas Schuler, *New Community Networks: Wired for Change* (Reading, Mass.: Addison-Wesley, 1996), 25.

57. Schuler, *New Community Networks*, 296.

58. Michael Gurstein, "Community Informatics: Enabling Community Uses of Information and Communications Technology," in *Community Informatics: Enabling*

Communities with Information and Communications Technologies, ed. Michael Gurstein (Hershey, Pa.: Idea Group Publishing, 2000), 1–31.

59. Douglas Schuler, *CSCW for the "Real World": Towards Computer-Supported Community Work*. Unpublished manuscript, 1999.

60. Schuler, chapter 14.

61. Vincent Mosco, "Myth-ing Links: Power and Community on the Information Highway," *The Information Society* 14 (1998): 57–62.

I

THE QUESTION OF COMMUNITY AND DIGITAL TECHNOLOGY

2

The Vanishing Table, Or Community in a World That Is No World

Darin Barney

"Community," Albert Borgmann writes, "gathers around reality."[1] He is referring specifically to "the holy game of baseball," and the reality of "a thoughtful and graceful ballpark." As a site of common celebration, the ballpark—and Borgmann is careful to distinguish ballparks from artificially turfed, climate-controlled domes that are a technology for rendering the game into a commodity and spectators into customers—"inspires common pride and pleasure, a shared sense of season and place, a joint anticipation of drama." One might say the same of a local hockey rink in the midst of a Canadian prairie winter. In both cases, the "rich reality" of the site acts to "sponsor a sense of community"; they are places where "reality and community conspire."[2]

Borgmann's poetry tempts us immediately to ask whether unreal or virtual environments can sponsor community in the same way that common engagement with rich material reality can. This is the "virtual community" question: Can digital communication networks mediate the sort of relationships located by the ballpark and hockey rink? Do *virtual* reality and community also conspire? These are tempting questions but, as a point of departure, they are too limiting if our aim is to appreciate the impact of digital technology, in its various and comprehensive manifestations, on the character of human relationships. The utilities typically associated with "virtual community"— multiple-user domains, chat rooms, discussion lists—represent only a small portion of the application of digital technology to everyday life, and it is not clear that the most significant social questions about this technology concern, or are contained within, the online environment itself. Digital technologies also work upon life offline: The reality into which digital technologies intervene is not just virtual. They intervene not only as instruments people use, but also as part of the material environment in which life unfolds. Borgmann's insight is that human social relations (not to mention individual human souls) always depend for much of their character on the material conditions in which they arise and subsist. As Borgmann puts it: "There is in every case a symmetry between human life and its setting."[3] The question is, then, what setting does digital technology provide for human life?

As Borgmann points out, some realities—the artificial environment of the domed stadium—are impoverished rather than rich and, as such, lack the necessary resources for a fruitful conspiracy with community. I argue that digital technology impoverishes rather than enriches our shared reality, at least so far as the concrete material foundations of community are concerned.[4] My contention is that this impoverishment is revealed in the relationship between digital technologies and our engagement with a common world of "things." Much of the debate over the social implications of digital technology is framed in terms of an encounter between location and communication. On the one hand, critics argue that digital technologies undermine the spatio-temporal location of human sociability, and that this dynamic threatens community relationships. On the other hand, proponents suggest that these technologies compensate for dislocation by mediating communication between displaced individuals, and so contribute to, rather than detract from, the possibility of community in the contemporary setting. As I concede below, there is considerable truth in both these propositions, and it pays to think them through. Nonetheless, the location–communication dialectic does not fully account for the setting that new information and communications technologies provide for community. Specifically, it fails to reckon with the crucial relationship between technologies and things, and between things and community. In what follows, I will argue that digital technology, as it is elaborated in the context of contemporary liberal capitalism, provides a material setting in which the concretion of a common world of things is systematically evaded, and so conspires more readily with commodity than with community.

A WORLD THAT IS NO WORLD

Human beings are radically limited by their situation in space and time, but our experience of this situation can vary considerably, especially when it is mediated and rendered artificial by technology. Naturally, we experience time as a recurrence of organic cycles (i.e., bodily rhythms, alternating days and nights, seasons, lifetimes) at rates specific to particular locations, and space as the extent of our regular habitation (i.e., where we live) and the distance over which we can reasonably travel, communicate, or see. Combined, these experiences of time and space as essentially limiting elicit a sense of "place" that localizes the organization and coordination of the common attention and activities of human communities. We are, by nature, local.

That being said, we are no longer natural, and perhaps we have never been. As David Harvey has argued, the human experience of space and time cannot be effectively separated from the specific material and symbolic practices that structure and endow it with meaning in any given context. Consequently, a radically natural experience of time or space would be very difficult for a social being to achieve. Additionally, Harvey writes, "The material practices from which our concepts of space and time flow are as varied as the range of individual and collective experiences."[5] The human apprehension of space and time is invariably social and varies, it would seem, across space and time.

Nevertheless, there are consistencies in the modern Western experience of space and time, and the mediation of this experience by technology is perhaps chief among them. Technological mediation—the standardized measure of time by clocks, calendars, and zones; the invention of the telescope; the proliferation of mapping; the development of transportation and communication technologies—artificially transgresses the natural limits of place, enabling the constitution and coordination of human attention and activity on scales and speeds greater than that of which nature provides and fits us. The name Harvey gives to this dynamic is "time-space compression," which he defines as follows:

> Processes that so revolutionize the objective qualities of space and time that we are forced to alter, sometimes in quite radical ways, how we represent the world to ourselves. I use the word "compression" because a strong case can be made that the history of capitalism has been characterized by speed-up in the pace of life, while so overcoming spatial barriers that the world sometimes seems to collapse inward upon us.[6]

In Harvey's view, intensification of the dynamic of time–space compression is the distinctive mark of postmodernity. Several others have also identified the construction of spatial and temporal experience as central to the trajectory of the modern West. Notable among these is Anthony Giddens, who identifies "time-space distanciation" as among the definitive marks of late modernity. In this dynamic, the localized experience of space and time characteristic of traditional societies is "disembedded" under the universalizing influence of symbolic tokens (e.g., national and international currencies) and technocratic systems.[7] For Giddens, the generalization of this dynamic under the auspices of globalization holds significant progressive potential.

If there is a consensus among those who reflect upon the social impact of digital media, it is that these technologies—despite whatever else they do—operate on our experience of space and time. In the digital age, social, political, and economic attention and activity are increasingly concentrated on and mediated by flows of data that race across vast distances in an instant. Under these conditions, the human experience of time and space as essentially localizing is fairly annihilated. As Manuel Castells puts it, when operated on by network technology, "Localities become disembodied from their cultural, historical, geographic meaning . . . inducing a space of flows that substitutes for the space of places. Time is erased in the new communication system. . . . The space of flows and timeless time are the material foundations of a new culture . . . the culture of real virtuality."[8] In this configuration of human experience, places are less important than processes; time, traversed by speed, becomes timelessness; and, as a material basis for individual lifestyles, connected mobility is more valuable than enduring, stable location. Indeed, under these dynamic conditions, location is typically experienced as a material liability rather than a source of strength and meaning.

Digital networks are neither the only nor the first technology to participate in the dislocation of human attention and activity. That modern technologies of mass and personal transport have enabled transgression of the limits imposed by distance is obvious. However, communication media have also always been technologies that work on the material of space and time. This was the crucial insight of Harold Innis.[9] According to Innis, communication media can be biased toward either the integrity through time of that which they mediate (time-biased media) or its portability through space (space-biased media). Time-biased media, such as stained glass windows and statuary, emphasize location and continuity and are not configured for reach or speed; space-biased media, such as mass printing on paper, money, electrical transmission, and broadcasting, emphasize the movement of large quantities of information across considerable distances at great speeds. In other words, time-biased media defer to the natural limits of space and time within which human beings are situated, while space-biased media operate to overcome these.

In Innis's view, the bias of a medium of communication emerges from equal parts technological and social determination. Technically, a medium such as the printed page (or a computer file) has the capacity to store a great deal of information for a very long period of time as well as enable its transport across great distances quite quickly. Which of these capacities ultimately defines the bias of the medium depends on which has a better rapport with the priorities of the society in which it is situated. The biases of communication media thus settle into a mutually reinforcing dynamic with the culture, politics, and economy of their age to establish what Innis called a "monopoly of knowledge."[10] In his view, the most stable and hospitable societies are those in which the monopoly of knowledge effects a balance between time and space bias—between concern for continuity and the extension of reach. Modern Western society, Innis lamented, has failed to achieve such a balance. Instead, the modern appetite for size and speed fairly overwhelms genuine attention to continuity or location, a condition both reflected in, and mediated by, an uninterrupted trajectory of space-biased communication technologies: the moveable-type printing press and paper; electric telegraphic transmission (which liberated communication from transportation); and electronic broadcasting.

As suggested above, digital communication technologies are probably best understood as a part of this trajectory of space-biased media rather than as a departure from it. Computerized networks introduce unprecedented levels of speed, automation, and reach into human communication, which decreases the need to synchronize and localize activity in particular places. Despite (or perhaps because of) their formidable capacity for storage and retrieval, these technologies also devalue the preservation of communicated information. The cultural priority of speed over continuity in communication is evident in the contrast between the frustration people demonstrate when their "downloads" of massive volumes of digital information are anything other than instantaneous, and the cavalier ease with which they unceremoniously "delete" these same volumes of information when they are no longer needed or desired. What, we might ask, could be more distant from our natural experience of space and time than the ability to receive in mere seconds, from a source across the globe, hundreds of "pages" rich in images and text that we feel quite comfortable to obliterate almost immediately should they not meet with our approval? That we expect instantaneous data flows rather than being astonished by them, and that we feel no hesitation in regularly destroying reams of digitally encoded information, are marks of both the vitality of space-bias in contemporary Western society and of the rapport that has been established between this society and the particular capacities of this technology. The space-biases of digital networks emerge as the perfect technological complement to the twenty-four-hour casino of global capitalism and culture, wherein everything is on, or on sale, all the time, everywhere, and nothing lasts too long. This is the acceleration of a dynamic identified by Innis over fifty years ago, just as that other great communication technology that would save modern communities—television—was about to take hold: "It is possible that we have become paralyzed to the extent that an interest in duration is impossible or that only under the pressure of extreme urgency can we be induced to recognize the problem."[11]

But what is the problem? Why does it matter that digital technologies accelerate a radical dislocation of our experience of space and time? On the basis of his sweeping history of Western civilization, Innis concludes that the cultural conditions attending monopolies of knowledge biased toward temporal continuity differ substantially from those biased toward spatial expanse. Societies with time-biased monopolies of knowledge—typically ancient societies—tended toward modesty of scale; localized attention; decentralized, personified political authority; personalized exchange relations; religiosity; celebration, tradition, and custom as practical, living embodiments of collective memory; nonspecialization; and community. Societies with space-biased monopolies of knowledge—most modern Western societies—tend toward grossness of scale; dislocated, cosmopolitan attention; centralized, rational-bureaucratic political authority; impersonal, commercial exchange relations based on the abstract forms of money and commodity; secularism; spectacle and consumption; specialization; and individual freedom and autonomy. Innis's "Plea for Time"[12] should not be understood as some romantic nostalgia for naive communalism. His view was that healthy societies are those that manage a balance between time-bias and space-bias, and that imbalance in one direction or the other— either the universal, homogenous republic of choice or the close, inward parochialism of the Hutterite colony—is fatal to human flourishing. Cosmopolitanism needs to be balanced by local traditions in order to prevent it from becoming deracinated homogeneity; and rootedness needs to be balanced by openness to diversity lest it descend into idiocy and bigotry. Either extreme is untenable in the long run.

That being said, as Innis once wrote: "Each civilization has its own methods of suicide."[13] If modernity is on the precipice it is because of the overwhelming space-bias of its dominant culture, abetted by communication technologies that comport with and mediate this imbalance. One need not accept these apocalyptic stakes to ask whether digital technologies are unfolding in such a way that they will right, or increase, this imbalance. As argued above, the infrastructural role these technologies play in political, economic, and cultural globalization seems to suggest that their destiny lies in continuing the trajectory of imbalanced space-bias that has characterized the modern West. We must assess the prospects of community under the auspices of this technology in this light. If digital technologies are predominantly space-biased, and if Innis is correct that communication media and practices that radically dislocate our experience of space and time are historically inimical to community, then we would do well to keep our expectations for community in the digital age relatively modest.[14]

Unless Innis is wrong and temporal/spatial orientations do not really matter to community. In 1916, John Dewey—in a statement echoed decades later by the likes of Jürgen Habermas and Benedict Anderson—asserted that "persons do not become a society by living in physical proximity, any more than a man ceases to be socially influenced by being so many feet or miles removed from others. A book or a letter may institute a more intimate association between human beings separated thousands of miles from each other than exists between dwellers under the same roof."[15] Forty years ago, Melvin Webber raised the possibility that modern urbanization, characteristically associated with decline in organic communal relationships, provided for "community without propinquity."[16] Communities need not be geographically localized, he argued, nor do they require immediate, face-to-face encounters.[17] Subsequently, Barry

Wellman and Claude Fischer argued that localized community as a basis for human association and sociability had long been literally dis*placed* into multiple networks of interpersonal ties that are not organized spatially.[18] Communication, it would seem, can compensate for dislocation.

Few would deny that most people in modern Western cities and suburbs (and perhaps even small towns) have little knowledge of, serious encounter with, or moral investment in the neighbors with whom they co-inhabit days and nights in buildings, blocks, or neighborhoods. To equate community with neighborhood, town, or city under these conditions is effectively to say that community simply designates an arbitrary physical boundary that contains very few substantial human relationships. Those who study social networks suggest that aspatial personal networks comprised of ties of varying degrees of intimacy and activity provide the very communal resources and experiences that local neighborhoods do not: support, sociability, information, and a sense of belonging.[19] In this vein, Wellman and Keith Hampton point out that "most of the social support, and much of the information and resources that people require to function in their day-to-day lives comes from sources outside of the local setting," and therefore, "community is best seen as a network—not as a local group."[20] This is probably true, and it substantiates rather than contradicts the argument that most human social relationships in the modern era are dislocated in space and time, essentially placeless. Whether this is cause for relief or concern depends on what one thinks a sense of place lends to human life, and on what one presumes to be the consequences of radical displacement and dislocation.

In any case, it is clear that these individuated networks of spatially dislocated interaction and association have been enabled, from the outset, by a variety of transportation and communication technologies, including especially automobiles, airplanes, and telephones. It is also clear that digital communication technologies are the perfect instrument of what Wellman has labeled "networked individualism"—sociability based on highly dynamic, spatially dislocated, nested networks of social ties constructed through individual choice and interests and maintained by communication.[21]

Some recent influential studies of Internet users are worth noting in this context: the first conducted by a group led by Barry Wellman using data from a large survey of visitors to the National Geographic website, a second by the Pew Internet and American Life Project, and a third by Keith Hampton based on his investigation (in which Wellman also participated) of a wired subdivision in suburban Toronto dubbed "Netville."[22] As one might expect, each of these studies found evidence that Internet users in significant numbers employ the medium to contact friends, family, groups, and organizations online. Digital communication media networks thus enable networked individuals to establish and maintain social ties with a variety of people, organizations, and associations.

What about specifically local or community concerns? In their work on the National Geographic survey, Wellman and his colleagues initially concluded that "the Internet is increasing interpersonal connectivity and organizational involvement. However this increased connectivity and involvement not only can expose people to more contact and more information, it can reduce commitment to community."[23] Subsequently, these authors revised their conclusion somewhat, emphasizing the correlation between frequent Internet use and a strong sense of *online* community, and suggesting that increased online activity "neither turns people on nor turns them off from an *overall* sense of community."[24] Whatever the case, the issue is moot because location as a basis for human associational or community life has long since ceased to matter. As the authors explain: "The security and social control of all-encompassing communities have given way to the opportunity and vulnerability of networked individualism. People now go through the day, week, and month in a variety of narrowly defined relationships with changing sets of network members."[25] In this sense, the Internet is playing precisely the role it ought to with respect to human sociability, enabling spatially and temporally dislocated associations and relationships.

The findings of the Pew study confirm this. While its author suggests that the results indicate "many Americans are using the Internet to intensify their connection to their local community,"[26] a closer look reveals that "many" might not mean very much. The study estimates that 90 million Americans use the Internet to contact groups. Later in the report we find that only 26 percent of these—roughly 23 million people—report that the Internet has helped them connect to "nearby groups" and, of these, "only 6% say it has helped them 'a lot' in getting them in touch with locally based groups."[27] The report concludes: "On balance, however, the vast majority of Internet users say the Internet is a useful tool for becoming involved in things going on *outside* their community. Two-thirds (67%) of Internet users say the Net helps them get involved in things outside their community, compared to only 9% who say it helps them get involved in things close to home."[28]

Hampton and Wellman's Netville studies complicate the issue somewhat. Netville is the fictitious name these researchers have given to a subdivision of 109 homes outside Toronto in which households were equipped by a consortium of technology and communication companies with advanced computer and network technologies. Homeowners moving to Netville would have free access to these advanced technologies and services in exchange for their agreement to have their use-patterns monitored and studied by the consortium (which also included select academic researchers). For what have been described as "various organizational reasons internal to the Magenta Consortium," 40 percent of Netville households were denied access to the network infrastructure despite initial assurances they would be fully wired—a glitch that served the happy purpose of providing researchers with a ready-made, nonwired control group against which they could compare the behavior of the wired residents.[29] In many respects, Hampton and Wellman's findings were predictable and consistent with those discussed above. Starting from the assumption that moving to a new neighborhood strains the ability of people to maintain their existing social ties, Hampton and Wellman found that the use of Internet communications alleviated this strain, particularly in relation to maintenance of ties across considerable distances. While the use of these technologies had no effect on distinctly local ties (within 50 kilometers), in the case of both midrange (50–500 kilometers) and distant (more than 500 kilometers) ties, wired residents of Netville fared better in terms of contact and support than nonwired residents.[30] These findings are consistent with the claim that the primary utility of digital communication technology—or, more specifically, e-mail—in relation to community under contemporary conditions is its effectiveness in mediating aspatial, far-flung associational or social networks.

There is, however, another finding that has emerged from the Netville studies that merits attention here. Hampton and Wellman have found that Netville's wired residents "neighbor" more extensively and more intensively than their nonwired counterparts. According to the study, "wired Netville residents on average know the names of 25 neighbors as compared to 8 for the non-wired, they visit each other's homes 50% more often, and the neighbors they know are spread more widely throughout Netville."[31] On this basis, Hampton suggests that new communication technologies "may hold as much promise of reconnecting us to communities of place as they do in liberating us from them," and that "the introduction of ICTs [information and communication technologies] specifically designed to facilitate communication and information sharing in a residential setting could reverse the trend of neighbourhood non-involvement."[32] The numbers regarding neighboring are certainly intriguing, and it does seem that digital communications contributed to localizing Netville, but Hampton does well to phrase his generalizations based on these findings in measured terms. It is not clear why a person who can recite twenty-five names she has seen repeatedly on a list of e-mail recipients should qualify as a better neighbor than one who can recall the names of eight people she has encountered in other ways; it is not surprising that contact through a digital network yields relationships that are more spatially dispersed throughout the neighbourhood than those produced by conversation that takes place over a fence; and it is not clear that the difference between 3.2 visits with the neighbors per year and 4.8 visits per year is really that significant.[33] In any case, we must keep in mind that while Netville is a real place, the conditions under which it has developed as a neighborhood are highly artificial. It may be the case that relatively well-distributed access to a dedicated, localized communications network that provides access to neighborhood content and contact can mediate a

replacement of community relations, especially amongst a relatively homogenous social group[34]—but it is not all clear that these characteristics pertain
to the dominant characteristics of Internet design and use, or of society, beyond the cul-de-sacs of Netville.

Nevertheless, what does emerge quite clearly from these studies is confir-
mation that community in North America has been progressively displaced
into dislocated, individualized social networks, and that digital communication and other technologies have contributed to the viability of this condition. However, as Castells writes in reflecting on this very phenomenon, "the
costs for society are still unclear."[35] Whatever community will be for those
who fully inhabit and partake of the digital age, it will be so under sociotechnical conditions of radical dislocation and displacement, compensated for by communication technologically enabled to surmount these very
conditions. Whether this compensation is full or partial, and whether it entails its own pathologies, is a separate question. Already in 1955, Martin Heidegger could observe: "All that with which modern techniques of communication stimulate, assail and drive man—all that is already much closer to man
today than his fields around his farmstead, closer than the sky over the earth,
closer than the change from night to day, closer than the conventions and
customs of his village, than the tradition of his native world."[36] Under these
conditions—arguably accentuated by digital technology—if community is to
exist at all, it will exist in a form appropriate to "the illusion of a world that
is no world."[37]

The Vanishing Table

Insofar as the argument that twins community with location is premised on
the assumption that dislocation makes authentic communication impossible, it
is untenable. Technology, as is its way, has made the seemingly impossible—
routine dialogic communication despite dislocation—seem possible and, in so
doing, breaks the location–community nexus, at least to the extent that regu-
larized dialogic communication is understood as definitive of community.
However, if we consider that community requires more than dialogic communication, there may be something else to say about its relationship with digital
technology. This section explores the possibility that meaningful engagement
with a common world of things is just as important to community as is communication or dialogue, and that the implications of digital technology for the
prospects of such an engagement are quite profound.

Concern with the distinctly modern phenomenon of technologically mediated wordlessness has not been restricted to reflection upon space and
time. For example, Hannah Arendt—the great theorist of worldlessness—
was concerned not so much with dislocation in place and time as with modern estrangement of human beings from a common world comprised of con-

crete material things. In Arendt's view, to dwell in the world was to be both related to, and separated from, others by concrete, enduring things that are the product of human work.[38] In laboring, we attend to the biological, animal needs of existence by producing items for consumption; in work—artful fabrication of objects for enduring use but not consumption—we build a common world that is the stage of our common interests, our "being among men (*inter homines esse*)" as Arendt puts it.[39] Referring to "the fabrication of human hands," she writes: "To live together in the world means essentially that a world of things is between those who have it in common, as a table is located between those who sit around it. The world, like every in-between, relates and separates men at the same time."[40] A "common world of things" that exists between human beings and nature provides a stable basis for dwelling in common interest—that is, in community—insofar as concrete things outlast individuals and their private needs, appetites, and passions. According to Arendt: "A community of things which gathers men together and relates them to each other depends entirely on permanence."[41] Human beings come and go but the world endures, at least insofar as the world is a world and not just, say, a cache of resources. As Arendt puts it:

> It is this durability which gives the things of the world their relative independence from men who produced and use them, their "objectivity" which makes them withstand, "stand against" and endure, at least for a time, the voracious needs and wants of their living makers and users. From this viewpoint, the things of the world have the function of stabilizing human life, and their objectivity lies in the fact—in contradiction to the Heraclitean saying that the same man can never enter the same stream—men, their ever-changing nature notwithstanding, can retrieve their sameness, that is their identity, by being related to the same chair and the same table.[42]

This, then, is the distinction between "the labor of our bodies" and "the work of our hands": The former gathers resources that disappear in consumption while the latter fabricates a common world of enduring things around which disappearing beings are gathered. Things are for use, not consumption: "Their proper use does not cause them to disappear and they give the human artifice the stability and solidity without which it could not be relied upon to house the unstable and mortal creature which is man."[43] Absent concrete, enduring things, "no common world and no public realm is possible."[44]

For Arendt, the modern human condition is marked by a crumbling of the common world of things:

> What makes mass society so difficult to bear is not the number of people involved, or at least not primarily, but the fact that the world between them has lost its power to gather them together, to relate and to separate them. The weirdness

of this situation resembles a spiritualistic séance where a number of people gathered around a table might suddenly, through some magic trick, see the table vanish from their midst, so that two persons sitting opposite each other were no longer separated but also would be entirely unrelated to each other by anything tangible.[45]

This worldlessness has a number of related causes, chief among them the elevation of the activities of labor (attention to biological appetite and necessity) over work (fabrication of objects) and action (Arendt's category for political deliberation and practical deeds), and a corresponding colonization of modern public life by activities of commerce strictly for the purpose of private consumption, whether immediate or deferred as accumulation.[46] Under this regime, work dissolves into mere labor, and the solidity and "intrinsic worth" of useful things dissolves into the "everchanging relativity" of commodity values established via the estimation of private, subjective tastes in public markets.[47] So reconfigured, things lose their objective quality and cannot serve as a firm basis for a common world that outlasts us. The end of production ceases to be the crafty fabrication of a useful thing that will endure, and becomes instead the technological generation of valuable commodities that disappear through consumption to make way for more commodities. The table degenerates from something concrete to gather around into an abstract value to be bought and sold by individuals. As a commodity exchanged, the table is passed from one laborer to another, from producer to consumer, but it does not remain between them as a thing that joins and separates them in common interest. Thus the material basis of community is compromised by the dissolution of the common world of things.

Technology plays no small role in this dynamic. The "problem of technology," according to Arendt, "is not so much whether we are the masters or slaves of our machines, but whether machines still serve the world and its things, or if, on the contrary, they and the automatic motion of their processes have begun to rule and even destroy world and things."[48] Her answer to this question is decisive: "For a society of laborers, the world of machines has become a substitute for the real world, even though this pseudo world cannot fulfill the most important task of the human artifice, which is to offer mortals a dwelling place more permanent and more stable than themselves."[49] If this is true, the implications for community are potentially profound.

These implications have been elaborated carefully by Albert Borgmann, who supplements Arendt's attention to things with a concern for the practices that safeguard them, and with a more radical understanding of commodity. Borgmann distinguishes between things and "devices." A thing "is inseparable from its context, namely, its world and from our commerce with the thing and its world, namely, engagement."[50] Devices, on the other hand, remove the world's material from its context and make it available to us in the form of commodities that alleviate the burdens of living in the world. Devices conceal the actual operations that accomplish this procurement and, in so doing, "dissolve the coherent and engaging character of the pretechnological world of things. In a device, the relatedness of the world is replaced by a machinery, but the machinery is concealed, and the commodities, which are made available by a device, are enjoyed without the encumbrance of or the engagement with a context."[51] To use Borgmann's example, a central heating plant is a device that "procures mere warmth and disburdens us of all other elements."[52] The heating plant conceals from consumers the manner in which heat is produced, and seems only to ask of them that they consume the warmth it makes available. By decontextualizing the production of warmth, the central heating plant disburdens us of the world without engaging us with it. The stove, on the other hand, is a thing that accomplishes more than just making warmth available. It also provides a focal point for engagement with its world via a set of focal practices that coheres around the stove: attending to the seasons, chopping wood, filling the wood box, building and tending the fire, gathering around the hearth. Practices, in this sense, are what things are for (just as availing us of commodities is what devices are for). Focal things are not produced for the sake of their production—they are not merely "stages on which nothing is ever enacted"[53]—but rather to center focal practices. In return, "A practice keeps faith with focal things and saves them for an opening in our lives."[54]

Borgmann's characterization of focal things and practices is rich:

> We might say this about focal things in general. They are concrete, tangible and deep, admitting of no functional equivalents; they have a tradition, structure, and rhythm of their own. They are unprocurable and finally beyond our control. They engage us in the fullness of our capacities. . . . A focal practice, generally, is the resolute and regular dedication to a focal thing. It sponsors discipline and skill which are exercised in a unity of achievement and enjoyment, of mind, body and the world, of myself and others, and in a social union.[55]

In focal things and the practices that guard them, reality is experienced as commanding and eloquent, quite unlike the commanded, muted reality that is opened to technological procurement as commodity under the device paradigm. Borgmann's list of focal things and practices includes the trout and fly-fishing, the wilderness and hiking, the horse and horsemanship, the instrument and musicianship, the meal and the culture of the table. There are potentially many others. However, in a technological world, devices and the commodities they make available typically displace focal things, and the disciplined burden of engaged, focal practice loses out to the ease of disburdened consumption. Technological devices make food readily available in the form of commodities that are convenient to consume ("fast" and prepared foods) but relieve us of the burdens (patience, skill, tradition, manners) of cultivating, gathering, and preparing food, and of eating it together around the same table. The table vanishes as a focal thing when the practices that focus upon it disappear into the brilliant ease offered by technological devices and commodities. In this instance we are deprived, technologically, of a site of engagement with the commanding and eloquent reality of the world, and of communion with other people. A focal practice such as the culture of the table, on the other hand, "discloses the significance of things and the dignity of humans, it engenders a concern for the safety and well-being of things and persons."[56] Clearly, there is something at stake for community here. The question is whether digital technology is oriented primarily toward devices and commodities, or toward focal things and practices.

Borgmann's later work refers to the "isolation of focal things and the diaspora of focal practices" under the auspices of postmodernity and its technologies.[57] Computerized information technology looms large here. As used by most people, the computer—like the central heating plant and its warmth—makes information and communication readily available as commodities, but it conceals (behind "Windows," ironically) the complex work of this accomplishment and the context in which it emerges. We need only to consider the strangeness (the *alienation*) of being able to do something so fantastic as to exchange complex messages with thousands of people all over the globe instantly and simultaneously, or to access representations of the entire content of a library or art gallery from a wafer thin disk (or from a URL) on our desktops, *without the execution of any substantial skill, craft, or knowledge whatsoever*, to appreciate the manner in which this device tears things from their context and estranges people from the commanding reality of the world. "Whatever is touched by information technology," Borgmann writes, "detaches itself from its foundation and retains a bond to its origin that is no more substantial than the Hope diamond's tie to the mine where it was found."[58] Information gathering and communication are mental activities, but their prosecution unfolds in the context of the concrete reality of the world, which includes time, toil, distance, and the presence and accommodation of others. The question is whether the mediation of these activities by digital networks is engaged with, or disengaged from, that reality: This will determine whether we are engaged in a focal practice, or disengaged, when we are gathering information and communicating with these devices. According to Borgmann, we can judge the focal significance of mental activity "by the force and extent with which it gathers and illuminates the tangible world and our appropriation of it."[59] The very appeal of network technology for most of its users is precisely that, despite the brilliance of its communication and information capacities, it still manages to leave darkened the tangible reality of just exactly how it appropriates the world.

Digital devices make extraordinary communication and information available to us as commodities, which is to say in a form that disburdens us of the challenges of the world and its reality. A commodity is, by definition, a convenience, something the purpose of which is to make life easier. The word "commodity" derives from the Latin root *commodus*, for that which has due measure, is suitable, convenient, or accommodating. It is typical to think of commodities exclusively in the classical Marxian sense as objects exchanged for money. Indeed, it is basically this conception of the commodity that underlines Arendt's diagnosis of the fate of things under the dominion of market relations, a diagnosis that speaks across decades to tell us a great deal about the escalating privatization and commercialization of the public sphere under the auspices of digital technology.[60] Still, the more radical notion of commodity as *that-which-is-commodious* can supplement our appreciation of digital media as technologies of worldlessness. In Borgmann's formulation, commodity—"the commodious way in which devices make goods and services available"[61]—is intrinsic to the modern technological dispensation. The "primary character" of technological commodities is "their commodious and consumable availability with the technological machinery as their basis and with disengagement and distraction as their recent consequences."[62] From this perspective, the commodity is not so much, or not solely, an object of exchange, but a quality that serves to disburden its possessor of the material difficulties of being in the world.

Whether the Internet becomes an exclusively commercial domain or not, digital technology certainly bears the marks of commodity in the sense of disburdenment, and its commodiousness extends beyond the ease with which it enables commercial exchange. Without digital devices, it would not be very easy to send identical messages from my desk in Ottawa to the desks of scores of political scientists scattered throughout Canada in the blink of an eye; or to receive a package of news reports from disparate sources, customized to my interests, on my computer every morning, (almost) no matter where I am in the world; or to gather, from my chair in the space of an hour, current documents from twenty governments around the world outlining their plans for the elaboration of digital infrastructure. Digital devices make all this easy. They are very convenient. That is what they are for. However, in the overwhelming convenience with which they make information and communication available to us, these devices deprive us of the more substantial engagements opened up to us when we confront the challenges of communication and information in the commanding reality of the world instead of devising ways around it.

We might consider here the different experiences of the student who comes to seminar and sits around the table with her fellows and hashes out the meaning of Heidegger's notion of "the fourfold," and the student who chooses to forgo seminar and get "the information" by e-mailing the professor or finding something about it on the Web. Let's assume, for the sake of argument, that these two students end up with roughly the same information about "the fourfold." What is the meaningful distinction between these two experiences? Obviously, one is easier, more convenient than the other. Showing up on time, staying alert for three hours, speaking, listening, deliberating, thinking—it's all hard work. Sending a one line e-mail ("I was just wondering, what's the fourfold?") and *not* waiting for the reply (the asynchronous genius of e-mail relieves us of the discipline of waiting patiently), or plugging "Heidegger's fourfold" into a search engine, at the time and place of one's choosing, is much more convenient. The other, perhaps more significant, difference is that one experience entails a focal practice while the other does not. As a thing, the seminar table gathers a focal practice: a practice with a tradition of its own; a practice the risks of which excite and engage the full capacities of those who undertake it; a practice that demands and nurtures dedication, resolve, discipline, and skill; a practice that presences mind and body, self and others, and culminates in the celebration of a common achievement. Something, perhaps, like a community. In addition, in this practice, very little of what is involved in reaching the collective outcome is concealed: Everything is on the table. This practice is what the seminar table, as a focal thing, is for.

The computer, in this example, is a device for avoiding the practice of the seminar by making the information available in a more convenient form. The computer can certainly deliver information about "the fourfold"—albeit information shorn of context and stripped of the markers of its achievement. It can also make the seminar table vanish and, with it, the practice that the table focuses. We might keep this in mind when we hear arguments that suggest the virtue of digital technology is that it makes it *easier* to be a member of a community, as in the following account of online community provided by Barry Wellman and Milena Gulia:

> With more ease than in most real life situations, people can shop around for resources within the safety and comfort of their homes or offices. Travel and search time are reduced. It is *as if* most North Americans lived in the heart of densely-populated, heterogeneous, physically-safe, big cities rather than in peripheral, low-density, homogeneous suburbs.[63]

The prospect here is that the device that makes community more convenient— by delivering it to shoppers as a commodity—may also be the device that drains community of the practices that give it substance and meaning.

This conflation of community and commodity brings us full circle in the discussion about things. For Arendt, when the work of our hands is given over to exchange wholly for the purposes of individual consumption, whether immediate or deferred as accumulation, when things lose their inherent worth as use-objects and are reduced to mere subjective values, we lose the shared world of stable, enduring things that relate and separate us in common interest. This worldlessness long preceded the onset of the digital age, although, I would venture, computer technologies certainly extend and accelerate it. What is left for community under these conditions? According to Arendt: "Historically, we know of only one principle that was ever devised to keep a community of people together who had lost their interest in the common world and felt themselves no longer related and separated by it." She refers here to Christian charity, "a bond between people strong enough to replace the world."[64] The virtue of charity abides, and it binds when it is offered and received, but it suffers in the context of a secular, bureaucratic, acquisitive society. So we are left to ask: What might now keep communities together despite the loss of interest in a common world of things that can relate and separate us?

The Internet, of course. Digital communication technologies, so complicit in the dissolution of the common world of things, are also well suited to make community available in the reduced form of commodious communication between networked individuals. The commodity of digital communication need not be limited to the vulgarities customarily associated with electronic commerce—software downloads, pornography, and customized Nike running shoes—but can be extended to include all manner of communicable, consumable, valued but expendable resources made conveniently available by this medium. As Wellman and Gulia argue, and as numerous other studies have confirmed: "Companionship, emotional support, services and a sense of belonging are abundant in cyberspace."[65] Contrary to what many critics of virtual community might imagine, these communal resources are easy, not hard, to find on the Internet because the medium eliminates many of the concrete challenges that make community in the real world so very hard to practice. True, the practice of community is strengthened by rising to, rather than evading, such difficulties, and doing away with them effectively removes the things that support the practice by challenging it. Nevertheless, homilies about the virtue of hard work (and the voices of our mothers telling us that "nothing worth doing is easy") are unlikely to persuade in the face of a good bargain, which is exactly what digital devices offer up when it comes to community.

Technologically mediated communication may indeed mitigate the negative impact of dislocation on community, especially in contexts where community is reduced to its communicative, dialogic aspects. It is not so clear that communication can adequately compensate for the loss of a common world of things, particularly communication mediated by technological devices that are also complicit in that loss. Phrased differently, it is not clear that community can bear the loss of focal things and focal practices with the same resilience with which it has borne the trauma of dislocation. It is difficult to say for certain whether the binding and separating action of common things is ultimately indispensable to community. My suggestion here is simply that community is impoverished, not necessarily eliminated, by technologically sponsored wordlessness, and that digital media participate in this sponsor-ship. It is certain that community is impossible without communication; it may also be the case that communication is meaningless without a world. To comprehend the relationship between digital technologies and community, we must hold these two propositions together, as Arendt does when—describing communication as "the premise for the existence of man"—she writes: "Existence itself is, by its very nature, never isolated. It exists only in communication and in awareness of other's existence. . . . Existence can de-velop only in the shared life of human beings inhabiting a given world com-mon to them all."[66]

My argument is that digital technologies affect both communication and its material setting. Specifically, in their very action as devices of commodious communication, these technologies simultaneously undermine our inhabita-tion of a common world of things. Thus, they provide a setting in which community appears as communication, but communication without a world that gives it meaning. It is worth pointing out that after the table vanishes, those once gathered around and separated by it still share a location, and they can still communicate; what sort of an association they might then have depends on what, absent the table, they would say to each other, why say-ing it would matter, and what it would mean to them. These things are hard to predict. Still, as a contrast to the sort of association in which communica-tion is easy but things are scarce, we might consider the community experi-enced by two neighbors who, on the heels of eight-hour shifts and forty-minute commutes, get their respective kids fed, bathed, kissed, and bedded, and then stand in the cold, joined and separated by fifty feet of ice they have just cleared and flooded for tomorrow's shinny, in silent recognition of that which they hold, and which holds them, in common. It remains to be seen whether community as commodious communication, between individuals dislocated in a world that is no world, will produce such wonders.

NOTES

1. Albert Borgmann, *Crossing the Postmodern Divide* (Chicago: University of Chicago Press, 1992), 136.

2. Borgmann, *Crossing*, 135.

3. Borgmann, *Crossing*, 96.

4. It is customary at this point to offer a "definition" of community that will inform the discussion to follow. I will refrain from doing so, largely because I think this is a rare instance in which strict definition is counterproductive. It has been my experi-ence that when one begins with a clear definition of community, consideration of subsequent argument is sacrificed to irresolvable contestation of that definition, es-pecially if it sets a high standard. In fact, the notion of "community" is so contested and variable that to choose one definition over another is essentially arbitrary, a

rhetorical strategy enlisted to lend normative support to the author's critique or endorsement of the operation of these technologies. In lieu of this, I would encourage the reader to engage with what follows in light of whatever understanding of community he or she regards as common and reasonable.

5. David Harvey, *The Condition of Postmodernity* (Oxford: Basil Blackwell, 1989), 211.

6. Harvey, *Condition,* 240.

7. Anthony Giddens, *The Consequences of Modernity* (London: Polity, 1990).

8. Manuel Castells, *The Rise of the Network Society* (London: Blackwell, 1996), 375.

9. Harold A. Innis, *The Bias of Communication* (Toronto: University of Toronto Press, 1951).

10. Innis, *Bias,* 4.

11. Innis, *Bias,* 88.

12. Innis, *Bias,* 61–91.

13. Innis, *Bias,* 141.

14. Directly or indirectly, Innis's concerns about dislocation are at the base of much of contemporary concern with the negative impact of digital communication technologies on community. See, for example, Catherine Frost, "How Prometheus is Bound: Applying the Innis Method of Communications Analysis to the Internet," *Canadian Journal of Communication* 28, no. 3 (2003), 9–24.

15. John Dewey, *Democracy and Education* (New York: Macmillan, 1964), 4–5. See also Jürgen Habermas, *The Structural Transformation of the Public Sphere,* trans. Thomas Burger (Cambridge: MIT Press, 1999); and Benedict Anderson, *Imagined Communities: Reflections on the Origin and Spread of Nationalism* (London: Verso, 1999).

16. Melvin Webber, "Order in Diversity: Community without Propinquity," in *Cities and Space,* ed. L. Wirigo (Baltimore: Johns Hopkins University Press, 1963).

17. For commentary on Webber's argument in light of contemporary conditions, see Craig Calhoun, "Community without Propinquity Revisited: Communications Technology and the Transformation of the Urban Public Sphere," *Sociological Inquiry* 68, no. 3 (August 1998), 373–97. Calhoun applauds Webber's "appreciation of the growing choice, flexibility, and multiplicity of relational groupings" available in modern urban and organizational situations. However, he also points out that "the conception of community with which [Webber] worked was remarkably vague and weak. Community meant no more to Webber than clusters of personal relationships characterized by some common identity and perhaps a bit of emotional warmth" (374).

18. Barry Wellman, "The Community Question," *American Journal of Sociology* 84 (1979), 1201–31; Claude Fischer, *To Dwell Among Friends: Personal Networks in Town and City* (Chicago: University of Chicago Press, 1982). See also B. Wellman, P. Carrington, and A. Hall, "Networks as Personal Communities," in *Social Structures: A Network Approach,* ed. B. Wellman and S. D. Berkowitz (Cambridge: Cambridge University Press, 1988).

19. Barry Wellman, "The Network Community," in *Networks in the Global Village,* ed. Barry Wellman (Boulder, Colo.: Westview, 1999).

20. Keith Hampton and Barry Wellman, "The Not So Global Village of Netville," in *The Internet and Everyday Life,* ed. Barry Wellman and Caroline Haythornethwaite (Oxford: Blackwell, 2002).

21. Barry Wellman, "Physical Place and Cyberspace: The Rise of Networked Individualism," *International Journal of Urban and Regional Research* 1 (2001).

22. John B. Horrigan, "Online Communities: Networks that Nurture Long-distance Relationships and Local Ties," Pew Internet & American Life Project, Washington, D.C., 2001; Barry Wellman, Anabel Quan Haase, James Witte, and Keith Hampton, "Does the Internet Increase, Decrease, or Supplement Social Capital? Social Networks, Participation, and Community Commitment," *American Behavioural Scientist* 45, no. 3 (November 2001), 436–55; Anabel Quan Haase, Barry Wellman, James Witte, and Keith Hampton, "Capitalizing on the Internet: Social Contact, Civic Engagement, and Sense of Community," in *The Internet and Everyday Life*, ed. Barry Wellman and Caroline Haythornethwaite (Oxford: Blackwell, 2002), 291–324; Keith Hampton, "Living the Wired Life in the Wired Suburb: Netville, Globalization and Civil Society," Doctoral Dissertation, Department of Sociology, University of Toronto, 2001; Keith Hampton and Barry Wellman, "Long Distance Community in the Network Society: Contact and Support Beyond Netville," *American Behavioural Scientist* 45, no. 3 (November 2001), 476-95.

23. Wellman et al., "Does the Internet Increase, Decrease, or Supplement Social Capital?" 450–51.

24. Haase et al., "Capitalizing on the Internet," 318. Emphasis added.

25. Wellman et al., "Does the Internet Increase, Decrease, or Supplement Social Capital?" 451.

26. Horrigan, "Online Communities," 2.

27. Horrigan, "Online Communities," 17.

28. Horrigan, "Online Communities," 25. Emphasis added.

29. Hampton and Wellman, "Long Distance Community," 481.

30. Hampton and Wellman, "Long Distance Community," 486–91.

31. Hampton and Wellman, "Long Distance Community," 486.

32. Keith Hampton, "Place-Based and IT Mediated 'Community,'" *Planning Theory & Practice* 3, no. 2 (2002), 228–31.

33. Figures taken from Hampton, "Living the Wired Life," 117.

34. Hampton and Wellman report that Netville residents were "similar in terms of age, education, and family status . . . largely lower middle class, English–speaking, and married." Most residents had children living at home, and most were white. Hampton and Wellman, "Long Distance Community," 481. One would presume that residents of Canada's first wired suburb were also relatively technologically literate.

35. Manuel Castells, *The Internet Galaxy: Reflections on the Internet, Business, and Society* (Oxford: Oxford University Press, 2001), 133.

36. Martin Heidegger, *Discourse on Thinking*, trans. John Anderson and E. Hans Freund (New York: Harper & Row: 1966), 48.

37. Heidegger, *Discourse on Thinking*, 48.

38. For another, related discussion of things and their relation to dwelling, see "The Thing" and "Building, Dwelling, Thinking" in Martin Heidegger, *Poetry, Language, Thought*, trans. Albert Hofstadter (New York: Harper & Row, 1971). According to Heidegger, things "gather" or "stay" "the fourfold" of "earth and sky, divinities and mortals," 171.

39. Hannah Arendt, *The Human Condition* (Chicago: University of Chicago Press, 1958), 51.

40. Arendt, *Human Condition*, 52.

41. Arendt, *Human Condition*, 55.

42. Arendt, *Human Condition*, 137.

43. Arendt, *Human Condition*, 136.

44. Arendt, *Human Condition*, 55.

45. Arendt, *Human Condition*, 52–53.

46. This point requires elaboration. Arendt understood that an artisan requires a market in which to exchange things with others. "The point," writes Arendt, "is that *homo faber*, the builder of the world and the producer of things, can find his proper relationship to other people only by exchanging his products with theirs, because these products themselves are always produced in isolation." Thus, "his public realm is the exchange market, where he can show the products of his hand and receive the esteem which is due him." The problem occurs, however, when the *whole* of public life is given over to commerce, and when the entire purpose of commercial exchange is mere consumption. "Historically," according to Arendt, "the last public realm, the last meeting place which is at least connected with the activity of *homo faber*, is the exchange market on which his products are displayed. . . . Its end came with the rise of labor and the labor society which replaced conspicuous production and its pride with 'conspicuous consumption' and its concomitant vanity." Arendt, *Human Condition*, 160–62.

47. Arendt, *Human Condition*, 164–65. In this sense, esteem is displaced from the worker to whom it is due and onto the product itself.

48. Arendt, *Human Condition*, 151.

49. Arendt, *Human Condition*, 152.

50. Albert Borgmann, *Technology and the Character of Contemporary Life: A Philosophical Inquiry* (Chicago: University of Chicago Press, 1984), 41.

51. Borgmann, *Technology*. 47.

52. Borgmann, *Technology*, 42.

53. Borgmann, *Technology*, 222.

54. Borgmann, *Technology*, 209.

55. Borgmann, *Technology*, 219.

56. Borgmann, *Technology*, 220.

57. Borgmann, *Crossing*, 122.

58. Albert Borgmann, *Holding on to Reality: The Nature of Information at the Turn of the Millennium* (Chicago: University of Chicago Press, 1999), 5.

59. Borgmann, *Technology*, 217.

60. See Darin Barney, "Invasions of Publicity: Digital Networks and the Privatization of the Public Sphere," in *New Perspectives on the Public Private Divide*, ed. Law Commission of Canada (Vancouver, Canada: UBC Press, 2003).

61. Borgmann, *Technology*, 42.

62. Borgmann, *Technology*, 259n5.

63. Barry Wellman and Milena Gulia, "Net Surfers Don't Ride Alone: Virtual Communities as Communities," in *Communities in Cyberspace*, ed. Peter Kollock and Marc Smith (New York: Routledge, 1999), 171–72.

64. Arendt, *Human Condition*, 53.

65. Wellman and Gulia, "Net Surfers Don't Ride Alone," 186.

66. Hannah Arendt, "What Is Existential Philosophy?" *Essays in Understanding: 1930–1954* (New York: Harcourt, Brace and Co., 1993), 186. This comes in the context of Arendt's endorsement of Jasper's placement of communication at the heart of the philosophic (and existential) enterprise over Heidegger's solitary contemplation—the latter, in her view, resulting in worldlessness and withdrawal.

3

Is the Internet the Solution to the Problem of Community?

Albert Borgmann

The nineteenth century was the first to feel the force of the radical transformations that came in the train of the industrial revolution. Its theorists and critics were well aware of the magnitude of these changes, and writers such as Thomas Carlyle, Karl Marx, and Friedrich Nietzsche left us observations, distinctions, and criticisms that have kept their relevance to this day. In this stream of reflections, there was a current that was concerned to articulate the fundamental shift in the human condition clearly and precisely. Henry Sumner Maine made one such attempt in his *Ancient Law* of 1861, where he famously concluded that the change was *"a movement from Status to Contract."*[1] Twenty-six years later, Ferdinand Tönnies tried to capture that same movement in a distinction whose terms, in German as well as in English, have remained both obvious and precise—the distinction between "Gemeinschaft und Gesellschaft," that is, between community and society.[2] Community by itself, of course, is a term of many senses—fifty-five if we are to agree with George Hillery.[3] It is the conjunction with *society* that gives *community* firm contours.

What Tönnies calls a community, Maine calls a *gens* or a house. It is one step up from the most basic of social units, the families.[4] While Maine thinks of the Roman houses or *gentes* as the illustration of a community, for Tönnies the leading example is a German village or town, and for us it may well be a Native American band. Remarkably, Maine's ascending order of families, houses, tribes, and the commonwealth perfectly fits the Blackfoot order of families, bands, tribes, and the Blackfoot Confederacy.[5]

In any case, a traditional community's members share their ethnicity, their ancestry, their religion, their customs, and some of their property. A community is small enough for each to know everyone and for all to be tied together by bonds of solidarity if not also of affection. The industrial *Grossstadt* or metropolis is the paradigm of society. The individuals of a big city are for the most part anonymous to one another. There is a diversity of races, practices, and religions.

In society, property is always private, either in the personal or in the economic and corporate sense. There is, strictly speaking, no commons, no property that is shared undivided and maintained by people who know one another and take joint responsibility for what they own in common. Roads and national forests are commons only in the technical but still important sense that they are open to all without registration or payment.

When we move the notions of community and society into the history of ideas, the distinction begins to show a normative edge. In the community-member relation, it is the community that is primary and assigns each person his or her place, function, and responsibility. The very notion of *member* suggests an organism whose parts serve the whole and perish when severed from it. The society-individual relation reflects the modern conception of the human being as the autonomous individual that begins with Hobbes and culminates in Kant. The individual is now the fundamental bearer of moral authority, and a society or a state owes whatever powers and rights it has to a grant and an agreement of individuals.

Hegel was an early and vigorous critic of individualism, but the force of his objections was overshadowed in Anglo-American philosophy by a controversy that took place *within* liberal democratic individualism, the disagreement between utilitarians and Kantians. The question was no longer whether a human being is essentially a member of a community or a self-determining individual, but rather whether the welfare of society could take precedence over the basic rights and well-being of some of that society's individuals.

Around 1980, *community* became a normative term in the critique of liberal democratic conceptions of the individual. The impetus came from Hegel, more particularly from Charles Taylor's work on Hegel. In the brief version of his work, Taylor had this to say about the autonomy of the self:

> The self which has arrived at freedom by setting aside all external obstacles and impingements is characterless, and hence without defined purpose, however much this is hidden by such seemingly positive terms as "rationality" or "creativity." These are ultimately quite indeterminate as criteria for human action outside of a situation which sets goals for us, which thus imparts a shape to rationality and provides an inspiration for creativity.[6]

Michael Sandel in turn was influenced by Taylor and extended the critique of the liberal self to the advocacy of the communal self and of what he called the strong view of community:

On this strong view, to say that the members of a society are bound by a sense of community is not simply to say that a great many of them profess communitarian sentiments and pursue communitarian aims, but rather that they conceive their identity—the subject and not just the object of their feelings and aspirations—as defined to some extent by the community of which they are a part. For them, community describes not just what they *have* as fellow citizens but also what they *are*, not a relationship they choose (as in a voluntary association) but an attachment they discover, not merely an attribute but a constituent of their identity.[7]

In 1981, Alasdair MacIntyre published a critique of the modern self that followed Aristotle and Thomas of Aquino more than Hegel. He called the self that is the same in everyone the *democratized self* and characterized it in terms by now familiar: "This democratized self which has no necessary social content and no necessary social identity can then be anything, can assume any role or take any point of view, because it *is* in and for itself nothing."[8]

For MacIntyre, the moral virtues are the counterforces to the ravages of modernity. Still, communities are needed if morality and civility are to survive: "What matters at this stage is the construction of local forms of community within which civility and the intellectual and moral life can be sustained through the new dark ages which are already upon us."[9] Thus was contemporary communitarianism born. It prospered throughout the eighties and early nineties, not least through the energy and resourcefulness of Amitai Etzioni.[10] It reached a high point in 1990 when the movement got its own journal, *The Responsive Community*. What propelled communitarianism was its promise to furnish, or perhaps uncover, a social vision that was less individualist than liberalism and less invidious than conservatism. In fact, the communitarians took much trouble and pride in proposing a set of social policies that were distinctively different from the positions on the left and on the right.

While conservatives for the most part looked benevolently on communitarianism, the liberals mounted a two-pronged attack. One prong was the charge of authoritarianism.

When Sandel said that people "discover" the attachments that are constituents of their identity, those bonds must evidently derive from the traditional communities people are born into. Marilyn Friedman did not mince her words when she replied: "Besides excluding or suppressing outsiders, the practices and traditions of numerous communities are exploitative and oppressive towards many of their own members."[11] Martha Nussbaum had it at MacIntyre in a similar vein:

In political terms, his view appears to endorse existing hierarchies, and to cast doubt on the coherence of radical social critique. It has been widely used by conservative thinkers in the United States, and fits neatly into a resurgence of "communitarian" thinking in U.S. conservative politics that stresses traditional "family values," questions the equality of women and homosexuals, and is at least tepid in its defense of racial equality.[12]

The other prong of the liberal critique was directed at the particulars of the communitarian program. Samuel Walker summarized the criticisms thus:

> In the end, the Communitarian Network Platform offers little in the way of specific proposals that would achieve its own goal of healthier communities. Several problems pervade the proposals in the Platform. On some issues, such as divorce, the proposals offer little more than feel-good rhetoric. On others, such as family leave, they refuse to confront the conservative political forces that have in fact blocked the development of a strong national network of social services. On the issue of crime policy, the Platform uncritically adopts conservative rhetoric without examining the evidence.[13]

It is fair to say that communitarianism no longer holds the attention of the intellectual community. In fact, commenting on the excitement a friend of communitarianism (Robert Putnam) has generated, a British writer remarked sniffily: "Perhaps we shouldn't get too excited. New Labour has a history of courting glamorous U.S. academics with fix-all solutions. Who now remembers Amitai Etzioni and his unsettling creed of communitarianism?"[14] This is surely unfair. A look at recent issues of *The Responsive Community* shows that significant writers continue to look at contemporary culture and current events from the communitarian point of view.

Moreover, the claim that communal life is uniquely beneficial to human flourishing has received unexpected support from evolutionary theory. Humans have evolved, and hence prospered, under specific circumstances, and most of their ailments today are due to the ignorant if not reckless abandonment of the salutary conditions of what has been called "the ancestral environment." That setting had a strictly physiological aspect— the conditions of nutrition and exercise. Seventy-five percent of mortality in advanced industrial countries is due to the fact that we fail to eat and to do what our Paleolithic ancestors did.[15] The physiological errors, however, can be corrected through "the Paleolithic prescription" of nutrition and exercise.[16]

This failure or fit between how we have evolved and how we live is the subject of "mismatch theory" or "discordance theory."[17] The part of the theory that is directly relevant to communitarianism deals with social and mental aspects. It points out that humans have evolved and now do well in small groups of friends and relatives and in a community of "intimacy and stability."[18] Much in society is injurious to communal well-being, and there is no ready Paleolithic prescription to heal those injuries—anxiety, depression, loneliness, aimlessness, and suicide.[19]

The problem of community, then, is that we need it but cannot have it. We need it to escape the anomie of individualism and the disorientation of anonymity, and to gain a sense of belonging, support, consistent affection, and, as Darin Barney has argued so well, of mutual obligation.[20] In short, our well-being requires community in this morally and socially normative sense. Yet the liberal critics are correct in stressing the validity and universality of equality, dignity, and liberty. These norms are the precious achievement of modernity. They constitute an epochal moral fact that invites explication and illumination, but in the end neither requires nor allows for a proof. The best evidence for the force of these norms is to see how all people of good will react when they see them violated. They rise up as one person to redress the injustice. But how can a privileged and surveyable group and a sense of particular and mutual benevolence arise when, from the moral point of view, all humans are exactly alike and have entirely the same claims on one another?

Not only the moral realm is inhospitable to community; so is the material setting of modern society. The best companions for anyone's community, relatives and friends, are dispersed and, what is worse, mobile. You may decide to up and leave well-loved work and a familiar town to be close to your children in the Midwest. But what if their dream is to live on the coast? Will you ask them to stay, given the investment in your recent move? Or will you reduce your life to that of a camp follower? And what if one daughter decides to move east and one west?

The Internet promises to provide the solution to the problem of community. To begin with, it appears to constitute in its text-based version the Rawlsian veil of ignorance that conceals the morally arbitrary and irrelevant features of a person—gender, skin color, accent, looks, height, wealth, and class.[21] It declassifies human beings into purely moral agents. And then it seems to reconcile the notions of freedom and obligation. A person is free to assume whatever obligations come with being a member of a chat group, a mailing list, or a Multi-User Domain (MUD). More particularly, the Internet preserves the kind of freedom that constitutes the paradigmatic form of modern liberty—freedom as unencumberedness, the freedom not only to initiate obligations but also to terminate them at will. You can leave a cybercommunity without having to apologize, suffer reproach, be disinherited, file for divorce, or pay child support. Most obviously, the Internet copes with dispersion by connecting people into a community no matter their location. It dissolves the communally injurious or irrelevant contingencies of space.

If all this seems too good to be true, let me remind you of some space of the truly cooperative and constructive achievements that have taken place in cyberspace. It has provided a habitat for what Andrew Feenberg has called "secondary instrumentation," the appropriation of a technology by a community for purposes of political activity, social support, or environmental protection.[22] In fact, the Internet became what it is through the pioneering and democratizing efforts of small groups.

The Internet, furthermore, has enlivened our ties to family and close friends. My wife and I would participate less in the lives of our daughters, take less pleasure in the growth of our grandchildren, and be less au courant with our relatives across the Atlantic were it not for e-mail and Web pages. In this way the Internet works as the telephone has worked—it supports but does not produce communities.[23]

Finally, there has been surprising social and linguistic creativity in e-mail, chat groups, and MUDs. New forms of acquaintance and exchange, new skills of conducting and comprehending conversations, and new ways of conveying information and emotion have sprung up on the Internet and are developing further as we speak here.[24]

In any discussion of community and the Internet, the Well looms large. It was certainly a splendid example of secondary instrumentation. A handful of inspired people wrested ongoing and online conversations from an obstreperous and, by contemporary lights, primitive electronic technology. It was a model and inspiration for subsequent efforts, and in its fifteen years of flowering it displayed most of the strengths and weaknesses that distinguish Internet communities. Thanks to Katie Hafner's great little book we now have a sympathetic and insightful record and interpretation of the Well's fortunes.[25]

For many of its participants, the Well provided, at least for a while, a fascinating social experience.[26] It generated friendships, marriages, messages of compassion, and works of charity.[27] It produced exchanges that sparkle with wit and inventiveness.[28] It also liberated people from the burdens of their physical appearance or psychological inhibitions. So, at any rate, Hafner suggests:

> The Well was a medium in which personalities quickly became evident—wisdom, humor, insight, and eloquence, or the dearth of such qualities, surfaced swiftly and purely, not filtered through the many physical attributes that color our perceptions of people when we meet them face-to-face. Perhaps those who shone online fell flat or went unnoticed in real life. Being online was an opportunity for the shy, self-conscious, or socially awkward to wield power, to command respect and gain popularity. The soft-spoken could dispense their quiet wisdom without interruption. By the same token, many people who tended to dominate in real-life conversation could find themselves at a loss when unable to call upon their mellifluous voices, fascinating faces, or sweeping physical gestures to give weight to hollow words.[29]

Finally, the recalcitrance of the fairly demanding software that delimited the Well's universe of discourse enforced a respectable level of technological engagement among its inhabitants.

The Well also displayed the problems that have haunted Internet communities ever since. Some of these are internal to communication in cyberspace. Others intrude from the surrounding culture. As for the internal ailments, the common claim that Internet communication has a socially or morally purifying and equalizing effect has another side to it. It is trivially true that text based communication filters out a person's actual physical appearance. But what remains and comes through is both a thinner and a more intense version of a person's character. A real bully will be a worse bully on the Internet. The Well had famously feisty characters and offensive posts.[30] Correspondingly, shy persons suffer more when attacked than self-assured people, and the shy ones retreat from the rough-and-tumble of belligerent posting. There is of course an initial phase of posting when a person's character is as yet undefined and untested. The bitterly resentful and mercilessly offensive Mark Ethan Smith (a woman actually) first appeared on the Well, in Hafner's words, as "another articulate, thoughtful poster."[31] But in the end and deep down, as Hegel scholars have reminded us, we crave recognition, the acknowledgement of who we are in fact.[32] Hence a person's character sooner or later wants out or cannot help itself from coming through, and so did "Mark Ethan Smith's" real identity.

Insidious outbursts would usually be reined in or stopped in face-to-face situations by the community itself. Virtual communities, to the contrary, would regularly be destroyed by such conflagrations were it not for moderators or wizards—resourceful people of good judgment who wield technologically effective power to stop messages or expel members. The Well depended entirely on the untiring work of moderators—evidence that the commercial spirit of a virtual community is weak and brittle.[33] "Most online groups," as Peter Kollock and Marc Smith put it, "have the structure of either an anarchy or a dictatorship."[34] So it appears, at any rate, when community extends beyond a definite utilitarian purpose and is expected to engage people's deeper concerns and loftier aspirations. But even a utilitarian scheme of sharing music via the Internet, such as Gnutella, is lop-sided toward taking rather than giving and could succumb to the Prisoner's Dilemma, where the multiple calculus of individual advantage is ruinous to the common good.[35]

In any event, the profound themes of the human condition—birth, friendship, love, marriage, parenthood, death—fail to sustain community and engagement in cyberspace, and communities break up into smaller communities, called "conferences" on the Well, some public and some private. The result in the case of the Wall, as Hafner reports, was injurious: "While the concept of a private conference was attractive, private conferences had had an eviscerating effect on the rest of The Well. Although there's nothing necessarily bad about breaking off into smaller groups if the core group is growing too large and impersonal, the net result was atomization."[36]

In *republic.com*, Cass Sunstein argues that this atomization is spreading through the Internet and imperils civic welfare, as people, focusing on their favorite topic with like-minded people, fail to experience unplanned encounters with diversity, and also fail to share the broadly common and unifying experiences that invigorate and steady civil society.[37] His claim has been roundly attacked and rejected and is surely untenable in this narrow version.[38] But surfing the Internet will likely aggravate the popular disinclination to immerse oneself in extended and demanding writings on social and political issues, and it weakens participation in the rump communities of family and friends.[39]

The enclitic character of virtual communities revealed itself particularly in the early exciting and engaging phase of the Well. What irrigated its flourishing did not flow from newly discovered virtual sources but from old-fashioned, face-to-face parties.[40] The excitement of the Well and the real life parties declined together.[41] Social capital, says Putnam, "may turn out to be a *prerequisite for*, rather than a *consequence of*, effective computer-mediated communication."[42] Perhaps the most damning comment on the sustainability of a vital virtual community came from one of its formerly most enthusiastic supporters, Howard Rheingold. Hafner reports:

> Rheingold had all but stopped posting to The Well as a daily practice, too, blaming the exodus of himself and others on what he characterized as the tired, predictable feel to the place. Rheingold gave this explanation, in an article in *Wired* magazine in July 1999: "After more than a decade on The Well, I found that I could predict who would react and how. And so I started asking myself: Why bother? Eventually I turned into little more than a lurker."[43]

Virtual communities are threatened from without as much as from within. A community in the normative sense needs a commons in at least the technical sense, a meeting place that is not under the direction of a corporation and not subject to profitability. The Well would have been impossible had not the federal government created something like an electronic commons by forcing Bell Telephone System to open its wires to traffic other than the one that the Bell Systems had exclusively favored—the analog wave forms of human speech. In 1968, AT&T was forced to permit the attachment of modems to the receivers so that digital messages could be sent across their wires. Before 1968 a modem would have been an illegal "foreign attachment."[44]

The Internet developed into a uniquely open and inviting commons, thanks to its end-to-end structure—the logic of the Internet itself is simple and general and leaves sophistication and specialization to the end points it connects.[45] Cyberspace, of course, consists of many more networks. In addition to Bell's systems, there are cable connections, satellite links, and the rest of the electromagnetic spectrum, occupied by radio, television, telephone, and more. Today, the tendency throughout cyberspace is toward control by corporate interests, and the consequence is a powerful bias away from accessibility and openness toward those uses that are most profitable.[46]

No virtual noncommercial community would have the money nor, very likely, the authorization to install its own communication links. But even if a stable commons is assured, a virtual community, to be truly independent of commercial intrusions, needs a server and a staff to see to its technical and social well-being. Throughout its existence, the Well had to struggle with the expenses of its substructure.[47] When millionaire Bruce Katz took over, poured millions of dollars into the Well, and tried to make it into a viable business, dissent and resentment rose from the depths of the Well.[48] Yet when finally the Well was sold to *Salon* in 1999, relief and pleasure were the common reactions.[49] To become part of an "online literary magazine" seemed like a congenial and reassuring solution. But hardly had the Well found refuge in the *Salon* when the storms of commercial exigency began to batter the refuge too.[50]

The intrinsic and extrinsic perils that beset virtual communities suggest that in the struggle between electronic community and the paradigmatic culture of technology, community has lost, or at any rate, has so far failed to prevail. In fact, it is one and the same culture that has eroded community from within and from without.

To put this in a larger context, we must remember that there was a twofold promise at the dawn of the common information era, sometime between 1975 when the first home computer, the Altair 8800, became available, and 1985 when the Well was founded.[51] Computers then represented the freshest and most advanced technology, and one thing it promised was insightful engagement with technology. A device such as the Altair 8800 was sophisticated enough to count as a bona fide computer and simple enough to be intelligible all the way down. As computers became more powerful, they presented another promise—to provide the framework for a new kind of community.

The promise of insightful engagement with technology collided head-on with the paradigmatic promise of technology, the promise of liberty and prosperity. Liberty was understood as liberation first from the burdens of hunger, disease, and confinement, and eventually from whatever task seemed aggravating or annoying. The notion of prosperity that agrees with liberation understood as disburdening consists of pleasures unmixed with any exertion or pain and unconstrained by time or location.

When you consider some of the great constants of the human condition—travel, nourishment, dwelling, entertainment—you can see how they were transformed from engagements into consumption goods. This transformation was made possible through increasingly powerful and sophisticated substructures that took on the burdens of availability and comfort. Take transportation. Two hundred years ago, most people traveled on foot. In the first half of the nineteenth century, railroads and streetcars became available. Late in the nineteenth century, the automobile came on the scene, and in 1908 the production of the Model T began. A car was then as intelligible and potentially engaging as the Altair 8800 was some sixty years later.

From then on, cars became ever faster, more comfortable, easier to operate, and safer. Over the course of the next eighty years, however, it became increasingly difficult to understand an automobile and to acquire the skills and tools to maintain it. A typical car of today is a marvel of comfort and convenience. It is also, for most people, as far as its mechanics and electronics are concerned, an impenetrable mystery. In the abstract, at least, a different development is conceivable. We might have valued technological literacy and mechanical competence above convenience and comfort and made intelligibility and lay-reparability overriding considerations. These standards are in fact honored in the construction of certain wind turbines and in the home power movement.[52]

Computer science and technology are both typical of the paradigmatic tendency in one regard and untypical in another. From the scientific and medical point of view, ever more powerful computers were desirable for high-minded reasons—the nobility of knowledge and the well-being of humans. But more powerful computers require higher-level languages, and looking through those languages all the way down to the machine language and the logic gates of a Pentium chip became impossible and unnecessary. In computer science and technology, the ascent to high-level languages, programs, and software packages is not, however, a descent into comfort and convenience. Expertise and engagement rather rise along with the growing distance to Boolean algebra and semiconducting switches.

As for the average consumer, the exponentially growing power of computers that is reflected in Moore's Law has chiefly redounded to the ease, speed, and enrichment of operation. Some of the best and brightest brainpower in this country is devoted to making computer interfaces still more intuitive and foolproof. In leisure time, therefore, computers are primarily used not for exercising skills, but for consuming commodities. There was a time when the Well and AOL were similar in size and structure. The Well tried to cling to community. AOL went after consumption.

Whatever is not made fast on the slopes of contemporary culture by stakes of excellence is overcome by consumption gravity and slides toward commodification. AOL is ready to give things a helpful push. At the height of cyberenthusiasm in 1999, AOL proclaimed its mission thus: "To build a global medium as central to people's lives as the telephone or television and even more valuable."[53] AOL was candid in its designs on people's time and life. One of its explicit goals was this: "It will develop new services to lure users to stay on line as long as three hours a day—the current average is 55 minutes—and, in the process, make advertising revenues as important to the company as subscriber fees."[54] Stephen Case, AOL's chairman, declared: "Our goal is to establish AOL as a more important part of tens of millions of people's every day life."[55] That year, AOL Time Warner's stock peaked at $95 a share. Late in 2002 the stock was trading at around $15. Within the year, it had been as low as $8.70.

Even before 9/11, sobriety had begun to settle on cyberintoxication. The dreamers had to wake up—venture capital ceased to flow, dozens of high-tech companies went bankrupt, and AOL is trying to regain its footing. And yet the fluorescent pleasures of cyberspace consist so well with the progressive dematerialization of technology and reality, and accord so well with the energy and resilience of capitalism, that renewed and successful efforts of the kind AOL has planned will almost certainly come to pass. Thus the economic and technical obstacles to community-building on the Internet are unlikely to be permanent.

There are those intrinsic limits to electronic communities. We can summarize and bring them into relief by distinguishing three kinds of communities—instrumental, final, and commodified. Instrumental communities, as the term suggests, are a means toward an end beyond or antecedent to the community. Such a community can serve social or technical ends. Thus family members or friends who love one another, and would do so regardless of the Internet, can use e-mail and websites to support and intensify relations among one another. This is the social case. The technical case is composed of communications that serve a medical or professional purpose or some research project, hobby, or the like. They are not primarily social because anyone can join who is devoted to the issue served by the community in question.

Of course the social and technical concerns can shade over into one another, though these are clearly distinct cases at the endpoints of this continuum. What sets all of them apart from final communities is the fact that final communities are ends rather than means, or, more precisely, they are the groups of people where one finds or works out one's reason for living. It is possible, to be sure, to articulate and live the meaning of one's life in solitude. But most of us have a family or a circle of friends with whom we do the things that make life worth living. We cannot imagine those things apart from our spouses, partners, children, or close friends. If we were to lose either those loved ones or the things and practices that unite us with them, we would fall into utter despair unless or until time would repair our losses in some way. The point is that final communities require the fullness of reality, the bodily presence of persons, and the commanding presence of things. Any attempt to secure the fulfillment of one's deepest capacities and aspirations in and through cyberspace will founder on the shoals of commodification.

The most common and precise sense of commodification is economic.

To commodify something economically is to pull something that is outside of the market into the market. As Marx liked to point out, in preindustrial rural life, almost everything was produced at home—food and clothing most importantly. Today most people buy rather than make their bread, wine, coats, hats, and so on, and this is possible only because of the massive commodification that occurred in nineteenth century Europe and North America. We all accept this kind of commodification. No one today refuses to buy shirts because spinning, weaving, and sewing have been commodified.

Commodification in the precise and technical sense of economics begins to acquire moral force when it comes to certain goods and services that we think should not be for sale, such as sex, bearing a child (surrogacy, so called), heirlooms, public lands, and political influence.[56] But such cases fail to capture the distinctive ethical significance that comes into play when commodification is used as a term of cultural criticism. What then is cultural commodification? It occurs when a thing or a practice is stripped of its customary context and support and made available in a reduced form that in the common cultural understanding is thought to be less cumbersome and more enjoyable. The burdens formerly borne by environment and engagement are transferred to a machinery (in a wide sense of the term) so that commodification and mechanization always go hand in hand.[57] Economic and cultural commodification largely overlap, but not entirely. Produce at the farmer's market is commodified economically—it is for sale, but not culturally—the context of place, season, and community is intact; the engagement of the growers is socially mediated when producers and customers talk about planting, pest control, fertilizing, and harvesting. Conversely, much of what is present on television is commodified culturally—it is present without context and exertion, but not economically—you do not have to pay for conventional television; it is a commons of consumption.

The Internet is culturally commodifying by its nature. It frees us from the limitations of space and time. Where research, utility, or social bonds provide a firm context, the commodifying tendency of the Internet does not matter and is in fact a useful feature. But the most intriguing promise of the Internet is to give us much more, to provide what appears to be best of two worlds—the ease and the riches of commodification and the profound fulfillment of a final community. What happens in fact is that commodification reduces ourselves and those we encounter on the Internet to glamorous and attractive personae. Commodification becomes self-commodification, but shorn of context, engagement, and obligation, of our achievements and failures, of our friends and enemies, of all the features that time has engraved on our faces and bodies—without all that we lack gravity and density.

Anecdotal evidence suggests that the initial encounter with a polished, if thin, self is pleasant and can be exciting, but at length the charm of a cyber-self begins to fade. The fate of purely electronic communication seems to be the ennui Katie Hafner reports in the case of Howard Rheingold. There is no good social science evidence about the emotional effects of prolonged socializing in cyberspace. Information about extensive use of the Internet is coming in, and although the case is by no means settled, the emerging contours of research appear to match the anecdotal ones. Use of the Internet at home leaves people feeling lonely and unhappy.[58]

The Internet truly serves final communities not as a focus but as a foil. It furnishes a background that highlights the necessary conditions of a community of meaning and fulfillment. Such a community needs to do justice to our evolutionary requirements. It has to be tangible and surveyable and peopled by persons we know and love. It has to respond to our moral and cultural aspirations in being centered on some of the great things of nature, art, or religion. Finally, it must be equal to the landmarks of modern ethics. Membership in a final community must be voluntary. The dignity of everyone needs to be guarded. And when a final community extends beyond family and close friends, it must have open membership. Devotion to the community's central concern must be the only requirement of membership.

NOTES

1. Henry Sumner Maine, *Ancient Law*, ed. Frederick Pollock (London: John Murray, 1912 [1861]), 174.

2. Ferdinand Tönnies, *Gemeinschaft und Gesellschaft* (Darmstadt: Wissenschaftliche Buchgesellschaft, 1979 [1887]).

3. George A. Hillery Jr., "Definitions of Community," *Rural Sociology* 20 (1975), 111–23.

4. Maine, *Ancient Law*, 123–74.

5. For a picture of Blackfoot social organization, see James Welch, *Fools Crow* (New York: Viking Penguin, 1987 [1986]).

6. Charles Taylor, *Hegel and Modern Society* (Cambridge: Cambridge University Press, 1979), 157.

7. Michael J. Sandel, *Liberalism and the Limits of Justice* (Cambridge: Cambridge University Press, 1982), 150.

8. Alasdair MacIntyre, *After Virtue* (Notre Dame, Ind.: Notre Dame University Press, 1981), 30.

9. MacIntyre, *After Virtue*, 245.

10. Michael D'Antonio, "I or We," *Mother Jones*, available at www.motherjones.com/mother_jones/MJ94/dantonio.html (accessed February 8, 2002).

11. Marilyn Friedman, "Feminism and Modern Friendship," in *Communitarianism and Individualism*, ed. Shlomo Avineri and Avner de-Shalit (Oxford: Oxford University Press, 1992), 107.

12. Martha Nussbaum, "Virtue Revived," *Times Literary Supplement* (July 3, 1992), 10.

13. Samuel Walker, *The Rights Revolution* (New York: Oxford University Press, 1998), 161.

14. Tristram Hunt, "Robert Putnam," *New Statesman* online, available at www

.chorion.org/core/files/culture/putnam2.txt (accessed November 7, 2002).

15. S. Boyd Eaton, Marjorie Shostak, and Melvin Konner, *The Paleolithic Prescription* (New York: Harper & Row, 1988), 62. See also Randolf M. Nesse and George C. Williams, *Why We Get Sick* (New York: Vintage Books, 1996).

16. Eaton et al., *Paleolithic*, 274–78.

17. Eaton et al., *Paleolithic*, 38–46; Robert Wright, "The Evolution of Despair," *Time* (August 28, 1995), 50–52.

18. Eaton et al., *Paleolithic*, 27–29 and 33–34; Wright, "Evolution," 53; Nesse and Williams, *Why We Get Sick*, 215–21; for an early statement, see Marshall Sahlins, *Stone Age Economics* (New York: Aldine de Gruyter, 1972), 1–39.

19. Wright, "Evolution," 50–57. See also references in note 17.

20. Darin Barney, "Communication vs. Obligation: The Moral Status of Virtual Community," in *Globalization, Technology, and Philosophy*, ed. David Tabachnick and Toivo Koivukoski (New York: SUNY Press, 2004).

21. John Rawls, *A Theory of Justice*, 2nd ed. (Cambridge: Harvard University Press, 1999), 118–23.

22. Andrew Feenberg, *Questioning Technology* (New York: Routledge, 1999), 131–47.

23. Robert Putnam, *Bowling Alone* (New York: Simon and Schuster, 2000), 168–69.

24. David Crystal, *Language and the Internet* (Cambridge: Cambridge University Press, 2001).

25. Katie Hafner, *The Well* (New York: Carroll and Graf, 2001).

26. Hafner, *The Well*, 23 and 30–33.

27. Hafner, *The Well*, 56–58.

28. Hafner, *The Well*, 27–30 and 51–52.

29. Hafner, *The Well*, 25. See also pp. 30 and 160.

30. Hafner, *The Well*, 34–37, 42–43, 81–82, and 115–18.

31. Hafner, *The Well*, 34.

32. Charles Taylor et al., *Multiculturalism: Examining the Politics of Recognition*, 2nd ed., ed. Amy Gutmann (Princeton: Princeton University Press, 1994).

33. Hafner, *The Well*, 55, 106–7, and 110–12.

34. Marc A. Smith and Peter Kollock, eds., *Communities in Cyberspace* (New York: Routledge, 1999), 13.

35. John Markoff, "More Taking Than Giving on the Web," *New York Times On the Web*, available at http://archive.nytimes.com/library/tech/00/08/biztech/articles/21shar.html (accessed February 6, 2004).

36. Hafner, *The Well*, 163.

37. Cass Sunstein, *republic.com* (Princeton: Princeton University Press, 2001). This (alleged) phenomenon has been called "cyberbalkanization." See Putnam, *Bowling Alone*, 177–78.

38. James Fallows, "He's Got Mail," *New York Review of Books* (March 14, 2002), available at www.nybooks.com/articles/151807 (accessed November 7, 2002).

39. Langdon Winner, "Enthusiasm and Concern: Results of a New Technology Poll," available at www.oreilly.com/people/staff/stevet/netfuture/2000/current/html (accessed February 29, 2000). Norman H. Nie and Lutz Ebring, "Internet and Society: A Preliminary Report," February 17, 2000, available at stanford.edu/group/sigss (accessed February 17, 2000).

40. Hafner, *The Well*, 10, 40, 44–47, 54, and 161.

41. Hafner, *The Well*, 163.

42. Putnam, *Bowling Alone*, 177.

43. Hafner, *The Well*, 178.

44. Lawrence Lessig, *The Future of Ideas* (New York: Random House, 2001), 45. See also p. 30.

45. Lessig, *The Future*, 34–39 and 88–89.

46. In addition to Lessig, see Charles C. Mann, "Who Will Own Your Next Good Idea?" *Atlantic* (September 1998), 57–82, and Jonathan Zittrain, "Balancing Control and Anarchy on the Internet," *Chronicle of Higher Education* 13 (October 2000): 320.

47. Hafner, *The Well*, 37, 39, and 69–70.

48. Hafner, *The Well*, 135–49.

49. Hafner, *The Well*, 169–73.

50. Felicity Barringer, "Salon Dismisses 13 Workers In Effort to Fight Shortfall," *New York Times* (June 8, 2000), section C, 8; Felicity Barringer, "Salon Will Start Charging its Web Readers," *New York Times* (2 October 2001), section C, 4.

51. See Albert Borgmann, *Holding On to Reality* (Chicago: University of Chicago Press, 1999), 162–65.

52. Gordon G. Brittan Jr., "Wind, Energy, Landscape," *Philosophy and Geography* 4 (2001): 169–84. Jesse Tatum, *Energy Possibilities* (Albany: SUNY Press, 1995).

53. Saul Hansell, "Now, AOL Everywhere," *New York Times* (July 4, 1999), section 3, 1.

54. Hansell, "Now, AOL Everywhere," section 3, 1.

55. Hansell, "Now, AOL Everywhere," section 3, 6. See also Seth Schiesel, "Planning the Digital Smorgasbord," *New York Times* (June 11, 2001), section C, 1 and 7.

56. Michael Walzer, *Spheres of Justice* (New York: Basic Books, 1983), 100–103.

57. See my *Technology and the Character of Contemporary Life* (Chicago: University of Chicago Press, 1984), 40–48.

58. See note 38 above.

4

Nihilism on the Information Highway: Anonymity versus Commitment in the Present Age

Hubert Dreyfus

Oh God said to Abraham, "Kill me a son." . . .
Well Abe says, "Where do you want this killin' done?"
God says, "Out on Highway 61."
Well Mack the Finger said to Louie the King
I got forty red, white, and blue shoe strings
And a thousand telephones that don't ring
Do you know where I can get rid of these things
And Louie the King said let me think for a minute son.
And he said yes, I think it can be easily done
Just take everything down to Highway 61.

Now the rovin' gambler he was very bored
He was tryin' to create a next world war
He found a promoter who nearly fell off the floor
He said I never engaged in this kind of thing before
But yes I think it can be very easily done
We'll just put some bleachers out in the sun
And have it on Highway 61.

—Bob Dylan, "Highway 61 Revisited"

In his essay, *The Present Age*,[1] written in 1846, Kierkegaard warns that his age is characterized by a disinterested reflection and curiosity that levels all differences of status and value. In his terms, this detached reflection levels all qualitative distinctions. Everything is equal in that nothing matters enough that one would be willing to die for it. Nietzsche gave this modern condition a name; he called it nihilism.

Kierkegaard blames this leveling on what he calls "the Public." He says that "in order that everything should be reduced to the same level, it is first of all necessary to produce a phantom, its spirit a monstrous abstraction . . . and that phantom is *the Public*" (*Present Age*, 59). But the real villain behind the Public, Kierkegaard claims, is "the Press." He warned that: "Europe will come to a standstill at the Press and remain at a standstill as a reminder that the human race has invented something which will eventually overpower it" (*Journals and Papers*, vol. 2, 483), and he adds: "Even if my life had no other significance, I am satisfied with having discovered the absolutely demoralizing existence of the daily press" (*Journals and Papers*, vol. 2, 163).

But why blame leveling on the public rather than on democracy, technology, consumerism, or loss of respect for the tradition, to name a few candidates? And why this monomaniacal demonizing of the Press? Kierkegaard says in his journals that "it is the Press, more specifically the daily newspaper . . . which make[s] Christianity impossible" (*Journals and Papers*, vol. 2, 163). This is an amazing claim. Clearly, Kierkegaard saw the Press as a unique cultural/religious threat, but it will take a little while to explain why.

It is no accident that, writing in 1846, Kierkegaard chose to attack the Public and the Press. To understand why he did so, we have to begin a century earlier. In *The Structural Transformation of the Public Sphere*, Jürgen Habermas locates the beginning of what he calls the "Public Sphere" in the middle of the eighteenth century.[2] He explains that, at that time, the press and coffeehouses became the locus of a new form of political discussion. This new sphere of discourse was radically different from the ancient polis or republic; the modern public sphere understood itself as being outside political power. This extrapolitical status was not just defined negatively as a lack of political power, but seen positively. Just because public opinion is not an exercise of political power, it is protected from any partisan spirit. Enlightenment intellectuals saw the Public Sphere as a space in which the rational, disinterested reflection that should guide government and human life could be institutionalized and refined. Such disengaged discussion came to be seen as an essential feature of a free society. As the Press extended public debate to a wider and wider readership of ordinary citizens, Burke exalted that, "in a free country, every man thinks he has a concern in all public matters."[3]

Over the next century, thanks to the expansion of the daily press, the Public Sphere became increasingly democratized until this democratization had a surprising result that, according to Habermas, "altered [the] social preconditions of 'public opinion' around the middle of the [nineteenth] century."[4] "[As] the Public was expanded . . . by the proliferation of the Press . . . the reign of public opinion appeared as the reign of the many and mediocre."[5] Many people, including J. S. Mill and Alexis de Tocqueville, feared "the tyranny of public opinion,"[6] and Mill felt called on to protect "nonconformists from the grip of the Public itself."[7] According to Habermas, Tocqueville insisted that "education and powerful citizens were supposed to form an *elite public* whose critical debate determined public opinion."[8]

The Present Age shows just how original Kierkegaard was. While Tocqueville and Mill claimed that the masses needed elite philosophical leadership and, while Habermas agrees with them that what happened around 1850 with the democratization of the Public Sphere by the daily press is an unfortunate decline into conformism from which the Public Sphere must be rescued, Kierkegaard sees the Public Sphere as a new and dangerous cultural phenomenon in which the nihilism produced by the Press brings out something that was deeply wrong with the Enlightenment idea of detached reflection from the start. Thus, while Habermas wants to recapture the moral and political virtues of the Public Sphere, Kierkegaard warns that there is no way to salvage the Public Sphere because, unlike concrete and committed groups, it was from the start the source of leveling.

This leveling was produced in several ways. First, the new massive distribution of desituated information was making every sort of information immediately available to anyone, thereby producing a desituated, detached spectator. Thus, the new power of the Press to disseminate information to everyone in a nation led its readers to transcend their local, personal involvement and overcome their reticence about what didn't directly concern them. As Burke had noted with joy, the Press encouraged everyone to develop an opinion about everything. This is seen by Habermas as a triumph of democratization, but Kierkegaard saw that the Public Sphere was destined to become a detached world in which everyone had an opinion about and commented on all public matters without needing any first-hand experience, and without having or wanting any responsibility.

The Press and its decadent descendant, the talk show, are bad enough, but this demoralizing effect was not Kierkegaard's main concern. For Kierkegaard, the deeper danger is just what Habermas applauds about the public sphere—as Kierkegaard puts it, "a public . . . destroys everything that is relative, concrete and particular in life" (*Present Age*, 62). The public sphere thus promotes ubiquitous commentators who deliberately detach themselves from the local practices out of which specific issues grow and in terms of which these issues must be resolved through some sort of committed action. What seems a virtue to detached Enlightenment reason, therefore, looks like a disastrous drawback to Kierkegaard. Even the most conscientious commentators don't have to have first-hand experience or take a concrete stand. Rather, as Kierkegaard complains, they justify their views by citing principles. Since the conclusions such abstract reasoning reaches are not grounded in the local practices, its proposals would presumably not enlist the commitment of the people involved, and consequently would not work even if enacted as laws. As Kierkegaard puts it in *The Present Age*: "A public is neither a nation, nor a generation, nor a community, nor a society, nor

these particular men, for all these are only what they are through the concrete; *no single person who belongs to the Public makes a real commitment*"
(63, my italics).

More basically still, that the Public Sphere lies outside of political power
meant, for Kierkegaard, that one could hold an opinion on anything without
having to act on it. He notes with disapproval that the public's "ability, virtuosity and good sense consists in trying to reach a judgment and a decision
without ever going so far as action" (*Present Age*, 33). This opens up the possibility of endless reflection. If there is no need for decision and action, one
can look at all things from all sides and always find some new perspective.
Accumulating information thus postpones decision indefinitely because, as
one finds out more, it is always possible that one's picture of the world and,
therefore, of what one should do will have to be revised. Kierkegaard saw
that, when everything is up for endless critical commentary, action can always be postponed. "At any moment reflection is capable of explaining
everything quite differently and allowing one some way of escape " (*Present
Age*, 42). Thus one need never act.

All that a reflective age like ours produces is more and more knowledge.
As Kierkegaard put it, "by comparison with a passionate age, an age without
passion gains in *scope what it loses in intensity*" (*Present Age*, 68). He adds:
"We all know . . . the different ways we can go, but nobody is willing to
move" (*Present Age*, 77). No one stands behind the views the Public holds,
so no one is willing to act. Kierkegaard is clear that "reflection by transforming the capacity for action into a means of escape from action, is both cor-
rupt and dangerous" (*Present Age*, 68) He wrote in his journal: "Here . . . are
the two most dreadful calamities which really are the principle powers of
impersonality—the Press and anonymity" (*Journals and Papers*, vol. 2, 480).
Therefore, the motto Kierkegaard suggested for the Press was: "Here men
are demoralized in the shortest possible time on the largest possible scale, at
the cheapest possible price" (*Journals and Papers*, vol. 2, 489).[9]

In *The Present Age*, Kierkegaard succinctly sums up his view of the relation of the Press, the Public Sphere, and the leveling going on in his time.
The desituated and anonymous press and the lack of passion or commitment
in our reflective age combine to produce the Public, the agent of the nihilistic leveling: "The Press is an abstraction . . . which in conjunction with the
passionless and reflective character of the age produces that abstract phantom: a public which in its turn is really the leveling power" (64). Kierkegaard
would surely have seen in the Internet—with its websites full of anonymous
information from all over the world and its interest groups that anyone in the
world can join without qualifications, and where one can discuss any topic
endlessly without consequences—the hi-tech synthesis of the worst features
of the newspaper and the coffee house.[10] Indeed, thanks to the Internet,
Burke's dream has been realized. In newsgroups, anyone, anywhere, any-

time can have an opinion on anything. All are only too eager to respond to the equally deracinated opinions of other anonymous amateurs who post their views from nowhere. Such commentators do not take a stand on the issues they speak about. Indeed, the very ubiquity of the Net tends to make any such local stand seem irrelevant.

What Kierkegaard envisaged as a consequence of the Press's indiscriminate and uncommitted coverage is now fully realized on the World Wide Web. Thanks to hyperlinks, meaningful differences have, indeed, been leveled. Relevance and significance have disappeared. And this is an important part of the attraction of the Web. Nothing is too trivial to be included. Nothing is so important that it demands a special place. In his religious writing, Kierkegaard criticized the implicit nihilism in the idea that God is equally concerned with the salvation of a sinner and the fall of a sparrow. "For God there is nothing significant and nothing insignificant," he said. On the Web, the attraction and the danger is that everyone can take this godlike point of view. One can view a coffeepot in Cambridge or the latest supernova, look up references in a library in Alexandria, find out what fellowships are available to his specific profile, or direct a robot to plant and water a seed in Austria, not to mention plow through thousands of ads, all with equal ease and equal lack of any sense of what is important. The highly significant and the absolutely trivial are laid out together on the information highway in just the way Abraham's sacrifice of Isaac, red, white, and blue shoe strings, a thousand telephones that don't ring, and the next world war are laid out on Dylan's nihilistic Highway 61.

Kierkegaard even foresaw that the ultimate activity the Internet would encourage would be speculation on how big it is, how much bigger it will get, and what, if anything, all this means for our culture. This sort of discussion is, of course, in danger of becoming part of the very cloud of anonymous speculation Kierkegaard abhorred. Ever sensitive to his own position as a speaker, Kierkegaard concluded his analysis of the dangers of the present age and his dark predictions of what was ahead for Europe with the ironic remark that: "In our times, when so little is done, an extraordinary number of prophecies, apocalypses, glances at and studies of the future appear, and there is nothing to do but to join in and be one with the rest" (*Present Age*, 85).

The only alternative Kierkegaard saw to the Public's leveling and paralyzing reflection was for one to plunge into some kind of activity—any activity—as long as one threw oneself into it with passionate commitment. In *The Present Age*, he exhorts his contemporaries to make such a leap:

> There is no more action or decision in our day than there is perilous delight in swimming in shallow waters. But just as a grown-up, struggling delightedly in the waves, calls to those younger than himself: "Come on, jump in quickly"— the decision in existence . . . calls out. . . . Come on, leap cheerfully, even if it

means a lighthearted leap, so long as it is decisive. If you are capable of being a man, then danger and the harsh judgment of existence on your thoughtlessness will help you become one. (36–37)

Such a lighthearted leap out of the shallow, leveled present age into deeper water is typified for Kierkegaard by people who leap into what he calls the *aesthetic sphere of existence*. Each sphere of existence, as we shall see, represents a way of trying to get out of the leveling of the present age by taking the risk of making some way of life absolute.[11] In the aesthetic sphere, people make enjoyment of what is interesting the center of their lives.

Such an aesthetic response is characteristic of the Netsurfer for whom information gathering has become a way of life. Such a surfer is curious about everything and ready to spend every free moment visiting the latest hot spots on the Web. He or she enjoys the sheer range of possibilities. For such a person, just visiting as many sites as possible and keeping up on the cool ones is an end in itself. The qualitative distinction that staves off leveling for the aesthete is the distinction between those sites that are *interesting* and those that are *boring*, and, thanks to the Net, something interesting is always only a click away. Life consists of fighting off boredom by being a spectator of everything interesting in the universe and of communicating with everyone else so inclined. Such a life produces what we would now call a postmodern self—a self that has no defining content or continuity, and so is open to all possibilities and to constantly taking on new roles.

But we have still to explain what makes this use of the Web attractive. Why is there a thrill in being able to be up on everything no matter how trivial? What motivates a passionate commitment to curiosity? Kierkegaard thought that in the last analysis, people were addicted to the Press, and we can now add the Web, because the anonymous spectator *takes no risks*. The person in the aesthetic sphere keeps open all possibilities and has no fixed identity that could be threatened by disappointment, humiliation, or loss.

Life on the Web is ideally suited to such a mode of existence. On the Internet, commitments are at best virtual commitments. Sherry Turkle has described how the Net is changing the background practices that determine what kinds of selves we can be. In *Life on the Screen*, she details "the ability of the Internet to change popular understandings of identity." On the Internet, she tells us, "We are encouraged to think of ourselves as fluid, emergent, decentralized, multiplicitous, flexible, and ever in process."[12] Thus, "the Internet has become a significant social laboratory for experimenting with the constructions and reconstructions of self that characterize postmodern life."[13]

Chat rooms lend themselves to the possibility of playfully inhabiting many selves, none of whom is recognized as one's true identity, and this possibility actually introduces new social practices. Turkle tells us: "The rethinking of human . . . identity is not taking place just among philosophers but 'on the ground,' through a philosophy in everyday life that is in some measure both proved and carried by the computer presence."[14]

She notes with approval that the Net encourages what she calls "experimentation" because what one does on the Net has no consequences. For that very reason, the Net frees people to develop new and exciting selves. The person living in the aesthetic sphere of existence would surely agree, but according to Kierkegaard, "As a result of knowing and being everything possible, one is in contradiction with oneself" (*Present Age*, 68). When he is speaking from the point of view of the next higher sphere of existence, Kierkegaard tells us that the self requires not "variableness and brilliancy," but "firmness, balance, and steadiness" (*Either/Or*, vol. 2, 16, 17).

We would therefore expect the aesthetic sphere to reveal that it was ultimately unlivable. Indeed, Kierkegaard held that if one leapt into the aesthetic sphere with total commitment, expecting it to give meaning to one's life, it was bound to break down. Without some way of telling the significant from the insignificant and the relevant from the irrelevant, everything becomes equally interesting and equally boring, and one finds oneself back in the indifference of the present age. Writing from the perspective of an aesthete experiencing the despair that signals the breakdown of the aesthetic sphere, he laments: "My reflection on life altogether lacks meaning. I take it some evil spirit has put a pair of spectacles on my nose, one glass of which magnifies to an enormous degree, while the other reduces to the same degree" (*Either/Or*, vol. 1, 46).

This inability to distinguish the trivial from the important eventually stops being thrilling and leads to the very boredom the aesthete Netsurfer dedicates his life to avoiding. So, if one throws oneself into it fully, one eventually sees that the aesthetic way of life just doesn't work to overcome leveling. Kierkegaard calls such a realization *despair*. Thus, Kierkegaard concludes: "Every aesthetic view of life is despair, and everyone who lives aesthetically is in despair whether he knows it or not. But when one knows it, a higher form of existence is an imperative requirement" (*Either/Or*, vol. 2, 197).

That higher form of existence Kierkegaard calls *the ethical sphere*. In it, one has a stable identity and one engages in involved action. Information is not played with, but is sought and used for serious purposes. As long as information gathering is not an end in itself, whatever reliable information there is on the Web can be a valuable resource serving serious concerns. Such concerns require that people have life plans and take up serious tasks. They then have goals that determine what needs to be done and what information is relevant for doing it.

Insofar as the Internet can reveal and support making and maintaining commitments for action, it supports life in the ethical sphere. But Kierkegaard would probably hold that the huge number of interest groups on the Net committed to various causes, and the ease of joining such groups, would eventually bring about the breakdown of the ethical sphere. The multiplicity of causes and the ease of making commitments, which should have supported action, will eventually lead either to paralysis or an arbitrary choice as to which commitments to take seriously.

To avoid arbitrary choice, one might—similar to Judge William, Kierkegaard's pseudonymous author of the description of the ethical sphere in *Either/Or*—turn to facts about one's life to limit one's commitments. Thus, Judge William says that his range of possible relevant commitments is constrained by his abilities and his social roles as judge and husband. Or to take a more contemporary example, one could choose which interest groups to join on the basis of certain facts about one's life situation. After all, there are not merely interest groups devoted to everything from bottle caps to cultural stars like Kierkegaard.[15] There are interest groups, for example, for the parents of children with rare and incurable diseases. So the ethical Net enthusiast might argue that to avoid leveling, all one need do is to choose to devote one's life to something that matters based on some accidental condition in one's life.

But the goal of the person in the ethical sphere, as Kierkegaard defines it, is to be morally mature, and Kant held that moral maturity consists in the ability to act lucidly *and freely*. To live ethically, then, one cannot base the meaning of one's life on what accidental facts impose their importance. Judge William is proud of the fact that, as an autonomous agent, he is free to give whatever meaning he chooses to his talents and his roles and all other facts about himself. He claims that, in the end, his freedom to give his life meaning is not constrained by his talents and social duties, unless he chooses to make them important.

Judge William sees that the choice as to which facts about his life are important is based on a more fundamental choice of what is worthy and not worthy, what is good and what is evil, and that choice is up to him. As Judge William puts it: "The good *is* for the fact that I will it, and apart from my willing, it has no existence. This is the expression for freedom. . . . By this the distinctive notes of good and evil are by no means belittled or disparaged as merely subjective distinctions. On the contrary, the absolute validity of these distinctions is affirmed" (*Either/Or*, vol. 2, 228).

But Kierkegaard would respond, if everything were up for choice, including the standards on the basis of which one chooses, there would be no reason for choosing one set of standards rather than another.[16] Besides, if one were totally free, choosing the guidelines for one's life would never make any serious difference, as one could always choose to rescind one's previous choice. A commitment does not get a grip on me if I am always free to revoke it.[17] Indeed, commitments that are freely chosen can and should be revised from minute to minute as new information comes along. The ethical thus ends up in despair because either I am stuck with whatever happens to be imposed on me as important in my life (for example, some life-threatening disease) and so I'm not free, or else the pure power of the freedom to make and unmake commitments undermines itself. As Kierkegaard puts the latter point: "If the despairing self is *active*, . . . it is constantly relating to itself only experimentally, no matter what it undertakes, however great, however amazing and with whatever perseverance. It recognizes no power over itself; therefore in the final instance it lacks seriousness. . . . The self can, at any moment, start quite arbitrarily all over again" (*Sickness unto Death*, 100).

Thus the *choice* of qualitative distinctions that was supposed to support serious action undermines it, and one ends up in what Kierkegaard calls the "despair of the ethical." One can take over some accidental fact about one's life and make it one's own only by freely *deciding* that it is crucially important, but then one can equally freely decide it is not, so in the ethical sphere all meaningful differences are leveled by one making one's freedom absolute.

According to Kierkegaard, one can only stop the leveling of commitments by being *given* an individual identity that opens up an individual world. Fortunately, the ethical view of commitments as freely entered into and always open to being revoked does not seem to hold for those commitments that are most important to us. These special commitments are experienced as gripping our whole being. Political and religious movements can grip us in this way, as can romantic relationships and, for certain people, such vocations as science or art. When we respond to such a summons with what Kierkegaard calls infinite passion, that is, when we respond by accepting an *unconditional commitment*, this commitment determines what will be the significant issue for us for the rest of our life. Such an unconditional commitment thus blocks leveling by establishing qualitative distinctions between what is important and trivial, relevant and irrelevant, serious and playful in my life. Living by such an irrevocable commitment puts one in what Kierkegaard called the "Christian Sphere of Existence."[18]

Of course, such a commitment makes one vulnerable. One's cause may fail. One's lover may leave. The detached reflection of the present age, the hyperflexibility of the aesthetic sphere, and the unbounded freedom of the ethical sphere are all ways of avoiding one's vulnerability. But it turns out, Kierkegaard claims, that, for that very reason, they level all qualitative distinctions and end in the despair of meaninglessness. Only a risky unconditioned commitment and the strong identity it produces can give an individual a world organized by that individual's unique qualitative distinctions.

This leads to the perplexing question: What role, if any, can the Internet play in encouraging and supporting unconditional commitments? A first suggestion might be that the movement from stage to stage would be facilitated by living experimentally on the Web, just as flight simulators help us learn to fly. One would be solicited to throw oneself into enjoying Netsurfing until it became boring, then into freely choosing which interest group was important until that choice revealed its absurdity. Finally, one would be driven to let oneself be drawn into a risky unconditional commitment as the only way out of despair. Indeed, at any stage from looking for all sorts of interesting websites as one surfs the Net, to striking up a conversation in a chat room, to joining an interest group to deal with an important problem in one's life, one might just find oneself being drawn into a lifetime commitment. No doubt this might happen—people do meet in chat rooms and fall in love— but it is relatively rare.

Kierkegaard would surely argue that, while the Internet, like the Public Sphere and the Press, does not *prohibit* unconditional commitments, in the end, it *undermines* them. Like a simulator, the Net manages to capture everything but the risk.[19] Our imaginations can be drawn in, as they are in playing games and watching movies, and no doubt, if we are sufficiently involved to feel as if we are taking risks, such simulations can help us acquire skills. But insofar as games work by temporarily capturing our imaginations in limited domains, they cannot simulate serious commitments in the real world. Imagined commitments hold us only when our imaginations are captivated by the simulations before our ears and eyes. And that is what computer games and the Net offer us. But the risks are only imaginary and have no long-term consequences.[20] The temptation is to live in a world of stimulating images and simulated commitments and thus to lead a simulated life. As Kierkegaard says of the present age, "It transforms the real task into an unreal trick and reality into a play" (*The Present Age*, 38).

The test as to whether one had acquired an unconditional commitment would come only if one had the passion and courage to transfer what one had learned on the Net to the real world. Then one would confront what Kierkegaard calls "the danger and the harsh judgment of existence." But precisely the attraction of the Net, like that of the Press in Kierkegaard's time, inhibits that final plunge. Indeed, anyone using the Net who was led to risk his or her real identity in the real world would have to act against the grain of what attracted him or her to the Net in the first place.

So it looks as though Kierkegaard may be right. The Press and the Internet are the ultimate enemy of unconditional commitment, and only the unconditional commitment of what Kierkegaard calls the religious sphere of existence can save us from the nihilistic leveling launched by the Enlightenment, promoted by the Press and the Public Sphere, and perfected in the World Wide Web.

NOTES

1. The following works by Søren Kierkegaard are cited parenthetically in the text: *The Present Age*, trans. Alexander Dru (New York: Harper and Row, 1962); *Journals*

and Papers, ed. and trans. H. V. Hong and E. H. Hong (Bloomington: Indiana University Press, 1967); *Edifying Discourses*, ed. P. L. Holmer (New York: Harper Torchbooks, 1958); *Either/Or*, trans. D. E. Swenson and L. M. Swenson (Princeton: Princeton University Press, 1959); and *The Sickness unto Death: A Christian Psychological Exposition for Edification and Awakening*, trans. A. Hannay (London/New York: Penguin, 1989).

2. Jürgen Habermas, *The Structural Transformation of the Public Sphere* (Cambridge: MIT Press, 1989).

3. Habermas, *Structural Transformation*, 94.

4. Habermas, *Structural Transformation*, 130.

5. Habermas, *Structural Transformation*, 131, 133.

6. Habermas, *Structural Transformation*, 138.

7. Habermas, *Structural Transformation*, 134.

8. Habermas, *Structural Transformation*, 137.

9. Kierkegaard would no doubt have been happy to transfer this motto to the Web, for just as no individual assumes responsibility for the consequences of the information in the Press, no one assumes responsibility for even the accuracy of the information on the Web. Of course, no one really cares if it is reliable because no one is going to act on it. All that matters is that everyone passes the word along by forwarding it to other users. The information has become so anonymous that no one knows or cares where it came from. Just to make sure no one can be held responsible, in the name of protecting privacy, identification codes are being developed that will ensure that even the sender's address will remain secret. Kierkegaard could have been speaking of the Internet when he said of the Press: "It is frightful that someone who is no one . . . can set any error into circulation with no thought of responsibility and with the aid of this dreadful disproportioned means of communication" (*Journals and Papers*, vol. 2, 481).

10. Although Kierkegaard does not mention it, what is striking about such interest groups is that no experience or skill is required to enter the conversation. Indeed, a serious danger of the Public Sphere, as illustrated on the Internet, is that it undermines expertise. As we saw in chapter 2, acquiring a skill requires interpreting the situation as being of a sort that requires a certain action, taking that action, and learning from the results. As Kierkegaard understood, there is no way to gain practical wisdom other than by making risky commitments and thereby experiencing both success and failure, otherwise the learner will be stuck at the level of competence and never achieve mastery. Thus the heroes of the Public Sphere who appear on serious radio and TV programs have a view on every issue, and can justify their view by appeal to abstract principles. However, they do not have to act on the principles they defend and therefore lack the passionate perspective that alone can lead to egregious errors and surprising successes and so to the gradual acquisition of practical wisdom.

11. Given Kierkegaard's use of the term "Sphere," precisely because reflection is the opposite of taking any decisive action, and therefore the opposite of making anything absolute, what Habermas calls the Public Sphere is not a sphere at all. A related nonsphere worth noting because it has become popular on the Net is de Chardin's Noosphere, which has been embraced by the Extropians and others who hope that, thanks to the World Wide Web, our minds will one day leave behind our bodies. The Noosphere, or mind sphere (in Ionian Greek *noos* means "mind"), is supposed to be

the convergence of all human beings in a single giant mental network that would surround the earth to control the planet's resources and shepherd a world of unified
love. According to Teilhard, this would be the Omega or End-Point of time.

From Kierkegaard's perspective, the Noosphere—where risky, embodied locality
and individual commitment would have been replaced by safe and detached ubiquitous contemplation and love—would be a confused Christian version of the Public
Sphere.

12. Sherry Turkle, *Life on the Screen: Identity in the Age of the Internet* (New York:
Simon and Schuster, 1995), 263–64.

13. Turkle, *Life on the Screen*, 180. A year after the publication of her book, Turkle
seems to be having doubts about the value of such experiments. She notes: "Many of
the people I have interviewed claim that virtual gender-swapping (pretending to be
the opposite sex on the Internet) enables them to understand what it's like to be a
person of the other gender, and I have no doubt that this is true, at least in part. But
as I have listened to this boast, my mind has often traveled to my own experiences
of living in a woman's body. These include worry about physical vulnerability, fears
of unwanted pregnancy and infertility, fine-tuned decisions about how much make-
up to wear to a job interview, and the difficulty of giving a professional seminar while
doubled over with monthly cramps. Some knowledge is inherently experiential, dependent on physical sensations" ("Virtuality and its Discontents: Searching for Community in Cyberspace," *The American Prospect* no. 24 [Winter 1996]).

14. Turkle, *Life on the Screen*, 26.

15. When I typed in Søren Kierkegaard, Google found 3450 hits; Alta Vista found
7452.

16. Jean-Paul Sartre develops the idea of the absurdity of fully free choice in *Being and Nothingness*.

17. Sartre gives the example in *Being and Nothingness* of a gambler who, having
freely decided in the evening that he will gamble no more, must, the next morning,
freely decide whether to abide by his previous decision.

18. There are two forms of Christianity for Kierkegaard. One is Platonic and disembodied. It is best expressed in St. Augustine. It amounts to giving up the hope of
fulfilling one's desires in this life and trusting in God to take care of us. Kierkegaard
calls this "Religiousness A," and says it is not the true meaning of Christianity. True
Christianity, or Religiousness B, for Kierkegaard, is based on the Incarnation and consists in making an unconditional commitment to something finite, and having the
faith-given courage to take the risks required by such a commitment. Such a committed life gives one a meaningful life in this world.

19. An attempt at inducing a sense of online risk was made in Ken Goldberg's telerobotic art project: Legal Tender (www.counterfeit.org). Remote viewers were presented with a pair of purportedly authentic U.S. $100 bills. After registering for a pass-
word sent to their e-mail address, participants were offered the opportunity to
"experiment" with the bills by burning or puncturing them at an online telerobotic
laboratory. After choosing an experiment, participants were reminded that it is a Federal crime to knowingly deface U.S. currency, punishable by up to six months in
prison. If, in spite of the threat of incarceration, participants click a button indicating
that they "accept responsibility," the remote experiment is performed and the results
shown. Finally, participants were asked if they believed the bill and the experiment

were real. Almost all responded in the negative. So they either never believed the bills were real or were setting up an alibi if they were accused of defacing the bills. In either case, they hadn't experienced any risk and taken any responsibility after all.

20. As Turkle puts it: "Instead of solving real problems—both personal and social— many of us appear to be choosing to invest ourselves in unreal places. Women and men tell me that the rooms and mazes on MUDs are safer than city streets, virtual sex is safer than sex anywhere, MUD friendships are more intense than real ones, and when things don't work out you can always leave" ("Virtuality and its Discontents: Searching for Community in Cyberspace," *The American Prospect* no. 24 [Winter 1996]).

5

Workers as Cyborgs: Labor and Networked Computers

Mark Poster

FROM WORKER TO CYBORG

Information technologies are indeed changing the world. The introduction of the computer and now the linkage of computers to the global network of the Internet vastly alter the patterns of life that have become customary in modern society. Individuals are now connected to one another and to the events and places around the world with an effective, instantaneous apparatus of information machines. The location in space of the individual body no longer limits the possibilities for that person to engage in relations with others, to act as a consumer, to participate in cultural or political events, or to connect with others having the same special interest. These changes also affect the domain of work.

In the relatively short span of a decade or two, the workplace has been transformed. Networked computers are ubiquitous in large corporations, medium- and small-size companies, mom-and-pop retail outlets, restaurants, even gas stations—in short, anywhere that humans work. From the clay tablets of the ancient world, to the introduction of double-entry bookkeeping in the Renaissance, to the typewriter in the late nineteenth century, to the cash register in the early twentieth century and the copy machine in the 1950s, information machines have accompanied the activities of human labor. Without belittling the importance of these earlier technologies of writing, calculating, recording, and copying, it is fair to say that they pale in significance compared to the influence of networked computers. Earlier information machines might be regarded as tools to assist human workers; networked computing promises radically to displace humans from the activities of producing commodities. The keyboard writing, if I may paraphrase an old homily, is clearly on the screen. The current situation of labor then must be viewed in light of the grand transformation going on around us. In this context we may well ask: How does networked computing affect workers?

Before exploring in detail the changes wrought by networked computing upon the domain of work, I wish to underline some important general features of what is at stake in this innovation. Human labor has entailed the application of muscle to the transformation of natural objects into usable goods. True enough, intelligence has always been at play in the process of work, finding the best and easiest method to produce the desired result. In addition, animals and tools have for eons been employed to assist mankind. Yet information about work remained limited by its confinement to the brain. Of course, memory has helped. Collective traditions of village, town, and guild extend the memory capacity of the single brain and are passed on in the training practices for new generations. Devices for recording labor practices are another form of extended memory, but these have been very slow to find a place in the routines of work. As late as the eighteenth century, Diderot's *Encyclopedia* was an early compendium on craft labor practices, breaking with guild traditions that kept them secret. Applying scientific methods to labor practices—a further example of information functions applied to work—began with Frederick Taylor first only in the early twentieth century.

Computerized information today is applied to human and machine labor with breathtaking rapidity. What distinguishes this effort from recording methods in books or applying systematic methods is that the computer, a machine, takes pride of place over the worker as well as over the mechanical machine. Hence we must understand labor as a product still of humans and mechanical machines, but even more as an accomplishment of information machines. These complex objects seriously upset the habits of mind we apply to the work world. Whether one conceives of work in the capitalist model of costs of production or the Marxist model of the organic composition of labor, information machines disrupt our models of comprehending work. When computers are central to production, it becomes difficult to measure costs and performances of either humans or machines. Information machines do not fit well into our frames of reference about work. Thus to add an information machine to a workplace is quite different from adding another worker or another mechanical machine.

Networked computing not only introduces into work the ontological oddity of the information machine, it also changes the territorial and temporal specificity of labor. Networked computing deterritorializes labor, rendering irrelevant the location on Earth of the work being done. Similarly it retemporalizes labor by introducing a register of instantaneousness that is comprehensible as computer time but not as human or even machine time. Because computers process information almost at the speed of light, this temporality is inserted into the calmer, more recognizable pace of the Newtonian temporalities of humans and machines. Further, information technology opens up to human inspection the microworld, with nanotechnology and other advanced procedures promising to profoundly transform entire regions of experience such as work, human reproduction, and medicine. In these ways, networked computing alters the cultural frame of labor, restructuring it in shapes that are not readily discernible.

Because networked computing inserts information machines into work and reorders the basic conditions of time and space, it also reconfigures the basic categories of mind and body, subject and object, that we unconsciously deploy in understanding the meaning of labor.

DIGRESSION ON METHOD

Information technology is an emergent phenomenon, one that is undergoing continuous and basic changes. If technologies such as the automobile and even the airplane have achieved a level of stability, such is not the case with networked computing. Because of the fluidity of the phenomenon, methods of analysis that measure it, usually in quantitative terms, are deeply limited. For example, studies in the 1990s measured the demography of online users, showing consistently that the population was affluent, young, white American males. All sorts of conclusions were drawn from these studies about the limitations of computer technology. By the end of the decade, women surpassed men and non-Americans surpassed Americans as online users. The elderly, the less affluent, and minority groups increased as a percent of total users. What is more, the purposes of online use have changed drastically as the technology developed. The introduction of the graphic user interface of the World Wide Web in 1993 added to networked computing sounds and images and altered completely the nature of online applications. One must then be careful in drawing conclusions from statistical measures in the realm of information technology.

Even methods of extrapolation are risky. Not only is information technology disseminating ever more widely around the globe and among different groups, it is also changing its fundamental character. As new applications are developed and as new technologies merge with older ones, the very character of networked computing changes.

THE CLASS STRUGGLE BY E-MAIL

In more traditional work locations, disruptions are almost as intense as in cyberspace. At major high-tech corporations such as IBM and 3Com, with the introduction of e-mail back in the Neolithic era of computing in the mid 1980s, management sought to modernize the practice of the suggestion box by replacing paper with electronic messaging. Without wasting time by moving the piece of paper with the proposal for change to the physically located suggestion box, the worker now simply sent an e-mail to management while seated at his or her workstation. At the forefront of the production of information machines, IBM and 3Com could certainly be proud of this innovation in working conditions. Yet with the aid of e-mail, workers took the occasion to embroider the idea of a suggestion box into a broad soapbox for critique. In their e-mails, workers reviewed management, most often finding fault, much to their superiors' embarrassment. Unlike the suggestion box, the complaining e-mails were widely distributed throughout the workplace, becoming a bulletin board for publicly posting the foibles of the leaders of the firm. Commentators observed that not only did e-mail save time, but "it encourage[d] workers of all ranks to change the rigid, hierarchical nature of communication."[1]

Within a few years, management at IBM learned its lesson. As a leader of the information technology sector, with computer messages surpassing phone calls within the company, it could not easily eliminate internal e-mail for workers. Instead it introduced software controls over its in-house conferences. By 1993, a system known as VOODOO (Virtual Organizer Optimizer Disk Organizer Optimizer) was introduced, which automatically monitored e-mails for offensive language, controversial topics, and the like. The program even discouraged irony and sarcasm. VOODOO did not last long, but controls are still in place over worker critiques of management.[2] Thanks to the widespread dissemination of computers and e-mail software, the 1980s and early 1990s saw a contest between management and workers over free expression and control of electronic communications internal to the firm.

In a recent case, workers invoke the National Labor Relations Act of 1935 in an effort to stop management from monitoring and censoring e-mail. The issue in many of these cases concerns again the right of workers to criticize management. Workers who were fired because of their carping e-mails have been reinstated or compensated as a consequence of rulings that invoke the National Labor Relations Act. This act ensures that workers have the right to communicate among themselves, and with these rulings by the National Labor Relations Board, e-mail is recognized as a valid means of communication. The surveillance of workers' e-mail by software programs, as well as the electronic surveillance of work with techniques, for example, of counting keystrokes, remains outside the jurisdiction of these decisions.[3]

If management appears to have gotten the upper hand by the end of this period, the struggle, if one may call it that, moved to another level with the birth of the World Wide Web in 1993. Now workers might have homepages on the Web outside the purview of management. Unhappy workers were henceforth able with impunity to vent their spleen for all the world to see. The scene of control shifted from management to Internet Service Providers (ISPs). When disgruntled workers used the Web to engage in "cybersmearing," raising questions about the economic status of the firm, which at times had repercussions on the stock market, pressure was placed on ISPs to monitor its users. Yahoo, for example, posted rules that prohibit messages that are "unlawful, harmful . . . defamatory, libelous . . . or otherwise objectionable."[4] Such protests took a much wider turn when, in June 2000, a virus (known as the "I Love You" virus) that disabled computers of major corporations and nations was attributed to a resentful man from the Philippines whose dissertation was rejected by his advisory committee. Workers with modest programming skills were perceived as a threat to the world's most powerful institutions.

CULTURES OF WORK

When the conditions of labor are so drastically restructured by information technology, we can expect disorientation and disruptions at the phenomenological level. And there are many of these. First of all, at locations most sensitive to these transformations, the breaks are greatest. In the labor of writing software programs, we find entirely new patterns and cultures of work. The figure of the nerd and the hacker are basically new types of workers. In the development of the computer industry during the 1970s and 1980s, a distinctive culture of work arose. Software programs were produced by highly educated workers who were trained in the new languages of machines. These workers were writers, after all, people who inscribed symbols, except these symbols were designed to control information machines—that is, were designed to be read not by an educated public, but by machines. One can say that programmers pioneered a new relation between humans and machines. They deployed cognitive abilities to communicate with inorganic objects. And they did so in a way that these objects would be empowered, so to speak, to perform tasks on information. Surely this is all very confusing.

Programmers were aware that they were participating in something new and even revolutionary. The ambience of Silicon Valley in Northern California resonated with the counterculture and New Left movements of the 1960s and 1970s, interpreting their highly technical activity as a continuation of the antiauthoritarian spirit and Aquarian sensibility. During the antiwar movement in 1970, one such hacker-professor at University of California, Irvine announced to the striking students, with the gravity of Trotsky or Lenin speaking to the workers' councils in 1917, that a computer connection now linked UC Irvine with Stanford University and UC Los Angeles. We now had available, he intoned as if an oracle, a means of communication with northern California that was not controlled by the media and could not be monitored by the FBI. By dint of networked computers, the movement was now autonomous, he thought, with its own links between campuses. The completion of the revolutionary takeover was only a matter of time.

The style of work in this nascent industry resembled nothing of the Fordist industrial factory or the offices of corporate America. Writing code requires great concentration and intellectual stamina. Programmers wrote for long hours brooking no supervision. It was as if software companies employed a bevy of talented literary people. One cannot exert Taylorist disciplines over the likes of Ernest Hemingway.[5] These workers had skills that were over the heads of management. In addition, these workers were comparatively young. To this day, programming and computer skills vary inversely with age. The figure of the young millionaire who earned his/her money rather than inherited it was born in the computer industry in the 1980s and 1990s. A young Steve Jobs working in his garage is legend. Many basic features of the Internet were developed by graduate students in their twenties: Multi-User Domains (MUDs), MUDs Object-Oriented (MOOs), Usenet, Internet Relay Chat (IRC), and the like. Teenagers with programming skills continue to threaten major corporations and even industries, such as Shawn Fanning at nineteen writing Napster, a program to facilitate sharing music files, and Jon Johansen, a Norwegian, at fifteen writing DeCSS, a program designed to defeat copy protection on DVDs. In addition, young people have been responsible for introducing viruses that paralyze major computer networks of the government and the economy (Robert Morris, a graduate student at Cornell) or invade sensitive computer sites (Kevin Mitnick arrested at age twenty-five by the FBI). With no experience of the corporate world of work, these youngsters with their programming skills wreaked havoc on the time-worn practices of capitalist modernity.

INFORMATICS AND CONTROL

If the culture of programmers introduced transgressions into the workplace, so did the business organization of high technology companies. The top-down, pyramid authority structures of industrial capitalism, with their continuous deskilling of workers, are not suited to information technology companies. From the outset, a much looser and perhaps more democratic structure arose in this industry. An early proponent of the democratization thesis concerning information technology is Shoshana Zuboff in her important book, *In the Age of the Smart Machine: The Future of Work and Power.*[6] Zuboff argues that the introduction of computers into the workplace and the general application of information technology make more democratic communications possible. With workers having access to computers, the larger processes of the firm's activities can be made available at each desktop. Instead of a hierarchical organization in which each level knows only what is particular to it, the computerized firm becomes, at every stage of activity, open for all to see. Zuboff writes, "Shared universal transparency can create a sense of mutual participation in and responsibility for operational and behavioral events. Joint access to the behavioral text can mean opportunities for joint learning."[7] When all departments, from purchasing to sales and customer service, have access to information about a work order—what Zuboff calls the "behavioral text"—a new degree of collective intelligence is brought to bear on economic operations. A process of dialogue might then open about the work order that would be impossible without computerization. The practice of negotiating and giving input from many points in the firm in turn might lead to a deeper sense of shared responsibility, again rendering obsolete the older structure of hierarchy.

Critics have been quick to point out problems with Zuboff's position. Stanley Aronowitz, for instance, argues against Zuboff's claim that informatics creates "a richer social text," claiming on the contrary that computer-mediated texts are "merely a kind of collective privatization, not a genuine democratic development."[8] This position, I believe, misses the point of Zuboff's contention. Information technology, she shows, changes the very nature of work in a fundamental way. In a stunning example from the paper industry, Zuboff describes the change in labor from an artisanal method in which workers touched, felt, and sensed the quality of paper at various stages of its formation, judging when the materials were ready for the next process to be applied, to an informaticized method in which workers monitored computer screens to ensure proper quality of production. In the latter case, the worker becomes a symbol manipulator, working cognitively rather than sensually. Once the paper worker operates on information machines, he or she is extracted from physical location and may easily have knowledge of the entire process of production. Work becomes the use of language and any worker who has facility with aspects of the language in question has a degree of power.

Critics of Zuboff also complain that far from democratizing the workplace, information technology makes possible new degrees of control by management over the worker, affords new ways through which the least movement of the worker can be monitored, recorded, and analyzed for performance evaluation. The computer affords management the ultimate power of knowing everything about the worker's activity by yielding it an absolute panoptic gaze. At issue here is what Michel Foucault called a "technology of power," a system of control of a few over many by a combination of discourses and practices.[9] In the nineteenth-century prison, Foucault surmised, a new form of power was constructed in which inmates could be monitored by a guard in a central tower without themselves being able to determine if the guard was on duty, was watching them or not. The purpose of this design, invented by Jeremy Bentham, was to instill into the prisoner the sense of constantly being watched. This internal authority, Bentham gauged, was the first step toward reform. Such a surveillance technique was supplemented by the development of the case file, thanks to the emerging field of criminology, in which records were kept on each convict. In addition, a fixed schedule of activities was introduced, also designed to discipline the criminal and introduce regularity into the life of the deviant. The regime of the panopticon thus brought to bear a system of power that would "correct" "abnormal" behavior. Foucault conjectured that the panopticon was disseminated throughout modern society—in hospitals, schools, factories, and the military—establishing a new form of social control he called "discipline."

There is little doubt that management has deployed panoptic methods in the course of the past century and a half, and it is now becoming clear that the introduction of information technology furthers the spread of this type of control. In fact Zuboff is well aware of the phenomenon of the panopticon, devoting a chapter to "The Information Panopticon." But she notes that the

> rendering of panoptic power reflects an important evolution of the original concept. It rests on a new collectivism in which "the many" view themselves and each views "the other." Horizontal visibility is created even as vertical visibility is intensified. The model is less one of Big Brother than of a workplace in which each member is explicitly empowered as his or her fellow worker's keeper. Instead of a single omniscient overseer, this panopticon relies upon shared custodianship of data that reflect mutually enacted behavior. This new collectivism is an important antidote to the unilateral use of panoptic power, but it is not a trouble-free ideal. Horizontal transparency breeds new human dilemmas as well.[10]

This analysis of the panopticon enhanced by information technology is not often noted by critics who simply observe that workers may, after the introduction of the computer into the firm, be monitored more effectively. They fail to see that workers also, in this system, take on the position of the observer and may watch management and other workers. It is most important in the discussion of information technology to take cognizance not only of the way the new machines alter existing positions of work, but also the way they enable new kinds of workers and new organizational forms of work practices. Sensitivity to new patterns of exploitation must be accompanied, as in Marx's analysis of early industrial capitalism, by an awareness of new possibilities for democratization. Otherwise analysis is limited to what Nietzsche called *resentiment*, discursively effecting not liberatory change but paralysis and defensiveness.

DIGITAL ORGANIZATIONS

But then there is the "real" world, which means Microsoft Corporation. If any company represents metonymically the information technology revolution, it is not IBM but Microsoft. And a glimpse of the Redmond, Washington, monster yields a picture that is not at all pretty. Readers of Douglas Coupland's *Microserfs*, portraying in intimate detail the daily life of Bill Gates's company, come away with a sad, disconsolate sense of lost opportunity.[11] Just as William Gibson's 1984 book *Neuromancer*, a punk science fiction novel, defined the Internet as "cyberspace" more compellingly than any computer scientist, social scientist, or humanist, so *Microserfs* depicted through a work of imagination the reality of labor in the greatest software company, indeed, as of 1999, the most highly capitalized corporation on the globe. Microsoft Corporation embodies the victory of old style entrepreneurship over the more beneficent possibilities opened by the introduction of information technology. The commodities created by Microsoft—first DOS, then Windows, then the rest of the applications (Word, Excel, Access, Internet Explorer, and so forth)—have domesticated as much as possible information technology to preexisting forms of economic activity and organization.

Notwithstanding Microsoft and other firms that have adapted new technologies as much as possible to Taylorist business organization, there are those who discern large opportunities for change in the domain of labor through the digitalization of information. Don Tapscott's *Digital Economy*, written for a popular audience with executives in mind, and Manuel Castells's *The Information Age*, a massive three volume compendium written for an academic audience, both herald fundamental changes in the economy, both depict this change as a consequence of the introduction of digital information technology, and both insist on the salience of the network, one global in scope, as the basis for a new economic order. Tapscott points out that some 60 percent of the workforce now manipulate symbols and 80 percent of new jobs are in this sector.[12] Less than 20 percent of workers are in the traditional primary and secondary sectors of agriculture, manufacturing, and mining. Castells adds a level of subtlety to these familiar figures by arguing that "the shift from industrialism to informationalism is not the historical equivalent of the transition from agricultural to industrial economies, and cannot be equated to the emergence of a service economy." At issue is not a shift in job activities because workers still perform in agriculture and manufacturing. The change is at another level. He writes, "What has changed is not the kind of activities humankind is engaged on, but its technological ability to use as a direct productive force what distinguishes our species as a biological oddity: its superior capacity to process symbols."[13] For Castells, and this is most important in understanding the effect of information technology upon labor, information technology means humanization. Labor now is directed more specifically than in the past upon the unique feature of our species: the brain.

The significance of Castells's observation is immense. Those who defend older forms of industrialism often do so with the claim that it is more humane, that computers somehow dehumanize work. The argument here is the reverse: Any animal may exercise muscle but no other species approaches the human ability with language. The move from an industrial to an informational economy is one toward the human. By implication, the direction and control of the new economy would have to proceed on principles different from those of the past. When muscle was shaped and organized by management, a certain pattern of hierarchy was installed and might be considered appropriate, a top-down system with clear lines of authority and responsibility, in short, a disciplinary regime as Foucault suggested. But when symbolization is the key to economic success, both Castells and Tapscott argue, a less rigid system of control is required, one that allows for inputs from many points in the structure, one that permits and even fosters the unknown, the invention, the creative insight to emerge from any position of speech and command respect regardless of the status of the speaker.

But Castells makes a fundamental error in his assessment of the humanization of the new digital economy. Paradoxically he fails to account for information machines. The "superior capacity of humans to process symbols" is a judgment relative to other living species. It is highly suspect when applied to computers. The new economy is one not of humanization but of posthumanization, of the deep symbiosis of humans with machines. It is not, as the Luddites argue, a dehumanization; that might have been true of industrialism, which organized production around the capacity of the mechanical machine. The digital economy, by contrast, organizes production around the partnership of humans with information machines. And it should be clear by now that two further tendencies are at play that Castells does not consider enough. First, the machines are becoming better and better at symbolization so that they will surpass human capacities in many areas of language use, if they have not done so already. Second, the humans are also likely to change with the advance of the genome project and the progressive understanding of DNA. We can no longer assume a world of fixed species with fixed traits, such as symbol processing, but must acknowledge that machines and humans are in the midst of a profound process of distinct but interrelated transformation.

The global network further complicates the position and character of labor. The combination of globalized production with world-wide communications removes spatial and temporal limitations that have characterized all previous economic systems. It is true that transportation methods have developed over thousands of years, enabling the trading of goods across local boundaries. It is also true that the industrial revolution considerably expanded the transport system by allowing motorized movement. The addition of networked computing lifted things up to a new level. Economic activities now could be coordinated regardless of location, with more workers commuting by modem, more processes administered by computer, and more transactions occurring over phone lines.[14] With the increasing amount of production and trade across national borders, more and more workers find themselves in competition with workers from other lands and working for firms based in other countries. The condition of work is now part of what Manuel Castells calls "the network society." He claims that "relationships between capital and labor (all kinds of capital, all kinds of labor) are organized around the network enterprise form of production. This network enterprise is also globalized at its core, through telecommunications and transportation networks. Thus, the work process is globally integrated, but labour tends to be locally fragmented."[15] Labor then finds itself in a new economic context, one that it is sorely unprepared for.

Generally speaking, the American labor movement responded to the network enterprise defensively. The North American Free Trade Agreement (NAFTA) and the General Agreement on Tariffs and Trade (GATT), two trade agreement systems of the 1990s that recalibrated economies to the condition of globalization by removing obstacles to trade, were broadly opposed by the unions. Demonstrations in Seattle in early 2000 against globalization via the meetings of the World Bank (WB) and World Trade Organization (WTO) included important participation by labor. The left generally hailed these protests as a sign that workers, ecologists, and many other groups had awakened to dangers of global capital. Before the demonstrations, few Americans knew much about the World Trade Organization; afterward the scene had been changed. A new awareness of the network society was thrust upon the populace. But the import of the meetings and the protests are not at all clear. Did they in fact represent the rebirth of the workers' movement, or were they the last gasp of that movement as it developed in the context of the industrial revolution?

The inequities of global capitalism are beyond question. The income gap is growing rapidly within the United States. As Don Tapscott, hardly a far left critic of capitalism, points out, "1 percent of American households own nearly 40 percent of the nation's wealth. The top 20 percent of American households . . . own 80 percent of the country's wealth. Wealth and income skewing is accelerating faster in the United States than in any other developed nation."[16] The situation is even worse globally. Estimates are that 85 percent of global wealth is consumed by 20 percent of population; the bottom 20 percent have 1.5 percent of world income. Although some Asian nations have vastly improved their economies since the 1970s, and although there are significant pockets of wealth in some Latin American countries, by and large, the North–South divide has grown deeper in terms of material conditions. Globalization and free trade, at least up to this point, appear to be benefiting primarily those already rich and harming those already poor. Proponents of globalization argue that a planet with free trade must increase the wealth of all nations while critics point to the unseemly facts of the present.

Yet the condition for the American worker wrought by the global network is itself globalized. Workers making shoes in Texas are in direct competition with workers making shoes in Bangkok. In fact they may be working for the same company. Yet the standards of living in the two places are vastly different, as are the wages. The hard question to face is how to take the new circumstances into consideration. A policy of defensive resistance by American workers is likely doomed to failure. If we examine the preparedness of the labor movement to develop a far-sighted and effective response, we see serious problems. As Eric Lee points out, labor unions as late as 2000 do not even have websites. There is little information-sharing across national boundaries; almost no databases exist of union activity, working conditions, and the like. Lee proposes the development of "online global labor press, archive/discussion group/journal and early warning network on trade union rights." And even these elementary steps, he judges, are "premature" given the indifference and ignorance of the union movement about new information technologies.[17]

Even in these dire circumstances, there are those who see the new global order as an opportunity rather than as a threat. Peter Waterman argues that capitalists pushing for global markets are inadvertently creating conditions for an international workers' movement. He calls for "new global solidarity" in the face of the march of the market.[18] Workers globally are now de facto in conditions of collective production. Thrust upon them by the greed and dynamics of capitalism, "workers of the world" is now a phrase that resonates not simply as a noble ideal but also as an empirical reality. For Waterman, looking backward to Marx, the laws of motion of the capitalist mode of production are producing the global conditions for its overcoming. If he is right, the question remains how the workers are to become aware of these circumstances and how are they to build a political movement to attain that end. One thing is sure: The *only* way a movement can be constructed of workers on a global scale is through the Internet. Network computing alone affords workers of different nations the possibility of communicating, accumulating mutually relevant knowledge and building a political movement. Given the slowness of at least the American labor movement to adapt the Internet to its purposes, the situation at present is bleak indeed.

If the deployment of information technology by the labor movement is a key in the response of labor to globalization, another condition that might also be understood as cultural is equally critical. Workers must see their identities as constructed through information technologies and in need of transformation from national to global configurations. Castells is cogently aware of the question of identity in relation to the network society. He contends,

> In a world of global flows of wealth, power, and images, the search for identity, collective and individual, ascribed or constructed, becomes the fundamental source of social meaning. . . . Identity is becoming the main, and sometimes the only, source of meaning in a historical period characterized by widespread destructuring of organizations, delegitimation of institutions, fading away of major social movements, and ephemeral cultural expressions. . . . It follows [that there exists] a fundamental split between abstract, universal instrumentalism, and historically rooted, particularistic identities. *Our societies are increasingly structured around a bipolar opposition between the Net and the Self.*[19]

The difficult problem that Castells puts in abstract language is that workers need to abandon their national identities and find a new source of identity as points in the network.

SOFTWARE AND YOU

This is a colossal conundrum. Cultural change of this sort is difficult, disorienting, and confusing. Information technology introduces restructured cultural space, putting into proximity phenomena that hitherto remained separate, and restructured culturally defined temporality, bringing into simultaneity events that previously appeared in a sequential or linear manner. Changing cultural configurations of time and space transform the individual's sense of self. As the self is composed of relations with others that serve to orient the individual in the world, new linkages such as remote intimacy upset the stability and coherence of everyday life.

Social scientists are discovering the profundity of these changes in microstudies of the workplace and information technology. Jackie Zalewski and Anteaus Rezba studied a hospital in the Midwest that introduced a software program for ordering supplies from the Internet. Previously, workers from various departments of the hospital filed new requests with the purchasing department, which then procured the supplies from vendors. This procedure led to face-to-face meetings between workers in purchasing and other sections of the hospital. Relationships developed over the years between purchasing agents and others so that if someone needed certain supplies more quickly than usual, these special requests could be accommodated. Zalewski and Rezba note also that the earlier system was inefficient and one of the motivations for management to introduce the new software. They also point out that the older procedures were more difficult than the new ones for management to control.[20]

Making purchases directly on the Web thus eliminated a network of personal contacts and relationships. To order equipment and supplies, workers now interface silently with a software program. The new system was more efficient and also, Zalewski and Rezba point out, facilitated management's greater control of the workers. Theorizing from the perspectives of Marcel Mauss, Raymond Williams, and Harry Braverman, among others, the researchers embed their findings in a narrative of worsening labor conditions. Information technology, they argue, furthers the alienation of the worker. They write,

> In general, electronic communications are void of personal nuances characteristic of face to face communications. Specifically, they lack framing, such as "Hello. How are you today?" This is, in large part, a function of the standard format of electronics' applications and Accolade's mandate to use them as the primary form of communications between departments. As a result, electronic communications can be characterized as instrumental, their content generally relays a Departmental supply need. Because the electronic system has the unique capacity to direct and document the actions of workers in the supply chain, obligations formerly developed between workers through verbal communications are replaced, to a large degree, by "an obligation to the System."[21]

While the authors are careful to present their work impartially, a narrative of decline and dehumanization creeps into their analysis.

The same cast is given by more well-known students of the labor process. Stanley Aronowitz and William DiFazio's *The Jobless Future* (1994) studies the introduction of information technology among architects and engineers in both the public and private sector in mid Atlantic states. After extensive interviews and analyses conducted over several years, they conclude that "computerized engineers and architects lose professional status by becoming more tightly controlled by managers. . . . Our studies showed that the Panopticon is not easily dislodged, that even the most revolutionary technology can be recruited in the interest of reproducing power, in this case to further degrade the labor of engineers, and even to be used as an instrument of proletarianization."[22] Although some of the workers in the study prefer the new technology, the students of labor, sensitive as they are to workers' rights, present a narrative of decline and a logic of suspicion about the motives of managers.

Information technology may not always fit easily into the interests of the rulers of industry. Joan Greenbaum studied the introduction of information technology since the beginnings of the introduction of computers into the workplace. She indicates how early mainframes fit into management strategies in very different ways from desktop or microcomputers. The latter provide workers with more flexibility and independence, certainly not a deliberate goal of management. In the next phase, desktop computers were connected by Local Area Networks (LANs). Network software attempts to bring workers again under more centralized control, but at the same time it enables the dispersion of the workplace in space. Greenbaum points out that "network software, user-friendly interfaces and integrated application packages reflect the interests of organizations to bind divided office labor back together, and simultaneously spread the results of this labor out over geographically dispersed areas of separate out-sourced units."[23] A new condition of spatial separation is made possible by networked computing, and this condition leads to unintended consequences with ambivalent implications. Linking dispersed workers precipitates new communications and new organizational possibilities. In Greenbaum's words, "The design concept of communication, like that of automation, may be running into conflict with the objectives of companies to compete in post-industrial capitalism, for it could be opening up possibilities for more bottom up communication and thus slowing down or interfering with management controlled objectives."[24] Here we have a more complicated perspective on the impact of information technology, one that points to the possibilities for new labor forms within networked computing.

POSTMODERN PERSPECTIVES

A review of some examples of labor studies concerning information technology indicates the need for vigilance concerning concepts and narrative structure. The story of networked computers in the workplace cannot be concluded at this moment. We are in the midst of a great transformation, to allude to the visionary writing of Karl Polanyi, whose outcome is far from certain. Information technology challenges us to expect the unexpected and search for concepts that allow the researcher to grasp the new as well as the old. At the theoretical level, Nick Dyer-Witheford provides a good instance of combining older theoretical perspectives with newer understandings of the possibilities for labor in the present conjuncture. He writes,

> At each point [in the circuit of capital] we will see how capital uses high technologies to enforce command, by imposing increased levels of workplace exploitation, expanding its subsumption of various social domains, deepening its penetration of the environment, intensifying market relations, and establishing an overarching, panoptic system of measurement, surveillance, and control through digital networks. . . . I argue that the development of new means of communication vital for the smooth flow of capital's circuit—fax, video, cable television, new broadcast technologies, and especially computer networks—also creates the opportunity for otherwise isolated and dispersed points of insurgency to connect and combine with one another.[25]

To take advantage of the economies of computerization, Dyer-Witheford continues, capitalism is compelled to promote a cadre of highly trained and skilled workers, what he calls "a virtual proletariat," a workforce strewn with new forms of resistance such as hacking. Far from a docile, disciplined, and controlled labor force, acts of noncompliance and outright resistance may be seen, he claimed, as increasing. *La perruque*, as per Michel de Certeau's term for informal, dilatory resistance, finds new avenues in the world of high technology.[26] Even traditional forms of labor protest are making their way into the high technology sector, as in the strike by Verizon workers in August of 2000. Some 86,000 workers went on strike, surprising the information industry behemoth, which relied on traditions of relatively, docility, and booming economic success. Equally, however, phone- and Internet-sex workers in Germany protest their conditions and demand fully parity with workers in more traditional sectors, and a judge in Kassel agreed with them.[27] Citing numerous examples of countermovements and oppositions that take advantage of networked computing, Dyer-Witheford foresees networked computing as having the unintentional consequence of creating the conditions for major changes in labor struggles. He opines that "somewhere between the ethereal activism of radio and computer networks, and the weary odysseys of proletarians trekking from San Salvador to Vancouver or from Manila to Kuwait City, a new global class composition is being born."[28] Whether or not a "new global class composition is being born," the advance in Dyer-Witheford's analysis rests with his awareness of the changes in spatial and temporal configurations introduced by network computing.

Like Castells, Dyer-Witheford leaves the cultural level of the question relatively unexamined. The formation of new identities, in Castells's term, or new class composition, in Dyer-Witheford's more Marxist language, rests with mediation of the medium, as we return necessarily to Marshall McLuhan's categories. The self is reconstructed in relation to information machines, machines that introduce a profound symbiosis with the human. While the emerging configuration of labor is necessarily, as Castells and Dyer-Witheford agree, a global one, it is also a posthuman one, uniting in depth technology with humans. The study of information technology and labor therefore must account for the assemblage of human and machine in new configurations of time and space, body and mind, subject and object, all of which, by the way, lie completely outside the intentions of managers and capitalists. In these new conditions, new forms of subjectivity must surely arise, those that are far more complex than the centered identities of the modern epoch. The mechanisms through which these multiple, dispersed, machine-linked subjectivities are constructed is a prime area for research and analysis in the domain of labor and information technology.

NOTES

1. Barbara Kantrowitz, "A New Way of Talking," *Newsweek* (March 17, 1986), 71.

2. Janny Scott, "On-Line, and Maybe out of Line Talking by Computer Has Changed the Way Workers Behave (and Misbehave)," *Los Angeles Times* (September 24, 1993), sec. A, 1.

3. Anush Yegyazarian, "Nosy Bosses Face Limits on E-Mail Spying—Workers Gain New Freedoms," *PC World* (September 2000), 62.

4. Greg Miller, "Online Power Gives David a Little Leverage on Goliath," *Los Angeles Times* (February 1, 1999), A7.

5. Andrew Ross, "Hacking Away at the Counterculture," in *Technoculture*, ed. Constance Penley and Andrew Ross (Minneapolis: University of Minnesota Press, 1991), 107–34.

6. Shoshana Zuboff, *In the Age of the Smart Machine: The Future of Work and Power* (New York: Basic Books, 1988).

7. Zuboff, *Smart Machine*, 361.

8. Stanley Aronowitz and William DiFazio, *The Jobless Future: Sci-Tech and the Dogma of Work* (Minneapolis: University of Minnesota Press, 1994), 102.

9. Michel Foucault, *Discipline and Punish: The Birth of the Prison*, 1st American ed. (New York: Pantheon Books, 1977).

10. Zuboff, *Smart Machine*, 351.

11. Douglas Coupland, *Microserfs* (New York: HarperCollins, 1995).

12. Don Tapscott, *The Digital Economy: Promise and Peril in the Age of Networked Intelligence* (New York: McGraw-Hill, 1996), 7.

13. Manuel Castells, *The Rise of the Network Society* (Cambridge, Mass.: Blackwell Publishers, 1996), 92.

14. Martin Carnoy et al., *The New Global Economy in the Information Age* (University Park: Pennsylvania State University Press, 1993).

15. Manuel Castells, "Materials for an Exploratory Theory of the Network Society," in *American Cultural Studies: A Reader*, ed. John Hartley and Roberta Pearson (New York: Oxford University Press, 2000), 421.

16. Tapscott, *The Digital Economy*, 285.

17. Eric Lee, "Trade Unions, Computer Communications, and the New World Order," in *Labour Worldwide in the Era of Globalization: Alternative Union Models in the New World Order*, ed. Ronaldo Munck and Peter Waterman (New York: St. Martin's Press, 1999), 242.

18. Peter Waterman, "The New Social Unionism: A New Union Model for a New World Order," in *Labour Worldwide in the Era of Globalization: Alternative Union Models in the New World Order*, ed. Ronaldo Munck and Peter Waterman (New York: St. Martin's Press, 1999), 254.

19. Castells, *Network Society*, 3, emphasis in original.

20. Jackie Zalewski and Anteaus Rezba, "'Where the Links Were Broken': Mandating Efficiency through an Electronics Supply Chain," unpublished manuscript (2000): 1–13.

21. Zalewski and Rezba, "Where the Links," 11.

22. Aronowitz and DiFazio, *Jobless Future*, 104, 131.

23. Joan Greenbaum, "From Chaplin to Dilbert: The Origins of Computer Concepts," in *Post-Work: The Wages of Cybernation,* ed. Stanley Aronowitz and Jonathan Cutler (New York: Routledge, 1998), 178.

24. Greenbaum, "From Chaplin to Dilbert," 181.

25. Nick Dyer-Witheford, *Cyber-Marx: Cycles and Circuits of Struggle in High-Technology Capitalism* (Urbana: University of Illinois Press, 1999), 92–93.

26. Michel de Certeau, *The Practice of Everyday Life*, trans. Steven Rendall (Berkeley: University of California Press, 1984).

27. Reuters. "Germany Decides Online Sex Workers Have Rights," *New York Times* (August 11, 2000), sec. Business: 1.

28. Dyer-Witheford, *Cyber-Marx*, 147.

6

Our Split Screens

Sherry Turkle

Computers influence our thinking about life and mind. They may do this quite directly. Research in artificial intelligence and artificial life explicitly tries to build machines that model the human mind and processes of evolution. Computational media also influence our thinking through their presence in everyday life. They are betwixt and between categories, animate yet not alive, thoughtful but not conscious, capable of intelligent reasoning but not (yet) minds. As boundary objects, they have a particular vocation as "objects-to-think-with." As almost-psychological machines, computational objects are evocative. When we interact with computers, when we project ourselves into the worlds they offer, the machines provoke reflection on self, life, and mind. In this sense, life on the screen brings philosophy into everyday life.[1]

These days, we are actors in a wide variety of computational landscapes—for example, we put ourselves in the virtual spaces of simulation games and create representations of ourselves in virtual communities on the Internet. Such involvements have complex "identity effects." At the same time that our "lives on the screen" facilitate an increased fluidity of identity play, we are immersed in simulations whose underlying mechanisms we do not understand and that may encourage us to see the world in simpler rather than more complex terms.

VIRTUAL PERSONAE ENTER THE HUMAN LIFE CYCLE

Cycling Through

In cyberspace, as is well known, the body is represented by one's own textual description, so the obese can be slender, the beautiful plain. The fact that self-presentation is written in text means that there is time to reflect upon and edit one's "composition," which makes it easier for the shy to be outgoing, the "nerdy" sophisticated. The relative anonymity of life on the screen—one has the choice of being known only by one's chosen "handle" or online name—gives people the chance to express often unexplored aspects of the self. Additionally, multiple aspects of self can be explored in parallel. Providers of online services offer their users the opportunity to be known by several different names. For example, it is not unusual for someone to be BroncoBill in one online context, ArmaniBoy in another, and MrSensitive in a third.

In the early 1990s, I studied a form of networked software known as MUDs (short for Multi-User Dungeons or Multi-User Domains). Using this software, people log in from all over the world, each at his or her individual machine, to join online virtual communities that exist only through and in the computer. MUDs are social virtual realities in which hundreds of thousands of people participate. The key element of "MUDding," the creation and projection of a "personae" into a virtual space, also characterizes simpler online communities such as bulletin boards, newsgroups, and "chat" rooms. MUDs may seem exotic, but they embody the general social and psychological dynamics of online life.[2]

When you join a MUD, you create a character or several characters, and you specify their genders and other physical and psychological attributes. Other players in the MUD can see this description. It becomes your character's self-presentation. In traditional role playing games in which one's physical body is present, one steps in and out of a character; MUDs, in contrast, offer a parallel life. Often, players on MUDs and the most avid participants in online life are people who work with computers all day at their "regular" jobs. As they play on MUDs, they may periodically put their characters to "sleep," remaining logged on to the game but pursuing other activities. From time to time, they return to the game space. In this way, they break up their work days and experience their lives as a "cycling through" between the real world and a series of simulated ones. The experience of "cycling through" is not limited to MUDs. One IRC (Internet Relay Chat) participant describes her experience of online talk: "I go from channel to channel depending on my mood. . . . I actually feel a part of several of the channels, several conversations. . . . I'm different in the different chats. They bring out different things in me." Identity play can happen by changing names and by changing places.

The "cycling through" behavior we see in virtual communities is made possible by the existence of what have come to be called "windows" in modern computing environments. Windows are a way of working with a computer that makes it possible for the machine to place you in several contexts at the same time. As a user, you are attentive to only one of the windows on your screen at any given moment, but in a certain sense, you are a presence in all of them at all times. You might be writing a paper in bacteriology and using your computer in several ways to help you: You are "present" to a word-processing program on which you are taking notes and collecting thoughts; you are "present" to communications software that is in touch with a distant computer for collecting reference materials; and you are "present" to a simulation program that is charting the growth of bacterial colonies when a new organism enters their ecology. Each of these activities takes place in a "window" and your identity on the computer is the sum of your distributed presence.

The development of the windows metaphor for computer interfaces was a technical innovation motivated by the desire to get people working more efficiently by "cycling through" different applications, much as time-sharing computers cycle through the computing needs of different people. But in practice, windows have become a potent metaphor for thinking about the self as a multiple, distributed, "time-sharing" system. The self is no longer simply playing different roles in different settings, something that people experience when, for example, one wakes up as a lover, makes breakfast as a mother, and drives to work as a lawyer. The life practice of windows is of a distributed self that exists in many worlds and plays many roles at the same time.

This notion of the self as distributed and constituted by a process of "cycling through" undermines many of our traditional notions of identity. Identity, after all, from the Latin *idem*, literally refers to the sameness between two qualities. On the Internet, however, one can be many and usually is. If traditionally, identity implied oneness, life on today's computer screen implies multiplicity, heterogeneity, and fragmentation.

When people adopt an online persona they cross a boundary into highly charged territory. Some feel an uncomfortable sense of fragmentation, some a sense of relief. Some sense the possibilities for self-discovery, even self-transformation. I have been studying people in the process of creating online personae since the early 1990s. They are able to articulate how the very process is personally evocative. A twenty-six-year-old graduate student in history says, "When I log on to a new MUD and I create a character and know I have to start typing my description, I always feel a sense of panic. Like I could find out something I don't want to know." A woman in her late thirties who just got an account with America Online (AOL) used the fact that she could create five account "names" as a chance to "lay out all the moods I'm in—all the ways I want to be in different places on the system." Another named one of the accounts after her yet-to-to-born child: "I got the account right after the amnio, right after I knew it would be a girl. And all of a sudden, I wanted that little girl to have a presence on the Net, I wrote her a letter and I realized I was writing a letter to a part of me." A twenty-year-old undergraduate says, "I am always very self-conscious when I create a new character. Usually, I end up creating someone I wouldn't want my parents to know about. It takes me, like, three hours." In these ways and others, many more of us are experimenting with multiplicity than ever before.

A Case Study of a Life on the Screen

"Case" is a 34-year-old industrial designer happily married to a female coworker. Case describes his RL (short for "real life") persona as a "nice guy," a "Jimmy Stewart type like my father." He describes his outgoing, assertive mother as a "Katherine Hepburn type." For Case, who views assertiveness through the prism of this Jimmy Stewart/Katherine Hepburn dichotomy, an assertive man is quickly perceived as "being a bastard." An assertive woman, in contrast, is perceived as being "modern and together." Case says that although he is comfortable with his temperament and loves and respects his father, he feels he pays a high price for his low-key ways. In particular, he feels at a loss when it comes to confrontation, both at home and at work. Online, in a wide range of virtual communities, Case presents himself as females to whom he refers as his "Katherine Hepburn types." These are strong, dynamic, "out there" women. They remind Case of his mother who "says exactly what's on her mind." He tells me that presenting himself as a woman online has brought him to a point where he is more comfortable with confrontation in his RL as a man. Additionally, Case has used cyberspace to develop a new model for thinking about his mind. He thinks of his Katherine Hepburn personae as various "aspects of the self." His online life reminds him of how Hindu gods could have different aspects or subpersonalities, or avatars, all the while being a whole self.

Case's inner landscape is very different from those of a person with multiple personality disorder. Case's inner actors are not split off from each other or his sense of "himself." He experiences himself very much as a collective whole, not feeling that he must goad or repress this or that aspect of himself into conformity. He is at ease, cycling through from Katherine Hepburn to Jimmy Stewart. To use the psychoanalyst Philip Bromberg's language, online life has helped Case learn how to "stand in the spaces between selves and still feel one, to see the multiplicity and still feel a unity." To use the computer scientist Marvin Minsky's language, Case feels at ease cycling through his "society of mind," a notion of identity as distributed and heterogeneous.[3] Identity, from the Latin *idem*, has been typically used to refer to the sameness between two qualities. On the Internet, however, one can be many and usually is.

Most recently, Ray Kurzweil, inventor of the Kurzweil reading machine and artificial intelligence researcher, has created a virtual alter ego: a female rock star named Ramona. Kurzweil is physically linked to Ramona. She moves when he moves; she speaks when he speaks (his voice is electronically transformed into that of a woman); she sings when he sings. What Case experienced in the relative privacy of an online virtual community, Kurzweil suggests will be standard identity play for all of us. Ramona can be expressed "live" on a computer screen as Kurzweil performs "her" and as an artificial intelligence on Kurzweil's web site.

In Western thinking about the self, "multiplicity" is a term that carries with it several centuries of negative associations; contemporary theorists are having an easier time with descriptions of multiplicity that stress the virtue of flexibility. We see this in the work of such authors as Kenneth Gergen, Emily Martin, and Robert Jay Lifton.[4] The essence of the "acceptable," flexible self is not unitary, nor are its parts stable entities. A person cycles through its aspects and these are themselves ever-changing and in constant communication with each other. The philosopher Daniel Dennett speaks of the flexible self in his "multiple drafts" theory of consciousness. Dennett's notion of multiple drafts is analogous to the experience of several versions of a document open on a computer screen where the user is able to move between them at will. Knowledge of these drafts encourages a respect for the many different versions while it imposes a certain distance from them.[5] The historian and theorist Donna Haraway, picking up on this theme of how a distance between self states may be salutary, equates a "split and contradictory self" with a "knowing self." She is optimistic about its possibilities: "The knowing self is partial in all its guises, never finished, whole, simply there and original; it is always constructed and stitched together imperfectly; and *therefore* able to join with another, to see together without claiming to be another."[6] What most characterizes Dennett's and Haraway's models of a knowing self is that the lines of communication between its various aspects are open. The open communication encourages an attitude of respect for the many within us and the many within others.

Screen Identities as Objects-To-Think-With

I first met notions of "decentered" identity, most notably that there is no such thing as "the ego"—that each of us is a multiplicity of parts, fragments, and desiring connections—in the intellectual hothouse of Paris in the mid 1970s. These ideas presented the world according to such authors as Jacques Lacan, Gilles Deleuze, and Félix Guattari. At the time that I met these ideas, my "French lessons" remained abstract exercises. These theorists of poststructuralism spoke words that addressed the relationship between mind and body, but from my point of view had little to do with my own.[7]

In my lack of personal connection with these ideas, I was not alone. To take one example, for many people it is hard to accept any challenge to the idea of an autonomous ego. While in recent years, many psychologists, social theorists, psychoanalysts, and philosophers have argued that the self should be thought of as essentially decentered, the normal requirements of everyday life exert strong pressure on people to take responsibility for their actions and to see themselves as unitary actors. This disjuncture between theory (the unitary self is an illusion) and lived experience (the unitary self is the most basic reality) is one of the main reasons why multiple and decentered theories have been slow to catch on—or when they do, why we tend to settle back quickly into older, centralized ways of looking at things.

When twenty years later, I first used my personal computer and modem to join online communities, I had an experience of this theoretical perspective that brought it shockingly down to earth. I used language to create several characters. My actions were textual—my words made things happen. I created selves that were made of and transformed by language. And in each of these different personae, I was exploring different aspects of my self. The notion of a decentered identity was concretized by experiences on a computer screen. In this way, cyberspace became an object to think with for thinking about identity. In cyberspace, identity was fluid and multiple, a signifier no longer clearly points to a thing that is signified, and understanding is less likely to proceed through analysis than by navigation through virtual space.

Appropriable theories, ideas that capture the imagination of the culture at large, tend to be those with which people can become actively involved. They tend to be theories that can be "played" with. So one way to think about the social appropriability of a given theory is to ask whether it is accompanied by its own objects-to-think-with that can help it move beyond intellectual circles.

For example, the popular appropriation of Freudian theory had little to do with scientific demonstrations of its validity. Freudian theory passed into the popular culture because they offered robust and down-to-earth objects-to-think-with. The objects were not physical but almost-tangible ideas such as dreams and slips of the tongue. People were able to play with such Freudian "objects." They became used to looking for them and manipulating them, both seriously and not so seriously. And as they did so, the idea that slips and dreams betray an unconscious started to feel natural.

In Freud's work, dreams and slips of the tongue carried the theory. Today, life on the computer screen carries theory. People decide that they want to interact with others on a computer network. They get an account on a commercial service. They think that this will provide them with new access to people and information, and of course it does. But it does more. When they log on, they may find themselves playing multiple roles; they may find themselves playing characters of the opposite sex. In this way they are swept up by experiences that enable them to explore previously unexamined aspects of their sexuality or that challenge their ideas about a unitary self. The instrumental computer, the computer that does things *for* us, has another side.

It is also a subjective computer that does things *to* us—to our view of our relationships, to our ways of looking at our minds and ourselves.

Online experiences with "parallel lives" are part of the significant cultural context that supports new ways of theorizing about nonpathological, indeed healthy, multiple selves.

"Dr. Sherry"

There is another sense in which life online can challenge our sense of identity. This was dramatized for me when one day on a MUD, I came across a reference to a character named "Dr. Sherry," a cyber-psychotherapist who has an office in the rambling house that constitutes this MUD's virtual geography. There, I am informed, Dr. Sherry administers questionnaires and conducts interviews about the psychology of MUDding. I have every reason to believe that the name "Dr. Sherry" refers to my fifteen-year career as a student of the psychological impact of technology. But I didn't create this character. Dr. Sherry is me but she is not mine. On the MUD, my character has another name—and does not give out questionnaires or conduct interviews. Dr. Sherry is a character name someone else created in order to quickly communicate an interest in a certain set of questions about technology and the self. I experience Dr. Sherry as a little piece of my history spinning out of control. I try to quiet my mind—I tell myself that surely one's books, one's public intellectual persona, are pieces of oneself in the world for others to use as they please. Surely this virtual appropriation is flattering. But my disquiet continues. Dr. Sherry, after all, is not an inanimate book, an object placed in the world. Dr. Sherry is a person, or at least a person behind a character who is meeting with others in the world. Well, in the MUD world at least.

I talk my disquiet over with a friend who poses the conversation-stopping question: "Well, would you prefer if Dr. Sherry were a 'bot' [an intelligent computer program that roams cyberspace] trained to interview people about life on the MUD?" This had not occurred to me but in a flash I realize that this, too, is possible. It is even likely to be the case. Many bots or "puppets" roam this MUD. Characters played by people are mistaken for these little artificial intelligences. I myself have made this mistake several times when a character's responses seemed too automatic. And sometimes bots are mistaken for people. I have made this mistake too, fooled by a bot that offered me directions or flattered me by remembering our last interaction. Dr. Sherry could indeed be one of these. I am confronted with a double that could be a person or a program.

People decide that they want to interact with others in a multi-user computer environment. They think that they will have new access to people and information—and there is little question that they do. But they find themselves playing in MUDs. They find themselves assuming multiple personae on computer networks. They are swept up in experiences that challenge their ideas about a unitary self. They meet their double and it is a cyborg.

IDENTITY, MORATORIA, AND PLAY

For some people, cyberspace is a place to "act out" unresolved conflicts, to play and replay characterological difficulties on a new and exotic stage. For others, it provides an opportunity to "work through" significant personal issues, to use the new materials of cybersociality to reach for new resolutions. These more positive identity-effects follow from the fact that for some, cyberspace provides what Erik Erikson would have called a "psychosocial moratorium," a central element in how Erikson thought about identity development in adolescence.[8] Although the term "moratorium" implies a "time out," what Erikson had in mind was not withdrawal. On the contrary, the adolescent moratorium is a time of intense interaction with people and ideas. It is a time of passionate friendships and experimentation. The adolescent falls in and out of love with people and ideas. Erikson's notion of the moratorium was not a "hold" on significant experiences but on their consequences. It is a time during which one's actions are, in a certain sense, not counted as they will be later in life. They are not given as much weight, not given the force of full judgment. In this context, experimentation can become the norm rather than a brave departure. Relatively consequence-free experimentation facilitates the development of a "core self," a personal sense of what gives life meaning that Erikson called "identity."

Erikson developed these ideas about the importance of a moratorium during the late 1950s and early 1960s. At that time, the notion corresponded to a common understanding of what "the college years" were about. These days, the idea of the college years as a consequence-free "time out" is more problematic. To mention only two factors, college is pre-professional and AIDS has made consequence-free sexual experimentation an impossibility. But if our culture no longer offers an adolescent moratorium, virtual communities often do. It is part of what makes them seem so attractive.

Erikson's ideas about stages did not suggest rigid sequences. His stages describe what people need to achieve before they can easily move ahead to another developmental task. For example, Erikson pointed out that successful intimacy in young adulthood is difficult if one does not come to it with a sense of who one is, the challenge of adolescent identity building. In real life, however, people frequently move on with serious deficits. With incompletely resolved "stages," they simply do the best they can. They use whatever materials they have at hand to get as much as they can of what they have missed. Now virtual social life can play a role in these dramas of self-reparation. Time in cyberspace reworks the notion of the moratorium because it may now exist on an always-available "window."

Having literally written our online personae into existence, they can be a kind of Rorschach. We can use them to become more aware of what we project into everyday life. We can use the virtual to reflect constructively on the real. Cyberspace opens the possibility for identity play, but it is very serious play. People who cultivate an awareness of what stands behind their screen personae are the ones most likely to succeed in using virtual experience for personal and social transformation. And the people who make the most of their lives on the screen are those who are capable of approaching it in a spirit of self-reflection. What does my behavior in cyberspace tell me about what I want, who I am, what I may not be getting in the rest of my life?

SIMULATION AND ITS DISCONTENTS

Alive/Not Alive

In Piaget's classic studies of the 1920s on how children thought about what was alive, the central variable was motion. Simply put, children took up the question of an object's "life status" by asking themselves if the object could move of its own accord. When in the late 1970s and early 1980s I studied children's reactions to a first generation of computer objects that were physically stationary but that nonetheless accomplished impressive feats of cognition (talking, spelling, doing math, and playing tic-tac-toe), I found that the focus had shifted to an object's psychological properties when children considered the question of its aliveness. So although the presence of computational objects disrupted the classical Piagetian story for talking about aliveness, the story children were telling about computational objects in the early 1980s had its own coherency. Faced with intelligent toys, children took a new world of objects and imposed a new world order, based not on physics but on psychology.

In the 1990s, that order has been strained to the breaking point. Children will now talk about computers as "just machines," but describe them as sentient and intentional. Faced with ever more complex computational objects, in particular with the world of screen simulations that model evolution (for example, Tierra) and social process (the games in the "Sim" series—SimCity, SimLife, and the Sims), children are now in the position of theoretical bricoleurs or tinkerers, "making do" with whatever materials are at hand, "making do" with whatever theory can fit a prevailing circumstance. They cycle through evolution and psychology and resurface ideas about motion in terms of the communication of bits.

My current collection of comments about life by children who have played with small mobile robots, the games of the Sim series, and Tierra includes the following notions: the robots are in control but not alive, would be alive if they had bodies, are alive because they have bodies, would be alive if they had feelings, are alive the way insects are alive but not the way people are alive; the Tierrans are not alive because they are just in the computer, could be alive if they got out of the computer and got onto America Online, are alive until you turn off the computer and then they're dead, are not alive because nothing in the computer is real; the Sim creatures are not alive but almost-alive, they would be alive if they spoke, they would be alive if they travelled, they're alive but not "real," they're not alive because they don't have bodies, they are alive because they can have babies, and finally, for an eleven year old who is relatively new to SimLife, they're not alive because these babies don't have parents. She says: "They show the creatures and the game tells you that they have mothers and fathers but I don't believe it. It's just numbers, it's not really a mother and a father." There is a striking heterogeneity of theory here. Different children hold different theories, and individual children are able to hold different theories at the same time.

Cyborg Babies

In the short history of how the computer has changed the way we think, it has often been children who have led the way. For example, in the early 1980s, children, prompted by computer toys that spoke, did math, and played tic-tac-toe, disassociated ideas about consciousness from ideas about life, something that historically had not been the case. These children were able to contemplate sentient computers that were not alive, a position that grownups are only now beginning to find comfortable. Today's cyborg children are taking things even further; they are pointing the way toward a radical heterogeneity of theory in the presence of computational artifacts that evoke "life." In his history of artificial life, Steven Levy suggests that one way to look at where artificial life can "fit in" to our way of thinking about life is to envisage a continuum in which Tierra, for example, would be more alive than a car, but less alive than a bacterium.[9] My observations suggest that children are not constructing hierarchies but are heading toward parallel, alternating definitions.

Today's adults grew up in a psychological culture that equated the idea of a unitary self with psychological health, and in a scientific culture that taught that when a discipline achieves maturity, it has a unifying theory. When adults find themselves cycling through varying perspectives on themselves ("I am my chemicals" to "I am my history" to "I am my genes") they usually become uncomfortable.[10] But such alternations may strike the generation of cyborg children who are growing up today as just the way things are.

Children speak easily about factors that encourage them to see the stuff of computers as the same stuff of which life is made. Among these are the ideas of shape shifting and morphing. Shape shifting is the technique used by the evil android in *Terminator II* to turn into the form of anything he touched—

including people. A nine year old showed an alchemist's sensibility when he explained how this occurs: "It is very simple. In the universe, anything can turn to anything else when you have the right formula. So you can be a person one minute and a machine the next minute." Morphing is a general term that covers form changes that may include changes across the animate/inanimate barrier. A ten-year-old boy had a lot to say about morphing, all of it associated with the lifestyle of "The Mighty Morphin' Power Rangers," a group of action heroes who turn from teenagers to androidal/mechanical "dinozords" and "megazords" and back. "Well," he patiently explains, "the dinozords are alive; the Power Rangers are alive, but not all the parts of the dinozords are alive, but all the part of the Power Rangers are alive. The Power Rangers become the dinozords. It's all the same stuff," he says, "just yucky computer 'cy-dough-plasm.'" This comment is the expression of a cyborg consciousness as it expresses itself among today's children: a tendency to see computer systems as "sort of" alive, to fluidly cycle through various explanatory concepts, and to willingly transgress boundaries.

To sum up: When today's adults cycle through different theories, they are uncomfortable. Such movement does not correspond to the unitary visions they were brought up to expect. But children have learned a different lesson from their cyborg objects. Donna Haraway characterizes irony as being "about contradictions that do not resolve into larger wholes . . . about the tension of holding incompatible things together because both or all are necessary and true."[11] In this sense, today's cyborg children, growing up into irony, are becoming adept at holding incompatible things together. They are cycling through the "cy-dough-plasm" into fluid and emergent conceptions of self and life. Even the operating systems they work with encourage them to accept and use what they are shown at any given time—to take things at interface value.

The Life of an Orgot

In the 1980s, most computer users who spoke of transparency were referring to a transparency analogous to that of traditional machines, an ability to open the hood and poke around. But when users of Macintosh computers began to talk about transparency in the mid 1980s, they were talking about seeing their documents and programs represented by attractive and easy-to-interpret icons. They were referring to an ability to make things work without needing to go below the screen surface. This was, somewhat paradoxically, a kind of transparency enabled by the screen's opacity. Today, the word "transparency" has taken on its Macintosh meaning in both computer talk and colloquial language. In a culture of simulation, when people say that something is transparent, they mean that they can see how to make it work, not that they know how it works.

"Your orgot is being eaten up," flashes the message on the screen. It is a rainy Sunday afternoon and I am with Tim, 13. We are playing SimLife, Tim's favorite computer game, which sets its users to the task of creating a functioning ecosystem. "What's an orgot?" I ask Tim. He doesn't know. "I just ignore that," he says confidently. "You don't need to know that kind of stuff to play." I suppose I look unhappy, haunted by a lifetime habit of not proceeding to step two before I understand step one, because Tim tries to appease me by coming up with a working definition of "orgot." "I think it is sort of like an organism. I never read that, but just from playing, I would say that's what it is."

The orgot issue will not die. A few minutes later the game informs us: "Your fig orgot moved to another species." I say nothing, but Tim reads my mind and shows compassion: "Don't let it bother you if you don't understand. I just say to myself that I probably won't be able to understand the whole game any time soon. So I just play." I begin to look through dictionaries in which orgot is not listed and finally find a reference to it embedded in the game itself, in a file called "READ ME." The text apologizes for the fact that orgot has been given several and in some ways contradictory meanings in this version of SimLife, but one of them is close to organism. Tim was right—enough.

Tim's approach to SimLife is highly functional. He says he learned his style of play from video games: "Even though SimLife's not a videogame, you can play it like one." By this he means that in SimLife, like video games, one learns from the process of play. You do not first read a rulebook or get your terms straight. Tim is able to act on an intuitive sense of what will work without understanding the rules that underlie the game's behavior. When Tim is populating his universe in a biology laboratory scenario, he puts in fifty each of his favorite creatures, trilobytes and sea urchins, but only twenty sharks. I listen to him thinking aloud about that decision: "I don't want fifty of those, I don't want to ruin this." Twenty is less than fifty and time will tell if it is the right amount. "My trilobytes went extinct," Tim says. "They must have run out of algae. I didn't give them algae. I forgot. I think I'll do that now." Tim can keep playing even when he has no very clear idea what is driving events. While I was fruitlessly looking up "orgot," Tim got deep into an age of the dinosaurs scenario in SimLife. On the positive side, a player like Tim is learning to think about complex phenomena as dynamic, evolving systems. From one point of view, he has made far better use of his time than I have.

And yet, Tim's videogame habits of mind also raise larger questions. When his sea urchins become extinct, I ask him why.

> Tim: I don't know, it's just something that happens.
> ST: Do you know how to find out why it happened?
> Tim: No.

ST: Do you mind that you can't tell why?
Tim: No. I don't let things like that bother me. It's not what's important.

When Piaget studied children's notions of causality, a child's world was full of things that could be understood in simple, mechanical ways. A bicycle could be understood in terms of its pedals and gears and a wind-up car in terms of its clockwork springs. In the late 1970s to early 1980s, the people who built or bought the first generation of personal computers understood them down to the bits and bytes. The operating systems that followed were far more complex, but invited that old-time, reductive understanding. Today, computer users such as Tim can completely ignore such understandings. Tim can stay on the surface, taking things at (inter)face value.

In the 1980s, the controversy in the world of computers and education was about whether computer literacy should be about programming. Would an emphasis on programming skills in the curriculum teach something important, or would it, as some feared in the parlance of the time, turn children into "linear thinkers." Today, the debate about computers in education centers around the place of educational software and simulations in the curriculum. Tim's response to SimLife (a level of comfort with play; not much understanding of the model that underlies the game) is not unusual. Just as some teachers do not want to be "reduced" to instructing children in a computer "appliance," many resent providing instruction in a learning environment that often strikes them as an overblown videogame. The question of simulation is posed from preschool through the college years. Why should four year olds manipulate virtual magnets to pick up virtual pins? Why should seven year olds add virtual ballast to virtual ships? Why should fifteen year olds pour virtual chemicals into virtual beakers? Why should eighteen year olds do virtual experiments in virtual physics laboratories? The answer to these questions is often: because the simulations are less expensive, because there are not enough science teachers. But these answers beg a large question: Are we using computer technology not because it teaches best but because we have lost the political will to adequately fund education?

Readership in a Culture of Simulation

Simulation, whether in a game like SimLife or in a physics laboratory or computer-aided-design application, does teach users how to think in an active way about complex phenomena as dynamic, evolving systems. And they also get people accustomed to manipulating a system whose core assumptions they may not understand and that may or may not be "true." Simulations enable us to abdicate authority to the simulation; they give us permission to accept the opacity of the model that plays itself out on our screens. Simulation games are not just objects for thinking about the real world but also cause us to reflect on how the real world has itself become a simulation game.

The seduction of simulation invites several possible responses. One can accept simulations on their own terms, the stance that Tim encouraged me to take. This might be called "simulation resignation." Or one can reject simulations to whatever degree possible, the position taken by a group of my colleagues at MIT, physicists who saw simulation as a thoroughly destructive force in science education. This might be called "simulation denial." But one can imagine a third response. This would take the cultural pervasiveness of simulation as a challenge to develop a new social criticism. This new criticism would discriminate among simulations. It would take as its goal the development of simulations that help their users understand and challenge their model's built-in assumptions.

I think of this new criticism as the basis for a new class of skills: *readership skills for the culture of simulation.* On one level, high school sophomores playing SimCity for two hours may learn more about city planning than they would pick up from a textbook; but on another level, they may not know how to think about what they are doing. When I interview a tenth grader named Marcia about SimCity, she boasts of her prowess and reels off her "top ten most useful rules of Sim." Among these, number six grabs my attention: *"Raising taxes always leads to riots."*

Marcia seems to have no language for discriminating between this rule of the game and the rules that operate in a "real" city. She has never programmed a computer. She has never constructed a simulation. She has no language for asking how one might write the game so that increased taxes led to increased productivity and social harmony. And she certainly does not see herself as someone who could change the rules. Like Tim confronted with the orgot, she does not know how to "read" a simulation. Marcia is like someone who can pronounce the words in a book but doesn't understand what they mean. She does not know how to measure, criticize, or judge what she is learning. As we face computers and operating systems of an increasingly dizzying size and complexity, this possibility feels so remote that it is easy to dismiss such yearnings as old fashioned. But Marcia's situation—she is a fluent user but not a fluent thinker—reposes the question in urgent terms. Marcia may not need to see the registers on her computer or the changing charges on a computer chip, but she needs to see *something.* She needs to be working with simulations that teach her about the nature of simulation itself, that teach her enough about how to build her own that she becomes a literate reader of the new medium.

Increasingly, understanding the assumptions that underlie simulation is a key element of political power. People who understand the distortions imposed by simulations are in a position to call for more direct economic and political feedback, new kinds of representation, more channels of information. They may demand greater transparency in their simulations; they may demand that the games we play, particularly the ones we use to make real life decisions, make their underlying models more accessible.

We come to written text with centuries-long habits of readership. At the very least, we have learned to begin with the journalist's traditional questions: who, what, when, where, why, and how? Who wrote these words, what is their message, why were they written, how are they situated in time and place, politically and socially? A central goal for computer education must now be to teach students to interrogate simulations in much the same spirit. The specific questions may be different but the intent is the same: to develop habits of readership appropriate to a culture of simulation.

CODA: GLOBAL COMPUTING AND THE WORLD OF SCARY/SAFE

The pioneers of computing, and those who referred to themselves as computer "hackers" (when this term connoted virtuosity not criminality), had a style of computer mastery that played with risk and virtuosity by flying by the seat of their pants. If they were addicted to computing, it was as a medium for playing with the issue of control, and playing with control meant constantly walking that narrow line between having it and losing it. MIT hackers called this "sport death." One described it by saying: "The essence of sport death is to see how far you can push things, to see how much you can get away with." Programming evoked the thrill of walking on the edge of a cliff, of being able "to hold the system in your head for that half second, and hope you can save it, but knowing that it might all crash." It has been called the psychology of "scary/safe." Life is danger and triumph, screen to screen of it. The computer and its simulated worlds can provide defenses for our anxieties.

A first line of defense can be to deny vulnerability. It is reassuring to have a medium that offers reassurance through a promise of total mastery. It is reassuring to play in safe microworlds where the rules are clear. On the global scene, computer gaming, computer programming, and virtual realities share a great deal with the rule-driven and bounded world of Tolkien's *Lord of the Rings*. The commonalities were not lost on the earliest generations of computer enthusiasts. In the early 1970s, the computer scientists at Stanford University's artificial intelligence laboratory were so enamored of *The Lord of the Rings* that they built three elven fonts for the Stanford printers. Two of the researchers wrote a Tolkienesque, single-player quest game that became known as "Adventure" as it spread worldwide via the nascent Internet. The personal computer movement of the 1970s and early 1980s was deeply immersed in Tolkien and translated his fantasy worlds into hugely popular (and enduring) role-playing games such as "Dungeons and Dragons."

What the magic of Tolkien shares with the magic of computer code is that each offers fantasy objects that one can control and the opportunity to assert and reassert mastery. Each episode of *Fellowship* presents a danger; each has a resolution in mastery. You go from one block of intransigent code to another. You debug one part of the program, you debug another. Each screen, each level of a computer game is danger, each screen is mastered in its turn, and you always return to danger again. Life is exhausting, but the repetition of microworld triumphs is reassuring. In the fellowship of the microchip, you may crash but ultimately you win.

We used to call hackers "computer people." No more. In a certain sense, if we take the computer to be a carrier of a way of knowing, of a way of seeing the world and what is important, we are all computer people now. Our global immersion in code bears more than a family resemblance to our global immersion in games and fantasy. Computer programs and Middle Earth are compelling on a global scale. They are complex, multilayered, and self-referential. However, we are at a moment in history when playing in closed systems of our own devising reinforces dangerous habits of mind. When we think about Tolkien and when we think about computing, we are not thinking about ambivalence, about complex human relationships, about battles that don't end in infinite justice. But the simple clarities of our globalized computer worlds depend on their virtuality. The real world is messy and painted in shades of gray. In that world we need to be comfortable with ambivalence and contradiction. We need to be able to put ourselves in the place of others in order to understand their motivation. Above all, we need to resist binary formulations. For these things we can't look to computation any more than we can look to Middle Earth.

Walt Whitman once wrote: "There was a child went forth every day. And the first object he look'd upon, that object he became." We make our technologies, our objects, but then the objects of our lives shape us in turn. Our new screen worlds have scintillating, pulsating surfaces. They invite playful exploration. They are dynamic, seductive, and elusive. It is not clear what we are becoming when we look upon them.

NOTES

1. Sherry Turkle, *The Second Self: Computers and the Human Spirit* (New York: Simon and Schuster, 1984); Sherry Turkle, *Life on the Screen: Identity in the Age of the Internet* (New York: Simon and Schuster, 1995).

2. Turkle, *Life on the Screen*, 1995.

3. Philip Bromberg, "Speak That I May See You: Some Reflections on Dissociation, Reality, and Psychoanalytic Listening," *Psychoanalytic Dialogues* 4, no. 4 (1994): 517–47; Marvin Minsky, *The Society of Mind* (New York: Simon and Schuster, 1987).

4. Kenneth Gergen, *The Saturated Self: Dilemmas of Identity in Contemporary Life* (New York: Basic Books, 1991); Emily Martin, *Flexible Bodies: Tracking Immunity in America Culture—From the Days of Polio to the Days of AIDS* (Boston: Beacon Press, 1994); Robert Jay Lifton, *The Protean Self: Human Resilience in an Age of Fragmentation* (New York: Basic Books, 1993).

5. Daniel Dennet, *Consciousness Explained* (Boston: Little, Brown and Company, 1991).

6. Donna Haraway, "The Actors are Cyborg, Nature Is Coyote," and "The Geography Is Elsewhere: Postscript to 'Cyborgs at Large'" in *Technoculture*, ed. Constance Penley and Andrew Ross (Minneapolis: University of Minnesota Press, 1991).

7. Sherry Turkle, *Psychoanalytic Politics: Jacques Lacan and Freud's French Revolution*, 2nd rev. ed. (New York: Guilford, 1990).

8. Erik Erikson, *Childhood and Society*, 2nd rev. ed. (New York: Norton, 1963).

9. Steven Levy, *Artificial Life: A Report from the Frontier Where Computers Meet Biology* (New York: Vintage, 1992), 6–7.

10. Peter Kramer, *Listening to Prozac* (New York: Penguin, 1993), xii–xiii.

11. Haraway, "Actors Are Cyborg," 148.

II

OBSERVING ONLINE COMMUNITIES

7

Virtual Togetherness: An Everyday Life Perspective

Maria Bakardjieva

The objective of this chapter is to explore some dimensions of the virtual community concept that relate to empowering possibilities for appropriating the Internet by domestic users. I contend that users' participation in what has been called "virtual communities"[1] over the Internet constitutes a cultural trend of "immobile socialization," or in other words, socialization of private experience through the invention of new forms of intersubjectivity and social organization online.

When I suggest the term immobile socialization, I intentionally reverse Williams's concept of "mobile privatization."[2] Unlike broadcast technology and the automobile that, according to Williams, precipitated a withdrawal of middle-class families from public spaces of association and sociability into private suburban homes, the Internet is being mobilized in a process of collective deliberation and action in which people engage from amidst the private realm. Whether an analyst would decide to call the electronic forums in which this is happening communities or not depends on the notion of community she is operating with. What has to be noted is that by engaging in different forms of collective practice, online users transcend the sphere of narrowly private interest and experience. Why do they do that? What does it mean to them? How does it reflect on the public understanding of the Internet? The concept of "virtual community" has been only of limited help to the understanding of this practice and I will try to explain why in what follows.

Few studies of virtual communities have attempted to relate online community engagement with users' everyday life situations, relevancies, and goals.[3] Most of the existing research has concentrated on the group cultures originating from the interactions of online participants, thus treating online group phenomena in isolation from the actual daily life experiences of the subjects involved.[4] My attempt in this chapter is to initiate an exploration of the experiences and motivations that lead Internet users to get involved, or the opposite, to stay away from forms of virtual togetherness. I believe it is important to understand what kinds of needs and values and under what circumstances virtual communities serve. This will open a realistic perspective on the significance of this practice in the social shaping of the Internet.

My reflections are based on an ethnographic study of the experiences of twenty-one domestic users of the Internet in Vancouver. The respondent group was formed through self-selection. The conditions for participation stipulated that 1) respondents should not have a professional involvement with the Internet, 2) they pay for their Internet access themselves, and 3) they use the Internet more than three times a week. Data were collected through in-depth individual interviews with users and group interviews with their family members where appropriate. Observational tours of the domestic space where the computer connected to the Internet was located and of the computer "interior" (bookmarks, address books, etc.) were also performed.[5]

On the basis of this material, I offer a typology of different forms of online involvement with others demonstrating that virtual community is not always the most accurate notion for describing people's actual social activities online. In fact, virtual togetherness has many variations, not all of which live up to the value-laden name of community. This fact, however, does not undermine the idea of collective life in cyberspace. On the contrary, I call for appreciation of the different forms of engagement with other people online (virtual togetherness) that exist and the different situated needs they serve. In these multifarious practices, I recognize new vehicles that allow users to traverse the social world, penetrate previously unattainable regions of anonymity, and expand their restorable social reach.[6] In light of this formulation of the meaning of virtual togetherness, I question the dichotomy between the private and the public that is at the root of both virtual utopia and dystopia.

THE VIRTUAL COMMUNITY DEBATE

Raymond Williams, tracing the etymology of the word "community," notes that it is "the warmly persuasive word to describe an existing set of relationships; or the warmly persuasive word to describe an alternative set of relationships" that "seems never to be used unfavorably and never to be given any positive opposing or distinguishing term."[7] Williams's account of the historical evolution of the usage of the word reveals its interpretative flexibility and hence its socially constructed character. There is no "genuine" fact of nature or social history that the word "community" denotes. There is no consensually accepted definition of its meaning. Different social actors have appropriated the word at different points in history with different concrete contexts, goals, and oppositions in mind.

A similarly complex constructive process can be discerned in the case of the notion of "virtual" or "online" community. The engineers and researchers who were the first to build, experience, and study the Internet, along with other technologies for computer-mediated communication, employed the concept of community in order to legitimate their project and to demonstrate its significance and nobility.[8] They portrayed membership in virtual community as liberating, equitable, and empowering. In response, critics have zealously defended an idealized notion of "real" community signifying a state of immediacy and locality of human relationships that resists technological mediation.[9]

In a recent paper, Wellman and Gulia have pointed out a common weakness of both sides of this debate.[10] These positions are premised on a false dichotomy between virtual communities and real life communities. Wellman's community studies carried out through the methods of network analysis, as well as Anderson's anthropological studies,[11] have demonstrated in their specific ways that the majority of the so-called real life communities are in fact virtual in the sense that they are mediated and imagined. Wellman and Gulia argue: "In fact most contemporary communities in the developed world do not resemble rural or urban villages where all know all and have frequent face-to-face contact. Rather, most kith and kin live farther away than a walk (or short drive) so that telephone contact sustains ties as much as face-to-face get-togethers."[12] In a curious concord between the two quite distinct schools of thought, Anderson insists: "All communities larger than primordial villages of face-to-face contact (and perhaps even these) are imagined."[13]

Furthermore, Wellman and Gulia charge, most accounts of virtual community have treated the Internet as an isolated phenomenon without taking into account how interactions on the Net fit with other aspects of people's lives: "The Net is only one of many ways in which the same people may interact. It is not a separate reality," Wellman and Gulia observe.[14]

These other aspects of people's lives constitute the crucial background against which questions regarding the social and individual significance of online communities can be raised and answered. Virtual communities cannot be declared inferior to real life communities simply because they lack face-to-face materiality. They cannot be celebrated as liberating or empowering by nature either, as people bring to them stocks of knowledge and systems of relevance generated throughout their unalterable personal histories and social experience. They cannot be studied and characterized exclusively by what is produced online, as the cultures enacted online have their roots in forms of life existing in the "real" world.

Finally, and this is the central thesis that I propose here, the concept of (virtual) community, with all the normative load it carries, has led analysis into a not particularly productive ideological exchange disputing the possibility for genuine community to be sustained through computer networks. This has deflected attention from the fact that a continuum of forms of being and acting together is growing from the technology of the Internet. I will refer to this emerging range of new social forms as "virtual togetherness" in order to avoid the normative overtones present in the concept of community. Community, whatever definition one may choose to give it, would then be one possible form of virtual togetherness among many.

The opposite of virtual togetherness (and community) is not "real" or "genuine" community, as the current theoretical debate suggests, but the isolated consumption of digitized goods and services within the realm of particularistic existence. The issue then is not which (and whether any) form of togetherness online deserves the "warmly persuasive"[15] label of community. The challenge to analysts is to understand and appreciate the significance of these various forms of transcending the narrowly private existence and navigating the social world for individual participants, for society at large and for the shaping of the Internet.

BETWEEN CONSUMPTION AND COMMUNITY

In this section I present an emergent continuum in users' understanding and actual practice with regard to the Internet spanning the poles of consumption and community. The important distinction between these two modes of Internet use, in my view, consists of the absence in the former and presence in the latter of users' participation and involvement with one another. The degree of immediacy and depth of this involvement, as I show below, varies in the different versions of virtual togetherness discernible in my respondents' accounts. It may or may not meet a normative standard of "genuine community." But in all forms of virtual togetherness, unlike in the consumption mode, users *produce* something of value to others—content, space, relationship, and/or culture. I believe that the legitimacy and the practical possibility of this participatory mode of Internet use is what needs to be defended against the assault of consumption and its related practices. By simply denying the value of virtual togetherness (community) critics lighthandedly undermine the strongest alternative of the narrowly consumptive model of Internet development.

THE INFOSUMER: THE RATIONALIST IDEAL OF INTERNET USE

Without specific questioning, accounts of participation in virtual groups came up in the stories of some of the people I interviewed. Invited to explain how they used the Internet, they started with their online groups. With others, no mention of any social life online was ever made. My pointed question about whether they took part in virtual groups or forums received sometimes very skeptical and even derogatory/nihilistic responses:

> I am reading a few groups, not much. But again, nothing intrigues me to participate. So I don't know how widespread is that communal thing. I have no idea. I haven't participated. Chats, I find, are a horrible waste of time! I tried it once or twice and said, forget it! [What is so disappointing about it?] Oh, the subjects, the way they talked about it. . . . (Reiner, 62, retired mechanical engineering technician)

> I am aware, like you say, of newsgroups or usegroups, whatever they are called, I tried, two or three years ago, some and I just didn't care. The crap that came back and the depth of the level of knowledge didn't really strike me, it wasn't worth going through these hundreds of notes—somebody asking this or that to find. . . . But I couldn't find any substantive issues and I did not care, I did not want to use it to advertise my own knowledge, so I just left them alone. (Don, 60, psychological counselor)

Gary, a 65-year-old retired naval radio operator, summed up this particular position regarding Internet group discussions in a useful model. According to him, a good radio operator sends as little as possible, but receives maximum:

> Because the radio operator is there just to get all the information he can about the weather, the time signal, about what's happening in different countries and orders from different places. And if he can get that efficiently without going on the air too much, then it is to the benefit of everybody. If everybody is on the air asking questions, then you cannot hear really anything but miles and miles of questions being asked. That's why the etiquette of the professional radio operator was to say as little as possible, like telegrams used to be. . . . To me, it is a matter of getting information across.

Coming from this perspective, Gary scorned the "noisy people out there on the Internet," "the empty heads" who were there first: "There are always people who just have their mouth hanging out and they are just talking, and talking, and talking, and just creating a lot of babble" (Gary).

These kinds of empty-heads produced "garbage upon garbage" on the Internet, a low level content that Gary refused to engage with. He believed that his contributions, had he made any, would not have been appreciated. To post in newsgroups, for him, would have been like "casting pearls before swine—that means it is pretty pointless to be intellectual when you are dealing with people who just want to talk about garbage."

A closer look at the "radio operator" perspective reveals its underlying communicative values to be "substantive issues," "information," and "efficiency."

The respondents in this category upheld a rationalist ideal of information production and exchange and expected the content of Internet discussions to live up to that ideal. Their high standards prevented them from contributing to any group discussions because of an "expert knowledge or nothing" attitude. These respondents repudiated sociability understood as the pursuit of human contact, acquaintance, friendship, solidarity, and intimacy as legitimate motives for using the Internet. The users in this category were turning to the Internet for timely, accurate, reliable information and, quite naturally, were finding it in the online offerings of traditional information institutions such as news agencies, radio stations, newspapers, and government sites.

INSTRUMENTAL RELATIONS: RATIONAL INTERACTION

In Martha's narrative, one could notice the persisting authority of the rationalist ideal with information as its central value, although acceptance of other people on the Internet, not necessarily experts and expert organizations, as sources of information and ideas was also showing through. Information remained the leading motive stated for going on the Internet, however "talking to people online" was not perceived as its antithesis: "My son has an attention deficit disorder . . . and it was really interesting to get online and to talk to people from all over the world about this issue. It was called the ADD forum—a really good way for providing information" (Martha, 41, meatwrapper for Safeway). At one turn of the conversation, when Martha admitted that she missed the ADD forum available only through CompuServe, she made haste to emphasize: "It wasn't chatting to meet people and get to know people. It was chatting about ideas and exchanging information," thus paying tribute to the rationalist ideal.

Similarly, John, a 73-year-old retired mechanical engineer, perceived his participation in a mailing list for motorglider hobbyists as a valuable resource in problematic situations when decisions regarding new equipment had to be made or technical problems needed to be solved. He approached newsgroups in the same way—in cases when he needed a question answered, a problem solved, a new experience illuminated: his wife's diabetes, a new type of apple tree he wanted to plant, his new communication software, and the like. He enjoyed the helpfulness and solidarity demonstrated by the people who took the time to answer his queries in their specifically human and social aspects, but admitted that once the problem was solved, the interpersonal communication would fade away:

> We don't normally communicate socially—how are you, what's the weather. . . .
> It's usually when a technical question comes up. After that question is solved, we
> may talk a little bit about how old we are, what we did. But once the problem is

solved this fades away. But yet, those people are still in the background. And when I am looking at postings and see their name, a bell rings. (John)

John himself would only respond to questions others had asked on the mailing list when he had "something positive" to say and believed that this reserved culture of positive, substantive contributions made his mailing list work well.

Merlin, a 58-year-old unemployed mechanical engineer, was also quite scrupulous as far as the quality of information exchange in his virtual group was concerned. He insisted he was on this mailing list in order "to learn," "to expand my understanding of the electrical components used in the electric car." He saw the list as a "semi-professional community" and only felt the right to contribute when "somebody says something wrong or asks a question, especially connected to hybrids, because I have thought about it, I haven't done any real calculations, [only] very simple calculations which answered some questions that were asked." Despite the preponderance of strictly technical content on the list, the personalities of participants had come through and Merlin had developed curiosity as to what kind of people some of the discussants were. When he had happened to be in the proximity of some of the guys on the list, he had driven by their houses or shops and had met some of them. Putting a face to an e-mail address or alias, a living image and context to stories told on the list, seemed to have been a transforming experience in terms of how Merlin felt about his list:

> Now, I have met these people, so it actually means a lot more to me, now that I have met [emphasizes] . . . I thought Jerry was a wealthy guy, in fact, you have to categorize him as poor, he is a postman and he hasn't worked for over a year; he is obviously not rich. And I have seen him, and I have seen his wife Shauna, I actually saw his two daughters in passing. I have seen the truck, the car, that had this plasma fireball incinerated inside of the car, I saw the battery—there were three batteries welded together in a T-junction, I mean really, to do that damage, it really had to have a lot of energy. (Merlin, 56, unemployed mechanical engineer)

Thus, unexpectedly, the rationalist model of Internet use (Merlin insisted on his loyalty to it) was showing cracks where it would have seemed most unlikely—on a technical discussion list.

PEOPLE AND IDEAS IN VIRTUAL PUBLIC SPHERES

For Patrick (33, electronics technician) and Myra (28, doctoral student in physics) "chatting about ideas" was one of the main attractions of newsgroups. In this communication model, the high standing of information, ideas, and knowledge was preserved, however it was inextricably linked to interest in people as knowers, interpreters, discussion partners, and opponents. The contact between the two of them (Patrick and Myra) was actually established when Myra found in the Albanian newsgroup she was reading a posting from a guy who wanted to "ask some questions about Albania to an Albanian, to a guy or girl who knew about the country." Reflecting over a gratifying exchange they had in an Internet newsgroup, they described it like this: "We started talking about serious politics . . . Albanian, Eastern European. We were talking—long, long, long messages—political analysis, how this or that could be. No jokes, no stupidities like oh, I find you attractive, nothing like that" (Myra, 28, Albanian background, doctoral student in physics). In her description of another newsgroup exchange with a previously unknown contributor, Myra stressed both the quality of the ideas that were articulated in the posting and the relationship established between its author and herself as a reader:

> There is a guy in the Russian group—and I saw a couple of postings of his and, of course, I sent him a message, a personal one and I said well, I am delighted, I like them and he replied—oh, I am delighted that you appreciate them. So you kind of establish a closer contact. We don't write to each other or anything but when I see a posting by him, I will go and read it. (Myra)

Myra used to write a lot in Albanian newsgroups and mailing lists (trying to express her opinion regarding various, mostly political, issues), but the highly controversial nature of the political topics she was addressing attracted flamers and later, after she responded in a way she thought due, intolerable disciplinary measures. Patrick, for his part, admitted that he was visiting newsgroups to some extent also for the controversy: "But I like provocative topics and if someone starts flaming me, fine, I get what I deserve. . . . I have been flamed and certainly will be flamed. I don't avoid that."

Both Patrick and Myra thought of newsgroups not simply as an information resource, but also as a space for intellectual sociability and political debate, a "public forum" in Patrick's own words, where diverse opinions could meet and clash as a matter of course. The point of being there was to get exposed to others' perspectives and to argue for your own, to build alliances with like-minded people and enjoy intellectually stimulating encounters.

An online political discussion that had gone the extra mile to involve subsequent organization and collective action of participants was represented by the mailing list Theodore belonged to. The participants in that discussion had gone beyond the process of collective sense-making of events and issues. An agreement over needs and directions of political organizing had grown out of their exchange and debate. The grassroots group Ethiopian National Congress had brought together face-to-face Ethiopian refugees scattered all over the world who had reached agreement over their common cause and course of action in their virtual togetherness:

> Individuals on the list started talking about this thing and said we should do something about it and so it started as a virtual organization and it transformed itself, there was a meeting in July of last year in LA—the initial meeting for individuals to get together and discuss this thing and then there was another meeting in 1997, October, where the actual organization was proclaimed and established in Atlanta. (Theodore, 45, parking patroller)

THE CHATTER: SOCIABILITY UNBOUND

The cases discussed so far are derived in a significant way from the rationalist model of Internet communication, albeit implanting in it interpersonal interaction and sociability in different degrees and variations. When one turns to listen to Sandy (35, telemarketer for a telecommunications company), one realizes that a qualitative break with the rationalist model has taken place. Sandy spoke for a markedly different model of Internet communication, one that had sociability as its central value. Ironically, Sandy was introduced to the Internet in relation to a university course she was taking. That means finding information had been the foremost function of the medium her attention was drawn to. However, it didn't take long before Sandy discovered chat room and became fascinated by what they had to offer. In her open and emotional statement Sandy showed no signs of guilt or remorse for abandoning the rationalist model of Internet use. In fact, she did not seem to notice the major subversion to which she was subjecting the medium as perceived from the "radio operator" perspective. She was happy to be one of those noisy people who were out there "talking, and talking, and talking" (see Gary's quote above). Sandy's main reason for being on the Net was "meeting people in there and having a great time talking to them" (see Martha's statement in the opposite sense above).

> I was drawn to the rooms that were like the parent zone, health zone, and things like that, just general interest. . . . I would talk to people in there and then I met this guy who lives in Ontario and his wife and they had a room called the Fun Factory. It was about ten of us. We just hung out there, we went in there and just chatted about life. All kind of fun things—we goofed around, told jokes, stories, whatever. The same ten people. Oh, I still talk to them all. In fact we've flown and we have met each other and some of us . . . Lots of times other people came in, but this was the core.

What started as "goofing around" ended up having dramatic consequences for Sandy's "real" life. In Sandy's own reflection, as a direct result of her

hanging out in chat lines, her marriage fell apart completely. That was because online she met "really good people" who helped her to regain her self-
confidence: "Then all of a sudden I was reminded that I was a real person
[emotional tone] with real emotions, and real feelings and I was likable by
people." Furthermore, one of her new online friends was the first person to
whom she revealed that her husband was beating her: "And he just said—
get out! You have to get out, Sandy, you cannot stay there! And he and I became really close good friends and he convinced me that life could go on
and even that I would lose a lot of materialism, I would gain so much more
if I could fight this fight and get out. And I did. I left."

Another person who became a close friend and shared a lot in Sandy's
marital problems was also instrumental in helping her with the technological challenges of the Internet. He was a computer professional who taught
Sandy the technical knowledge and skills that she needed to move and act
freely online. Starting from a close, personal relationship established online,
Sandy had occasionally gone full circle back to hard information. "And he
made it easy. I would say 'I don't think I can do that,' and he would say—'I
remember you saying that about such and such, but if you just think about
how it works.' And he would explain to me how it worked. And then I would
go and do it myself."

The chat room Sandy was describing could hardly meet the high standards
of community raised by the critics of the idea of virtual community. According to Sandy, the interactions in that room had been vibrant, and yet superficial, intense, and fleeting at the same time: "In the room it was mostly goofing around, cracking jokes. And also there was always stuff going on in the
background in private conversations and then you'd have the public room.
And often you would have three or four private conversations going at the
same time as the room." What actually was happening in this environment
was people meeting strangers and treating them not simply with civility, but
as someone "like myself," someone who could laugh at the same jokes, talk
about the same topics of interest, and then walk away and go on with his/her
own life. That is, what the room was providing for its visitors was an environment for "fluid sociability among strangers and near-strangers."[16] Speaking about the sociability of premodern cities, Ariès writes: "This is a space of
heterogeneous coexistence, not of inclusive solidarity or of conscious collective action; a space of symbolic display, of the complex blending of practical motives with interaction ritual and personal ties."[17]

The chat room Sandy described also displayed social proximity found
across physical distance. Sandy's account indicated that the people she was
meeting in her chat room were socially and culturally close to her: they liked
rock and roll, Star Trek, and kayaking. They had computers of the same
make and similar kinds of marital problems. The spirit of sociability sustained in the chat room was a product of the shared desire of these people

to overcome the privateness of their existence, to socialize about some of their most personal experiences, anxieties, and troubles. The merry superficiality of the chat room was only the first level of contact where, through the display of one's personality in public, interpersonal affinities were sought and negotiated. The deeper effects of this activity were playing themselves out at the level of the private conversations breaking off from the party and even further, into participants' actions in the offline world. These were effects concerning again the private spheres of the individuals involved. However, the return to the private to deal with its challenges was performed at a different level, bringing in a reaffirmed self, reflexivity, and new interpretative frameworks for addressing vital problems of everyday life acquired in the social online relationships.

When I spoke with Sandy, the Fun Factory chat room had died out—its participants had left. Sandy emphasized that she did not want to chat online that much any more, "at least for now. I think I want to establish social relationships in the real world instead of in the virtual world right now. That's important for me where I am right now. I still want to keep in contact with the friends that I have met online and I do that by e-mail now instead of chat rooms."

In Sandy's case, the involvement in a form of virtual togetherness had clearly been a situational phenomenon. The problems and relevance systems of a particular situation in her life—the isolation brought about by an abusive marriage—had led Sandy to seek sociability, recognition, social support, and intimacy in the more or less anonymous virtual association of people she could meet through the online chat programs. In her virtual togetherness with the other members of the chat room, Sandy found the means to deal with the problems she was presently facing. In a changed situation, she was consciously choosing a different route and different means for building togetherness with people. Yet as one can notice in her statement, she cherished the relationships she had created online and worked to translate them into a different format. Her virtual friendships were in the process of becoming "real," and as such, notably, sustained through other communication technologies—e-mail and telephone, a transformation that once again exposes the fragility of the constructed boundary between real and virtual togetherness.

THE COMMUNITARIAN

With Ellen (49, former editor), the concept of community dominated the conversation from the first question on. Ellen hooked up to the Internet from home after she became housebound with a diagnosis of a rare but crippling chronic illness. Her explicit motivation for becoming an Internet user was to be able to connect to a support group. She simply felt "very desperate for information and help." "Getting information" and "getting support" were two inseparable reasons for her to go online. Thus, Ellen joined an invisible dispersed group of people who were logging on everyday to get the "gift of making this connection" with each other:

> To discover that thousands of people are going through exactly the same incredible experience and nobody in their family understands, their husbands and wives don't understand, the doctor doesn't believe them and they have this terrible difficulty of functioning. And yet, there is this tremendously strong community of people who have never met and probably will never meet but who are so loyal to each other and have such a strong support because it is a lifeline for all of us.

The mailing list Ellen described was experienced as a safe environment by these people, a place where they felt comfortable saying: "I've had a really bad day, I had to go see a specialist and I had such a difficulty and couldn't breathe and it was such a challenge to get there and then the doctor was awful to me. And then I got home and my husband was complaining because the house wasn't clean." And immediately after a complaint such as this would pop up in members' mail boxes, there would be a flurry of supportive responses. Loyalty, high tolerance for "dumping," safety, family-like atmosphere, compassion—these were all attributes Ellen used to describe the quality of interaction in her "wonderful group."

The real-life effects consisted in "a lot of confidence," "getting my life in proportion again," "getting a sense of myself" (compare this with an almost identical formulation by Sandy), and "feeling much less a failure." Learning a lot about the disease was among the benefits of list membership, however Ellen took care to distinguish the particular kind of learning that was taking place there: "I learnt so much from these people who had had the disease for years. I had tried to get hold of some medical information. But getting online is different because there for the first time you get information from people who have trodden this path already!" For good or ill as the case may be, the victims of the disease Ellen had were short-circuiting the medical establishment and the expert knowledge produced by it and were learning from each other. More accurately, they were collectively appropriating and using expert knowledge in ways they had found relevant and productive in their own unique situations as sufferers and victims.

A similar sense of gain from online support group discussions came through clearly in the comments of Mathew, a 37-year-old amputee. According to him, people with similar health problems learned from each other about the existence of a variety of treatment options, which, consequently, empowered them vis-à-vis the medical profession. Matthew challenged the very notion of a patient. In his understanding, people with health problems were clients, customers, and in the best case, collaborators with doctors, nurses, and prosthetists. To be able to act in this capacity however, they needed to be informed and acculturated in their disability. This is, Matthew believed, why online support groups are instrumental. "I learned more about being an amputee in the one year of being on the mailing list than through-out the twenty years I had had the problem," Matthew insisted passionately.

What distinguished Ellen's experience from other, more detached, forms of learning such as those described by previous respondents was the fact that the people she was interacting with over time had come to constitute a collective entity with its own distinctive culture. Her online group had a relatively stable membership communicating on a daily basis and feeling responsible for each other's well-being. Both commonality of interest and diversity could be found in that group. Most of its participants were people seeking alternative ap-proaches for dealing with chronic disease. In Ellen's estimate, most of them were highly educated and articulate, and most of them were women. At the same time, members of the group came from different religious backgrounds and life experiences in terms of education, profession, family, and so on. Yet characteristically, they were entering their shared space ready and eager to lis-ten to interpretations coming from viewpoints different from their own. Ellen says: "Like this woman in Israel, a Hebrew scholar, a convert to Judaism, she has the most fascinating perspective on things. There are amazing things com-ing from her. . . . But nobody has ever tried to push one point of view above another. There has been very much a sense of sharing."

Ellen's account describes, I would argue, a "warmly persuasive" version of a robust online community characterized by interpersonal commitment and a sense of common identity. Ellen's Internet was thus markedly different from the rationalist model of Internet communication defended by the info-sumers. The users who denied the communal aspects of the Internet came from a strictly utilitarian and/or rationalist value orientation. They sought positive, reliable, scientific, professionally presented information, and were able to find it in the virtual projections of institutions such as online maga-zines and newspapers, radio, and television stations' sites, government sites, news agencies, and scientific publications. To most of these users, news-groups and mailing lists had little to offer and respectively, communal forms were put under question in principle. The everyday practice of the info-sumer, I suggest, is organized by and continuously reproduces the con-sumption model of the Internet as a social institution.

On the other hand, representatives of disenfranchised groups—in my study these were clearly Ellen and Matthew, both disabled, but also in some sense Sandy (a victim of spousal abuse) and Merlin (unemployed for a long term)— were using the technology as a tool to carve spaces of sociability, solidarity, mutual support, and situated, appropriative learning in communion with oth-ers. As I tried to show, these two forms of Internet use were not separated by empty space but by a whole range of intermediate modalities. Martha and John appreciated the empowerment stemming from the opportunity to draw on the knowledge, experience, and practical help of otherwise anonymous people in the areas of their specific interests and concerns. Myra, Patrick, and Theodore were new immigrants struggling to make sense of the dramatic political events that had befallen their native countries, as well as to sustain a meaningful balance between disparate, even conflicting, sides of their cultural identities. In this process, they were leaning on both the informational and the communal affordances of the Internet, thus forging a medium for political debate and civic involvement.

Common for all the modalities of virtual togetherness described here is the fact that actions and interactions in online forums were closely intertwined with participants' projects and pursuits in their offline lives. Martha carried over information and advice on attention deficit disorder received through her CompuServe chat room into the discussions and publications of her local parent support group. Jane (35, homemaker) used Internet sources for ideas to implement in her arts and crafts group at the local church. Theodore directed a radio program for the Ethiopian community in Vancouver drawing on the themes and issues discussed in his mailing list. In many cases, for example with Merlin and Sandy, relationships established online had been followed up in face-to-face contacts. With John, there was no distinct boundary between virtual and real links. He moved seamlessly between involvement in actual events with his fellow hobbyists and the electronic communication that sustained their organization. As much as these banal everyday activities may contrast the exotic aura of some virtual community accounts, they powerfully demonstrate the artificiality of the split between virtual and real. With Ellen, who felt more at home in her virtual community than in any face-to-face group, a very specific configuration of situational factors had brought forth this rather extreme form of virtual togetherness: a rare disease, physical and social isolation, a vital need to come to terms with a radically new experience combined with mastery of language and expression (recall that Ellen was a philologist, editor, and writer). And it should be noted that even in this case, online community was not displacing face-to-face community where the latter did or could have existed. It was rather filling the void left by the impossibility of face-to-face community or the inability of existing face-to-face communities to satisfy important needs of the individual.

BETWEEN THE PUBLIC AND THE INTIMATE: GRADIENTS OF IMMEDIACY

In his *Television: Technology and Cultural Form*, Williams draws attention to the condition of "mobile privatization" characterizing everyday life in an earlier phase of industrial capitalist society and sees the technology of broad-casting as a resolution, at a certain level, of the contradictory pressures gen-erated by this condition:

> This complex of developments included the motorcycle and motorcar, the box camera and its successors, home electrical appliances, and radio sets. Socially, this complex is characterized by the two apparently paradoxical yet deeply con-nected tendencies of modern urban industrial living: on the one hand mobility, on the other hand the more apparently self-sufficient family home. The earlier period of public technology, best exemplified by the railways and city lighting, was replaced by a kind of technology for which no satisfactory name has yet been found; that which served an at once mobile and home centered way of liv-ing: a form of *mobile privatization*. Broadcasting in its applied form was a so-cial product of this distinctive tendency.[18]

The lives of the Internet users I talked to did not seem to match this descrip-tion precisely. First of all, these people were not sufficiently mobile—their au-tomobiles could not take them to places socially denied to them. Secondly, they felt ambiguous about the self-sufficiency of the private homes in which their existence was circumscribed. They were ready and eager, each one to a different extent and different degree of rationalization, to trade that private-ness for human contact, community, and broader social involvement. Their Internet-based practices could be characterized as constituting an attempt at "immobile socialization." Users employed the medium for associating with other people and social entities without leaving, which represented a resolu-tion, at a certain level, of the pressures present in their original situations.

The practice of immobile socialization, I argue, undermines a second di-chotomy that has been employed to frame the discussion of the social mean-ing of the Internet—that between the public and the private. Critics such as Kumar have seen growing Internet use as contributing to the "increased pri-vatization and individualization" of existence and the "evacuation and di-minishing of the public sphere of contemporary western societies."[19] Enthu-siasts, on the other hand, have anticipated invigorated public life and a "network nation."[20] Neither of these bulk qualifications accurately reflects the actual practice of users. What I found in my respondents' accounts was evidence of active and discriminating crafting of boundaries and definitions of relationships between individuals and individuals and groups. These boundaries delineated spaces of social interaction, intermeshing the public and the private in ways unimaginable without the new communication medium.

Most of the people I interviewed, especially the women, spoke about an ini-tial shock and fear for their privacy when using the Internet. As new users, they found it hard to imagine exactly how visible and socially consequential their various actions and interactions were. Sandy recollected her early anxiety with amusement: "I remember when the modem hooked up the first time I was scared. I thought: Oh, no! I thought everyone was gonna know everything about me for some reason." Jane, a 36-year-old homemaker, was still at the stage where making a comment in a newsgroup or participating in a chat line felt "creepy." "So, I just made a comment. But I didn't like the idea because I realized later that anybody could read my comment and send me e-mail. . . . I didn't make any other comments."

With experience, users developed strategies for careful control of the degree of exposure they allowed on the Internet in particular action contexts. Martha's approach involved complex manipulation of two e-mail addresses, one "anonymous" and the other indicating her real name:

> The address I have at the VCN[21] forwards mail . . . to my home address. When the people I am contacting are a nonprofit website I can contact them either way—from my home address or the VCN one. I like to have that anonymity. Then any mail that goes to the VCN, the people that have sent it don't know where it goes to until I contact them.

Similarly, when Myra wanted to respond to a request for information posted in a newsgroup by an unknown person hidden behind a nickname, she reasoned: "Robert Redford [poster's nickname]! . . . Let's see what his true name is. (I am a scientist after all.) At the same time I wanted to be safe and because I had several accounts scattered around the world, I wrote to him from an account that I had in Italy. And on the next day when I checked that account, I found a message from that guy that I also thought was a Pole." The mystery guy and Myra started a serious political discussion (referred to earlier in this chapter), which went in concentric circles from public issues to private thoughts and feelings:

> And then after months, because he was always asking questions: how are things over there. . . . After months, I started joking and said, well, the next message I expect something like ten questions from you. And here come ten questions: How tall are you? What kind of wine do you like? Do you like sailing? . . . things like that. So it got more into [I suggest personal, she doesn't accept it, preferring] ordinary human terms rather than talking about big issues.

Myra was drawing the trajectory of a fascinating gradual movement between the public and the private, or as Schutz would put it, between different gradients of immediacy spanning the distance between the most anonymous—"an Albanian, a girl or guy who knew about the country," "that guy that I also thought was a Pole"—and the most intimate, as we will see shortly. Communication media varied accordingly. They were used with subtle discretion to carefully negotiate transcendence of social and cultural boundaries, one infinitesimal step at a time:

And then it was almost a year after we started talking. . . . I don't know, maybe I was bored again or I had other problems in my life when I decided again, well, what's this guy, let's hear his voice. Let's make him a real thing rather just an Internet header. So I asked him may I give you a call and he said yes. I was a little shy, because I knew nothing about his *private* [emphasis mine] life. You don't want to intrude into somebody's life and we were just friends, not even friends, not even close friends. But he said "yes" and I call him, and I talk to this guy who happens to have an accent, we talked about some rubbish, I guess. I don't even remember, nobody would have guessed then that things would get . . . (Myra)

As the story progressed, the phone conversations between the two of them became a regular event, alternating between long Internet chats, e-mails, and again hours-long phone conversations. Then, pictures were exchanged, then a marriage proposal from him came by e-mail in the form of a joke: "And it was easier to make that joke on the Internet than on the phone" (Patrick). Then, "things started getting more and more romantic" (Myra). And finally, a visit was arranged:

Myra: At the beginning of March of 1997 I came to Vancouver. We met at the airport and that was it.
Maria: How did you find each other after having had all the correspondence? Did reality change your image of the other person?
Patrick and Myra: No.
Myra: I remember that I was very tense, of course.
Patrick: Me too [unclear].
Myra: I remember I got through the gates. The first thing that I saw was him. He was coming toward me. We just hugged and we kept walking. I was talking all the time because otherwise I would explode. It was my usual way of talking—making fun of everything including myself. He was used to that, I guess. He wasn't surprised that I was behaving . . .
Maria: How long did it take from the first time you exchanged messages to that moment?
Myra: A year and a half.

As I explained earlier, in Sandy's story the interaction in the semipublic space of the chat room consisted of "mostly goofing around, cracking jokes." In the private background, however, joking was turning into deeply intimate revelations:

Roland's and mine relationship was mostly joking around, but we, at some point, got quite deep into his relationship with his wife and my relationship with my husband. . . . He was married and going through really tough times with his wife, so he and I got really good friends and we e-mailed each other back and forth every day and just having that relationship with him made me feel alive! And made me realize how much really I had going for me because after my husband diminished my self-worth and self-respect so low.

Sandy went all the way from "cracking jokes" in public to a romantic relationship with one of her new friends from the chat group. The dynamic of the story of that relationship was similar to Myra and Patrick's—long chats, coming to know each other's life stories in detail, exchange of pictures, and finally, a face-to-face meeting. The end of it all, however, was not quite so happy as in the previous case. Sandy's virtual friend, C. K., had taken advantage of the manipulative powers of the Internet to lead numerous women into believing that each of them was the only one he was attracted to and exchanged intimate correspondence with. By accident, Sandy made a discovery on his computer, which opened her eyes to the fact that C. K.'s compassion and caring had been shared with many other women all over North America at exactly the same time that their romance was in full swing. In a theoretically quite interesting move, Sandy chose to publicize her deeply private pain. Enraged, she sent a message to these women explaining what C. K. was actually doing, thus creating a powerful, even if short-lived, united front against the trickster: "None of them [the women she e-mailed] hated me, they were really angry with him. He took some pretty big flak over."

In the context of her disease-related mailing list having hundreds of readers and dozens of contributors all around the world, Ellen also traversed a spiral of public to private and back to public communications. Initially, she was "intimidated by the very hugeness" of the list and did not feel confident enough to contribute. However, in the midst of the big group discussion, after a while, Ellen would notice people that she "would resonate with." "I would find myself looking through the list of messages for their names—just to see whether they have written that day." And finally one day, she contacted a couple of people through the so-called back channels by sending them a private e-mail. This contact coincided with the creation of a new sublist by one of the women Ellen had gotten in touch with. About seventeen people who found through the big list that they shared similar interests and approaches to healing formed a semiprivate group branching off from the open public forum and initially exchanged carbon copied e-mails with each other.

As the interest in that group turned out to be quite high, after some time it had to be transformed into a new "official" (as Ellen put it) mailing list based on a server at St. John's University in Boston. This meant that from a closed, private discussion, the list was going back into the public realm where everyone could read and join it. Some members feared that this would compromise the quality of the exchange, as well as the openness and the depth of the interpersonal sharing. The group deliberated on the problem and finally decided that it was "the idea of keeping it private versus having new blood, and new information, and new ideas. Also importantly, being able to offer what we had to more people." They chose publicness and initially Ellen was ambivalent about it: "I felt very uncomfortable with the idea of becoming public. I wasn't sure I could continue posting because I am a very, very private person. I don't like the feeling of being on stage. It is a very personal medium—I find that people write very personal messages. They really reveal themselves very deeply."

Eventually, feeling that the characteristic "very nice atmosphere and a sense of camaraderie and common ground" of the list was preserved, Ellen overcame her reservations and continued to be an active contributor. Thus, after finding reaffirmation of her interests and values in other individuals and later, in a close in-group, Ellen took her deeply private thoughts and sensations out of her walk-in closet (where her old Mac was located) and came out on the stage of the public realm, empowered as an actor. After some time on the new list, someone suggested that the members exchanged personal biographies. This made Ellen reflect on the dialectic of public and private, self-presentation and knowledge of the other person in the online environment:

> I found it so fascinating to read—first of all, what everyone chooses to say about themselves; and also think about what I want to convey about myself—here I am in this unique online environment where I can't be seen, I can't be heard and yet I want to convey something about myself. . . . I kept them all. So that gave us more of a sense of the individual lives and of being a group.

What this public–private–intimate continuum helps us realize is that, analogous to the consumption versus community continuum, there is no critical point where a person or a group's behavior can be definitively characterized as private as opposed to public and vice versa. People plan and experience their social action as combining privacy and publicness in different proportions. The task typically assigned to the Internet is to bring the determination of this proportion under the user's control. To whom do I want to listen? Whom do I want to talk to? Whom do I allow to listen to me? For and with whom do I want to act? Who do I allow to act upon me? How big and open a collectivity do I want to act with? The different answers individual users give (more or less consciously) to these questions lead them to choose individual, private e-mails or e-mails carbon copied to a dozen people; posting to a closed or an open mailing list; lurking in a newsgroup or contributing to one; joining a mailing list; or, as a matter of fact, creating and moderation one as did Matthew, one of the men in my respondent group.

If we look at Myra and Ellen's examples closely, we recognize the multidimensionality of the notions of private and public. There are at least three senses in which publicness and privacy are perceived and respectively manipulated online: in terms of the forum, or space of gathering; in terms of the content of the communication; and in terms of the action taken—does it affect others or is it performed in perfect privacy, within the "lair of the scull," as Anderson has put it, describing the act of reading the newspaper.[22]

What emerges is a multidimensional scale on which privacy and publicness of social action can be gauged. At all stations of the processes of encountering others and interacting with them online, people are located in their private homes. From this position, they turn themselves, initially as simple consumers/readers, to forums that are public. Later, they reach out to another private individual sending him/her content that can itself be classified as dealing with issues of public or private concern. Thus all three components into which I have subdivided the process analytically—forum, action, and content—can be perceived as either public or private, and people carefully select the degree of openness of each component they want to permit at any particular moment. In this way the practice of immobile socialization allows for an infinitely diverse range of forms of interpersonal interaction, collective life, and public participation to proliferate.

CONCLUSION

In this chapter, I have attempted to display the limitations of a dichotomous understanding of online communication as well as of the normatively charged and vaguely defined concept of community as the standard against which social practice on the Internet is judged. Users approach the medium, as my data have shown, from a variety of situational motivations, needs, and ideologies. In doing that, they generate a rich repertory of use genres, each of which needs careful consideration and evaluation on its own merits. The preoccupation with ideologically constructed standards, such as virtual community versus real/genuine community and public participation versus privatization of experience, blinds commentators to the possibility for new, unexpected, unimaginable, and yet humanistic and empowering variations of technological practice to emerge.

It is my belief that careful examination of actual Internet use in its numerous forms should be organized by the task of discerning, recognizing, and articulating the empowering aspects of the technology as they arise out of the everyday lives of real people in particular situations. A struggle to direct resources toward the further development and reenforcement of these aspects of the Internet as a technology and a social institution can start from there.

A quote I found in Schutz's *Collected Papers* helped me summarize what my at times confusing journey through my respondents' social actions on the Internet had in fact helped me discover. In the conclusion of his analysis of Mozart's musical contribution, Schutz writes:

> I submit that Mozart's main topic is not, as Cohen believed, love. It is the metaphysical mystery of the existence of a human universe of pure sociality, the ex-

ploration of the manifold forms in which man meets his fellow-man and acquires knowledge of him. The encounter of man with man within the human world is Mozart's main concern. This explains the perfect humanity of his art.[23]

My study of the communicative and communal use of the Internet has uncovered a fascinating variety of forms in which individuals meet their fellow men and women and acquire knowledge of them opening up thanks to the new medium. The encounter with the Other, in singular and plural, within the human world, the filling of erstwhile regions of anonymity with detailed knowledge of the fellow human, is one of the most exciting promises of the Internet. Discovering and promoting these manifold forms of human encounter in a new technological environment is, I believe, the central task of a humanistic study and shaping of the Internet.

NOTES

1. Howard Rheingold, *The Virtual Community: Homesteading on the Electronic Frontier* (Reading, Mass.: Addison-Wesley, 1993).

2. R. Williams, *Television: Technology and Cultural Form* (London: Fontana, 1974).

3. An exception is Sherry Turkle, *Life on the Screen: Identity in the Age of the Internet* (New York: Simon and Schuster, 1995).

4. See two works edited by Steven G. Jones: *CyberSociety: Computer-Mediated Communication and Community* (Thousand Oaks, Calif.: Sage Publications, 1995) and *Virtual Culture: Identity and Communication in Cybersociety* (Thousand Oaks, Calif.: Sage Publications, 1997).

5. The call for participation in the study and a description of the research procedures can be viewed at www.ucalgary.ca/~bakardji/call.html.

6. A. Schutz and T. Luckmann, *The Structures of the Life-world* (Evanston, Ill.: Northwestern University Press, 1973).

7. R. Williams, *Keywords: A Vocabulary of Culture and Society* (New York: Oxford University Press, 1985), 76.

8. J. C. R. Licklider and R. W. Taylor, "The Computer as a Communication Device," *Science and Technology* 76 (1968): 21–31; R. Hiltz and M. Turoff, *The Network Nation: Human Communication via Computer* (London: Addison Wesley Publishing Company, 1968); Cerf, cited in J. E. Abbate, "From Arpanet to Internet: A History of ARPA-Sponsored Computer Networks, 1966–1988" (PhD diss., University of Pennsylvania, 1994); Rheingold, *Virtual*.

9. Albert Borgmann, *Crossing the Postmodern Divide* (Chicago: University of Chicago Press, 1992); Hubert L. Dreyfus, *Kierkegaard on the Internet: Anonymity vs. Commitment in the Present Age*, available at http://ist-socrates.berkeley.edu/~hdreyfus/html/paper_kierkegaard.html (accessed January 8, 2003); K. Kumar, *From Post-Industrial to Post-Modern Society: New Theories of the Contemporary World* (Cambridge, Mass.: Blackwell Publishers, 1995); Neil Postman, *Technopoly: The Surrender of Culture to Technology* (New York: Knopf, 1992); M. Slouka, *War*

of the Worlds: Cyberspace and the High-tech Assault on Reality (New York: Basic Books, 1995).

10. B. Wellman and M. Gulia, "Net-Surfers Don't Ride Alone: Virtual Communities as Communities," in *Networks in the Global Village: Life in Contemporary Communities*, ed. B. Wellman (Boulder, Colo.: Westview Press, 1999), 331–66.

11. B. Wellman, "The Community Question: The Intimate Networks of East Yorkers," *American Journal of Sociology* 84, no. 5 (1979): 1201–29; B. Wellman, "The Community Question Reevaluated," in *Power, Community, and the City*, ed. M. P. Smith (New Brunswick, N.J.: Transaction Books, 1988); B. Anderson, *Imagined Communities: Reflections on the Origin and Spread of Nationalism* (London: Verso, 1983).

12. Wellman and Gulia, "Net-Surfers," 348.

13. Anderson, *Imagined*, 18.

14. Wellman and Gulia, "Net-Surfers," 344.

15. Williams, *Keywords*, 76.

16. Philippe Ariès, quoted in Jeff Weintraub. "The Theory and Politics of the Public/Private Distinction." In Jeff Weintraub and Krishan Kumar, eds., *Public and Private in Thought and Practice: Perspectives on a Grand Dichotomy* (Chicago, London: University of Chicago Press, 1997), 1-42, esp. 25.

17. Quoted in Winetraub, 25.

18. Williams, *Television*, 20.

19. Kumar, *From Post-Industrial*, 163.

20. Hiltz and Turoff, *Network Nation*.

21. Vancouver Community Network.

22. Anderson, *Imagined Communities*.

23. A. Schutz, *Collected Papers II: Studies in Social Theory* (The Hague, Netherlands: Martinus Nijhoff, 1964), 199.

8

Gender and the Commodification of Community: Women.com and gURL.com

Leslie Regan Shade

This chapter chronicles the transformation of two online communities designed specifically for women (Women.com) and young girls (gURL.com), whose origin stories in the early to mid 1990s began as earnest attempts to produce feminist-oriented content for a demographic that was not then adequately represented on the Internet. Feminist pioneers created their communities in the heady days of Internet utopianism, when the North American female population of the Internet was paltry in comparison to its current gender parity. Women.com and gURL.com are interesting case studies because, as we shall see, both communities became part of the wave of dot.com euphoria, merging with other companies and creating commercial ventures, capitalizing on Internet stock speculation, and, in the process, diluting the nature of its feminist content to appeal to a mainstream female audience, thus targeting and commodifying a particular female demographic.

Women.com and gURL.com are cautious tales of how cutting-edge online feminist communities became part of the feminization of the Internet, by which I refer to the process whereby the creation of popular content privileges women's consumption, rather than encouraging their production or critical analysis. The corporate history of Women.com and gURL.com will be detailed, and the elements that shape their notion of community (such as discussion boards, content forums, user agreements, and privacy policies) will be analyzed. As will be shown, the case studies of Women.com and gURL.com illustrate how community has been transformed by the process of commodification, and how users are conceived not as active agents or citizens, but as consumers. What were once burgeoning feminist communities have since been transmogrified into female-oriented spaces where empowerment is often equated with consumer sovereignty.

WOMEN.COM

Did you expect a feminist revolution online, empowering women to toss aside those astrology readings and turn off Ally McBeal, to run for president on a platform of halting genital mutilation in Africa? Those who thought the Web would be more like *Ms.* than *Mademoiselle* —believing that all women were itching for more intellectualism—were deluded.[1]

Women.com emerged in 1993 as Women's WIRE (Worldwide Information Resource & Exchange). As this was before graphical interfaces and even the earliest incarnation of the World Wide Web, Mosaic, was popularized, Women's WIRE was launched as a dial-up service, and then moved on to the commercial bulletin board service CompuServe before establishing a presence on the Web in 1995. It used First Class software, which bundled together chat, message boards, libraries, and upload and download areas. Subscription costs were $15/month for two hours, with additional hours billed at $2.50/hour. Women's WIRE was founded by Ellen Pack, former chief operating officer at Torque Systems Inc., a software company, and Nancy Rhine, who worked in customer support at the Well, a famous online network known for its communitarian zeal, emanating from the Bay Area.[2]

In the early 1990s, estimates of women's online participation were approximately 15 percent of all Internet participants, with most women accessing the Internet through universities and in high-tech workplaces. Access to the Internet for women was an emerging social and political issue. Exemplary in this regard was a loose coalition of women called BAWIT (Bay Area Women in Telecommunications) who presented one of the earliest "manifestos" on gender issues in online communication at the Computers, Freedom, and Privacy Conference in 1993. Issues BAWIT identified included the need for women to become more active users and designers of computer networking, identification of online harassment and sexist forms of online interaction, the prevalence of pornography, and the paucity of women in computer science programs.[3] Early Internet content for women included a variety of feminist-oriented listservs and Usenet newsgroups, emphasizing academic and technical interests.[4]

In 1994, subscription information for Women's WIRE read:

WOMEN'S WIRE draws its content from the media, newswires, women's organizations, government sources and, most importantly, from its subscribers— offering a central source for the latest women's news and information. Topic areas include news & politics, the environment, parenting, education, health & fitness, technology, arts & leisure, careers & finance, and more. Subscribers can access the latest legislative updates, reports, health abstracts, event calendars, and other information resources on issues impacting women. In addition, there are cultural resources like book, music and movie reviews, and conversations on a multitude of topics. Not only that, but WOMEN'S WIRE offers Internet email, mailing lists, AP and Reuters newswires, and Usenet newsgroups, too![5]

Content on Women's WIRE emphasized current news and affairs and encouraged political activism. Subscribers were expected to participate and interact on diverse conferences and take a role in building community content. According to Ellen Pack, Women's WIRE started off with five hundred "founding subscribers" enlisted to develop an online community that would "foster diversity . . . people with something to contribute, personally, intellectually or through their involvements. While many subscribers will already be familiar with computer conferencing, our goal is to make it so easy to get around online that it's completely unnecessary to be technologically sophisticated."[6] The emphasis on creating community content was a natural for cofounder Nancy Rhine, who got her start in community development when she was a member of The Farm, an intentional community in Tennessee formed in 1971 famous for their role in promoting home births and midwifery.[7] When Rhine relocated to California, she joined other ex-Farm members who were at the Well, where she realized that "women, especially, would adopt the Internet on a global scale for exchanging ideas and information on everything from politics and discrimination issues to day-to-day child-rearing, career, and health information."[8]

According to Rhine, Women's WIRE became very popular as "word spread like wildfire as activist-minded women joined to converse with a global, online population that was 90 percent female. The support and excitement was palpable among the first thousand paying customers, as women realized what this tool could do to help them make a living, raise their kids, and find support and information of all kinds."[9]

In 1995 Women's WIRE established a presence on the World Wide Web, and in 1996 it received more than 7.5 million hits a month, which represented 300,000 individual visitors. Original content was repackaged with wire stories from Reuters, and distribution relationships, corporate partnerships, and advertisers, including Levi's, signed on.[10] In 1997 Women's WIRE changed its name to Women.com, which reflected their domain name. Marlene McDaniel became CEO and chairman. She had previously spent thirty years in the technology field (her senior executive marketing positions included stints at Sun Microsystems, 3Com, and publisher Ziff-Davis). At that time Women.com consisted of three separate entities: its popular Women's Wire online site, Beatrice's Web Guide (a guide to women's activities and websites), and *Prevention*'s Healthy Ideas (health tips from Rodale's health and fitness magazine).[11] Distribution agreements were later struck with AOL, Microsoft's WomenCentral and Yahoo!, a partnership with Bloomberg News, and agreements with foreign media companies in Japan, Korea, Malaysia, and Latin America.

Under McDaniel, Women.com merged with Hearst New Media & Technology HomeArts.com in 1999. Each company held an equal 50 percent stake in the venture. The terms of agreement with Hearst obliged Women.com to access content from Hearst, which included their cable, television, and magazine content, including their HomeArts.com site, their popular Astrology.com site, and distribution of online magazine sites including *Country Living Gardener, Country Living's Healthy Living, Good Housekeeping, Redbook,* and *Town & Country.*[12] Promotion of Women.com was via Hearst's television cable properties Lifetime, A&E, and the History Channel. Although Hearst's audience was more traditional and mainstream than Women.com's users, the business rationale was that an amalgamation of a wider female audience would create more advertising and e-commerce business ventures. About the revamped Women.com, McDaniel said: "It's a place to go where women can find a whole variety of things that appeal their interests. And it will give us the opportunity to serve our advertisers and our audience with better programming."[13]

By then, women's presence on the Internet had increased substantially, and corporations realized that one of the ways to attract more lucrative e-commerce traffic would be to target the "elusive" female market, purportedly responsible for over half of household purchases. Marketers dissected the female online population to ascertain what strategies to employ in their bid to capture their spending dollars. Advertisers eagerly signed on for partnerships and joint ventures, and several "one-stop shopping" women's portals were created, including competitors Oxygen Media and iVillage.com.[14] At that time, the climate for the women's commercial online climate was heating up. The media paid much attention to the $87.6 million IPO in March 1999 of iVillage.[15] The stakes were up for "supremacy in the online battle to attract women Web users, prized as a growing and highly coveted (read: they spend a lot)."[16] Women.com executives recognized this and participated in a joint study with Proctor & Gamble, the consumer products company, and Harris Interactive, a market research firm, to uncloak the psychographics of women's online behavior. Because men design most websites, McDaniel contended, "We want to understand how women use the Web to better design products and services for them."[17]

In the late 1990s, like so many Internet based ventures, Women.com decided to jump on the IPO bandwagon. Their 1999 IPO was launched at 3.75 million shares at $10 each. Early trading saw the stock price rise to almost $24. One month later the stock price was at 80 percent above initial offering price, but later plummeted to half of the IPO.

With the downturn in the Internet economy in 2000 and the intense competition for advertising monies, many women's Internet portals sunk and their stock valuation plummeted.[18] In 2001 Women.com and iVillage announced a $36M merger.[19] As reported in *The Wall Street Journal*, "the deal supports the notion that the Internet cannot sustain several major ad-dependent sites catering to the niche market of women's interest."[20]

iVillage was cofounded by Nancy Evans and Candice Carpenter in 1995. Carpenter had previously worked with Time-Life and cable home shopping channel QVC. Evans was a well-known publishing executive, having been a columnist for *Glamour* magazine, the editor-in-chief of the Book-of-the-Month Club, and a president and publisher of Doubleday. In 1995 Carpenter and Evans, noting the paucity of online content for women, created Parent Soup, dedicated to parenting resources for women, which later changed into iVillage.

When iVillage began selling common stock in 1999 as part of their initial public offering (IPO), the opening bid was $95.88, and by the end of the first day, Carpenter's stake—690,001 shares of stock—was worth over $80M.[21] Media attention was both adulatory and hostile because cofounders Candice Carpenter and Nancy Evans "were neither 'Webheads' nor computer geeks, but two women in their forties with controversial reputations rooted in the realm of books, magazines, and television."[22] The media paid particular attention to Carpenter, who also parlayed the media into a process she dubbed "self-branding."[23] Although Carpenter was frequently profiled in the media as one of the quintessential female Internet entrepreneurs, in November 2000 she left the company after receiving a one-time payment of $1.3 million.[24] Carpenter married, took the last name of her husband (Olson), and wrote a book published by McGraw-Hill, *Chapters: Create a Life of Exhilaration and Accomplishment in the Face of Change.* [25]

THE iVILLAGE COMMUNITY

iVillage pioneered "integrated sponsorships" wherein advertisers participate in creating online content and services; examples of early sponsorships included iVillage's Pet Channel, sponsored by pet food manufacturer Ralston Purina, and a "behavior modification program" sponsored by the milk industry consisting of e-mail reminders and message boards to drink three glasses of milk per day. Described as a "ganglion of corporate alliances and digital pathways that together form a network of seventeen Web sites, or 'channels,' through which the company seeks to build a community of women on the Internet,"[26] iVillage also had aspirations to "monetize" its community by selling enough products and advertising to create profits. It purchased Lamaze Publishing (publisher of information for new and impending parents) and The Newborn Channel, broadcaster of instructional information to new mothers distributed in hospitals across the United States. Like many emergent e-commerce ventures, iVillage attempted to exploit the "stickiness" factor—the attributes that draw users into the websites and keep them online for long sessions. Quantifying the number of "unique visitors" (also called "eyeballs") and page tracks is the Web equivalent to Nielson Media television ratings, and in its early days, iVillage reported more than 100 million page views per month.[27]

According to Cliff Figallo (an early member of the Well and known for his work on building online communities), since its founding in 1995, iVillage has adopted several different business models. These include its origins as an advertiser-sponsored community site, to e-commerce ventures targeting women as the main household purchasers, to its acquisition of Women.com when it moved to a paid subscription model, "leveraging on the needs and wants of the community."[28]

iVillage has several different types of community-related content, according to Kellie Gould, iVillage's senior vice president for programming: "about 3,000 message boards, about 900 weekly hosted chats, and we have roughly 2,500 'community leaders.'" These leaders and community managers are volunteers who lead and guide the weekly hosted chats, message boards, and interactive forums.[29] Gould refers to iVillage's content as "evergreen issues": "They're about parenting and dieting and financial management—these kinds of things are so important to women for so many years—and their needs change. What we're really excited about is offering that information throughout their lives."[30]

iVillage's strategy is what Figallo refers to as "a lifecycle approach to community," wherein women return to the community as they go through different stages of their lives, from marriage to pregnancy to child rearing to careers to divorce (see table 8.1 for details of iVillage community content).

Although iVillage boasts reaching 12.6 percent of the Internet population, claims that it ranks thirteenth among all digital media properties for women aged eighteen and older, and "is the leading destination and brand and touches 31 million unique people," it is not without its critics. Commented Janelle Brown: "Other than a certain emphasis on resourcefulness, do-it-yourself-ism and pro-female positivity, there isn't much difference between the front page of iVillage and the cover of *Family Circle*, that of Women.com and *Cosmopolitan* (whoops, *Cosmopolitan* is now part of Women.com)."[31] Indeed, a recent look at iVillage featured a Women.com link to a spread on "Rock Star Workouts! How to Get: Gwen's Abs, Britney's Bust, Madonna's Arms, and Shakira's Butt." Another feature, "Spring Cleaning for Real Women," linked to columnist "Clean-It Queen" Mary Ellen Pinkham, with sidebars to a feng shui quiz and links to purchase storage products ("Organizing your CD or video collection has never been easier!!").

Under the ownership of iVillage, Women.com has certainly shifted gears, going from intelligent women's commentary and oftentimes feminist content to a content slate concentrating on "gossip, sex & style." At Women.com "you can leave life's pressures behind, kick back and laugh at hilarious dating sto-

Table 8.1.   Commodifying Community: The View from iVillage

Magazine sites include *Cosmopolitan, Country Living, Good Housekeeping, House Beautiful, Marie Claire, Redbook, Town & Country,* and *Victoria.*

iVillage advertising partners include Clairol (hair coloring products), Country Crock (cooking and home decorating resources), Dewey Color System (psychological color profiling), eDiets (fitness and meal plans), Kraft (food processor and recipes), Match.com (dating service), Olay (facial and skin products), SmartSource (household consumer coupons), and WestPoint Stevens (home bed and bath linens).

Online integrated sponsorships and advertising include "deep integration of brand messages including sponsored content, customized bridge sites, special promotion, market intelligence, and problem-solving interactive tools." Marketing partners include Ford Motor Company; financial service companies PNC Bank, Visa, and Charles Schwab; consumer products companies Kimberly-Clark, Proctor & Gamble, Johnson & Johnson, and Unilever; pharmaceutical companies Pfizer and Glaxo-Wellcome; dog food company Ralston Purina; and online drugstore Planet R$_x$.

Nineteen iVillage channels are loosely organized around subject matter, including family, health, work, money, food, relationships, beauty, shopping, diet and fitness, travels, pets, and astrology. Channel features include interactive tools, access to experts, special features, and resources.

Member services include e-mail, games, coupons, newsletters, quizzes, and personals.

Community Challenges is a trademarked "behavior-changing program" featuring a "combination of defined steps and group collaboration" providing women "with a structured and supportive program through which to tackle—and conquer—common and pressing problems. Led by top experts, Community Challenges generally last six weeks and include weekly 'assignments' as well as special message boards and chats so that participants can interact with other women pursuing the same goals." Topics have included organizational skills, walking for fitness, and "thinking for thinness."

---

ries, get the hottest celebrity scoop, check out styles for your home and your closet, talk about sex, take revealing quizzes and amuse yourself with games that women love."[32] At *Girl Talk,* Sexual Bloopers are revealed (featuring bodily functions gone awry); *Date This Dude* allows women to vote for their favorite hottie; and Cosmo Sex reveals the secrets in Sex University (Oral Studies and Kinky Curriculum!). The site is littered with flash java-scripted pop-up and banner ads.

How is community conceptualized at Women.com and iVillage? Gustafson[33] has analyzed three popular women's sites—iVillage.com, Women.com, and Oxygen.com—to ascertain their rhetoric of community through design and its implication in the creation of the feminization of community online. She concludes that these sites, through their rules and coding practices, reinforce women's traditional roles as consumers. Integrated sponsorships and commercial partnerships are just one part of this package. Membership benefits include access to message boards, discounts, coupons, "freebies," interactive quizzes, newsletters, and the ability to create your own webpage. Becoming a member of iVillage (membership in Women.com is linked to iVillage) involves registering identification (name, e-mail address, gender, birth date, country, and zip code are required fields) and agreeing to the Terms of Service. "The Women's Network" (TWN) Terms of Service cover a range of issues; for instance, members who provide iVillage with false or misleading information may have their iVillage e-mail account and webpage terminated. Spam is not allowed, nor is anonymity or impersonating another member. Content is strictly enforced, as the following excerpt from the Terms of Service reads:

> Unlawful, harassing, libelous, defamatory, abusive, threatening, harmful, vulgar, obscene, profane, sexually oriented (unless within the scope of the topic area of a message board as determined by iVillage in its sole discretion), racially offensive, inaccurate, or otherwise objectionable material of any kind or nature or that encourages conduct that could constitute a criminal offense, give rise to civil liability or otherwise violate any applicable local, state, national or international law or regulation, or encourage the use of controlled substances. For purposes of the immediately preceding sentence, "masked" vulgarity, obscenity or profanity (e.g. "f*ck") is deemed to be equivalent to including the actual objectionable word, phrase or symbol in your post, message or otherwise on TWN. iVillage reserves the right to delete any such material from TWN.[34]

Messages posted on iVillage in public areas are the property of iVillage. Members thus waive their intellectual property rights and grant the use of any of their content to iVillage:

> Royalty-free, perpetual, irrevocable, non-exclusive right (including any moral rights) and license to use, reproduce, modify, adapt, publish, translate, create derivative works from, distribute, communicate to the public, perform and display the content (in whole or in part) worldwide and/or to incorporate it in other works in any form, media, or technology now known or later developed, for the full term of any Rights that may exist in such content.[35]

In their Privacy Policy, iVillage assures its members that information they collect is to provide a better community for their members:

> iVillage uses the information it gathers for several purposes, such as to understand more about our audiences' interests, to communicate with you and to give you a better experience when visiting the iVillage Network by personalizing tools, content, services and email messages. iVillage also uses this information to build new services and develop offers that iVillage believes are more relevant and valuable to you.[36]

However, at one time, a serious glitch at the iVillage website allowed women to view other users' personal messages.[37] This infraction was quickly resolved.

Members are told that information collected about them from either iVillage or third parties is collected from server logs and cookies. Information is aggregated to create anonymous statistical demographic profiles of the iVillage members, which is used to determine trends and market research for potential advertisers and partners. As Gustafson writes: "iVillage is perhaps the most overt in its intention to promote tailored marketing and encourage organized, traditionally feminine modes of consumption. Surveys and discussion groups may bond community members to one another, while serving the broader purpose of providing detailed marketing information."[38]

iVillage is heavily dependent on sponsorships and advertising, which represent 78 and 81 percent of their revenues. Advertising revenues derive from short- and long-term contracts, typically featuring banner advertisements on each page from which viewers may hyperlink to each advertiser's homepage. In their 2002 10K report to the Securities and Exchange Commission, it was stressed that iVillage's business depends on the market acceptance of the Internet as a medium for advertising. For year-end 2002 and 2001, revenues from the five largest iVillage customers accounted for approximately 38 and 37 percent of total revenues, respectively. The three largest advertisers (Proctor & Gamble, Hearst Communications, and Unilever) accounted for approximately 11, 11, and 10 percent of total revenues. According to the 10K filing, "iVillage has not achieved profitability and iVillage expects to continue to incur operating losses for the foreseeable future. iVillage incurred net losses of approximately $33.9 million for the year ended December 31, 2002, $48.5 million for the year ended December 31, 2001, and $191.4 million for the year ended December 31, 2000. As of December 31, 2002, iVillage's accumulated deficit was approximately $466.7 million."[39]

GURL.COM

The Internet simultaneously expands on and explodes the image of the teenybopper with a phone welded to her ear, giving teenage girls an open forum to talk to anyone about anything. With her personally crafted identity, a Web-wise girl can be free from the judgment she feels in real life and find out what she needs to know without worrying about whispers of her dilemma leaking out in gym class the next day. Girls no longer have to wait until they are twenty-seven (and drunk) to admit to a girlfriend that they masturbate. Now they can go online and get advice on how to get the most out of the showerhead technique.[40]

gURL.com began as a project initiated in 1996 by students Rebecca Odes, Esther Drill, and Heather McDonald at New York University's Interactive Telecommunications Program. According to Odes, "The lack of interesting media was the subject of a lot of high school late-night discussions. . . . After we started studying at NYU, we thought maybe the Web would be the place to do something different."[41]

gURL.com differed from other websites set up for teen girls because it presented a frank and feisty attitude toward dating, sex, and beauty. According to its creators, it was "committed to discussing issues that affect the lives of girls age 13 and up in a non-judgmental, personal way. Through honest writing, visuals and liberal use of humour, we try to give girls a new way of looking at subjects that are crucial to their lives. Our content deals frankly with sexuality, emotions, body image, etc."[42] Popular content included "Paper Doll Psychology," which allowed girls to dress a figure and receive a pseudo-psychological assessment of what the chosen outfit says about the outfitter. "The Boob Files" included first person essays on breasts, and "Deal With It" tackled issues regarding sexuality, parents, growing up, and the body.

The gURL.com founders were often featured as part of New York's Silicon Alley "digerati," multimedia artists who pioneered a hip new style on the burgeoning Web.[43] Drill, McDonald, and Odes parlayed their gURL.com content into a best-selling book, *Deal With It!*, published by Pocket Books.[44] For "mature teens," the book covered a gamut of issues, from sex and sexuality, to the body (functions and image), to careers. Described by *New York Magazine* as "Our Bodies Ourselves for teenagers—minus the 100% cotton," it received critical acclaim for its honesty and spunkiness. A few years later they created *The Looks Book*,[45] an eclectic examination of beauty throughout the ages, the body (images, parts, modification), and the creation of style (including Bombshell, Baby Doll, African Queen, California Girl, Chick Geek, and Modern Primitive). The books reinforced Odes' intention that "our job is not to give girls a reason to be online, but to have them realize that this message can exist offline."[46]

In December 1997, gURL.com was acquired by dELiA*s Corporation, a direct-market fashion retailer to teenage girls and young women. They folded gURL.com into their network of teen-centered Internet properties, the iTurf Network.[47] Two years later, iTurf issued an IPO for $92.4 million and stock sold for $66/share the first day. One of their initiatives was with Upoc, a wireless media company targeting youth, with the goal "to send updates on news, shopping and local events from the gURL.com Web site to pagers and mobile phones."[48]

With the downturn in Internet stocks a year later, dELiA*s shut down or sold off all their Internet properties except for gURL.com. Then in 2001, Primedia, a large special-interest magazine publisher, acquired gURL.com from dELiA*s for an undisclosed price. The purchase of gURL.com was meant to augment their existing teen properties, which they had started to build up in October 2000 when they brought in former MTV Networks Online president

Fred Seibert to head their Teen Internet Initiative, designed to leverage the Web assets of their offline publications, including *Seventeen, Teen Beat*, and *Tiger Beat* magazines.

Primedia's magazine holdings include over a hundred and fifty general interest publications covering an array of topics: entertainment, automobiles, sports, crafts and jewelry, equine, gardening, high technology, hunting and fishing, marine sports, motorcycles, quilting and sewing, shooting sports, action sports, and sports news. Primedia's Youth Entertainment Group includes several magazines focusing on music (*Bop, Teen Beat, Tiger Beat*) and teen celebrities (*Teen Stars, Teen, BB*) but also Channel One Network, a commercial newscast seen in many U.S. high schools, which has not been without its critics as a blatant example of the commercialization of public space.[49]

Cross-promotion of Primedia's holdings is evident with gURL.com and *Seventeen* magazine, with the ability for gURL.com members to contribute content to *Seventeen*, and with *Seventeen* ads appearing on the site. However, in April 2003 Primedia announced the sale of *Seventeen* and other branded properties to Hearst Publishing for $182.4M.[50] It is not yet known how this will affect gURL.com.

The demographic of tweens (preteens age eight to twelve) and teens in North America is huge. Generation Y, as it is often referred to, consists of 71 million teens and young adults in the United States alone. Between 1990 and 2000, the number of teens aged twelve to nineteen increased to 32 million, and it is expected to increase to 34.6 million by 2006. It is also a very multi- and intracultural demographic.[51] Concomitant with this increase in youth is an exponential growth in tween targeting and marketing. YTV (Youth Television Network) in Toronto estimates that, in Canada, tweens "control about $1.9 billion in spending every year," with $15 billion in the United States, from "gifts (particularly from doting grandparents who live longer and have fewer grandkids than their counterparts of a generation ago), allowances, [and] money from jobs such as babysitting and other spending money."[52] Globally, the youth market is growing dramatically, and represents "a ripe and growing consumer base for U.S. marketers, with $100 billion in spending power, even if they live in developing countries, among chaotic economic circumstances (in Argentina, for example), or in countries not considered the States' political allies."[53]

Targeting teenagers for their spending prowess in the marketplace is nothing new. Record has chronicled the post–World War II courting of the teen consumer, when advertisers seized teens as a viable consumer demographic. Particularly attractive were teenage women who were wooed by a bevy of products that were the precursor for their future role in the domestic sphere. The emergence of *Seventeen* magazine in 1944 exemplified how advertisers and publishers saw opportunities to enlist young women in "embracing white middle-class heteronormativity . . . [focusing] primarily on the young women's domestic role and her need to spend money in order to achieve domestic bliss."[54]

THE GURL.COM COMMUNITY

Unlike other web-based communities for young women, gURL.com has an edgier—and even feminist—attitude. Content is organized around the topics of everyday management ("Deal With It"), fashion and beauty ("Looks Aren't Everything"), Shopping ("Stop, Look, and Listen"), careers ("Where Do I Go From Here?"), celebrities ("Movers, Shakers, and Media Makers"), and Sports. Interactive features include advice columns, polls, "shout outs," comics, games, e-cards, and contests.

Drill, Odes, and McDonald were prescient in realizing that girls wanted to be not mere consumers of content, but creators. As Kearney has observed, young women have created a vibrant zine and e-zine culture, often parodying mainstream commercial culture and dominant discourses on femininity.[55] Early content on gURL.com was hailed for its irreverent nature and interactive features. Current games include "Make Your Own Rock Band," "Make Your Own Reality TV Show," and "Try the Prom Dress Selector." The "Deal With It!" section includes "Sucky Emotion Comics" and "Mizbehavior." Members may contribute comics and poems and are invited to give their opinions on various topics of current news interest; recent headlines have included "Georgians plan whites-only program," "War on the Environment," "Madonna Slams American Values," and "Senate Passes Bill Limiting Abortion."

Despite gURL.com's alliance with *Seventeen* magazine (banner ads entreating members to subscribe to the magazine appear throughout a gURL.com session), content encourages young women to think in careerist modes, and the "Movers and Shakers" section features interviews with women working in diverse fields: included have been a civil rights lawyer, a Congresswomen, a gURL.com web designer, a journalist, archeologist, writer, neuroscientist, and astronaut.

Membership in gURL.com is free and includes participation in chat rooms, access to free web pages, ability to participate in surveys, and publishing opportunities. To sign up for membership, users are asked for a nickname, password, first name, birth date, zip/postal code, state/province, and country, plus a current e-mail address. Users may opt out of receiving e-mail updates from gURL.com partners, and as well can opt out of participating in the gURL.com survey. Upon registering, members receive the following notice: "I agree to treat other gURL members with respect in all interactions: on the chat, in the shoutouts, in emails, etc. I am aware that attacking another gURL member is not allowed and that all comments of this nature will be removed, as will the people who say them."

A lengthy legal notice agreement is also appended, which tells the member that 1) they use gURL.com at their own risk and that "we cannot guarantee the accountability or reliability of any information obtained through gURL.com"; 2) intellectual property rights adhere to any text, images, or sounds transmitted through gURL.com, and that any content submitted through gURL.com remains the property of gURL.com—"a royalty-free, perpetual, irrevocable, worldwide, non-exclusive right and license to use, reproduce, modify, adapt, publish, translate, create derivative works from, distribute, perform, transmit and display such Content (in whole or part) and/or to incorporate it in other works in any form, media or technology now known or later developed for the full term of any Rights that may exist in such Content"; 3) gURL.com is not liable for any damages resulting from the use of gURL.com, such as downloading inappropriate or buggy content; and 4) modifications to the agreement can be made at any time.

After agreeing to these legal notices (it is doubtful that most young girls actually wade through the convoluted legalese), members are brought to their personal survey profile, where they are asked to give their opinion on what they like to do in their spare time (a wide range of choices are given, from reading, making crafts, cooking, e-mailing, to participating in an organized religion), what sorts of electronic devices they intend to purchase in the next six months, survey topics interested in (cars, foods, jobs/money, politics, shopping), whether or not she intends to go to college, modem speed, access to credit cards, how much money she spends in an average week, how much time she spends online per week, how often she visits gURL.com, and whether she reads *Seventeen* magazine.

Members can then create a gURL.com profile. They are asked to provide information on their age (junior high, high school, college, or older), provide personal comments without providing full name or real addresses, click on interests, sports, music, and arts genres preferred, academic interests, and choose an icon to represent themselves (includes cartoons of a sun, red lips, daisy, basketball, star, fox, television set, soccer ball, hamburger). Member services are plentiful, and members are encouraged to provide input on the types of features they want (see table 8.2).

A "Note to Parents" tells them that the operating ethos behind gURL.com is that "information is a positive thing":

> We created gURL to be an alternative to prescriptive traditional girls' magazines, and our site strives to present a variety of experiences that are relevant to teen girls. Because of this, gURL sometimes contains mature content dealing with sexuality, body image, emotions, self-destructive behavior, etc. Our honesty is part of what makes our site resonate with our audience. . . . We recognize that not every girl is ready to deal with these issues at the same age. If your daughter is younger than our recommended age or you think she is not ready to deal with mature content at whatever age, we suggest you direct her to another site.[56]

gURL.com adheres to the Children's Online Privacy Protection Act (COPPA), an FTC regulation that restricts the personal information children's websites

Table 8.2. Commodifying Community: The View from gURL.com

gURL Chat: Includes chat rooms and live chats. Chats are "a place where members of the gURL connection can chat with and meet each other. If that is not what you have in mind, i.e. you hope to meet boys or to cyber, please go elsewhere!" and "Live chats with celebrities, health experts, and goofballs."

gURL Grams: Allows members to send messages to each other.

gURL Profiles: When users are signing up for membership, they create a profile that "lists your likes, interests, and a personal message to the gURL community. Other members of the gURL community can view your profile and, from there, send you a gURL gram or add you to their friends list."

gURL Pages: Free websites for members.

Shout-Outs: These are bulletin boards where members can read, post, and respond to various topics. These include Shout Out to gURL—for advice on gURL.com; Shout Out for Advice—subtopics include dating, friends, school, family, bodies, emotions; Poetry Shout Out—subtopics include emotion, hate, love poems, my self, nature, relationships, the state of the world; Shout Out a Story—fiction, horror, mystery, romance, sci-fi, and fantasy; HTML Shout Out—learn and practice hypertext markup language; College Shout Outs—academics, getting in, freshman year, living situations, social stuff, vacation, working; Spirituality Shout Out—beliefs, religions, faith, God, the Bible, the occult, spiritual practices; Media Shout Out; Sports Shout Out.

gURL Mall: An online store where one can buy books (*Deal With It!*), subscribe to *Seventeen* magazine, order CDs from Sony Music, purchase *Seventeen* home bedding fashions (hyperlinked to retailer JC Penney), and other items. The Classifieds section also provides links to shopping and events sites.

gURL Contests: Includes links to various retail contests (CoverGirl Summer Stylin' Sweepstakes, Rockstar Sweepstakes, Clearasil's "Celebrate Your Prom in Style").

can collect from individuals under the age of thirteen. Their Privacy Statement says that "they sometimes collect personal information from our users," but that information collected during membership will not be sold to third parties outside Primedia "although you may occasionally receive mailings from advertisers." Members are cautioned to be aware of the privacy policies for sites outside of gURL.com.

Although gURL.com contends that its editorial content and expressed viewed are "independent of any influence by advertisers or marketing partners," one has to wonder if this is always the case. gURL.com persuades its members, through its various discursive strategies (particularly its hip language and humor and its recognition of the importance of popular culture in the everyday lives of girls) that they are part of a community whose viability and energy depends upon their contributions. But this captive community is also a temptation for online marketers who see a sizable demographic of affluent and active consumers.

gURL.com illustrates the increasing debate surrounding the ethics of online marketing targeted to children and young people. The blurring lines between content and advertising, particularly with media convergence, has created for many marketers a new and exciting challenge. But for others—academics and children's media advocates—the brave new world of digital media for children portends a perilous decline in non-commercial media spaces.[57]

CONCLUSION

Tracing the corporate history and examining their discourses of community reveal how Women.com and gURL.com exemplify both the feminization of the Internet and the commodification of community. The creation of consumer-oriented content targeting women and young girls by media behemoths and a new breed of competitive entrepreneurs is one facet of the feminization of the Internet. The other is the erasure of race and class. As Nakamura contends, "Gender and race can just as easily be co-opted by the e-marketplace. Commercial sites such as these tend to view women and minorities primarily as potential markets for advertisers and merchants rather than as 'coalitions.'"[58]

The commandeering of the semblance and sensibility of community has been an objective of many commercial sites on the Internet. This contrasts with utopian sentiments of virtual communities, wherein a gift economy flourishes regardless of geographic locale. The tension between the Internet as a marketplace of ideas constituted by citizens, versus the Internet as a mere market controlled by corporations, is expressed well by Fernback, who writes:

> When community becomes as purchasable as any other commodity, it loses its meaning as a fundamental social institution. . . . People are empowered as consumers rather than as citizens when they participate in communities that are designed to be advertising billboards. If we are empowered as consumers, we make democratic decisions based on our roles as consumers rather than as citizens. The audience becomes a market rather than a public.[59]

The late 1990s were heady days for the Internet. Fueled by media adulation, Wall Street hi jinks, and a faith in market incentives, digital capitalism, or as pundits dubbed it, the "new economy," became a short-lived bust. Described as a "technicist neo-liberal mythology,"[60] many of the products of the Internet, which burst onto the scene with much hype and hurrah, quickly went the way of vaporware—here today, gone tomorrow. The original feminist qualities inherent in Women.com—and to a certain extent gURL.com—have been, similar to our current cultural backlash—diluted and packaged for a homogeneously idyllic audience commodity. The question is: Will these "communities" be sustainable, given the vicissitudes of convergence, or will they be merely passing fads?

NOTE

1. Janelle Brown, "From Feminism to Fluff: Economics Forces Top Sites to Push Content into Line with Print Media," *The Vancouver Sun* (September 7, 2000): F14.

2. Howard Rheingold, *The Virtual Community: Homesteading on the Electronic Frontier*, rev. ed. (Cambridge: MIT Press, 2000).

3. Hoai-An Truong, "Gender Issues in Online Communications," version 4.3, 1993, available at www.cpsr.org/cpsr/gender/bawit.cfp93 (accessed May 1, 2003).

4. In August 1993, I delivered a talk on gender issues in networking at the first international conference on community networking (the International Free-Net Conference), at Carleton University in Ottawa, Canada. My paper detailed activity over the last few months on gender issues in computer networking, and discussed issues such as the participation of women in computer science and networking, social interactions, ethical issues including pornography, use of networks by women, and included a variety of references and online resources. The ASCII text of the talk circulated widely on the Internet for years and appeared in newsgroups, private e-mails, computer conferences, and later, on many sites on the Web. What was fascinating was the viral fashion in which the text circulated online, and the incredible interest and passion the topic—that of feminism and the Internet—generated. See *Gender Issues in Computer Networking*, available at www.cpsr.org/cpsr/gender/leslie_regan_shade.txt (accessed January 28, 2004).

5. See www.cs.berkeley.edu/~jmankoff/women.wire.txt (accessed January 28, 2004).

6. "Women's Wire Gets Serious about Business," *The Tampa Tribune* (accessed August 19, 1995).

7. See www.thefarmcommunity.com (accessed January 28, 2004).

8. Nancy Rhine, "Populist Activism—Online Facilitation," *TechTV* (2001), available at www.techtv.com/screensavers/print/0,23102,3335135,00.html (accessed May 1, 2003).

9. Rhine, "Populist Activism."

10. "Women's Wire Gets Serious."

11. Gary M. Sterne, "Women's Wire," *Link-Up* 15, no. 2 (March–April 1998): 20.

12. Jennifer Oldham, "Women.com, Hearst to Build Site for Women," *Los Angeles Times* (January 29, 1999); Greta Mittner, "Hearst.com Gives Muscle to Women.com," *Red Herring* (January 29, 1999), available at www.redherring.com/insider/1999/0129/vc-women.html (accessed May 1, 2003).

13. "Women.com Gets Makeover," *Wired News* (January 28, 1999), available at www.wired.com/news/culture/0,1284,17606,00.html (accessed May 1, 2003).

14. Leslie Regan Shade, *Gender and Community in the Social Construction of the Interne.* (New York: Peter Lang, 2002).

15. Erik Larson, "Free Money," *The New Yorker* (October 11, 1999): 76–85.

16. Chris Nerney, "Women.com IPO Turns Heads on Wall Street," *The Internet Stock Report* (October 15, 1999).

17. Lindsey Arendt, "How Women Buy, and Why," *Wired News* (November 17, 1999), available at www.wired.com/news/business/0,1367,32483,00.html (accessed May 1, 2003).

18. Shelley Emling, "Web Sites Battle to Lure Women: Many Full-Service Portals Are Struggling," *Edmonton Journal* (March 15, 2001): F2.

19. Jennifer Rewick, "iVillage.com to Buy Rival Women.com for $30 Million," *Wall Street Journal* (February 6, 2001): B8.

20. Rewick, "iVillage.com."

21. Larson, "Free Money," 85.

22. Larson, "Free Money," 76.

23. Larson, "Free Money," 76.

24. Brad Reagan, "Openers—Where Are They Now? (Candice Olson)," *Wall Street Journal* (February 11, 2002): R4.

25. Reagan, "Openers," R4.

26. Larson, "Free Money," 78.

27. Larson, "Free Money," 78.

28. Cliff Figallo, "iVillage: Investing in Community and Banking on Trust," *Econtent* 25, no. 6 (June 2002): 52–53.

29. Cliff Figallo, "iVillage," 52–53.

30. Cited in Figallo, "iVillage."

31. Brown, "From Feminism to Fluff."

32. From "Women.com—About Us," at www.women.com.

33. Karen E. Gustafson, "Join Now, Membership is Free: Women's Web Sites and the Coding of Community," 168–88 in *Women and Everyday Uses of the Internet: Agency and Identity*, ed. Mia Consalvo and Susanna Paasonen (New York: Peter Lang, 2002).

34. iVillage Terms of Service, June 22, 2001.

35. iVillage Terms of Service, June 22, 2001.

36. iVillage Privacy Policy, June 22, 2001.

37. Eugene Schultz, "More Privacy Breaches Occur," *Computers & Security* 21, no. 7 (2002): 583–84.

38. Gustafson, "Join Now," 183.

39. iVillage Form 10-K for Annual and Transition Reports Pursuant to Sections 13 or 15(d) of the Securities Exchange Act of 1934, for the fiscal year Ended December 31, 2002, available at www.edgar-online.com/bin/edgardoc/finSys_main.asp?dcn=0001125282-03-002637&nad= (accessed May 1, 2003).

40. Rebecca Odes, cofounder of gURL.com, quoted in Amanda Griscom, "Vital Signs: New Media Savants Check the Pulse of Silicon Alley," *The Village Voice*, January 19–25, 2000, available at www.villagevoice.com/issues/0003/griscom.php (accessed May 1, 2003).

41. Michael J. Martinez, "gURLs Online and Out Loud." *ABC News* (April 10, 1998), available at more.abcnews.go.com/sections/tech/dailynews/gurl980410.html (accessed May 1, 2003).

42. From www.gurl.com

43. Vanessa Grigoriadia, "Generation 1.0: Oldest Silicon Alley Veterans Tell All," *New York* (March 6, 2000).

44. See www.dealwithit.com.

45. See www.thelooksbook.com.

46. Quoted in Martinez, "gURLs Online."

47. Brian Morrissey, "Primedia Scoops Up gURL.com from Delias," *Silicon Valley Reporter* (May 29, 2001), available at siliconalley.venturereporter.net/issues/sar05292001.html#Headline8615 (accessed May 1, 2003).

48. Deborah Mendez-Wilson, "Targeting gen 'Y': You go gURL!" *Wireless Week* 6, no. 28 (July 10, 2000): 26.

49. See Ronald V. Bettig and Jeanne Lynn Hall, *Big Media, Big Money: Cultural Texts and Political Economics* (Lanham, Md.: Rowman & Littlefield, 2003) and Henry A. Giroux, *Impure Acts: The Practical Politics of Cultural Studies* (New York: Routledge, 2000).

50. Press release archive of April 24, 2003 at www.primedia.com.

51. Alison Stein Wellner, "The Teen Scene," *Forecast* 22, no. 9 (September 2002): 1.

52. Elizabeth Payne, "Tweens: The Latest Sale Bait: Too Young to Woo?" *Edmonton Journal* (April 28, 2002): D3.

53. Arundhati Parmar, "Global Youth United," *Marketing News* 36, no. 22 (October 28, 2002): 1, 49.

54. Angela R. Record, "Born to Shop: Teenage Women and the Marketplace in the Postwar United States," 181–95 in *Sex and Money: Feminism and Political Economy in the Media,* ed. Eileen R. Meehan and Ellen Riordan (Minneapolis: University of Minnesota Press, 2002), 188.

55. Mary Celeste Kearney, "Producing Girls: Rethinking the Study of Female Youth Culture," 285–310 in *Delinquents and Debutantes: Twentieth Century Girls' Cultures,* ed. Sherrie A. Inness (New York: NYU Press, 1998).

56. Note to Parents, undated, at www.gurl.com/more/about/noteto.html.

57. Kathryn C. Montgomery, "Digital Kids: The New On-line Children's Consumer Culture," 635–50 in *Handbook of Children and the Media,* ed. Dorothy and Jerome Singer (Thousand Oaks, Calif.: Sage, 2000).

58. Lisa Nakamura, "After/Images of Identity: Gender, Technology, and Identity Politics" 321–31 in *Reload: Rethinking Women + Cyberculture*, ed. Mary Flanagan and Austin Booth (Cambridge, Mass.: MIT Press, 2002), 328.

59. Jan Fernback, "Community as Commodity: Empowerment and Consumerism on the Web," pp. 224-230 in *Internet Research Annual Volume 1: Selected Papers from the Association of Internet Researchers Conference* 2000–2002, ed. Mia Consalvo et al. (New York: Peter Lang, 2004), 228-29.

60. Jean Gadrey, *New Economy, New Myth* (London: Routledge, 2003), 111.

9

Ethics on the Internet: A Comparative Study of Japan, the United States, and Singapore

Yumiko Nara and Tetsuji Iseda

This chapter reports some of the results from the international survey conducted by the Japanese Foundations of Information Ethics (FINE) Project, a five-year project on information ethics funded by the Japanese government from 1998 to 2003. While the survey investigated many aspects of behavior on the Internet, this chapter concentrates on the influence of everyday life on moral consciousness and behavior on the Internet.

It is not common in ethics to use a statistical social survey as key evidence. No doubt this is because ethical studies usually concern normative questions, and people's actual behaviors and opinions are therefore regarded as irrelevant: *is* does not determine *ought*. However, there are certainly cases where reliable normative judgment requires factual inputs. For example, the method of reflective equilibrium requires considered judgments as a basis, and if we are serious about this method we cannot ignore facts about how real people make such judgments, facts that can be surveyed. A more common use of factual inputs is involved in deriving concrete moral judgments from basic principles. We are concerned with issues arising from claims about Internet community: Is there such a thing, and if so, what should be done about it? In answering such questions, facts about online behavior play an important role. Here again a social survey can help us. Of course, there are many different sources of factual inputs such as introspection and laboratory experiments. A social survey is not good at in-depth investigation into our consciousness, but it is a good tool for identifying a general pattern in a society, especially correlations between various measurable variables.[1] This is valuable information that other types of factual input cannot provide.

In this chapter, we first introduce the outline of the study and the main variables to be analyzed. The main variables concern moral consciousness and behavior in everyday life (henceforth Everyday Ethics) and moral consciousness and behavior on the Internet (henceforth Information Ethics). We then look at some statistical correlations on the Internet and offer interpretations of them. One of the focuses here is the relationship between personal character (egoistic, sympathetic, conscientious, etc.) and Information Ethics. Finally, we review some objections and discuss the limits and possibilities of this kind of analysis.

THE ANALYTICAL FRAMEWORK OF THE RESEARCH

This survey was motivated by several hypotheses that together make up the general model behind the survey:

1. Moral awareness and behavior in Everyday Ethics influences Information Ethics.
2. The content, frequency, form of Internet use, and Internet literacy influence awareness and behavior in Information Ethics.
3. Personality (rationality, egoistic tendency, empathy, and conscientiousness) influences awareness and behavior in both Everyday and Information Ethics.
4. Recognition of salient features of the Internet (anonymity, invisibility, etc.) influences awareness and behavior in Information Ethics.

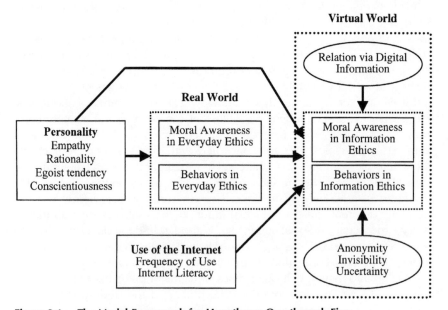

Figure 9.1.   The Model Framework for Hypotheses One through Five

These hypotheses can be summarized in a box-arrow diagram (figure 9.1). To anticipate, results of our analyses show that all four hypotheses are confirmed (at least to some extent), but the relationships are not as straightforward as expected.

METHOD

There are already some statistics on behavior on the Internet, but few studies concentrate on moral behavior. Studies that try to identify factors that influence moral awareness and behaviors on the Internet (Information Ethics as opposed to Everyday Ethics) are even rarer. This study intends to remedy the lack of information. This is an empirical study employing questionnaires to examine the status of Information Ethics and the factors that influence them. Also, this is an international study of information ethics comparing Japan, the United States, and Singapore.

The subjects of the survey were male and female Internet users, twenty to thirty-nine years old from all parts of Japan, the United States, and Singapore. They were picked randomly from panels composed by survey facilities ([J] NOS list, [US] Greenfield Online list, [S] ACNielsen Online list). Surveys were conducted in February and March of 2002, with slight differences in the survey period among the three countries ([J] 2002 February 7–27, [US] February 21–March 7, [S] February 21–March 4). For Japan, the questionnaire was sent and returned via ordinary mail; for the other two countries, subjects logged on to a questionnaire website with a log-in name and password. The sample size was 1,800 (with 1,278 usable samples) for Japan, 580 (with 505 usable samples) for the United States, and 1,365 (with 530 usable samples) for Singapore. Basic attributes of respondents are as follows—gender: female 66.0 percent and male 34.0 percent in Japan, 50.1 percent and 49.9 percent in United States, and 43.8 percent and 56.2 percent in Singapore; age: between twenty and twenty-nine years old 40.5 percent and between thirty and thirty-nine years old 59.5 percent in Japan, 39.2 percent and 60.8 percent in United States, and 45.8 percent and 54.2 percent in Singapore.

RESULTS

Construction of the Main Variables

First let us explain how we index the main variables to be analyzed statistically.[2] We asked the respondents to rate their behavior and awareness in both Information and Everyday Ethics by listing various items related to ethical behavior. Tendencies found in these answers are explained by other factors surveyed in the study. There are four categories of things to

Table 9.1.   Indexing the Variables: Behavior in Information Ethics

Q. How often have you done the following *on the Internet?*
Please circle the most suitable number for each item.
1. Very often   2. Often   3. Sometimes   4. Rarely   5. Never

a. Circulated incorrect information knowingly
b. Read other people's e-mail without their knowledge
c. Looked at pornographic websites on computers in your workplace or at school
d. Gave your password to other person/s
e. Accessed computers that you were not authorized to access
f. Tampered with data on other person's computer through the Internet
g. Sent a computer virus deliberately
h. Circulated somebody's name and phone number to a large number of unidentified people without his/her knowledge
i. Used pictures or texts from somebody's website for your own website without his/her knowledge (exclude cases in which permission was obtained)
j. Put pornographic pictures or texts on your freely accessible website

be explained, namely behavior in Information Ethics, moral awareness in Information Ethics, behavior in Everyday Ethics, and moral awareness in Everyday Ethics. Questions about Information Ethics behavior are reproduced in table 9.1, and similar questions are asked about the other three categories (for the list of behaviors in Everyday Ethics, see table 9.2). The latter three categories are also employed to explain the first category, namely behavior in Information Ethics.

To use these categories as dependent variables in a statistical analysis, we need a formula for calculating variables from the raw replies. Since the

Table 9.2.   Indexing the Variables for Behavior in Everyday Ethics

Q. How often have you done the following *away from the Internet?*
1. Very often   2. Often   3. Sometimes   4. Rarely   5. Never

a. Circulated incorrect information knowingly
b. Read somebody else's sealed letters and diaries without his/her knowledge
c. Given somebody's name and phone number to a third party without his/her knowledge
d. Spoken ill of others
e. Sent a letter anonymously
f. Deliberately broken somebody else's property or public property
g. Looked at a pornographic magazine in your workplace or at school
h. Stolen somebody else's property or public property
i. Cheated in an exam
j. Broken a promise
k. Kept a wallet you found on the ground
l. Injured somebody
m. Deliberately thrown trash somewhere other than in a trash can

choice of questions is somewhat arbitrary, we conducted a factor analysis for behavior in Information Ethics.[3] These questions consist of various kinds of action items. We divided them into several groups to cluster similar kinds of items. In order to define groups, we first carried out a factor analysis for ten items of behavior in Information Ethics; this result was then used to group other dependent variables (awareness in Information Ethics and behavior and awareness in Everyday Ethics).

Two factors were obtained from the factor analysis of behavior in Information Ethics. Factor 1 consists of "f. tampering with data on another person's computer through the Internet," "g. sending a computer virus deliberately," "h. circulating somebody's name and phone number to a large number of unidentified people without his/her knowledge," and "j. putting pornographic pictures or texts on your freely accessible web site." These four items are similar in that the action in question is other-regarding, having direct influence on other parties. Thus we call this factor "behavior in other-regarding Information Ethics" (BOI for short). On the other hand, Factor 2 consists of "b. reading other people's e-mail without their knowledge," "c. looking at pornographic websites on computers in your workplace or at school," "e. accessing computers that you are not authorized to access," and "i. using pictures or texts from somebody's website for your own website without his/her knowledge (excluding cases in which permission was obtained)." These items are similar in that the action in question is self-regarding—that is, it does not have other people as a direct target, and the morality implied is mostly a matter of self-restraint. Taking these considerations into account, we call this factor "behavior in self-regarding Information Ethics" (BSI for short).[4]

Based on this distinction, the other three categories are also divided into two groups; awareness in other-regarding Information Ethics (AOI), awareness in self-regarding Information Ethics (ASI), behavior in other-regarding Everyday Ethics (BOE) (consisting of questions c, f, l, and m), behavior in self-regarding Everyday Ethics (BSE) (consisting of b, g, i, and k) awareness in other-regarding Everyday Ethics (AOE), and awareness in self-regarding Everyday Ethics (ASE).

It is important to note in using this kind of measure whether these questions measure the same thing or not. The so-called "Cronbach's α" is a statistical indicator that measures the reliability of these measures. The values for Cronbach's α for each measure are as follows: .880 for BOI, .684 for BSI, .722 for AOI, .725 for ASI, .603 for BOE, .616 for BSE, .801 for AOE , and .772 for ASE. This means that for most of the variables the correlations between the questions are high enough to make the measure reliable; values for BOE and BSE are not high enough, which means we need to be careful in dealing with these variables.

To summarize, we constructed our variables by clustering items in each category. The clustering was done partly through looking at correlations among items and partly through conceptual similarities among them. The result shows that there is a divide between other-regarding behaviors and self-regarding behaviors, at least in Information Ethics.

Differences in Ethics Behavior and Awareness among Nations

Naturally, one of our main independent variables is the national factor. We conducted multivariate analysis of variance (MANOVA) for all four dependent variables (BOI, BSI, AOI, ASI, BOE, BSE, AOE, and ASE) by country (Japan, the United States, and Singapore). The purpose of analysis of variance (ANOVA), on which MANOVA is based, is to test for significant differences between means by comparing (i.e., analyzing) variances. More specifically, by partitioning the total variation into different sources, we are able to compare the variance due to the between-groups variability with that due to the within-group variability. Under the null hypothesis (that there are no mean differences between groups in the population), the variance estimated from the within-group variability should be about the same as the variance estimated from between-groups variability.

All results were highly significant ($p < 0.001$). (Each value of Wilks's λ is as follows: BOI .978, BSI .872, AOI .800, ASI .794, BOE .849, BSE .937, AOE .854, and ASE .809.) These results mean there are national differences in ethical behavior and awareness in both everyday life and on the Internet.

We also compared individual items of behavior and awareness in information and everyday ethics. For most items including them, the score was highest ("ethically desirable") for Japanese respondents, and lowest ("ethically undesirable") for U.S. respondents, both in behavior and awareness in Information Ethics.[5]

Recognition of Features of the Internet and Information Ethics

It is often pointed out that there are some salient features of the Internet, such as anonymity or invisibility. Recognition of these features may have decisive effects on behavior on the Internet. This is also an important element of our survey. Here, recognition of anonymity, invisibility, and uncertainty on the Internet is measured by the following questions.

What do you think about the Internet? Please choose the most suitable number for each item (the respondents are given a six-step scale from "1. strongly agree" to "6. strongly disagree").

a. Nobody can identify me on the Internet unless I use my real name.
b. My actions on the Internet are seen by somebody.
c. I don't understand well how the Internet works.

Table 9.3. Relation between Recognition of Feature of Internet and BOI/BSI

Dependent Variable	Independent Variable	Wilks's λ		
		Japan	US	Singapore
BOI	Invisibility	0.984	0.974	0.97
	Anonymity	0.987	0.772***	0.965
	Uncertainty	0.983	0.778***	0.981
BSI	Invisibility	0.991	0.962	0.961
	Anonymity	0.959***	0.905***	0.959
	Uncertainty	0.952***	0.893***	0.936

*** $p < 0.001$

Items a, b, and c are intended to ask about the perception of anonymity, invisibility, and uncertainty, respectively. Taking BOI and BSI as dependent variables, we conducted MANOVA to analyze the influence of recognition of anonymity, invisibility, and uncertainty. The results are shown in table 9.3.

To summarize the results: for Singapore respondents, recognition of these features does not influence either BOI or BSI. As for the U.S. respondents, anonymity and uncertainty have some significant effect on BOI and BSI. More concretely, for BOI, those who agree strongly with the anonymity claim tend to behave "undesirably" in all BOI items, and those who agree strongly with the uncertainty claim also tend to behave "undesirably" in all four items of BOI.

For Japanese respondents, anonymity recognition and uncertainty recognition have statistically significant influence only on BSI, not on BOI. To take individual items, "reading other people's e-mail without their knowledge" is more frequent among those who feel anonymity strongly. Those who do not feel uncertainty tend to perform the other three items in BSI more frequently.

Effects of Literacy and Frequency of Internet Use on Information Ethics

We also compared the influence of frequency of Internet use functions and Internet literacy on Information Ethics. The Internet use function is measured by a five-step scale from "very often" to "never" in terms of the following items:

a. electronic mail with a mobile/cellular phone
b. visiting websites with a cellular phone
c. electronic mail (e-mail) (other than with a cellular phone)
d. visiting websites to gather information (other than with a cellular phone)
e. visiting websites for fun (other than with a cellular phone)
f. creating and updating your own website
g. chat rooms
h. electronic bulletin boards

Internet literacy was measured by counting the number of things the respondent can do from the following list:

a. Attach files (pictures etc.) to an e-mail
b. Change your password for e-mail
c. Find a website by using a search engine
d. Create a website by yourself
e. Manage a network server
f. Compress a large file
g. Access a website via a proxy server
h. Eliminate a virus from a computer

It is expected that there is a rather strong correlation between the frequency of use of the Internet and Internet literacy. In fact, the correlation coefficients between the two variables are .489 for the Japanese, .348 for the United States, and .351 for Singapore respondents.[6] We conducted multiple regression analyses using these factors for each country. A multiple regression analysis is used when there is more than one independent variable. To learn the genuine influence of one variable on another, we need to exclude the possibility that the two variables have no direct relationship but are correlated with a third variable. This type of analysis subtracts the influence of such other variables, enabling us to see the genuine correlation between the two variables. For this analysis, we employed the above questions on use frequency and literacy as independent variables, and BOI and BSI as dependent variables. BOI is measured by giving a numerical value (1 point to "very often," 2 points to "often," and so on) and adding the points to the four questions associated with BOI. A similar maneuver is used for BSI as well.

BOI gave us different results for different countries. For Japanese respondents, the two independent variables do not have a statistically significant influence on BOI. For Singapore respondents, the use frequency has a weak but statistically significant influence (β = –0.109 and $p < 0.05$) on the negative side (the higher the use frequency, the less "desirable" the behaviors are), while literacy does not have a statistically significant influence. For the U.S. respondents, the results are interesting; the use frequency has a strong negative effect (β = –0.351 and $p < 0.001$), while literacy has a similarly strong positive effect (β = .222 and $p < 0.001$).

What about the influence on BSI? For Japanese respondents, both use frequency and literacy have a negative effect on BSI (the higher the use frequency or the higher the literacy, the less "desirable" the behaviors are). The effect of literacy (β = –0.148 and $p < 0.001$) is stronger than that of use frequency (β = –0.076 and $p < 0.05$) To the contrary, for the U.S. respondents, literacy has little effect on BSI (β = –0.001 ns), while use frequency has a strong effect (β = –0.338 and $p < 0.001$). The result from Singapore is somewhere in between. That is, the two independent variables both have an effect on BSI, but the strength of the effect has the opposite pattern from that of the Japanese respondents, the effect of use frequency ($\beta = -0.172$ and $p < 0.001$) being stronger than that of literacy ($\beta = -0.094$ and $p < 0.05$).

To summarize, we found some statistically significant correlations here. Frequency of use seems to have a consistently negative effect when the correlation is significant. The effect of literacy is not easily interpretable, but its positive effect for BOI in the United States and negative effect for BSI in Japan calls for attention.

Even though these factors are significant, coefficients of determination R^2 are small (BOI [j] 0.004ns, [US] 0.126***, [S] 0.010ns : BSI, [j] 0.038***, [US] 0.114***, and [S] 0.050***), which means that Internet literacy and use frequency are not sufficient to explain the behaviors in Information Ethics. Then what other elements can account for the differences? Next we look at BOE and BSE as independent variables influencing BOI and BSI.

The Relation between Information Ethics and Everyday Ethics

The correlation coefficients among eight variables (BOI, BSI, AOI, ASI, BOE, BSE, AOE, and ASE), have been calculated for each country and the results are summarized in tables 9.4 and 9.5. The correlation (Pearson's R) between two variables represents the degree to which they are related. Typically a linear relationship is measured with either Pearson's correlation or Spearman's rho. It is important to keep in mind that correlation does not necessarily mean cau-

Table 9.4. Relation between Information Ethics and Everyday Ethics: Correlation Coefficients among Variables Related to BOI

		(1) BOI	(2) AOI	(3) BOE	(4) AOE
Japan	(1) BOI	1.000	0.188***	0.075**	0.047
	(2) AOI		1.000	0.254***	0.409***
	(3) BOE			1.000	0.441***
	(4) AOE				1.000
US	(1) BOI	1.000	0.0.24	0.570***	0.083
	(2) AOI		1.000	0.118**	0.656***
	(3) BOE			1.000	0.236***
	(4) AOE				1.000
Singapore	(1) BOI	1.000	0.261***	0.263***	0.112**
	(2) AOI		1.000	0.209***	0.627***
	(3) BOE			1.000	0.291***
	(4) AOE				1.000

*** $p < 0.001$
** $p < 0.01$
* $p < 0.05$

Table 9.5.   Relation between Information Ethics and Everyday Ethics: Correlation Coefficients among Variables Related to BSI

		(1) BSI	*(2) ASI*	*(3) BSE*	*(4) ASE*
Japan	(1) BSI	1.000	0.289***	0.305***	0.234***
	(2) ASI		1.000	0.334***	0.622***
	(3) BSE			1.000	0.490***
	(4) ASE				1.000
US	(1) BSI	1.000	0.187***	0.652***	0.166***
	(2) ASI		1.000	0.116**	0.713***
	(3) BSE			1.000	0.201***
	(4) ASE				1.000
Singapore	(1) BSI	1.000	0.447***	0.478***	0.226***
	(2) ASI		1.000	0.324***	0.653***
	(3) BSE			1.000	0.349***
	(4) ASE				1.000

*** $p < 0.001$
** $p < 0.01$
* $p < 0.05$

sation. As you can see here, the behavior/awareness in everyday ethics (BOE, BSE, AOE, and ASE) significantly influences the behavior/awareness in Information Ethics (BOI, BSI, AOI, and ASI). This tendency is especially strong in the United States. A natural interpretation of the results suggests that Everyday Ethics provides the base line for Information Ethics.

As mentioned above, recognition of characteristics of the Internet (such as anonymity), frequency of use, and Internet literacy influence behaviors in Information Ethics. How strong are these influences, compared with the influence of Everyday Ethics? Figures 9.2 and 9.3 show the relative strength of the influence of these factors on BOI and BSI, using analyses of covariance structure. An analysis of covariance structure is a method for revealing causal structure between observed variables and constructed concepts. Structural equation models are most often represented graphically. Figures 9.2 and 9.3 are graphical examples of structural equation models.

In figure 9.1, the circled variables are latent variables, and those in the boxes are observed variables. Observed variables are replies to the questions, and directly measurable. Latent variables measure concepts constructed with the values of these observed variables. The arrow shows the presumed direction of influence, and the values are so-called standardized regression weights, which represent the strength of influence.[7]

The two figures show that both BOI and BSI are most strongly influenced by behaviors in Everyday Ethics. It is true that the recognition of characteristics of the Internet has a certain weak effect; that is, the more the respondents are aware of anonymity, invisibility, and uncertainty, the more "unde-

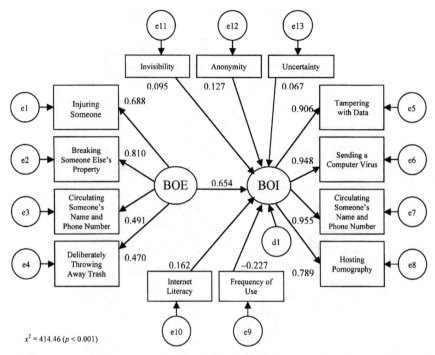

Figure 9.2. Various Effects for BOI: United States

sirably" they tend to behave. Among these factors, the recognition of anonymity has the strongest effect, with $\beta = -0.127$ for BOI. The influences of literacy and use frequency are also fairly strong. However, by far the strongest determinant for BOI and BSI are BOE ($\beta = 0.654$) and BSE ($\beta = 0.839$). This result suggests that people bring their ordinary pattern of behavior to the Internet, even though the circumstances are different there. Similar tendencies are observed with Singapore and Japanese respondents, though standardized regression weights are different; the influence of behavior in Everyday Ethics is much stronger than recognition of Internet characteristics, frequency, or literacy variables.

Of course, our findings are nothing more than a statistical result—that is, we can't specify the causal direction, so the results can be interpreted in many different ways (for example, behavior on the Internet may be influencing behavior in everyday life, rather than the reverse). What is more probable is that there is a third factor that influences both Everyday and Information Ethics. Personality is a candidate for such a factor. Each individual acts in accordance with his/her personality, common to the real and the virtual world. This may be the common factor behind BOE, BSE, BOI, and BSI.

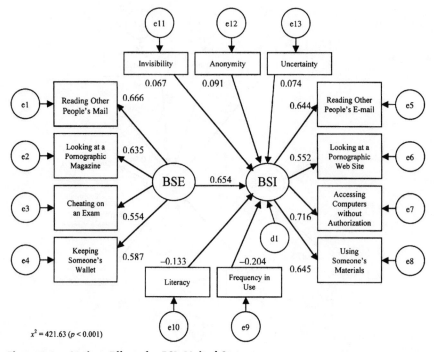

$x^2 = 421.63 \ (p < 0.001)$

Figure 9.3.   Various Effects for BSI: United States

Effect of Personality

If Everyday Ethics and Information Ethics are correlated, one possible explanation is that they are similar because they are based on the same personality. Thus we next look at the effect of personality on Information Ethics. We tested three personality types, which we call the rational egoist tendency, the empathetic tendency, and the conscientious tendency. Let us look at these three categories in turn. We focus here mainly on BOI and BSI.

Rational Egoism

The first type is the rational egoist tendency. How much does rational egoism influence our behavior? We measured the rational tendency and the egoist tendency separately, using six-step scales from "applies very well" to "doesn't apply at all." Rationality here means instrumental rationality, namely choosing rational means for the end. We use "To attain a goal, I assess the current situation carefully before acting" and two other questions to measure this tendency. Egoism is defined here as self-centeredness in relation to others and society. We used three questions for this tendency, including "I would like to live my life as it suits me even if that means that other people have to suffer."

Based on these measures, we divided the respondents into four groups for each country, to conduct ANOVA.[8]

Group 1: Low Egoism, Low Rationality
Group 2: Low Egoism, High Rationality
Group 3: High Egoism, Low Rationality
Group 4: High Egoism, High Rationality

The results of one-way ANOVA using BSI and BOI as dependent variables for the U.S. respondents were F = 1.916 (nonsignificant at 0.05 level) for BOI, and F = 3.632 (significant at 0.05 level) for BSI. Since the result was statistically significant for BSI, we did a follow-up test using Tukey's HSD test.[9] The test revealed the significant difference was located between Group 2 and Group 3. Even though we do not have the space to show the details, in general, Group 2 tends to have a high value (to be "ethically desirable") in both Everyday and Information Ethics, while Group 3 tends to have a low one (to be "ethically undesirable") in all three countries we study.

Thus, against our expectation, irrational egoism rather than rational egoism is the factor that is associated with "ethically undesirable" behaviors. We found that the egoist tendency has a stronger effect than rationality, and in the opposite (ethical) direction.

Empathetic Tendency

Our second personality factor is the empathetic tendency. Is empathy really an important background for ethical behavior? There are many different ways to define the empathetic tendency, and the one used here is that empathy is a tendency to think from the other's point of view. In our survey, the empathetic tendency is based on Davis's perspective taking scale.[10] We measured it with the following question and two other related questions: "Before criticizing somebody, I try to imagine how I would feel if I were in their place." Again, a six-step scale from "applies very well" to "doesn't apply at all" was used, and the result was summarized by giving numerical values to the sum of these answers.

We found that empathy has a fairly strong correlation with everyday ethics in all three countries. Here we discuss just one point that attracted our attention. We could not find a correlation between the empathetic tendency and BOI or BSI. We formed a further hypothesis: Empathy may function with difficulty on the Internet because of the lack of intimate feelings there. We can test this further hypothesis by taking into account the ease of developing intimate relationships on the Internet. The question used for this tendency was "Do you sometimes feel that it is easier to form close relationships with others on the Internet than otherwise?" Answers were ranked with a six-step measure from "strongly agree" to "strongly disagree." We conducted a one-way ANOVA on the following four categories:

Group 1: Low Empathy, Low Intimacy
Group 2: Low Empathy, High Intimacy
Group 3: High Empathy, Low Intimacy
Group 4: High Empathy, High Intimacy

The results of ANOVA for the U.S. respondents were $F = 2.015$ (nonsignificant at 0.05 level) for BOI, and $F = 5.014$ (significant at 0.01 level) for BSI. Again, we conducted a Tukey's HSD test as the follow-up on the BSI result, and it revealed that a significant difference was between Group 1 on the one hand and Groups 3 and 4 on the other.

These results show that if low empathy is accompanied with low intimacy (difficulty in having intimate relationship on the Internet), there seems to be a negative effect on BSI. This is still rather puzzling because empathy is expected to influence other-regarding behaviors. We do not pursue this question here.

Conscientious Tendency

Our final personality factor is conscientiousness, which is defined here as a tendency to choose a moral action because it is moral (not because of rational egoism, empathy, etc.). We used the following question to identify this tendency:

"There is a wallet on the road. There is nobody around. A person named B takes the wallet and keeps it." What do you think about this conduct?

1. I would do the same as B.
2. I wouldn't do the same as B because I might be found out.
3. I wouldn't do the same as B because I would be breaking the law.
4. I wouldn't do the same as B because the person who dropped the wallet would be upset.
5. Regardless of the reasons listed above, since it would be wrong no matter what, I wouldn't do the same as B.

We also asked a similar question for speaking ill of somebody in a chat room. Those who chose 5 are regarded as "conscientious." One-way ANOVA on BOI and BSI for the U.S. respondents resulted in highly significant differences: $F = 15.922$ for BOI and $F = 13.983$ for BSI, both significant at .001 level. Follow-up tests show that "conscientious" respondents tend to get higher scores in these behaviors. Also, though the results aren't shown here, similar patterns are observed both for Information and Everyday Ethics for all three countries. Basically the same results were obtained from the question on speaking ill of somebody in a chat room: $F = 7.7662$ for BOI and $F = 7.7581$ for BSI, again both significant at .001 level.

Here, we found a straightforward correlation between conscientiousness and "ethically desirable" behaviors cutting across different variables and different countries. Such a robust result should be paid due attention.

THE LIMITS AND POSSIBILITIES OF THE SURVEY RESEARCH APPROACH

Ethical Desirability of Dependent Variables

In this research we use behaviors in Everyday and Internet Ethics as dependent variables (variables to be explained). It is important to understand the import of the variables if we are to use the results correctly. In explaining these variables, we used expressions such as "tendency to behave ethically." Some readers may naturally object to such an ethical judgment. At the very least such a judgment should only be made after careful ethical considerations. Can we simply assume that some behavior is ethical just because it is generally considered ethical?

We must emphasize that this study is not committed to any special moral point of view. In this study we had to use expressions such as "high moral awareness" or "desirable behavior" to summarize the results, but these expressions describe rather than evaluate; in other words, these expressions are used in what Hare called the "inverted commas" sense.[11] This study is basically concerned with the correlations between various variables, but evaluations of the variables are a different matter. The groupings of variables such as BOI, BSI, and so on are also intended as descriptive categories based partly on conceptual similarities and partly on the actual correlations between the variables grouped together, rather than evaluative categories based on ethical desirability. Needless to say, we have to be very careful in making ethical judgments when we use these results to improve Information Ethics education.

Another related point to be clarified is the relevance of the dependent variables to morality. We expect some readers have the following doubt: If we want to know about the tendency to act ethically, shouldn't we base the analysis on what the person herself considers to be ethical, rather than what is generally considered as ethical? That is, if the person believes that sending computer viruses is ethical and does send them, is she not, in a sense, acting ethically? If we adopt this point of view, the way this study organizes the dependent variables may seem off target.

If we want to know about the tendency to do what the person herself regards as wrong, we can construct such a variable by combining moral awareness variables and moral behavior variables. The easiest way to do this is to subtract the moral behavior score of a given person from the corresponding moral awareness score (the details of such calculation can be debated, but we cannot get involved in such minute details here). Probably such a tendency is a better dependent variable for some occasions, but in other cases it can be misleading. The score for this tendency can be raised in two different ways, namely by lowering the moral behavior score or by raising the moral awareness score. Thus, when an independent variable influences moral awareness in a "good" way without changing moral behavior, the sum is such that the independent variable has a "bad" effect on the tendency to do what the person herself regards as wrong.

To give a concrete example, suppose that a person thinks that sending out computer viruses is not problematic (the moral awareness score = 1) and often does so (the moral behavior score = 1), without the influence of variable X. Suppose also that the same person would think that sending out computer viruses is more or less problematic (the moral awareness score = 4) but sometimes does so (the moral behavior score = 2), if she were under the influence of variable X. This variable intuitively seems to have a "good" influence on both moral awareness and behavior, but on the other hand it raises the tendency to do what the person regards as wrong (from $1 - 1 = 0$ to $4 - 2 = 2$).

We think that such considerations justify our decision to use simple moral awareness and behavior as our main dependent variables. At the same time, if we are really interested in such a tendency, the survey has the information for conducting an analysis of it too. Survey research is not as simplistic as it may seem, if we are flexible in the choice of analytic scheme.

The Use of Self-Declared Frequencies

In this survey, various behavioral variables are measured by respondents' own evaluations according to a six-step scale from "very often" to "never." What are we measuring by asking these questions? How much does the answer to such a question reflect the real frequency? There are alternative interpretations to be considered, as we argue below. While it is not possible to rule out all the alternative interpretations, the data itself offers some clues for dealing with some of them.

The first alternative we consider is the possibility that very conscientious people may overestimate the frequency of their "bad" behavior because of guilt feelings (let us call this Alternative Interpretation 1). That is, such a person may answer that she lies very often even though in fact she rarely tells a lie. If this interpretation is right, we can expect to find a correlation between a high score for the conscientious tendency and a low score ("bad" score) for moral behavior. However, the analysis of the data on speaking ill in a chat room or taking a wallet found on the road does not support this interpretation. That is, those who choose the "conscientious" reason tend to have a high ("good") score in moral behavior. This result becomes more understandable if we adopt a straightforward interpretation in which the score reflects the real frequency rather than Alternative Interpretation 1.

However, this argument will not persuade everyone. Even if Alternative Interpretation 1 fails, there is another alternative that gets around our reply. This interpretation (let us call it Alternative Interpretation 2) reflects the possibility that the reported frequency may reflect the ideal frequency, rather than the real frequency, of the behavior in question. If some of the respondents have the tendency to give "exemplary" replies that reflect what the person should do rather than what the person actually does, their choices have the effect of overestimating the frequency of moral behaviors.

Alternative Interpretation 2 can account for the results from the "chat" and "wallet" questions. If somebody has the tendency to give an exemplary answer, the person will choose the "conscientious" answer ("because it is bad no matter what,") regardless of her own real motives. Since such a person also gives exemplary ("good") estimates to moral behaviors, it is natural that we find a correlation between conscientiousness and a high score in moral behavior.

Our survey data supports this interpretation to some extent. In the survey, we asked whether the respondent feels bad after he or she tells a lie, and we offered the reply "never told a lie off of the Internet." The percentage of the respondent who choose this answer was 7.7 percent for Japanese, 10.5 percent for American, and 13 percent for Singapore respondents. The group of respondents who choose this answer tends to get higher than average scores both in moral awareness and moral behavior (the tendency is most remarkable in Singapore). Actually, this answer is used to measure whether the respondent is replying sincerely, with the assumption that everybody tells a lie from time to time; in other words, the respondent who says he or she "never told a lie" is regarded as a liar. This consideration suggests that at least some of the respondents are "exemplary answer" respondents. Of course there may be people who never tell a lie off of the Internet, but 10 percent is way too high as the percentage of such people.

Since this problem is related to the nature of respondents in general, what is questioned here is the very methodology of survey research method itself. However, it is unreasonable to require that a scientific study should be able to reply to all possible doubts. Otherwise all papers in physics would have to start by defeating the Cartesian demon. The important thing is to reply to answerable doubts to the extent the field of the study requires. We hope that the arguments given in this section help to see how this kind of study deals with answerable doubts.

CONCLUDING REMARKS

In this chapter, we summarized some of the findings from the analyses of our survey data. In spite of the limits discussed above, the findings are interesting, and we think they contribute to our understanding of behavior on the Internet. Behaviors in Self-regarding Information Ethics (BSI) and Behaviors in Other-Regarding Information Ethics (BOI) were our main variables to be explained. Various factors influence these variables, but by far the most important variables are the corresponding behaviors in Everyday Ethics (BSE and BOE respectively). Among the personality variables we looked at, the conscientiousness factor seems to be most important. These results suggest that the Internet is just an extension of our ordinary experience, and that people's behavior there is largely an extension of their behavior in everyday life.

NOTES

1. For those who are not familiar with statistical analysis, explanations of some technical terms are provided in these notes. A correlation in a statistical sense is a relationship between two variables. If two variables are positively correlated, that means that if one variable is higher, the other variable also tends to be higher.

2. When an experiment is conducted, some variables are manipulated by the experimenter and others are measured from the subjects. The former variables are called "independent variables" or "factors;" the latter are called "dependent variables" or "dependent measures."

3. A factor analysis is an analysis that tries to find the "factors" behind replies. This analysis is based on the assumption that actual replies are (somewhat inaccurate) measures of the psychological tendencies we are investigating. If respondents tend to answer multiple questions in a similar manner, these questions are seen as measuring the same factor and are grouped together.

4. The reader may wonder about two other questions in the list. As for d. (giving your password to other persons), it does not correlate strongly with either of the factors. A. (circulating incorrect information knowingly), does correlate strongly with Factor 2, but does not seem to have much in common with other questions in this group. We need to analyze this result carefully before we can interpret its significance.

5. We are not committed to any ethical position in this chapter, so "ethically desirable" simply denotes what seems to be ordinarily regarded as ethically desirable. No clear pattern was found for everyday ethics, but the total score was still highest for the Japanese respondents (except BSE) and lowest for the U.S. respondents.

6. The correlation coefficient ranges from -1 (total opposite) to 1 (total agreement). Roughly speaking, a value over .5 is usually regarded as a very strong correlation. These values are not all that strong, but they are strong enough to be significant.

7. A standardized regression weight is obtained by controlling for the influence of other independent variables, and the influence of each independent variable is

given in a pure form. This value ranges from -1 to 1, and the closer the value is to 1, the stronger is the correlation. The χ square value in the figures is an indicator of the degree of fitness of the model. If the significance level of this value is less than 0.05, the model can be regarded as suitable.

8. ANOVA is an abbreviation of "analysis of variance" and used to decide whether there is a statistically significant difference between the group means of more than two groups.

9. ANOVA can tell us that there should be some statistically significant differences among the groups, but does not tell us which ones are significantly different. There are various follow-up tests to locate where these differences are, and Tukey's HSD is one of most standard tests.

10. M. H. Davis, *Empathy: A Social Psychological Approach* (Oxford: Westview Press, 1994).

11. R. M. Hare, *Freedom and Reason* (Oxford: Oxford University Press, 1963).

III

THE DEMOCRATIC POTENTIAL OF THE INTERNET

10

Virtually Democratic: Online Communities and Internet Activism

Richard Kahn and Douglas Kellner

It has been slightly over a decade since the blossoming of hypertext and the utopian rhetoric of cyberdemocracy and personal liberation that accompanied the growth of the new online communities that formed the nascent World Wide Web. While the initial cyberoptimism of many ideologues and theorists of the "virtual" community now seem obviously partisan and dated, the continued growth of the Internet as globally popular, and as a tool for organizing new relations of information and social interaction, requires that "online communities" be continually retheorized from a standpoint that is both critical and reconstructive.[1]

The Internet remains a dynamic and complex space in which people can construct and experiment with identity, culture, and social practices.[2] It also makes more information available to a greater number of people more easily and from a wider array of sources than any instrument of information and communication in history.[3] On the other hand, information–communication technologies have been shown to retard face-to-face relationships,[4] threaten traditional conceptions of the commons,[5] and extend structures of Western imperialism and advanced capitalism to the ends of the earth.[6] The challenge at hand is to begin to conceive the political reality of emergent media such as the Internet as a series of places embodying reconstructed models of citizenship and new forms of political activism even as it reproduces logics of domination and becomes co-opted by hegemonic forces. In this sense, following Marcuse, we should look to how new technologies and communities are interacting as tentative forms of self-determination and control "from below"—recognizing that as today's Internet citizens organize politically around issues of access to information, capitalist globalization, imperialist war, and other forms of oppression, they represent important oppositional forms of agency in the ongoing struggle for social justice and a more participatory democracy.[7]

In contradistinction to the radical hopes potentially offered by the Internet, since George W. Bush ascended to the presidency in a highly contested election in 2000, the ideal and forms of democracy have taken a terrible beating.[8] The Bush administration arguably used the events of 9/11 to proclaim and help produce an epoch of Terror War, responding to the 9/11 terror attacks to invade, conquer, and occupy both Afghanistan and Iraq and to promote a new geopolitical doctrine of preemptive war.[9] In this context, the threat of constant terrorism has been used to limit the public sphere, curtail information and communication, legitimate government surveillance of electronic exchange, and cut back on civil liberties. Likewise, a panoply of neoliberal economic policies have been invoked and made law under the guise of promoting patriotism, supporting the war effort, and advancing domestic security. With democracy under attack on multiple fronts, progressive groups and individuals face the challenge of developing modes of communication and organization to oppose militarism, terrorism, and the threats to democracy and social justice.

While mainstream media in the United States have largely promoted Bush's militarism, economic and political agenda, and "war on terrorism," a number of online communities have attempted to develop alternative organs of information and communication, using the Internet and emergent technologies to produce new instruments and modes of democracy. As early as 1986 when French students coordinated a national strike over the Internet-like Minitel system, there are numerous examples of people redeploying information technology for their own political ends, thereby actualizing the potential for a more participatory society and alternative forms of social organization.[10] Since the 1990s, there have been growing discussions of Internet activism and how new media have been used effectively by a variety of political movements, especially to further participatory democracy and social justice.[11] Now, in the wake of the September 11 terror attacks and U.S. military interventions in Iraq and Afghanistan, a tide of political activism has risen with the Internet playing an important and increasingly central role.[12]

In late 2002 and early 2003, global antiwar movements began to emerge as significant challenges to Bush administration policies against Iraq and the growing threats of war. Reaching out to broad audiences, political groups like MoveOn (www.moveon.org), A.N.S.W.E.R. (www.internationalanswer.org), and United for Peace & Justice (www.unitedforpeace.org) used the Internet to circulate antiwar information, organize demonstrations, and promote a wide diversity of antiwar activities. One need only recall February 15, 2003's unprecedented public demonstration of millions around the world calling for peace in unison to realize that the new media represent a groundbreaking tool for global democracy. Indeed, after using the Internet to successfully organize a wide range of antiwar/globalization demonstrations, activists (including many young people) are now continuing to build a "virtual" bloc that monitors, critiques, and fights against the sort of aggressive versions of Western capitalism and imperialism being promoted by Bush, Blair, and their G8 counterparts.

Of course, we do not mean to imply that the Internet qua infrastructure is *essentially* participatory and democratic, as we recognize major commercial interests at play and that it is a contested terrain among competing groups from right to left. It is clear that decisive issues exist from public participation in Net design and access to how individuals and groups use and configure information and communication technologies.[13] Again, while it is essential that the progressive political uses of the Internet be enumerated, we recognize that this does not absolve its being critiqued and theorized as a tool and extension of global technocapitalism.[14] Accepting this, our point here is that the Internet is a "contested terrain" in which alternative subcultural forces and online communities are articulated in opposition to more reactionary, conservative, and dominant groups.

Online communities are arguably an increasingly important domain of the global Internet that are creating the base and the basis for an unprecedented worldwide antiwar/pro-peace and social justice movement during a time of terrorism, war, and intense political struggle. Correspondingly, the Internet itself has undergone radical transformations during this time toward becoming a more participatory and democratic medium. New forms of communicative design, such as blogs and wikis, have emerged as important developments of the Net's hypertextual architecture, and online phenomena such as hacker culture and Web militancy are no longer marginal technocultures known only to code geeks with a radical edge.[15] Contemporary Internet subcultures are potentially involved in a radically democratic social and educational project that amounts to the mass circulation and politicization of information and culture. Thus, it is our belief that many emergent online communities today are moving toward reaffirming and reconfiguring what participatory and democratic global citizenship will look like in our emergent global/local future, even as more reactionary and hegemonic political forces attempt to do the same. We will accordingly focus on how online communities use information and communication technologies (ICTs) to promote democracy and social justice on local and global scales.

GLOBALIZATION AND NET POLITICS

The Internet today has emerged as a complex assemblage of a variety of groups and movements, both mainstream and oppositional, reactionary and democratic, global and local. However, after the massive hi-tech sector bust at the start of the new millennium, and with economic sectors generally down across the board due to the transnational economic recession, the Terror War erupting in 2001, and the disastrous effects of Bushonomics, much of the corporate hype and colonization of the new media has waned. If the late 1990s represented the heyday for the commercialization of the Net, the Bush years have found the Internet more overtly politicized beyond questions of commerce alone.

Since 9/11, novel oppositions are forming around the online rights to freedom of use and information, as well as user privacy, that groups such as the Electronic Frontier Foundation (EFF), Computer Professionals for Social Responsibility (CPSR), and the Center for Democracy and Technology (CDT) have long touted.[16] When it emerged in late 2002 that the Bush administration was developing a Total Information Awareness project that would compile a government database on every individual with material collected from a diversity of sources, intense online debate erupted and the Bush administration was forced to make concessions to critics concerned about privacy and Big Brother surveillance.[17] Such online political oppositions directly pit subcultural groups, many who did not previously have an obvious political agenda, against the security policies of government. In this scenario, Internet corporations were often left in the middle with the option to side with the users whom they would court as consumers or with the political administrations that could regulate them (such as Microsoft's antitrust battle under the Clinton administration and then again under Bush).

Still, as the Internet has become more highly politicized, it has become harder for corporations to portray themselves simply as neutral cultural forces mediating electronic disputes between citizens and states. Using the corporate architecture of the Internet for forwarding corporate-wary agendas, Net users are beginning to globally develop and voice a maturing political awareness that perceives corporate and governmental behavior as intertwined in the name of "globalization." As part of the backlash against globalization over the past years, a wide range of theorists have argued that the proliferation of difference and the shift to more local discourses and practices define significant alternatives to corporate globalization. In this view, theory and politics should swing from the level of globalization and its accompanying, often totalizing and macrodimensions in order to focus on the local, the specific, the particular, the heterogeneous, and the microlevel of everyday experience. An array of discourses associated with poststructuralism, postmodernism, feminism, and multiculturalism focus on difference, otherness, marginality, hybridity, the personal, the particular, and the concrete over more general theory and politics that aim at more global or universal conditions. Likewise, a broad spectrum of Internet subcultures of resistance have focused their attention on the local level, organizing struggles around a seemingly endless variety of identity issues.

However, it can be argued that such dichotomies as those between the global and the local express contradictions and tensions between crucial constitutive forces of the present moment, and that it is therefore a mistake to reject a focus on one side in favor of an exclusive concern with the other.[18] Hence, an important challenge for developing a critical theory of globalization is to think through the relationships between the global and the local by observing how global forces influence and even structure an increasing number of local situations. This requires analysis of how local forces mediate the global, inflecting global forces to diverse ends and conditions, and producing unique configurations of the local and the global as the matrix for thought and action in the contemporary world.[19]

Globalization is thus necessarily complex and challenging to both critical theories and radical democratic politics. But many people these days operate with binary concepts of the global and the local, and promote one or the other side of the equation as the solution to the world's problems. For globalists, globalization is the solution, and underdevelopment, backwardness, and provincialism are the problem. For localists, the globalized eradication of traditions, cultures, and places is the problem and localization is the solution. But, less simplistically, it is the mix that matters, and whether global or local solutions are most fitting depends upon the conditions in the distinctive context that one is addressing and the particular solutions and policies proposed.

Specific locations and practices of a plurality of online communities constitute perhaps what is most interesting now about oppositional, subcultural activities at work within the context of the global Internet. Much more than other contemporary subcultures like boarders, punks, mods, or even New Agers, Internet communities have taken up the questions of local and global politics and are attempting to construct answers both locally and globally in response. Importantly, this can be done due to the very nature of the medium in which they exist. Therefore, while the Internet can and has been used to promote capitalist globalization, the current configuration of online communities is interested in the number of ways in which the global network can be diverted and used in the struggle against it.

TECHNOPOLITICS AND THE
ANTIGLOBALIZATION MOVEMENTS[20]

Successful use of the Internet by the EZLN Zapatista movement in Mexico dramatized its importance for progressive politics.[21] Beyond deploying the Internet as a technology for plotting political organization and for furthering communication, activists quickly drew upon the Zapatistas' imaginative use of the Internet to begin broadcasting their new messages to a potential global audience. In the late 1990s, activists began employing the Internet to foster movements against the excesses of corporate capitalism. A global protest movement surfaced in resistance to the World Trade Organization (WTO) and related globalization policies, while championing democratization and social justice, and this movement has resulted in historic spectacles of broad-based, populist demonstrations such as have never been seen before.

Beginning with the June 18, 1999, Carnival Against Capital! protest that secretly organized hundreds of thousands of protesters (including labor, environmentalist, feminist, anticapitalist, animal rights, anarchist, and other groups) throughout the world to demonstrate in emergent found solidarities, the Carnival continued with the infamous "Battle for Seattle" against the World Trade Organization (WTO) meeting in December 1999. Many web sites contained anti-WTO material and numerous mailing lists used the Internet to distribute critical material and to organize the 1999 protests. The result was the mobilization of caravans to take protestors to the sites, many of whom had never met and were recruited through the Internet.

Furthermore, the Internet provided critical coverage of the event, documentation of the various groups' protests, and debate over the WTO and globalization. Whereas the mainstream media presented the protests as "antitrade," featured the incidents of anarchist violence against property, and minimized police violence against demonstrators, the Internet provided pictures, eyewitness accounts, and reports of police brutality and the generally peaceful and nonviolent nature of the protests. While the mainstream media framed the protests negatively and privileged suspect spokespeople like Patrick Buchanan as critics of globalization, the Internet provided multiple representations of the spectacles of opposition, advanced reflective discussion of the WTO and globalization, and presented a diversity of critical perspectives.

The Seattle protests had some immediate consequences. The day after the demonstrators made good on their promise to shut down the WTO negotiations, Bill Clinton gave a speech endorsing the concept of labor rights enforceable by trade sanctions, thus effectively making impossible any agreement and consensus during the Seattle meetings. In addition, at the World Economic Forum in Davos a month later there was much discussion of how concessions were necessary on labor and the environment if consensus over globalization and free trade were to be possible. Importantly, the issue of overcoming divisions between the information rich and poor, and improving the lot of the disenfranchised and oppressed, bringing these groups the potential benefits of globalization, were also seriously discussed at the meeting and in the media.

More importantly, many activists were energized by the new alliances, solidarities, and militancy, and continued to cultivate an antiglobalization

movement. The Seattle demonstrations were followed by April 2000 struggles in Washington, D.C., to protest against the World Bank and International
Monetary Fund (IMF), and later in the year against capitalist globalization in
Prague and Melbourne; in April 2001, an extremely large and militant protest
erupted against the Free Trade Area of the Americas summit in Quebec City,
and in the summer of 2001 a sizeable demonstration took place in Genoa. In
May 2002 another huge event took place in Washington and it was apparent
that a new social movement was in the making that was uniting diverse opponents of capitalist globalization throughout the world via the Internet.
Similar demonstrations had taken place in Monterrey, Mexico, two months
earlier, and two more occurred during June 2002 at Calgary and Ottawa to
protest against the G8 Summit meeting in Canada. At the WTO trade talks in
Cancun in September 2003, leaders of the developing world concurred with
protestors and blocked expansion of a "free trade zone" that would mainly
benefit the United States and overdeveloped countries. Likewise, in Miami in
November 2003 the "Free-Trade Summit" collapsed without an agreement as
the police violently suppressed protestors. Each of these demonstrations was
comprised of people hailing from many locations intent on using the venue
as an opportunity to promote their voice and fight in common cause against
the perceived oppression by the dominant corporate culture.

Initially, the incipient antiglobalization movement was precisely that:
against globalization. The movement itself, however, became increasingly
global, linking together a diversity of movements into networks of affinity
and using the Internet and instruments of globalization to advance its struggles in this behalf. Thus, it would be more accurate to say that the movement
embodied a globalization-from-below that would defend social justice,
equality, labor, civil liberties, universal human rights, and a healthy planet on
which to live safely from the ravages of an uncontrolled capitalist globalization strategy.[22] Accordingly, the anticapitalist globalization movements began advocating common values and visions and started defining themselves
in positive terms such as the global justice movement.

Technopolitics became part and parcel of the involvement of Internet online communities, a mushrooming global movement for peace, justice, and
democracy that has continued to grow through 2004 and shows no sign of
ending. The emergent movements against capitalist globalization have thus
placed the issue of whether participatory democracy can be meaningfully realized squarely before us for our consideration. Whereas the mainstream media had failed to vigorously debate or even report on globalization until the
eruption of a vigorous anticapitalist globalization movement, and rarely, if
ever, critically discussed the activities of the WTO, World Bank, and IMF, there
is now a widely circulating critical discourse and controversy over these institutions. Whereas prior to the rise of the recent antiwar/prodemocracy
movements average citizens were unlikely to question a presidential decision

to go to war, now people do question and not only question, but protest publicly. While such protest has not prevented war, or successfully turned back globalized development, it has continued to evoke the potential for participatory democracy that can be actualized when publics reclaim technology, information, and the spaces in which they live and work.

HACKING THE SYSTEM TO BYTES:
TOWARD GLOBALIZATION-FROM-BELOW

To capital's globalization-from-above, subcultures of cyberactivists have been attempting to carry out globalization-from-below, developing networks of solidarity and propagating oppositional ideas and movements throughout the planet.[23] Against the capitalist organization of neoliberal globalization, a Fifth International, to use Waterman's phrase (1992), of computer-mediated activism is emerging that is qualitatively different from the party-based socialist and communist Internationals of the past. As the virtual community theorist Howard Rheingold notes, advances in personal, mobile informational technology are rapidly providing the structural elements for the existence of fresh kinds of highly informed, autonomous communities that coalesce around local lifestyle choices, global political demands, and everything in between.[24]

These multiple networks of connected citizens and activists transform the "dumb mobs" of totalitarian and polyarchical states into "smart mobs" of socially active personages linked by notebook computers, PDA devices, Internet cell phones, pagers, and global positioning systems (GPS). Thus, while emergent mobile technology provides yet another impetus toward experimental identity construction and identity politics, such networking also links diverse communities such as labor, feminist, ecological, peace, and various anticapitalist groups, providing the basis for a radically democratic politics of alliance and solidarity to overcome the limitations of postmodern identity politics.[25]

Of course, as noted previously, rightwing and reactionary forces can and have used the Internet to promote their political agendas as well. In a short time, one can easily access an exotic witch's brew of websites maintained by the Ku Klux Klan and myriad neo-Nazi assemblages, including the Aryan Nation and various militia groups. Internet discussion lists also disperse these views, and rightwing extremists are aggressively active on many computer forums.[26] These organizations are hardly harmless, having carried out terrorism of various sorts extending from church burnings to the bombings of public buildings. Adopting quasi-Leninist discourse and tactics for ultraright causes, these groups have been successful in recruiting working-class members devastated by the developments of global capitalism, which has resulted in widespread unemployment for traditional forms of industrial, agricultural, and unskilled labor. Moreover, extremist websites have influenced alienated middle-class youth as well (a 1999 HBO documentary "Hate on the Internet" provides a disturbing number of examples of how extremist websites influenced disaffected youth to commit hate crimes).

A recent twist in the saga of technopolitics, in fact, seems to be that allegedly "terrorist" groups are now increasingly using the Internet and websites to promote their causes. An article in the *Los Angeles Times* in 2001 reports that groups such as Hamas use their website to post reports of acts of terror against Israel, rather than calling newspapers or broadcasting outlets.[27] A wide range of groups labeled as "terrorist" reportedly use e-mail, listserves, and websites to further their struggles, causes including Hezbollah and Hamas, the Maoist group Shining Path in Peru, and a variety of other groups throughout Asia and elsewhere. The Tamil Tigers, for instance, a liberation movement in Sri Lanka, offers position papers, daily news, and free e-mail service. According to the *Los Angeles Times*, experts are still unclear "whether the ability to communicate online worldwide is prompting an increase or a decrease in terrorist acts."

Since September 11, 2001, there have been widespread discussions of how bin Laden's Al Qaeda network used the Internet to plan the 9/11 terrorist attacks on the United States, how the group communicated with each other, got funds, and purchased airline tickets via the Internet, and used flight simulations to practice their hijacking.[28] Since "Operation Enduring Freedom," news stories have documented how many pro–Al Qaeda websites continue to appear and disappear (such as www.Alneda.com), serving as propaganda conduits and potential organization channels for remaining terrorist cell members. By encrypting messages within what appears to be simple Web pictures, Al Qaeda (or any group or person) can transfer sensitive information that only requires the receiving party to download the picture and then decrypt it in order to reveal the secret message. The sheer volume of video and still picture information on the Internet helps to ensure that the information can be circulated even when perused by such powerful governmental surveillance systems as Echelon and Carnivore. But, apparently in response to the threat posed to U.S. War on Terror interests, the Bush administration has begun the attempt to discontinue websites that it suspects terror cells are frequenting to gain information that could be used in terrorist attacks.

Despite the expectation that any governmental administration would seek to target and disarm the information channels of its enemy, it is exactly the extreme reaction by the Bush administration to the perceived threats posed by the Internet that have the subcultural forces associated with the battle against globalization-from-above fighting in opposition to U.S. Internet policies. Drawing upon the expertise of a subculture of politically minded computer "hacktivists,"[29] people are progressively more informed about the risks involved in online communications, including threats to their privacy posed by monitoring government agencies such as the Office of Homeland Security, and this has led in turn to a wider, more populist opposition to Internet policing generally. A technical wing has become allied to those fighting for globalization-from-below, with groups such as Cult of the Dead Cow (www.cultdeadcow.com), Cryptome (www.cryptome.org), and the hacker journal *2600* (www.2600.org) serving as figureheads for a broad movement of exceptionally computer literate individuals who group together under the banner of HOPE (Hackers On Planet Earth) and who practice a politics called "hacktivism."

Hacktivists have involved themselves in creating open source software programs that can be used freely to circumvent attempts by government and corporations to control the Internet experience. Notably, and somewhat scandalously, hackers have released programs such as Six/Four (after Tiananmen Square) that combine the peer-to-peer capabilities of Napster with a virtual private networking protocol that makes user identity anonymous, and Camera/Shy, a powerful Web browser stenography application that allegedly allows anyone to engage in the type of secret information storage and retrieval that groups such as Al Qaeda have used against the Pentagon. Moreover, associated with the hacktivist cause are the "crackers" who create "warez," pirated versions of commercial software or passwords. While anathema to Bill Gates, there is no software beyond the reach of the pirate-crackers, and to the delight of the alternative Internet subculture, their often otherwise expensive programs are freely traded and shared over the Web and peer-to-peer networks across the globe. Hackers also support the Open Source movement, in which noncorporate software is freely and legally traded, improved upon at large, and available for general use by a public that agrees not to sell their improvements for profit in the future. Free competitors to Microsoft, such as the operating system Linux (www.linux.org) and the word processing suite OpenOffice (www.openoffice.org), provide powerful and economically palatable alternatives to the PC hegemon.

Another hacker ploy is the monitoring and exploitation for social gain of the booming wireless, wide-area Internet market (called Wi-Fi, WAN, or WLAN). Wi-Fi, besides offering institutions, corporations, and homes the luxury of Internet connectivity and organizational access for any and all users within the area covered by the local network, also potentially offers such freedoms to nearby neighbors and wireless pedestrians if such networks are not made secure. In fact, as the U.S. cybersecurity czar Richard Clarke noted in December 2002, an astounding number of Wi-Fi networks are unprotected and available for hacking. This led the Office of Homeland Security to label wireless networking a terrorist threat.[30] Part of what the government is reacting to is the activist technique of "wardriving," in which a hacker drives through a community equipped with a basic wireless antenna and computer searching for network access nodes.[31] Many hackers had been wardriving around Washington, D.C., thereby gaining valuable federal information and server access, prompting the government contractor Science Applications International Corporation (SAIC) to begin monitoring drive-by hacks in the summer of 2002.[32]

But not all war drivers are interested in sensitive information, and many more are simply interested in proliferating information about what amounts to free broadband Internet access points—a form of Internet connectivity that otherwise comes at a premium cost.[33] Thus, wireless network hackers are often deploying their skills toward developing a database of "free networks" that, if not always free of costs, represent opportunities for local communities to share connections and corporate fees. Such freenets represent inclusive resources that are developed by communities for their own needs and involve values like conviviality and culture, education, economic equity, and sustainability that have been found to be progressive hallmarks of online communities generally.[34] Needless to say, corporate Internet service providers are outraged by this anticapitalist development, and are seeking government legislation favoring prosecution of this mode of gift economy activism.

Hacktivists are also directly involved in the immediate political battles played out around the dynamically globalized world. Hacktivists such as The Mixter, from Germany, who authored the program Tribe Floodnet that shut down the website for the World Economic Forum in January 2002, routinely use their hacking skills to cause disruption of governmental and corporate presences online. On July 12, 2002, the homepage for the *USA Today* website was hacked and altered content was presented to the public, leaving *USA Today* to join such other media magnets as the *New York Times* and Yahoo! as the corporate victims of a media hack. In February 2003, immediately following the destruction of the Space Shuttle Columbia, a group calling themselves Trippin Smurfs hacked NASA's servers for the third time in three months. In each case, security was compromised and the web servers were defaced with antiwar political messages. Another repeated victim of hacks is the Recording Industry Association of America (RIAA), who because of its attempt to legislate P2P (peer to peer) music trading has become anathema to Internet hacktivists. A sixth attack upon the RIAA website in January 2003 posted bogus press releases and even provided music files for free downloading!

BLOGS AND WIKIS: HYPERTEXT GONE DEMOCRATIC

While movements emerging out of hacker culture such as the participatory movement for free and shared Internet bandwidth are promising indeed, free Internet connectivity in itself doesn't necessarily lead to social benefit if its only use is the sort of e-commerce typical of the late 1990s Web and to-day's E-bay. Importantly, however, emergent socially interactive forms of Internet media, such as blogs and wikis, have become widely popular communication tools alongside the ultimate "killer app" of e-mail. The mushrooming Internet community that has erupted around blogging is particularly deserving of analysis here, as bloggers have demonstrated themselves as technoactivists favoring not only democratic self-expression and networking, but also global media critique and journalistic sociopolitical intervention.

Blogs, short for "web logs," are partly successful because they are relatively easy to create and maintain—even for nontechnical web users. Combining the hypertext of webpages, the multiuser discussion of message-boards and listservs, and the mass syndication ability of XML and e-mail, blogs are also popular because they represent the next evolution of web-based experience. If the WWW was about forming a global network of interlocking, informative websites, blogs make the idea of a dynamic network of ongoing debate, dialogue, and commentary come alive and so emphasize the interpretation and dissemination of alternative information to a heightened degree. While recent mainstream coverage of blogs tends to portray them as narcissistic domains for one's own individual opinion, many group blogs exist, such as American Samizdat (www.drmenlo.com/samizdat), Metafilter (www.metafilter.com), and BoingBoing (www.boingboing.net), in which teams of contributors post and comment upon stories. The ever-expanding series of international Indymedia (www.indymedia.org) sites, erected by activists for the public domain to inform one another both locally and globally, are especially promising. But even for the hundreds of thousands purely individual blogs, forming groups of fellow blog readers and publishers is the norm, and blog posts tend to reference (and link) to an impressive degree social interaction amongst the group(s) proper.

One result of bloggers' fascination with networks of links has been the subcultural phenomenon known as Google Bombing. Documented in early 2002, it was revealed that the popular search engine Google had a special affinity for blogs because of its tendency to favor highly linked, recently updated Web content in its site ranking system. With this in mind, bloggers began campaigns to get large numbers of fellow bloggers to post links to specific postings designed to include the desirable keywords that Google users might normally search. A successful Google Bomb, then, would rocket the initial blog that began the campaign up Google's rankings to number one for each and every one of those keywords—whether the blog itself had important substantive material on them or not!

While those in the blog culture often abused this trick for personal gain (to get their own name and blog placed at the top of Google's most popular search terms), many in the blog subculture began using the Google Bomb as a tool for political subversion. Known as a justice bomb, this use of blogs served to link a particularly distasteful corporation or entity to a series of keywords that either spoofs or criticizes the same. Hence, thanks to a Google Bomb, Google users typing in "McDonald's" might very well get pointed to a much-linked blog post titled "McDonald's Lies about Their Fries" as the top entry. While Google continues to favor blogs in its rankings, amidst the controversy surrounding the so-called clogging of search engine results by blogs, it has recently taken steps to deemphasize blogs in its rating system and may soon remove blogs to their own search subsection altogether—this despite blogs accounting for only an estimated .03 percent of Google's indexed Web content.[35]

Google or not, many blogs are increasingly political in the scope of their commentary. Over the last year, a plethora of leftist-oriented blogs were created and organized in networks of interlinking solidarity, so as to contest what was perceived to be a politically domesticated forum of blogoshere conservative opinion. Post–September 11, with the wars on Afghanistan and Iraq, the phenomenon of Warblogging arose to become an important and noted genre in its own right. Blogs, such as our own BlogLeft (www.gseis .ucla.edu/courses/ed253a/blogger.php), became distinguished for providing a broad range of critical alternative views concerning the objectives of the Bush administration and Pentagon and the corporate media spin surrounding them. One blogger, the now famous Iraqi Salam Pax (www.dear_raed .blogspot.com), gave outsiders a dose of the larger unexpurgated reality as the bombs exploded overhead in Baghdad. Meanwhile, in Iran, Hossein Derakhshan became the first blogger to be jailed for "undermining national security through cultural activities."[36] In response to the need for completely anonymous and untraceable blogging (as in countries where freedom of speech is in doubt), open source software like invisiblog (www.invisiblog .com) has been developed to protect online journalists' identities.

Political bloggers have played a significant role in at least two other recent notable events—the focus of attention upon the racist remarks made by then Speaker of the House Trent Lott and the creation of a media uproar over the dishonest reporting exposed recently at *The New York Times*. In the first case, Lott's remarks had been buried in the back of the *Washington Post* until communities of bloggers began publicizing them, generating public and media interest that then led to his removal. In the second, bloggers again rabidly set upon the newsprint giant, whipping up so much controversy and hostile journalistic opinion that the *Times*'s executive and managing editors were forced to resign in disgrace. Noting the ability of blogs to coalesce groups around issues for political effect, the campaign for Howard Dean became an early blog adopter (www.blogforamerica.com), which successfully catalyzed his grassroots campaign. In turn, blogs became de rigueur for all political candidates

and have been sites for discussing the policies and platforms of various candidates, interfacing with local and national support offices, and in some cases
speaking directly to the presidential hopefuls themselves.[37]

As alluded to earlier, bloggers are cumulatively expanding the notion of
what the Internet is and how it can be used. Increasingly, bloggers are not
tied to their desktops, writing in virtual alienation from the world, but are
posting pictures, text, audio, and video on the fly from PDA devices and cell
phones. Large political events, such as the World Summit for Sustainable Development, the World Social Forum, and the G8 forums all now have wireless bloggers providing real time alternative coverage. One environmental
activist, a tree-sitter named Remedy, even broadcast a wireless account of
her battle against the Pacific Lumber Company from her blog (www.con-
trast.org/treesit), 130 feet atop an old growth redwood. She has since been
forcefully removed but continues blogging in defense of a sustainable world
in which new technologies can coexist with wilderness and other species.[38]

While the overt participatory politics of bloggers, as well as their sheer
numbers, makes the exciting new media tool called the wiki secondary to
this discussion, the inherent participatory, collective, and democratic design
of wikis have many people believing that they represent the coming evolution of the hypertextual Web. Taken from the Hawaiian word for "quick,"
wikis are popular innovative forms of group databases and hypertextual
archives that work on the principle of open editing, meaning that any online
user can not only change the content of the database (add, edit, or delete),
but also its organization (the way in which material links together and networks). Wikis have been coded such that they come with a built-in failsafe
that automatically saves and logs each previous version of the archive. This
makes them highly flexible because users are then freed to transform the
archive as they see fit, as no version of the previous information is ever lost
beyond recall. The result, then, is not only of an information-rich databank,
but one that can be examined as *in process*, with viewers able to trace and
investigate how the archive has grown over time, which users have made
changes, and what exactly they have contributed.

While initially conceived as a simple, informal, and free-form alternative to
more highly structured and complex groupware products such as IBM's Lotus Notes, wikis can be used for a variety of purposes beyond organizational
planning.[39] To the degree that wikis could easily come to supplant the basic
model of the website, which is designed privately, placed online, and then is
mostly a static experience beyond following preprogrammed links, wikis demand investigation by technology theorists as the next wave in the emerging
democratic Internet. An example of wiki power, in this respect, is the impressive Wikipedia (www.wikipedia.org), a free, globally collaborative encyclopedia project based on wiki protocol that would have made Diderot and
his fellow *philosophes* proud. Beginning on January 15, 2001, the Wikipedia

has quickly grown to include approximately 162,000 always-evolving articles in English (with over 138,000 in other languages) and the database grows with each passing day. With over 5,000 vigilant contributors worldwide creating, updating, and deleting information in the archive daily, the charge against wikis is that such unmoderated and asynchronous archives must descend into chaos and not information. However, as required by the growth of the project, so-called Wikipedians have gathered together and developed their own loose norms regarding what constitutes helpful and contributive actions on the site. Disagreements, which do occur, are settled online by Wikipedians as a whole in what resembles a form of virtualized Athenian democracy wherein all contributors have both a voice and vote.

IN CONCLUSION: SITUATING OPPOSITIONAL POLITICS ONLINE

The examples in this chapter suggest how new media developments in technoculture make possible a reconfiguring of politics and culture and a refocusing of participatory democratic politics for everyday life. In this conjuncture, the ideas of Guy Debord and the Situationist International are especially relevant with their stress on the construction of situations, the use of technology, media of communication, and cultural forms to promote a revolution of everyday life, and to increase the realm of freedom, community, and empowerment.[40] To a meaningful extent, then, the new information and communication technologies *are* revolutionary, they *do* constitute a dramatic transformation of everyday life in the direction of more participatory and democratic potentials. Yet it must be admitted that this progressive dimension coevolves with processes that also promote and disseminate the capitalist consumer society, individual and competition, and that have involved new modes of fetishism, enslavement, and domination yet to be clearly perceived and theorized.[41]

The Internet is thus a contested terrain, used by left, right, and center of both dominant cultures and subcultures to promote their own agendas and interests. The political battles of the future may well be fought in the streets, factories, parliaments, and other sites of past struggle, but politics is already mediated by broadcast, computer, and information technologies and will increasingly be so in the future. Our belief, and what we have attempted to show here, is that this is at least in part a positive development that opens radical possibilities for a greater range of opinion, new modes of virtual and actual political communities, and novel forms of direct political action. Those interested in the politics and culture of the future should therefore be clear on the important role of the alternative public spheres and intervene accordingly, while critical cultural theorists and activists have the responsibility of educating students around the cultural and subcultural literacies that ultimately amount to the skills that will enable them to participate in the on-going struggle inherent in cultural politics.[42]

Online activist subcultures have thus materialized in the last few years alone as a vital oppositional space of politics and culture in which a wide diversity of individuals and online communities have used emergent technologies to help produce new social relations and forms of democratic political possibility. Many of these subcultures may become appropriated into the mainstream, but no doubt novel oppositional cultures and different alternative voices and practices will appear as we navigate the increasingly complex present toward the ever receding future.

NOTES

1. See Howard Rheingold, *The Virtual Community: Homesteading on the Electronic Frontier* (Reading, Mass.: Addison-Wesley, 1993); John Perry Barlow, "A Declaration of the Independence of Cyberspace," available at www.eff.org/~barlow/Declaration-Final.html, 1996 (accessed July 2003); Bill Gates, *The Road Ahead* (New York: Penguin Books, 1996); Kevin Kelly, *New Rules for the New Economy* (New York: Viking Press, 1998).

2. Mark Poster, "Cyberdemocracy: The Internet and the Public Sphere," in *Internet Culture*, ed. D. Porter (New York: Routledge, 1997); Sherry Turkle, *Life on the Screen: Identity in the Age of the Internet* (New York: Touchstone Press, 1997).

3. Douglas Kellner, "The Media and Democracy," available at www.gseis.ucla.edu/faculty/kellner/papers/MEDIAdem2003.htm, 2003 (accessed January 30, 2004).

4. N. H. Nie and L. Ebring, *Internet and Society: A Preliminary Report* (Stanford, Calif.: The Institute for the Quantitative Study of Society, 2000).

5. C. Bowers, *Educating for Eco-Justice and Community* (Athens: University of Georgia Press, 2001).

6. D. Trend, *Welcome to Cyberschool: Education at the Crossroads in the Information Age* (Lanham, Md.: Rowman & Littlefield, 2001).

7. Herbert Marcuse, *Towards a Critical Theory of Society: Collected Papers of Herbert Marcuse, Vol. II*, ed. D. Kellner (New York: Routledge, 2001), 180–82.

8. Douglas Kellner, *Grand Theft 2000: Media Spectacle and a Stolen Election* (Lanham, Md.: Rowman & Littlefield, 2001).

9. Douglas Kellner, *From 9/11 to Terror War: Dangers of the Bush Legacy* (Lanham, Md.: Rowman & Littlefield, 2003).

10. See Andrew Feenberg, *Alternative Modernity* (Los Angeles: University of California Press, 1995), 144–66. For a pre-Internet example of the subversion of an informational medium, in this case, public access television, see Douglas Kellner, "Public Access Television: Alternative Views" available at www.gseis.ucla.edu/courses/ed253a/MCkellner/ACCESS.html (accessed January 30, 2004). Selected episodes are freely available for viewing as streaming videos at www.gseis.ucla.edu/faculty/kellner (accessed January 30, 2004).

11. Steven Best and Douglas Kellner, *The Postmodern Adventure* (New York and London: Guilford Press and Routledge, 2001); Nick Couldry and James Curran, eds.,

Contesting Media Power: Alternative Media in a Networked World (Lanham, Md.: Rowman & Littlefield, 2003).

12. Kellner, *From 9/11 to Terror War.*

13. Andrew Feenberg, *Questioning Technology* (New York: Routledge, 1999); C. Luke, "Cyber-schooling and Technological Change: Multiliteracies for New Times" in *Multiliteracies: Literacy, Learning, and the Design of Social Futures,* ed. B. Cope and M. Kalantzis (Australia: Macmillan, 2000), 69–105; Langdon Winner, "Citizen Virtues in a Technological Order" in *Controlling Technology,* ed. E. Katz, A. Light, and W. Thompson (Amherst, N.Y.: Prometheus Books, 2003), 383–402.

14. Best and Kellner, *Postmodern Adventure.*

15. "Blogs" are hypertextual web logs that people use for new forms of journaling, self-publishing, and media/news critique, as we discuss in detail below. For examples, see our two blogs: BlogLeft: Critical Interventions, www.gseis.ucla.edu/courses/ed253a/blogger.php, and Vegan Blog: The (Eco)Logical Weblog, www.getvegan.com/blog/blogger.php. "Wikis" are popular new forms of group databases and hypertextual archives, covered in more depth later in this paper.

16. The Internet has equally played a major role in the global environmental "right to know" movement that seeks to give citizens information about chemical, biological, and radiological threats to their health and safety. For example links, see www.mapcruzin.com/globalchem.htm.

17. Recently, a subversive initiative has been formed by a team at the MIT Media Lab to monitor politicians and governmental agents via a Web databank provided by global users. See Government Information Awareness at: http://18.85.1.51.

18. A. Cvetkovich and D. Kellner, *Articulating the Global and the Local: Globalization and Cultural Studies* (Boulder, Colo.: Westview, 1997); Manuel Castells, "Flows, Networks, and Identities: A Critical Theory of the Informational Society," in *Critical Education in the New Information Age,* ed. D. Macedo (Lanham, Md.: Rowman & Littlefield, 1999), 37–64.

19. A. Luke and C. Luke, "A Situated Perspective on Cultural Globalization," in *Globalization and Education,* ed. N. Burbules and C. Torres (New York: Routledge, 2000).

20. On technopolitics, see Douglas Kellner, "Intellectuals, the New Public Spheres, and Technopolitics," *New Political Science* 41–42 (Fall 1997): 169–88; J. Armitage, ed., Special Issue on Machinic Modulations: New Cultural Theory and Technopolitics," *Angelaki: Journal of the Theoretical Humanities* 4, no. 2 (September 1999); and Best and Kellner, *Postmodern Adventure.*

21. Best and Kellner, *Postmodern Adventure.*

22. J. Brecher, T. Costello, and B. Smith, *Globalization from Below* (Boston: South End Press, 2000); M. Steger, *Globalism: The New Market Ideology* (Lanham, Md.: Rowman & Littlefield, 2002).

23. On globalization, see Best and Kellner, *Postmodern Adventure*; Douglas Kellner, "Globalization and the Postmodern Turn," in *Globalization and Europe,* ed. R. Axtmann (London: Cassells, 1998); and Douglas Kellner, "Theorizing Globalization," *Sociological Theory* 20, no. 3 (November 2002): 285–305.

24. Rheingold, *The Virtual Community.*

25. See Nick Dyer-Witheford, *Cyber-Marx: Cycles and Circuits of Struggle in High-Technology Capitalism* (Urbana, Ill.: University of Illinois Press, 1999); Best and

Kellner, *Postmodern Adventure*; and R. Burbach, *Globalization and Postmodern Politics: From Zapatistas to High-Tech Robber Barons* (London: Pluto Press, 2001).

26. Extreme right wing material is also found in other media, such as radio programs and stations, public access television programs, fax campaigns, video, and even rock music productions.

27. *Los Angeles Times* (February 8, 2001), A1, A14.

28. Kellner, *From 9/11 to Terror War*.

29. On hacker culture, see P. Taylor, *Hackers: Crime and the Digital Sublime* (New York: Routledge, 1999); and P. Himanen, *The Hacker Ethic* (New York: Random House, 2001).

30. See www.wired.com/news/wireless/0,1382,56742,00.html (accessed February 2, 2004).

31. See www.wardriving.com (accessed February 2, 2004) and www.azwardriving.com (accessed February 2, 2004). Related to wardriving is "warspying," in which hactivists search a city looking for the wireless video signals being sent by all manner of hidden digital cameras. For more on this, see www.securityfocus.com/news/7931 (accessed February 2, 2004).

32. See www.securityfocus.com/news/552 (accessed February 2, 2004).

33. See www.freenetworks.org (accessed February 2, 2004).

34. Doug Schuler, *New Community Networks: Wired for Change* (Reading, Mass.: ACM Press and Addison-Wesley, 1996).

35. See Andrew Orlowski, "Google to Fix Blog Noise Problem," *The Register* (May 9, 2003) available at www.theregister.co.uk/content/6/30621.html (accessed February 2, 2004).

36. Now freed and living in exile in Toronto, "Hoder," as he is called, worked with the blogging community to launch a worldwide blogging protest on July 9, 2003 to commemorate the crackdown by the Iranian state against student protests on that day in 1999 and to call for democratic change once again in the country. See his blog at hoder.com/weblog.

37. See www.dailykos.com (accessed February 2, 2004) for an example.

38. See www.contrast.org/treesit (accessed February 2, 2004).

39. B. Leuf and W. Cunningham, *The Wiki Way: Collaboration and Sharing on the Internet* (Boston, Mass.: Addison-Wesley, 2001).

40. On the importance of the ideas of Debord and the Situationist International to make sense of the present conjuncture, see S. Best and D. Kellner, *The Postmodern Turn* (New York and London: Guilford Press and Routledge, 1997) chap. 3, and on the new forms of the interactive consumer society, see Best and Kellner, *Postmodern Adventure*.

41. Best and Kellner, *Postmodern Adventure*.

42. Douglas Kellner, "Technological Revolution, Multiple Literacies, and the Restructuring of Education," in *Silicon Literacies*, ed. Ilana Snyder (New York: Routledge, 2002), 154–69.

11

The Practical Republic: Social Skills and the Progress of Citizenship

Philip E. Agre

Political philosophy, for all its frequent brilliance, is also frequently innocent of the actual workings of politics. Exceptions are found, particularly among authors who do fieldwork.[1] But more often the arguments of the political philosophers are abstracted from everyday political life. To illustrate what I mean, I will discuss three prominent political theories: social capital, deliberative democracy, and civic republicanism. All three are the objects of vast literatures—the literature on social capital being relatively recent, that on deliberative democracy being ancient in its roots but explosive in the last couple of decades, and that on civic republicanism being one of the most venerable of any literature on earth. All of these literatures are brilliant, but all of them are analytically flawed. Each of them, I argue, suffers for lack of a theory of social skills—the practical skills of political life broadly construed. I conclude by sketching such a theory with particular reference to the United States, and by demonstrating that social capital, deliberative democracy, and civic republicanism must all be reconceptualized as a result of it.

SOCIAL CAPITAL

The concept of social capital draws on a long tradition, starting with medieval sources and Tocqueville. But the phrase "social capital," as well as its connection with the mapping of social networks, begins with Loury, for whom it served as part of an explanation of poverty in terms of poorly functioning community support systems.[2] Social capital for Loury was the sum total of other people's capital (e.g., equipment available for borrowing) to which an individual has access through social connections of friendship and association. A related concept, mainly intended to explain the persistence of social stratification, originates with Bourdieu and Passeron.[3] Social capital was then theorized more fully by Coleman and by such scholars of social networks as Lin.[4]

The idea of social capital entered broad circulation, however, with Robert Putnam's *Making Democracy Work*.[5] Half of good research is having a good question, and Putnam's question was this: Why does northern Italy work so much better than southern Italy, given that the two halves of the country share the same government, language, and religion? The answer, Putnam suggests, lies in a nonobvious aspect of culture. Southern Italy is clientelistic: When people in southern Italy have a problem, they look up and down social hierarchies. Northern Italy, by contrast, is associationistic: When people in the north have a problem, they look laterally to people like themselves. They form associations, and the social connections that result then become resources that the association's members can draw on in the future.[6] By "social capital," Putnam refers to two things: the stock of social network connections and the prevailing atmosphere of trust that is conducive to making such connections.[7] Thus, although the concept of social capital originates in social theory rather than in political philosophy, Putnam's conception of social capital is essentially political. Civic engagement is one of its elements, but even the founding of businesses and nonpolitical associations draws on the same generalized reservoir of trust and network connections as do formal political processes.

One problem with the concept of social capital is that it is not clear why we should call it "capital."[8] An individual's own social network, though lacking a price in the market, is arguably a type of capital, but "capital" is not the sort of thing that a society can have. And even if the sum total of a population's social networks were its collective capital, it is hard to understand why a prevailing sense of trust should be called "capital." At least one is stretching the term.

A more serious problem, in my view, is that "social capital" ought to include a third element that is often left out, namely social skills. Because Putnam was comparing northern and southern Italy as regions, we learn less about differences within those regions. In reality, life chances, even within a single region, depend heavily on one's ability to fashion the kinds of lateral connections that Putnam discusses. Those social skills are themselves a kind of capital—economists would call them "human capital" if they considered them at all—and social capital is only going to accrue to individuals who possess the skills to create it. Of course, the acquisition of such advanced social skills is related to associations and trust: If you associate with people who are skilled at organizing people, and you have relations of mutual trust with them, then perhaps you can acquire the necessary skills through apprenticeship or osmosis. Even so, access to the skills of creating social capital is hardly a given.

So the three elements of social capital—networks, trust, and social skills—are interrelated. And the element of social skills should not be taken for granted. Many people grow up in environments where the necessary social skills do not exist, either because everyone is too busy scratching out a subsistence living, or because they have acquired the social skills they need to live in a different kind of society, or because they have internalized conservative ideologies that keep them from creating associations that might threaten established interests. People from such a disadvantaged background might excel in school and get a good job, only to stall in their careers because they are not building strong networks.[9] People whose careers stall in this way are often mystified; they are working hard, doing what they are told, projecting a positive attitude, and generally exercising the skills that are required to get along in a clientelistic world. But they lack the skills of association. Indeed, they probably lack even a clue that the skills of association exist. They might decide that they are being discriminated against (which does happen, skills or no), or that they really do deserve the subordinate social status to which they had originally been assigned. Either would be a tragedy compared to a world in which the necessary skills are universal.

Intergovernmental and nongovernmental organizations have expressed great enthusiasm for the concept of social capital because it promises concrete guidance for social development projects, both in poor areas of industrial countries and in emerging democracies. Accordingly, these organizations have spent huge sums in recent years on social capital research, and several books about social capital have appeared, most famously Putnam's own extremely detailed study of the decline of social capital in the United States.[10] These intuitions are probably right, as far as they go. But social reform activities based on building social capital may not succeed, or may even reinforce existing social inequalities, unless explicit attention is paid to building the necessary social skills among those segments of the population that lack them. You can give people social capital, but it is better to teach them the skill of making social capital for themselves.

Why does the skill dimension of social capital receive so little press? It is hard to know for certain. But experts have generally forgotten what it is like to be beginners, and people who long ago learned the skills of association, or who acquired them tacitly through their socialization into the habitus of professionals, often have a hard time articulating the skills for others. This is a general pattern that De Soto also remarks on in his analysis of the institutional foundations of economic development: People in industrialized countries are so accustomed to a very complex institutional environment that they literally cannot comprehend life in a society where that environment is lacking.[11] Institutions consist first and foremost of social skills, and what Putnam really saw in Italy was institutions that are present in the north and not the south.[12]

DELIBERATIVE DEMOCRACY

From its earliest days to the present, democracy has always been attended by a certain myth: citizens gather around in the community meeting-house, they have an open and rational discussion, they come to a consensus or hold a pleasant vote, decisions get made, and everyone becomes a better person in the process. This powerful legitimating myth is called deliberative democracy, and it is almost unrelated to the reality of democracy in any time or place.[13] Of course, the more sophisticated theorists of deliberative democracy, such as Jürgen Habermas, do not present this picture as a descriptive theory but as a system of regulative norms. But even as a norm, deliberative democracy is so profoundly disconnected from reality that something must be analytically wrong with it.

Objections to the empirical utility of the myth of deliberative democracy are not new. Schudson, for example, presents a wide variety of debunking arguments from American history.[14] For example, he argues that the classical New England town meetings were largely staged events in which social hierarchies were placed on display.[15] And sophisticated, grounded accounts of democracy in practice are certainly available.[16] My target, then, is not the study of politics as such, but a relatively narrow tradition, albeit one of great importance historically.

The problems with the myth of deliberative democracy are numerous. It ignores the embedding of formal democratic processes in other social structures. It ignores the behind-the-scenes work, both strategic and tactical, in which any skilled citizen or politician engages before bringing an issue to a public forum. It neglects struggles over the constitutional framework that is supposed to organize deliberation in any democracy. And it ignores the plain fact that many people are afraid to speak at public meetings.[17] To disagree with the myth of deliberative democracy is not to endorse the opposite myth of a mass democracy manipulated by elites.[18] Rather, it argues that the neglected dimensions of democratic reality belong at the center of any realistic analysis.

I want to focus on one of these neglected dimensions: the issue of scale.[19] Democracy today occurs on a mass scale. Yet deliberative democracy takes as its paradigm the local group: the Greek polis, the small town, or (especially in northern Europe) the workplace. This attention to small-group democracy is not entirely wrong, of course. Dewey, for example, emphasized the small group because that is where children learn or do not learn the values of democracy. Classrooms that tacitly instruct children in authoritarian values are antidemocratic. Conservatives in the United States have emphasized political localism for their own, almost opposite reasons. The problem in either case is simply that society is big and interconnected. And the problem obviously comes to the fore in a society becoming rapidly globalized and wired, as the issues that citizens debate in a democracy become themselves increasingly intertwined with the issues that citizens debate in other places.

Of course, political parties and other structures of mobilization have existed for centuries, but now the interconnections through which political opinions and policies are formed are much more complex. The problem for political theory is not that political decision-making is moving upward in a hierarchy, away from local councils and toward a representative central government. The problem, rather, is that a wired society is making obtrusive the role of large-scale processes in organizing even very local decision-making. In a society where communications technologies are poorly developed, even in the early days of radio and television that provoked the literature on "mass society," it is possible to conceptualize the influences of large-scale processes on local decision-making in the nebulous form of "ideology." Ideologies waft outward from the center, or upward from the supposed masses, and influence individuals' general cognitive orientations, thus shaping the attitudes (e.g., democratic or deferential) that they bring to the affairs of their community. That, in its dimness, is the picture that centuries of political theory have left us.

The reality is different. Listen to real people argue about politics, and you will generally hear them recite arguments that they got from professional opinion-makers (politicians, pundits, journalists, scholars, workplace authorities, and so on) that they happen to agree with.[20] From the point of view of the deliberative democracy model, this observation is an embarrassment, if not an elitist insult. But it is nothing of the sort. Coming up with novel political arguments requires a lot of work. Human beings are finite, and nobody has the time or knowledge to invent thought-out arguments on every issue all by themselves. Even the professional arguers are mostly pooling arguments among themselves, for example by refashioning arguments they have appropriated from others and applying general schemata to particular cases. Political tendencies can be thought of as industries that generate arguments to suit their respective interests and strategies, and then deliver those arguments to their members. A political tendency, in this sense, requires an infrastructure (magazines, radio programs, associations, websites, think tanks, and so on), and a political infrastructure is successful if it delivers the right arguments to the right people at the right time. This has always been true. What is different now is simply the scale and speed with which debates collectively unfold in a society. Think, for example, of the titanic clash of party lines during the American election controversy of 2000.[21] Such episodes make clear that local debates are not constituted only by their members, or conditioned only by an evolving climate of competing ideologies, but are embedded—in great detail and in real time—in larger systems.[22]

Now, it may be argued that this new picture is still deliberative democracy, only shifted from the local group to what Kroeber called the superorganic level.[23] But that won't do. Central to deliberative democracy is a certain picture of the human person: self-possessed, fully rational, engaged with others, respectful of procedural rules, and so on. The capacity to participate in collective decision-making is, for the ideal of deliberative democracy, the highest state of human life, and people who cannot participate in collective decision-making (whether because of outside political constraints or for lack of the relevant skills or attitudes) are not fully realized human beings. This is why critiques of the deliberative democracy theory are taken so seriously: They explode a normative picture of human development, thereby leaving rudderless whole territories of social and educational thought. This is just as well, given the standard theory's tendency to abstract the citizen away from the individual's concrete identity and location in the social system.[24] Surely this reassertion of the collective level in politics diminishes the significance of the individual and obliterates the case for liberal political freedoms? Not so. Recognizing the embedded nature of political debate does explode a certain story about those topics, but it does not explode the topics themselves.

What does it do? To start with, viewing individual citizens as participants in debates on a collective level does not cast us into the outer darkness of antihumanist political theories, such as that of Foucault, that view the human individual as wholly the product of impersonal "discourses." One could make some minimal sense of the collective level of public deliberation, for example, simply by appealing to the metaphor of the "marketplace of ideas."[25] Under the marketplace metaphor, the individual, no longer centrally a producer of arguments, is at least a discerning consumer, picking and choosing from the arguments. The marketplace metaphor hardly does justice to the phenomena, given that the advertising and the goods are nearly the same. It does not explain the phenomena that are central to Foucault's theory: the ways that individuals' political participation is organized through their socialization into social roles such as professions. It eliminates any sense that the citizen has responsibilities, as opposed to private rights. It fails to suggest a satisfactory political analog to the marketplace's regulations against fraud. And it provides no account of the actual process of debate, as opposed to the forming of opinion. But it does provide something of an existence proof that a theory of collective political argument does not extinguish individual political agency. Perhaps in analyzing the tensions among the various received theories, we can transcend the deliberative model and set about reconstructing the values of democracy in the context of democracy as it is actually lived.

CIVIC REPUBLICANISM

A republic is the opposite of a monarchy. A republic, in other words, is a polity that does not have a king or queen. This may not seem like much of a definition, but so long as most of the world was ruled by monarchs—until well into the twentieth century—it was a powerful idea. The very possibility of a society without a monarch was already well known to the Greeks, however, and republicanism is a nearly continuous thread throughout the history of the West.[26]

In the United States, however, attempts to discuss republicanism are frustrated by the widespread idea that the United States is a republic because it is not a democracy. This unfortunate dichotomy originates with an isolated mistake in Madison that is representative neither of his philosophy generally nor of the history of political thought with which he was certainly familiar.[27] In fact, the concepts of republicanism and democracy are logically unrelated. Conservativism is rule by an elite, or a stratified social order administered by that elite, as opposed to democracy, which is rule by the people. Republicanism (which can be either conservative or democratic), for its part, is opposed to monarchy (which also can be either conservative or, in the case of a constitutional monarchy, democratic). Conservative philosophy stereotypes democracy as rule by the mob, the erosion of culture and morals by demotic values, and the leveling of aristocratic excellence into a general mediocrity.[28] Democracy is held to lead inevitably to tyranny, and rule by elites (which is what conservatives mean by representative government) is understood as a counterweight to the mindlessness and degradation of the mass.

Such distinctions having been drawn, we can consider the real ideas of civic republicanism. The word "civic" points to the positive agenda for society that is supposed to occupy the void left behind by the departing monarch. People are supposed to rule themselves, not be ruled by monarchs, and this obligation makes certain demands on them. Good citizens, it is said, place the welfare of the whole above their own private welfare as individuals. Of course, stated in that way the principle could mean several things. It is not, for example, communism. In particular, it is not an institutional question, such as whether private property should exist or what other laws should be passed; rather, it is a norm of political culture. Citizens, it is said, should pitch in, be public-spirited, and recognize that their fates are conjoined. If the modern ideal of market supremacy were actually true—that is, if it were even theoretically possible that each individual's welfare could be reduced to his or her own private property—then the civic values of republicanism would not be necessary. But the market ideal is not true, and civic republicanism, while not opposed to markets as such, is founded on its denial.

The history of civic republicanism has mostly been written, like most history, as a story of leaders. This is a vestige of the aristocratic worldview in which the fate of the polity depends on the personal qualities of the few who are in charge. Successful republican government has historically been regarded as a wonder, and credit for the wonder goes to the leaders who manage to hold it together. Or else it goes to institutions such as the separation of powers that compensate for human nature. While talented leaders and well-designed institutions are certainly necessary, however, they are more nearly products of republican society than producers of it. In reality, the success of republican government, like that of nearly any institution, is founded on ordinary people. The problem with the philosophy of civic republicanism, historically, is precisely its overemphasis on the civic values of placing the good of the whole above one's own. Civic-mindedness is certainly valuable, but a preoccupation with civic values as the central condition of republicanism speaks too much of a polemical defense against conservative pessimism about humanity, and too little of the actual practical work of republican self-government.

Once again—and there is a pattern here—what is missing is a clear conception of the individual citizen.[29] The word "citizen," like many words in politics, is unfortunate because it has two independent meanings: it is either a bundle of rights (such as the rights enjoyed by citizens of a country versus people who are in the country on visas or illegally) or a bundle of responsibilities (voting, being informed about public issues, engaging with fellow citizens, expressing views) and the construction of self that goes with them. The civic republican tradition, which has not (unlike democracy) been centrally concerned with spreading the rights of citizenship as widely as possible, has understood citizenship mainly in the latter sense, as a bundle of responsibilities. In many cases, citizenship has been understood as love of country, respect for the flag, civility in debate, and other injunctions that, while perhaps necessary, suggest more a fear of citizens rather than respect for them.[30] With rare exception, republicanism's understanding of the skills of citizenship has been superficial and formalistic. It is highly developed in some areas, for example in its inheritance from the tradition of rhetoric. It has also drawn on the lengthy tradition of advice manuals for rulers (as opposed to citizens). But it provides little guidance about the great majority of social interactions that organize political life outside the giving of speeches.

Republicanism also has a deeper meaning, one that begins to connect with the other themes that I have been developing. Republicanism is not simply the absence of monarchs—that is its negative meaning. It is also the capacity for collective self-government. Obeying a monarch is not simply a consciously chosen method of running a society; it is also an existential condition. No form of government is feasible in the long run unless the people regard it as legitimate, and the only way to legitimize monarchy is through internalized habits of deference—that is, through the deeply rooted belief that one is, by nature, inferior to the monarch, and by extension to the hierarchy of authorities that God Himself, through the agency of His monarch, has instituted. Republican conservatism is, in historical terms, a transitional form of society in which deference to authority remains but is legitimized by an abstract appeal to tradition rather than to the monarch. The historical significance of the United States, and its greatest contribution to the world, is that it broke with deference as an organizing principle of political culture.[31] From the cultural revolution of the 1790s, through the populist eras of the early and late nineteenth century, through the labor movement of the Depression to the civil rights era and the new social movements that followed it, the history of the United States has been a story of progress: the progressive undoing of internalized deference and the progressive realization of democratic republican values. Overcoming the habits of deference means realizing, at the deepest level, that one can, and deserves to, participate in determining one's own fate. Only when the lights go on in individuals' minds will they take the initiative to fulfill—indeed, to invent—the promise of citizenship.

MACHIAVELLIANISM

These considerations on republicanism provide a convenient occasion to discuss the most important modern analysis of social skill and its role in society, that of Fligstein.[32] Fligstein observes that social theory, despite its endless concern with the relationship of agency to social structure, has been remarkably unconcerned with either the nature or the substance of the skills that social agents employ. He has sought to remedy that omission by sketching a theory of social skill that draws on ideas from symbolic interactionism.[33]

Fligstein's starting point is the concept of a social field, which is roughly speaking an institution in which various social groups contest their respective interests. The social skills he describes are those of a "skilled actor" or "institutional enterpreneur" who negotiates the interactions between powerful and powerless groups within the social field in order to arrive at a set of rules to govern their future relationships. Social fields, he observes, tend to be highly stable. The opportunities for a skilled actor to change things tend to emerge in periods of crisis, especially when the territory of the social field is being invaded by some other social field. In those situations, the skilled actor can employ a wide range of interpersonal strategies, maintaining the appearance of community-mindedness by manipulating rules and tailoring communication to the beliefs and identities of each particular audience. Having thereby mediated the emergence of a new system of rules, the skilled actor must once again stabilize the field by instilling in the field's participants a new set of habits.

Fligstein's theory restores a missing piece to social theory. It does so, however, through a striking reinvention. Although he does not seem aware of it, Fligstein's theory is isomorphic, and in remarkable detail, to that of Machiavelli (whom he mentions only in passing, when observing that the skilled actor tries not to appear Machiavellian).[34] The skilled actor in Fligstein's account is analogous to Machiavelli's prince. The field is the Renaissance city–state. The powerful groups are the oligarchic families, and the powerless groups are the *populo*, mainly the guilds. The powerful groups/oligarchic families must negotiate among themselves, lest their rule collapse into factionalism. The various groups among the powerless/*populo* must also maintain solidarity to have any chance of curtailing the rule of the powerful. The "rules" that govern a field are the laws of the city–state. The field/city–state alternates in each theory between stasis and crisis; the crisis can be caused by internal dynamics but is more often caused by invasion. It is very hard to change the rule of a field/city–state while it is static. The would-be prince must wait for a crisis. The field/city–state is ruled not directly by the ruler, but through the mediation of a set of habits that the field/city–state instills in its participants/citizens. This, after all, is what the fifteenth century meant by republicanism. The elements that Fligstein takes from symbolic interactionism have been known since ancient Greece as rhetoric. The prince/skilled actor fashions appearances and manipulates rules/laws, operating largely by flattery. And he is very concerned to be seen as acting in the community interest, whether he is or not.

The one important divergence between the theories comes at the point where, each says, the prince/skilled actor's attempt to institute a new order can fail. The main motivation of Machiavelli and his readers is to prevent political crisis from producing a tyrant. For that reason, Machiavelli advises the prince to resort to violence when necessary to institute his new republican order. Fligstein and his readers are not motivated by the danger of a tyrant, at least not consciously, and that may explain why Fligstein observes much more dispassionately than Machiavelli that the prince/skilled actor's attempts can fail. He is not clear on what happens next, though from the logic of his argument I would assume either that the old order limps along in a reduced form, or else that the field is subsumed by its neighbors.

My purpose here is not to criticize Fligstein, who has done social theory a service by reviving a theme that was once central to Western theories of politics as a whole. Fligstein's accomplishment speaks volumes about the immense reorientation of political inquiry from a practical art to a distanced, abstract, and only marginally applicable would-be science. Even Marx, who was emphatic about the unity of theory and practice, provided his readers with almost no concrete instruction in the arts of politics.[35] It is time to repair the damage. Yet Machiavelli's theory, even when updated with modern social-theoretic vocabulary, is not the theory of social skill that a modern democracy needs. Machiavelli, like the great majority of authors of guides to practical skills before the modern era, wrote only for an elite. He presupposes that only one individual possesses the skills that he writes about. Everyone else is treated passively as raw material for the manipulations of the prince. This is not a theory of democracy. It is not even a theory of republicanism. What would a polity be like in which everyone had advanced social skills, and what would the ideal skills be like for a polity in which political skills are widespread?

CITIZENSHIP

The United States is a democratic republic, and it needs a democratic republican theory of the skills of citizenship.[36] Although such a theory cannot be simple, elements of it can be found in the correctives that I have offered to the ideas of social capital, deliberative democracy, and civic republicanism. What is needed is something like a manual—a how-to, that most American of genres. The central problem that the citizen faces is how to participate meaningfully in a society of hundreds of millions. It is a common and reasonable question: How does my voice count? Some theorists, in the tradition of Downs, actually seem to revel in the difficulty, making it seem mysterious that anyone should even find it worthwhile to vote, much less involve themselves in the minutiae of public issues.[37] That won't do.

Other theorists point more reasonably to the institutions of "civil society" that mediate between individuals and the state.[38] Perhaps the average citizen cannot have much effect on national legislation, but having an effect on the policy positions of one's profession, party, church, union, political club, interest group, or civic association is more imaginable. The concept of civil society has its weaknesses; it works better for some societies than for others.[39] But at least it provides a point of departure for a serious consideration of the practical work of politics in a complex modern society.

From the arguments above, it follows that a how-to for democratic republican citizenship would have several elements, including skills for building social capital and participating in the collective production and circulation of political arguments. I cannot provide such a how-to here, but I can sketch perhaps the central idea that is undreamt in the philosophies that I have been describing. That idea is as follows: It is central to the political process that individual citizens, in their public personae, are able to associate themselves with issues. Citizens, whether politicians or activists, make their political careers in entrepreneurial fashion by identifying issues that are coming to prominence, researching and analyzing them, staking out public positions on them, and building social networks of other citizens who have associated themselves with related issues, especially those whose positions are ideologically compatible.[40] Not only is this kind of issue entrepreneurship central to the making of public policy, but it is also central to the "politics," in the broad sense, of nearly every institutional field, from industries to research fields, from bureaucracies to artistic circles, from professions to social movements.

Ideologies, in their practical political aspect, are designed to rationalize and cement coalitions among issue entrepreneurs who have staked out a wide range of issues, and the social networks whose construction the ideologies facilitate then become the connective tissue of political movements.

This process is fractal: Its logic is essentially the same on the global stage as on the national, and it is essentially the same on a regional stage as on a local. What is more, it is essentially the same within a wide variety of institutional contexts. Thus, individuals can stake out issues and build political networks within their professions, their churches, their unions, their industries, or their political organizations. The politics of the local PTA is, in this regard, largely isomorphic to the politics of a national political party. Issue entrepreneurship, in this sense, is a pervasive organizing logic of a democratic republican society, and not the preserve of the social movement leader-hero or the occasional prince. The key is that political personae, political networks, and political issues, on every scale, are all constructed in the same process. This network among individuals who have publicly associated themselves with particular political issues—drawing on a mathematical metaphor,[41] call it an issue lattice—has four dimensions:

- In the vertical dimension, individuals who stake out a given issue on the national level will generally network with those who stake out the same issue on either the global or the regional level;
- In the geographic dimension, individuals who stake out issues in a given geographic jurisdiction will generally network with their counterparts in other jurisdictions;
- In the institutional dimension, individuals who stake out a given issue within one institutional context will generally network with those who stake out the same issue in other institutions; and
- In the ideological dimension, individuals who stake out ideologically related positions on different issues in similar institutional locations will generally network with one another.

This four-dimensional lattice structure is the essence of civil society.[42] Yet note how different it is from the three concepts that I described at the outset. First of all, the four-dimensional issue lattice is not simply a large quantity of social network connections, but a very definite network structure. Nor does it require high levels of trust, but rather a large number of particular negotiations and a great deal of issue-by-issue coalition-building stabilized by ideology. Above all, the issue lattice is sufficiently complex in its detailed workings that it will never emerge without high levels of political skill diffused throughout the society. From this perspective, the crucial type of capital that a society needs is not social networks but social skill; the rest, social networks included, will follow from the entrepreneurial energy of individuals and the cognitive and informational demands of republican politics. Social capital, on this theory, does not depend crucially on the founding of associations, in the sense of formal organizations among nominally equal citizens. Associations are usefully viewed as epiphenomena of the more fundamental skill of forming an issue lattice.[43]

Secondly, the four-dimensional issue lattice could hardly be more different from the idealized picture of deliberative democracy. Political decision-making, it turns out, is embedded in long-term relationships. Its center is ideology, not the making of particular political decisions. Whereas the deliberative democracy theory portrays every citizen as having the same relationship to every issue, in reality citizens tend to specialize in particular issues. This phenomenon follows naturally from the cognitive limits of citizens in complex societies, but it also follows from demands of the long-term construction of public political personae. Individuals fashion themselves into "brand names" by articulating positions on particular issues that will attract coherent groups of followers, whether as organization members, contributors, subscribers, volunteers, or voters. It follows that a central task for a citizen is to organize the circulation of arguments on an issue, both within the three-dimensional issue lattice and to the individuals who subscribe to the citizen's position. Of course, deliberative meetings still occur. The point is that these meetings are thoroughly embedded in longer-term, multiply scaled political processes that extend far beyond the walls of any given meeting house.

Finally, specifying the actual practice of citizenship shifts the focus of civic republicanism from civic values to the skills of civic life. Civic values are no doubt necessary, but their exercise is heavily embedded in the structure of relationships. This embedding helps to make civic values less mysterious: They become partly reducible to the negotiations through which coalitions are built, for example in the segmentary politics that continually ripple up and down the vertical dimension of the issue lattice. More importantly, the success of republican government no longer seems to depend on the altruism of civic selflessness, and instead to depend on the diverse incentives to pursue civic careers.[44] Of course, a polity of global scope without powerful norms of civic selflessness may no longer be republican in any recognizable sense. The question is not trivial: One must determine whether the classical ideal of the self-governing city–state is the very definition of republic, or whether that ideal was simply one means, limited by the available technology and the unequal distribution of entrepreneurial social skills, to a more fundamentally republican end.

The operation of issue lattices is, then, closely tied to the technologies of information and communication, and these technologies become especially important when we consider the democratic aspects of citizenship.[45] Historically, theories of political networks have focused their attention on the highest echelons of interest group politics, for example in the endlessly shifting alliances among interest groups in Washington.[46] In fact, similar issue-networking processes take place throughout the society, and civil society can be strengthened if access to the skills and technologies of building networks around political issues are further democratized. This includes the curricula of civics classes, of course, which ought to teach the practical skills of political organizing. But it should also include the curricula of professional schools, the citizenship tests given to immigrants, and many other contexts where the practical foundations of a democratic republic can be reinforced.[47] In particular, the issue entrepreneurship theory argues that the main democratic potential of technologies like the Internet does not rest in their ability to support deliberation.[48] Instead, it rests mainly in their ability to support the work of issue entrepreneurs: identifying and researching emerging issues, distributing analyses of current events to an audience, organizing events, and networking with other entrepreneurs in the issue lattice.

Politics has been understood since the Greeks as a practical skill, and so it may seem surprising that the most central skill of politics has remained largely unarticulated across centuries. But in hindsight it is not surprising at all. Civilization is the story of the human struggle to emerge from the moral darkness of conservatism, to turn the lights on in individual minds and overcome the habits of deference that turn people into machines. Democratic republicanism is a story not of perfection but of progress. It is a story that is written afresh in every era, and in every life. Technology provides most of the organizing themes for that story in our own era. But technology is not central; what is central are the choices that we make, each of us, in laying claim to the rights and responsibilities of citizenship in our own lives.

NOTES

I appreciate helpful comments from Michael Cornfield, David Ryfe, Karl Schafer, and Janos Simon.

1. Jane Mansbridge, *Beyond Adversary Democracy* (New York: Basic Books, 1980); Carmen Sirianni and Lewis Friedland, *Civic Innovation in America: Community Empowerment, Public Policy, and the Movement for Civic Renewal* (Berkeley: University of California Press, 2001).

2. Glenn Loury, "A Dynamic Theory of Racial Income Differences," in *Women, Minorities, and Employment Discrimination,* ed. Phyllis A. Wallace and Annette Le Mund (Lexington, Mass.: Lexington, 1977).

3. Pierre Bourdieu and Jean-Claude Passeron, *Reproduction in Education, Society, and Culture,* trans. Richard Nice (London: Sage, 1977).

4. James S. Coleman, *Foundations of Social Theory* (Cambridge, Mass.: Harvard University Press, 1990); Nan Lin, *Social Capital: A Theory of Social Structure and Ac-*

tion (London: Cambridge University Press, 2001). On the concept of social capital and its applications, see Partha Dasgupta and Ismail Serageldin, eds., *Social Capital: A Multifaceted Perspective*, (Washington, D.C.: World Bank, 2000); Ben Fine, *Social Capital versus Social Theory: Political Economy and Social Science at the Turn of the Millennium* (New York: Routledge, 2001); Robert D. Putnam, ed., *Democracies in Flux: The Evolution of Social Capital in Contemporary Society* (Oxford: Oxford University Press, 2002); Christiaan Grootaert and Thierry Van Bastelaer, eds., *The Role of Social Capital in Development: An Empirical Assessment* (Cambridge: Cambridge University Press, 2002); Lin, *Social Capital*; Robert I. Rotberg, ed., *Patterns of Social Capital: Stability and Change in Historical Perspective* (Cambridge: Cambridge University Press, 2001); and Michael Woolcock, "Social Capital and Economic Development: Toward a Theoretical Synthesis and Policy Framework," *Theory and Society* 27, no. 3 (1998): 151–208. On the background in Tocqueville see Axel Hadenius, *Institutions and Democratic Citizenship* (Oxford: Oxford University Press, 2001) and Harvey C. Mansfield and Delba Winthrop, "Editors' Introduction," in Alexis de Tocqueville, *Democracy in America*, trans. Harvey C. Mansfield and Delba Winthrop (Chicago: University of Chicago Press, 2000).

5. Robert D. Putnam, *Making Democracy Work: Civic Traditions in Modern Italy* (Princeton: Princeton University Press, 1993).

6. For critical discussion of Putnam's argument, see Bob Edwards and Michael W. Foley, "Social Capital and Civil Society Beyond Putnam," *American Behavioral Scientist* 42, no. 1 (1998): 124–39; Margaret Levi, "Social and Unsocial Capital: A Review Essay of Robert Putnam's *Making Democracy Work*," *Politics and Society* 24, no. 1 (1996): 45–55; and Filippo Sabetti, "Path Dependency and Civic Culture: Some Lessons from Italy about Interpreting Social Experiments," *Politics and Society* 24, no. 1 (1996): 19–44.

7. For Loasby, by contrast, social capital is located not in networks but in practical skills:

> Institutions are a response to uncertainty. They are patterns acquired from others that guide individual actions, even when these actions are quite unconnected with any other person. They economize on the scarce resource of cognition, by providing us with ready-made anchors of sense, ways of partitioning the space of representations, premises for decisions, and bounds within which we can be rational—or imaginative. They constitute a capital stock of other people's reusable knowledge, although, like all knowledge, this is fallible. In fact, just as Marshall recognized the importance for firms of supplementing their own internal organization with an external organization, so each of us finds life much more manageable if we supplement our own internally organized cognition with the externally organized social capital that is the accretion of many other people's cognition. We are therefore not restricted to our own apparatus of classification in trying to make sense of our surroundings.

Brian J. Loasby, *Knowledge, Institutions, and Evolution in Economics* (New York: Routledge, 1999), 46. Somewhat similarly, Ostrom locates social capital in the governance systems that local communities evolve for managing common resources such as water. Elinor Ostrom, "Social Capital: A Fad or a Fundamental Concept?" in *Social Capital: A Multifaceted Perspective*, ed. Partha Dasgupta and Ismail Serageldin (Washington, D.C.: World Bank, 2000). A significant difference between Putnam and these authors is that, for Putnam, social capital is sufficiently generic that it can readily be transferred from one institutional setting to another. For Loasby and Ostrom, by contrast, social capital consists of concrete practical skills that are embedded in particular institutions.

8. Kenneth J. Arrow, "Observations on Social Capital," in *Social Capital: A Multifaceted Perspective,* ed. Partha Dasgupta and Ismail Serageldin (Washington, D.C.: World Bank, 2000); Geoffrey M. Hodgson, *How Economics Forgot History: The Problem of Historical Specificity in Social Science* (New York: Routledge, 2001), 162; Stephen Samuel Smith and Jessica Kulynych, "It May be Social, but Why Is It Capital? The Social Construction of Social Capital and the Politics of Language," *Politics and Society* 30, no. 1 (2002): 149–86. But see also Lin, *Social Capital,* 19.

9. For extensive empirical evidence that the structure of social networks affects career advancement, see Ronald S. Burt, *Structural Holes: The Social Structure of Competition* (Cambridge: Harvard University Press, 1995); and Nan Lin, Karen S. Cook, and Ronald S. Burt, eds., *Social Capital: Theory and Research* (De Gruyter, 2001). For background, see James E. Rauch and Alessandra Casella, eds., *Networks and Markets* (New York: Russell Sage Foundation, 2001) and Neil J. Smelser and Richard Swedberg, eds., *The Handbook of Economic Sociology* (Princeton: Princeton University Press, 1994).

10. Robert D. Putnam, *Bowling Alone: The Collapse and Revival of American Community* (New York: Simon and Schuster, 2000). This new work makes a stronger empirical case for claims that Putnam originally put forth in his celebrated but controversial article alleging a decline of social capital in the United States. See Robert Putnam, "Bowling Alone: America's Declining Social Capital," *Journal of Democracy* 6, no. 1 (1995): 65–78. For critical analysis of Putnam's original argument, see Michael Schudson, "What If Civic Life Didn't Die?" *American Prospect* 25 (1996): 17–20.

11. Hernando De Soto, *The Mystery of Capital: Why Capitalism Triumphs in the West and Fails Everywhere Else* (New York: Basic Books, 2000).

12. Cohen and Fields argue that Putnam's theory of social capital as a generalized disposition toward association does not explain the economic success of Silicon Valley, with its high levels of network-building and near-zero levels of civic engagement. Instead, they argue that Silicon Valley's social capital cannot be dissociated from its unique ensemble of institutions. Those institutions include the great research universities, government research and development policies, venture capital, stock options, and the specific nature of the computer industry. The social capital of other economic and political regions, even ones as superficially similar as the Route 128 technology corridor near Boston, may well be embedded in quite different institutions. See Stephen S. Cohen and Gary Fields, "Social Capital and Capital Gains: An Examination of Social Capital in Silicon Valley," in *Understanding Silicon Valley: The Anatomy of an Entrepreneurial Region,* ed. Martin Kenney (Stanford, Calif: Stanford University Press, 2000).

Krishna also connects the concept of social capital to that of institutions. He usefully subdivides social capital into two kinds: institutional capital, which is the collection of formal mechanisms for organizing activity with which a given community has experience, and relationship capital, which is the collection of established personal relationships among the individuals in a community. The two forms of social capital are complementary, and each is necessary for a strong and flexible social system. This way of defining the concepts is somewhat problematic: Institutions comprise more than just formal rules, and relationships are generally organized by institutions. Even so, Krishna's analysis does provide one way of overcoming the industrial world's inattention to the institutional foundations of development. See Anirudh Krishna, "Creating and Harnessing Social Capital," in *Social Capital: A Multifaceted Perspective*, ed. Partha Dasgupta and Ismail (Washington, D.C.: World Bank, 2000). On the role of institutions in development, see Karla Hoff and Joseph E. Stiglitz, "Modern Economic Theory and Development," in *Frontiers of Development Economics: The Future in Perspective*, ed. Gerald M. Meier and Joseph E. Stiglitz (New York: Oxford University Press, 2001). On institutions in civil society, see Robert N. Bellah, "The Good Society: We Live through Our Institutions," in *The Essential Civil Society Reader: Classic Essays in the American Civil Society Debate*, ed. Don E. Eberly (Lanham, Md: Rowman & Littlefield, 2000) and Sheri Berman, "Civil Society and Political Institutionalization," *American Behavioral Scientist* 40, no. 5 (1997): 562–74.

13. Very unusually in the literature, Mansbridge actually found and studied two polities that approximate the deliberative myth. She emphasizes the ongoing work of maintaining relationships outside of the venues of formal decision-making, and she argues that the ideal of deliberation requires the citizens to have the same interests. For both these reasons, she concludes that the deliberative ideal is inapplicable to large-scale politics. Jane Mansbridge, *Beyond Adversary Democracy* (New York: Basic Books, 1980). On the idea that participation in politics makes one a better person, see Jane Mansbridge, "On the Idea That Participation Makes Better Citizens," in *Citizen Competence and Democratic Institutions*, ed. Stephen L. Elkin and Karol Edward Soltan (University Park: Pennsylvania State University Press, 1999). Although Mansbridge argues that the idea in its full-blown form is recent, elements of it are much older. On the concept of deliberative democracy generally, see James Bohman and William Rehg, eds., *Deliberative Democracy: Essays on Reason and Politics* (Cambridge: MIT Press, 1997); John S. Dryzek, *Deliberative Democracy and Beyond: Liberals, Critics, Contestations* (Oxford: Oxford University Press, 2002); Jon Elster, ed., *Deliberative Democracy* (Cambridge: Cambridge University Press, 1998); Amy Gutmann and Dennis Thompson, *Democracy and Disagreement* (Cambridge: Harvard University Press, 1996); Harold Hongju Koh and Ronald C. Slye, eds., *Deliberative Democracy and Human Rights* (New Haven, Conn.: Yale University Press, 1999); and Carlos Santiago Nino, *The Constitution of Deliberative Democracy* (New Haven: Yale University Press, 1996). On the related but distinct concept of participatory democracy, see Carol Pateman, *Participation and Democratic Theory* (Cambridge: Cambridge University Press, 1970). Of course, these theories of deliberative democracy vary, and not all of them subscribe to every element of the myth that I have described. The overall picture, though, is quite consistent. For diverse criticisms of Habermas's theory of deliberative democracy in particular, with Habermas's informative response, see Craig Calhoun, ed., *Habermas and the Public Sphere* (Cambridge: MIT Press, 1992).

14. Michael Schudson, *The Good Citizen: A History of American Public Life* (New York: Free Press, 1998); see also Michael Schudson, "Why Conversation Is Not the Soul of Democracy," *Critical Studies in Mass Communication* 14, no. 4 (1997): 297–309; and Michael Schudson, "Sending a Political Message: Lessons from the American 1790s," *Media, Culture, and Society* 19, no. 3 (1997): 311–30.

15. Schudson, *The Good Citizen*, 16–19.

16. See, for example, Johan P. Olsen, *Organized Democracy: Political Institutions in a Welfare State, the Case of Norway* (Bergen: Universitetsforlaget, 1983).

17. Mansbridge, *Beyond*, 60–64; Schudson "Conversation," 301–302.

18. It is, however, to acknowledge somewhat ruefully the empirical accuracy in most democratic polities to date of what Etzioni-Halevy calls the demo-elite theory. According to this theory, the feasibility of democratic government depends on the elites of many different institutional fields (business, education, the arts, and so on) having enough resources under their command to maintain their autonomy in relation to the state. If the state is able to undermine the autonomy of these institutions, then the result will be some form of corporatism, or worse. In a society where the social skills of association are unevenly distributed, being in essence restricted to the various elites, this conclusion most likely follows. Whether the autonomy of sectoral elites is a significant consideration in a society where political skills are universally taught in grade school is another matter. See Eva Etzioni-Halevy, *The Elite Connection: Problems and Potential of Western Democracy* (Cambridge, Mass.: Polity Press, 1993).

19. Craig Calhoun, "Community without Propinquity Revisited: Communications Technology and the Transformation of the Urban Public Sphere," *Sociological Inquiry* 68, no. 3 (1998): 373–97.

20. Gabriel Tarde, *On Communication and Social Influence: Selected Papers*, ed. Terry N. Clark (Chicago: University of Chicago Press, 1969). Originally published in French in 1898; cited in Schudson, "Conversation," 304–305.

21. Philip E. Agre, "Legitimacy and Reason in the Florida Election Controversy," *Social Studies of Science* 31, no. 3 (2001): 419–22.

22. Philip E. Agre, "Real-Time Politics: The Internet and the Political Process," *Information Society* 18, no. 5 (2002): 311–31.

23. Alfred L. Kroeber, "The Superorganic," *American Anthropologist* 19, no. 2 (1917): 163–213.

24. James Bohman, "Citizenship and Norms of Publicity: Wide Public Reason in Cosmopolitan Societies," *Political Theory* 27, no. 2 (1999): 176–202.

25. The phrase "marketplace of ideas" is widely attributed to John Stuart Mill (*On Liberty* [1859; reprint, London: Penguin, 1974]), but as Gordon observes, "this metaphor does not come from Mill's own text . . . and quite to the contrary . . . does not reflect accurately Mill's views on free speech." See Jill Gordon, "John Stuart Mill and the 'Marketplace of Ideas,'" *Social Theory and Practice* 23, no. 2 (1997): 235. The metaphor is also often falsely attributed to Milton's *Areopagitica*. It is best known from its use in Oliver Wendell Holmes's dissent in *Abrams v. United States*, 250 U.S. 616 (1919). Yet even there the precise phrase "marketplace of ideas" does not occur. Holmes in fact says "the ultimate good desired is better reached by free trade in ideas" and "the best test of truth is the power of the thought to get itself accepted in the competition of the market" (both at 630). The text is available at http://usinfo .state.gov/usa/infousa/facts/democrac/43.htm (accessed January 26, 2003).

26. On republicanism and its history, see William J. Connell, "The Republican Idea," in *Renaissance Civic Humanism: Reappraisals and Reflections*, ed. James Hankins (Cambridge: Cambridge University Press, 2000); Philip Pettit, *Republicanism: A Theory of Freedom and Government* (Oxford: Oxford University Press, 1997); Cass R. Sunstein, "The Enduring Legacy of Republicanism," in *A New Constitutional-*

ism: Designing Political Institutions for a Good Society, ed. Stephen L. Elkin and Karol Edward Soltan (Chicago: University of Chicago Press, 1993); Martin Van Gelderen and Quentin Skinner, eds., *Republicanism: A Shared European Heritage* (Cambridge: Cambridge University Press, 2002); and Maurizio Viroli, *Republicanism*, trans. Antony Shugaar (New York: Hill and Wang, 2002). An especially accessible history is William R. Everdell, *The End of Kings: A History of Republics and Republicans* (Chicago: University of Chicago Press, 2000). For the debate on the role of republican ideas in the founding of the United States, see Joyce Appleby, *Capitalism and a New Social Order: The Republican Vision of the 1790s* (New York: New York University Press, 1984); J. G. A. Pocock, *The Machiavellian Moment: Florentine Political Thought and the Atlantic Republican Tradition* (Princeton, N.J.: Princeton University Press, 1975); Paul A. Rahe, *Republics Ancient and Modern: Classical Republicanism and the American Revolution* (Chapel Hill: University of North Carolina Press, 1992); Daniel T. Rodgers, "Republicanism: The Career of a Concept," *Journal of American History* 79, no. 1 (1992): 11–38; Robert E. Shalhope, *The Roots of Democracy: American Thought and Culture, 1760–1800* (New York: Twayne, 1990); Gordon S. Wood, *The Creation of the American Republic, 1776–1787* (Chapel Hill: University of North Carolina Press, 1969); and Michael P. Zuckert, *Natural Rights and the New Republicanism* (Princeton: Princeton University Press, 1994).

27. William R. Everdell, *The End of Kings: A History of Republics and Republicans* (Chicago: University of Chicago Press, 2000), 5–6.

28. Joseph V. Femia, *Against the Masses: Varieties of Anti-Democratic Thought since the French Revolution* (Oxford: Oxford University Press, 2001).

29. On the concept of citizenship and its history, see Axel Hadenius, *Institutions and Democratic Citizenship* (Oxford: Oxford University Press, 2001); Michael Ignatieff, "The Myth of Citizenship," in *Theorizing Citizenship*, ed. Ronald Beiner (Albany: State University of New York Press, 1995; J. G. A. Pocock, "The Ideal of Citizenship since Classical Times," in *Theorizing Citizenship*, ed. Ronald Beiner (Albany: State University of New York Press, 1995); and Peter Riesenberg, *Citizenship in the Western Tradition: Plato to Rousseau* (Chapel Hill: University of North Carolina Press, 1992).

30. For a contemporary version of this, see Michael J. Sandel, *Democracy's Discontent: America in Search of a Public Philosophy* (Cambridge, Mass.: Harvard University Press, 1996).

31. Gordon S. Wood, *The Radicalism of the American Revolution* (New York: Knopf, 1992). See also Shalhope, *The Roots*.

32. Neil Fligstein, "Social Skill and the Theory of Fields," *Sociological Theory* 19, no. 2 (2001): 105–25.

33. An earlier version of the theory is presented in Neil Fligstein, "Social Skill and Institutional Theory," *American Behavioral Scientist* 40, no. 4 (1997): 397–405.

34. See, for example, Machiavelli's *Discourses on Livy*, Book 1, Chapter 9. The convergence of Fligstein's theory with the account of Machiavelli in Janet Coleman, *A History of Political Thought: From the Middle Ages to the Renaissance* (Oxford: Blackwell, 2000), is especially striking.

35. Jürgen Habermas, "Popular Sovereignty as Procedure," in *Deliberative Democracy: Essays on Reason and Politics*, ed. James Bohman and William Rehg (Cambridge, Mass.: MIT Press, 1997),51.

36. For a rare discussion of the role of social skill in democratic society, see Stephen L. Elkin and Karol Edward Soltan, eds., *Citizen Competence and Democratic Institutions* (University Park: Pennsylvania State University Press, 1999). On democratic republicanism, see C. Edwin Baker, *Media, Markets, and Democracy* (Cambridge: Cambridge University Press, 2001).

37. Anthony Downs, *An Economic Theory of Democracy* (New York: Harper, 1957).

38. Although the concept of civil society is arguably ancient, its extraordinary contemporary revival begins with John Keane, *Democracy and Civil Society: On the Predicaments of European Socialism, the Prospects for Democracy, and the Problem of Controlling Social and Political Power* (London: Verso, 1988); John Keane, ed., *Civil Society and the State: New European Perspectives* (London: Verso, 1988); and John Keane, *Civil Society: Old Images, New Visions,* (Stanford: Stanford University Press, 1998). See also Jeffrey C. Alexander, ed., *Real Civil Societies: Dilemmas of Institutionalization* (London: Sage, 1998); Jean L. Cohen and Andrew Arato, *Civil Society and Political Theory* (Cambridge, Mass.: MIT Press, 1992); Ernest Gellner, *Conditions of Liberty: Civil Society and Its Rivals* (New York: Allen Lane, 1994); John A. Hall, ed., *Civil Society: Theory, History, Comparison* (Cambridge: Polity Press, 1995); and Adam B. Seligman, *The Idea of Civil Society* (New York: Free Press, 1992). For a forcefully analytical argument for the central role of civil society in the contemporary trend toward democratization, see Graeme Gill, *The Dynamics of Democratization: Elites, Civil Society, and the Transition Process* (New York: St. Martin's Press, 2000). For historical perspectives, see Antony Black, *Guilds and Civil Society in European Political Thought from the Twelfth Century to the Present* (London: Methuen, 1984); John Ehrenberg, *Civil Society: The Critical History of an Idea* (New York: New York University Press, 1999); and Adam Ferguson, *An Essay on the History of Civil Society,* ed. Fania Oz-Salzberger (Cambridge: Cambridge University Press, 1995). The concept was also employed for rather different purposes by American conservative intellectuals in their campaign for welfare reform in the 1990s; see Peter L. Berger and Richard John Neuhaus, *To Empower People: From State to Civil Society,* 2nd ed., ed. Michael Novak (Washington, D.C.: American Enterprise Institute, 1996); Don E. Eberly, ed., *The Essential Civil Society Reader: Classic Essays in the American Civil Society Debate* (Lanham, Md: Rowman & Littlefield, 2000); and Harvey C. Mansfield and Delba Winthrop, editors' introduction to *Alexis de Tocqueville: Democracy in America,* trans. Harvey C. Mansfield and Delba Winthrop (Chicago: University of Chicago Press, 2000).

39. For comparative perspectives, see Simone Chambers and Will Kymlicka, eds., *Alternative Conceptions of Civil Society* (Princeton, N.J.: Princeton University Press, 2001); Chris Hann and Elizabeth Dunn, eds., *Civil Society: Challenging Western Models* (New York: Routledge, 1996); Jude Howell and Jenny Pearce, *Civil Society and Development: A Critical Exploration* (Boulder, Colo.: Rienner, 2001); Sudipta Kaviraj and Sunil Khilnani, eds., *Civil Society: History and Possibilities* (Cambridge: Cambridge University Press, 2001); and Michael G. Schechter, ed., *The Revival of Civil Society: Global and Comparative Perspectives* (New York: St. Martin's Press, 1999). For an especially forceful critique, see John L. Comaroff and Jean Comaroff, eds., *Civil Society and the Political Imagination in Africa: Critical Perspectives* (Chicago: University of Chicago Press, 2000).

40. It has often been observed that experts, for example the members of professions, play distinctive cognitive roles in society. See, for example, James Bohman, "Citizenship and Norms of Publicity: Wide Public Reason in Cosmopolitan Societies," *Political Theory* 27, no. 2 (1999): 176–202. My point here, though, is more general: A democratic republic will make available a repertoire of institutions and action-forms that enable any citizen, whether formally credentialed or not, to pursue a career as an issue entrepreneur.

On business entrepreneurship, see Richard Swedberg, ed., *Entrepreneurship: The Social Science View* (Oxford: Oxford University Press, 2000); and Mark Casson, *Enterprise and Leadership: Studies on Firms, Markets, and Networks* (Cheltenham, UK: Elgar, 2000). On entrepreneurship in the university context, see Burton R. Clark, *Creating Entrepreneurial Universities: Organizational Pathways of Transformation* (Oxford: Pergamon Press, 1998). In the context of cultural institutions, see Paul DiMaggio, "Culture Entrepreneurship in Nineteenth-century Boston: The Creation of an Organizational Base for High Culture in America," *Media, Culture, and Society* 4, no. 1 (1982): 33–50; and Paul DiMaggio, "Culture Entrepreneurship in Nineteenth-Century Boston, Part II: The Classification and Framing of American Art," *Media, Culture, and Society* 4, no. 4 (1982): 303–22.

In the context of social movements, see Mayer N. Zald and John D. McCarthy, eds, *Social Movements in an Organizational Society: Collected Essays* (New Brunswick, N.J.: Transaction, 1987); and Charles Spinosa, Fernando Flores, and Hubert L. Dreyfus, *Disclosing New Worlds: Entrepreneurship, Democratic Action, and the Cultivation of Solidarity* (Cambridge, Mass.: MIT Press, 1997). McCarthy and Zald use the phrase "issue entrepreneurs." Their emphasis, however, is on movements generally, and they do not develop a general theory of the issue entrepreneur as an individual, or of issue entrepreneurship as a form of social practice.

Political scientists also use the phrase to refer to politicians who build electoral coalitions by pioneering new political issues. Schneider and Teske, for example, draw out the analogy between politicians' issue entrepreneurship and the economic theory of business entrepreneurship. See Mark Schneider and Paul Teske, "Toward a Theory of the Political Entrepreneur: Evidence from Local Government," *American Political Science Review* 86, no. 3 (1992): 737–47.

In his lecture "Politics as a Vocation," Weber describes the professional political as an entrepreneur. Max Weber, "Politics as a Vocation," in *From Max Weber: Essays in Sociology*, ed. H. H. Gerth and C. Wright Mills (New York: Oxford University Press, 1946), 86, 102–105, 109. In each case, though, he is referring to the methods that politicians (and not citizens generally) use to turn political activity into a paying job. He also briefly discusses the business entrepreneur's role in politics, or lack thereof (85, 100).

41. Garrett Birkhoff, *Lattice Theory*, 3rd ed. (Providence, R.I.: American Mathematical Society, 1967).

42. In Burt's terms, citizens establish places for themselves in the issue lattice by filling structural holes–that is, networking among diverse individuals among whom the newly emerging issue creates opportunities for arbitrage, agenda-setting, and other forms of entrepreneurial gain. See Ronald S. Burt, *Structural Holes: The Social Structure of Competition* (Cambridge, Mass.: Harvard University Press, 1995).

Like the issue lattice theory, Lin's theory of social capital asserts that the social system is organized as a hierarchical social network. But Lin offers little explanation of how individuals attain their particular locations on one stratum or another except to say that they invest effort in establishing new social links with people on the strata above them. See Lin, *Social Capital*, 36–39.

43. The theoretical consequences of this point may be considerable. Even as it provides a substantive theory of the social mechanisms that underlie civil society, the theory of issue entrepreneurship also undermines to some degree the very concept of civil society as something distinct from, and set against, the institutions of the state. The pervasively fractal nature of issue entrepreneurship implies that the same social logic organizes political processes in every institution, including both state and nonstate institutions. What is more, the issue lattice of a functioning democratic republic knits the social networks of the state into those of nearly every other sphere of society. Although it is commonly held that democracy requires a robust civil society (see note 38), it is entirely possible that democracy in fact requires a robust political culture—a culture in which the skills of issue entrepreneurship are thoroughly ingrained in the language, values, and action forms of everyday life. Perhaps that kind of political culture must satisfy additional institutional constraints, such as a distinction and opposition between civil society and the state. But before the question can be usefully asked, categories such as association and civil society need to be rethought. As Habermas aptly notes, "as an organizational form, an association lacks the complexity necessary to structure the social fabric as a whole." Habermas, "Popular Sovereignty," 54.

Arguing from a conservative perspective, however, Zijdervald asserts that social networks are replacing the institutions within which people formerly found their positions in society. He worries, though, that mere networks may be incapable of serving the socializing, value-instilling function of traditional institutions. See Anton C. Zijdervald, *The Institutional Imperative: The Value of Institutions in Contemporary Society* (Amsterdam: Amsterdam University Press, 2000).

Similarly, Sandel argues that "by the mid- to late twentieth century . . . the [United States] proved too vast a scale across which to cultivate the shared self-understandings necessary to community in the formative, or constitutive sense. And so the gradual shift, in our practices and institutions, from a public philosophy of common purpose to one of fair procedures, from a politics of good to a politics of right, from the national republic to the procedural republic." Sandel, *Democracy's Discontent*, 93.

44. Habermas, "Popular Sovereignty" 59. Similarly, March and Olsen warn against a conflation between the quite distinct concepts of community membership and civic identity. James G. March and Johan P. Olsen, *Democratic Governance* (New York: Free Press, 1995), 38.

45. See Agre, "Real-Time Politics"; Darin Barney, *Prometheus Wired: The Hope for Democracy in the Age of Network Technology* (Chicago: University of Chicago Press, 2000); Barbara Becker and Josef Wehner, "Electronic Networks and Civil Society: Reflections on Structural Changes in the Public Sphere," in *Culture, Technology, Communication: Towards an Intercultural Global Village,* ed. Charles Ess (New York: State University of New York Press, 2001); Hubertus Buchstein, "Bytes That Bite: The Internet and Deliberative Democracy," *Constellations* 4, no. 2 (1997): 248–63; Ann M. Florini, "Who Does What? Collective Action and the Changing Nature of Authority," in *Non-State Actors and Authority in the Global System,* ed. Richard A. Higgott, Geoffrey R. D. Underhill, and Andreas Bieler (New York: Routledge, 2000); Kenneth L. Hacker

and Jan van Dijk, eds., *Digital Democracy: Issues of Theory and Practice* (London: Sage, 2001); Barry N. Hague and Brian Loader, eds., *Digital Democracy: Discourse and Decision Making in the Information Age* (New York: Routledge, 1999); Jens Hoff, Ivan Horrocks, and Pieter Tops, eds., *Democratic Governance and New Technology: Technologically Mediated Innovations in Political Practice in Western Europe* (New York: Routledge, 2000); Neil Netanel, "Cyberspace Self-Governance: A Skeptical View from Democratic Theory," *California Law Review* 88, no. 2 (2000): 395–498; and Pippa Norris, *Digital Divide: Civic Engagement, Information Poverty, and the Internet Worldwide* (Cambridge: Cambridge University Press, 2001).

46. See, for example, Edward O. Laumann and David Knoke, "Policy Networks of the Organizational State: Collective Action in the National Energy and Health Domains," in *Networks of Power: Organizational Actors at the National, Corporate, and Community Levels*, ed. Robert Perrucci and Harry R. Potter (New York: Aldine de Gruyter, 1989).

47. Berkowitz argues that proposals for deliberative democracy unfairly tilt the political playing field toward the very sorts of sophisticated and articulate individuals who tend to support them, and a similar objection might be raised to my own proposals here. In each case, though, the obvious response is the same: You cannot have a democratic republic without an educated citizenry, and one purpose of a democratic republican political theory is to sketch the syllabus for the necessary education. See Peter Berkowitz, "The Debating Society," *The New Republic* 215, no. 25 (November 1996): 36–42.

48. Agre, "Real-Time Politics," 311–12.

12

On Virtual, Democratic Communities

Amitai Etzioni

COMMUNITIES DEFINED

The very term "community" has often been criticized as a concept that is vague and elusive, as a term that either has not been defined or cannot be defined, and as one that is used because of its political appeal rather than its scholarly merit.[1] In response one should note, first of all, that terms commonly used in social science often resist precise definition, as in the case of such widely used concepts as rationality and class. And while "community" has often been used without an explicit definition, I have previously suggested the following definition. Communities are social entities that have two elements. One, a web of affect-laden relationships among a group of individuals, relationships that often crisscross and reinforce one another (rather than merely one-on-one or chainlike individual relationships). The other, a measure of commitment to a set of shared values, norms, and meanings, and a shared history and identity—in short, to a particular culture.[2]

Among those who responded to this definition of community, Benjamin Zablocki noted that while the definition is quite clear, few communities left in modern societies meet its requirements.[3] This is a common concern that has been with us since Emile Durkheim and Ferdinand Tönnies suggested that modern history is marked by a transition from Gemeinschaft to Gesselschaft. Others have viewed our society as a "mass" society composed of individuals without shared bonds or values. Actually, while there has been a decline in community, many social entities that fit the definition provided above abound even in large metropolitan areas. These communities are often ethnicity based. Communities such as this are found in Little Havana, Chinatown, Koreatown, Spanish Harlem, on the south shore of Boston, and in Williamsburg, New York, among many other locations. Others are composed of people who share a sexual orientation (for instance, gay communities) or an occupation (for instance, the medical staff of some hospitals).

Important for the discussion that follows is that communities, as defined, need not be local or residential. The faculty of some small colleges make one community even if they do not live next door to one another or on the campus. The same holds for the members of a labor union local.

The definition excludes interest groups. Groups of people who merely share an interest in lower tariffs, in gaining a tax deduction, and so on, as a rule do not a community make. They share no affective bonds nor a moral culture. (Of course, some social entities can both be a community and share some interests, but this does not negate the difference between these two concepts.) In short, communities can be defined and are far from defunct.

ARE THERE VIRTUAL COMMUNITIES?

Many of those who argue that there can be no true communities in cyberspace implicitly follow a different notion as to what a community is than the one relied on here (which, in my judgment, is quite close to what most people mean when they employ the term). These critics of virtual communities have in mind numerous accidental rather than essential features of offline communities, such as face-to-face meetings. One should grant that online communities do not have all the features of offline ones (nor do offline communities have all the features of online ones). But the question is: Can cyberspace meet the basic prerequisites of communities?[4]

The answer is affirmative, although one must grant that the needed prerequisites are not often provided, at least not in full. Indeed, there is a distinct inclination by commercial sites to pretend that community exists (because such claims bring "eyeballs" to one's site) where there is none. To provide but one example, GeoCities purports to provide neighborhoods and neighborhood clubs within their community, but these neighborhoods simply amount to collections of home pages and chat rooms that are about the same topic (for instance, Sunset Strip is a neighborhood of home pages and chat rooms devoted to the discussion of rock and punk rock).

More generally, a very large part of the communications and transactions on the Internet either are not interactive at all (placing an order for a consumer product) or are only point to point (exchange of e-mail messages), which by themselves do not make communities. In 1998, according to a survey conducted by the Pew Center for the People and the Press, the following percentages of online users engaged in the following activities at least once a week: 72 percent sent e-mail, 47 percent did research for work, and 38 percent got news on current events, public issues, and politics. Far fewer users participated in online group activities. Only 22 percent engaged in online forums or chat groups, and only 4 percent engaged in online political discussions.[5] A recent Gallup poll provided similar results, reporting that 95 percent of people online use the Internet to obtain information, 85 percent to send or receive e-mail, and 45 percent use it for shopping, while only 21 percent visit chat rooms.[6]

All that these facts show is that, just like offline interactions, the greater part of online interactions are not community focused. They do not, however, indicate that communities cannot be formed on the Internet.

There are numerous informal accounts of strong affective bonds, the first element of community, formed via the Internet as people who did not previously know one another meet on the Internet and form intense relationships. There are a fair number of reports of people who abandon their spouses on the basis of liaisons they formed online, and some of singles who met in cyberspace and married.

The second element, forming a shared moral culture, is met much less often. At first, it may seem that chat rooms could provide opportunities for developing such a culture (as well as affective bonds) because at first glance they bear some resemblance to communities: groups of people meet and interact. The main reason, in my judgment, that the hundreds of thousands of chat rooms that exist do not, as a rule, provide for shared cultures (nor affective bonds) is the way they are set up. Typically, chat room participants use aliases and are keen to maintain their anonymity. Exchanges are very brief and intersected by other exchanges that occur in the same "space." Participants tend to engage in very limited exchanges and often engage in a false presentation of self.[7] As a result, piecing together a picture of the person one deals with, which may well be a prerequisite for forming shared values (as well as affective relationships), is hampered. The situation is akin to meeting someone for the first time on a bar stool or on an airplane flight. Conversation tends to be superficial and no relationship develops.[8]

The conditions under which virtual communities would thrive are, in effect, the mirror opposite of chat rooms: membership would be limited in number and relatively stable, members would have to disclose their true identity, and it would be verified. In addition, the subjects explored would cover a broad range rather than be limited to a few such as stock tips or dating-related banter. The fact that so far these conditions are infrequently satisfied should not be viewed as suggesting that they cannot be met; it merely suggests that they do not readily lend themselves to profit-making (and hence are of little interest to those who run chat rooms on the Internet), and that they conflict with the individualistic ideologies of those who originally shaped the Internet.

While the said conditions for successful community building are rarely satisfied in full by such chat rooms, some are met via thousands of so-called clubs run by Yahoo!, Excite, and eCircles. Membership in these clubs is limited to a given number (say, two thousand). In some, users need to apply to become a member. While many of these clubs are listed in indexes maintained on the respective websites, one can refuse to list a club in order to protect it from open-ended participation.

At the same time, these clubs do not provide for disclosure of self or verified identity. In addition, the topics they specialize in are often quite narrow and limited; for example, examples of Excite clubs include Amateur Astronomers (1159 members), Amateur Models of Virginia (1046 members), and The Homebrewing Club (340 members).

ECircles has a more personal focus than other online club sites. It provides families and friends with private areas within cyberspace to meet and exchange messages, and is less interest or issue based. H-net runs some eighty clubs that fully meet the said conditions: not only is participation limited, but identities are disclosed. (Albeit the subjects under discussion are rather specialized, such as French literature in one club and certain periods of German history in another.) So far there are no studies of the community-building effects of these clubs, although personal observation suggests that they are considerably stronger than those of the typical chat rooms.

MediaMOO has been occasionally referred to as a true online community, although the extent to which it lives up to this description is unclear at least.[9] Howard Rheingold's accounts of online communities are often cited as examples of the possibility of developing close relationships and a rich emotional life online. For instance, he describes an online funeral he attended as a "rite of passage for all of [the virtual community] CIX, a time when the original members of the group felt closest to each other."[10] According to Rheingold, there were strong affective bonds among group members and there was a shared group history and culture (the group Rheingold describes qualifies as a real community according to the definition of community I proposed above).

Finally, one should also not overlook that some online communities work to complement and reinforce existing offline communities. (I refer to these as hybrid communities.) There is something artificial about the very way the question is typically posed, comparing virtual to other communities. After all, nobody lives in cyberspace; even the avatars in Neal Stephenson's *Snow Crash* are put on by three-dimensional people. The more realistic questions that arise concern community (and democracy) in a new world in which there are both on and offline group relationships. (Rheingold, who is a firm believer in the depth of online relationships and community, nevertheless describes how his online relationships often led to face-to-face meetings and friendships.)

Among the reports of neighborhood communities significantly reinforced by virtual links is the often-cited example of Blacksburg, Virginia. Around 87 percent of Blacksburg's residents are online,[11] and the town has an online community called Blacksburg Electronic Village (www.bev.net). Both the town and the various groups and neighborhoods in it benefit from their ability to post meetings, share information, and interact via the shared site.

All said and done, there are very few reports of full-fledged, purely online communities. It is rather difficult to establish whether the reason for this finding is that the Internet has not been set up to facilitate community building despite the fact that this could be quite readily done, or (as several have argued) there is something in its structure that inherently prevents true community formation. I personally hold that communities would thrive if stable and disclosed membership would be made relatively easy to attain, but this remains to be demonstrated. There is, though, little doubt that online communities can significantly reinforce offline ones.

Quantitative Data

The discussion so far has focused on so-called qualitative observations, one case at a time. There is, though, considerable quantitative data concerning the ability to form and sustain social relations on the Internet. Because these data concern not merely friendships (which can be merely between two people, and are hence point-to-point) but also families (which contain community-like web relationships), these data speak to the question of whether one of the key prerequisites of community building can be met online.

The question of whether cyberspace agitates social bonds or enriches it has been recently examined by several studies. One study, by Norman H. Nie and Lutz Erbring, has claimed to find that the Internet is detrimental to such bonding.[12] According to them, "the more hours people use the Internet, the less time they spend in contact with real human beings."

Nie and Erbring say, "Internet time is coming out of time viewing television but also out at the expense of time people spend on the phone gabbing with family and friends or having a conversation with people in the room with them." They acknowledge that most Internet users use e-mail, which increases their "conversations" with family and friends via this medium, "but you can't share a coffee or a beer with somebody on e-mail or give them a hug." In short, "The Internet could be the ultimate isolating technology that further reduces our participation in communities even more than did automobiles and television before it."[13]

The findings of the study are summarized as follows:

- 13 percent spend less time with family and friends
- 8 percent attend fewer social events
- 34 percent spend less time reading the newspaper
- 59 percent spend less time watching television

- 25 percent spend less time shopping in stores
- 25 percent are working more at home (without any decline in work at the office)[14]

What do Nie's and Erbring's figures actually show? In discussing the findings, one must note that they concern two groups of people: those who are not connected to the Internet (N=2,078) and those who are connected (N=2,035). The latter are further divided into light users (less than five hours per week; 64 percent of the "connected" sample) and heavy users (more than five hours per week; 36 percent of the "connected" sample).

Of all users only 9 percent said that they spend less time with their family, and 9 percent said they spend less with their friends, while nearly ten times more people—86 percent and 87 percent respectively—said that they spend the same amount of time with family and friends as before! Moreover, quite a few (6 percent and 4 percent respectively) reported that they spend more time with family and friends. The proper headline of their study should have been: "Internet does not significantly affect social life."

The picture does not change much even if one focuses on the heavy users. Only 10 percent of those who spend five to ten hours online per week reported that they spend less time with family and friends, and only 15 percent of those who are online ten or more hours per week said so.

The finding that some Internet users spend more time with family and friends may at first seem unlikely, but it is hardly so. The study itself shows that by far the largest effect of Internet activity for all users is to reduce the amount of time spent watching TV (46 percent of users) and shopping (19 percent). For heavy users, 59 percent spend less time watching TV and 25 percent spend less time shopping. (Obviously it takes less time to order things from eToys or Amazon than to go to a mall or store.) The study did not inquire into how the time saved in these ways is used and whether or not some of it is allocated to increasing social life.

Along the same lines, the study found—as is widely known—that people's most common use of the Internet is communicating via e-mail. This, too, is a time-saving device compared to letter writing and even phone calls. Ergo the Internet readily allows people to spend both more time on the Internet and more time socializing. In effect, the fact that people use the Internet largely for communication (90 percent use e-mail) and not shopping (36 percent buy products online) or banking (12 percent), and that most of this communication is with people they are familiar with rather than with strangers, strongly suggests that people relate to one another more rather than less because of the Internet.

A study on technology by the Kaiser Family Foundation, National Public Radio, and Harvard's Kennedy School of Government reported the following findings:

Despite their overall positive attitudes, Americans do see some problems with computers and technology. . . . More than half say computers have led people to spend less time with their families and friends (58 percent). Furthermore, slightly fewer than half (46 percent) of Americans say that computers have given people less free time, although 24 percent who say computers have given people more free time and 28 percent who say computers haven't made much of a difference.[15]

Note, though, that people were asked about computer use, not their Internet connections. The question people were asked was: Do you think the use of computers has given people more free time, less free time, or hasn't it made much difference? This kind of question makes people think about noninteractive uses of their computers, especially word processing, preparing documents, number crunching, and so on. Questions about use of the Internet, which is merely one function of computers, are more revealing.

A study released in May 2000 by the Pew Internet and American Life Project found clear evidence that email and the Web have enhanced users' relationships with their family and friends—results that challenge the notion that the Internet contributes to isolation. Significant majorities of online Americans say their use of email has increased the amount of contact they have with key family members and friends. Fifty-nine percent of those who exchange email with a family member say they are in contact with that relative more often thanks to email. Only 2 percent say they are in contact less often with this family member since they struck up their e-correspondence. Email users say virtually the same thing about the frequency of their contact with close friends via e-letters. Sixty percent of those who email friends say they communicate more often with a key friend now that they use email and 2 percent say they do so less often.

Additional Pew findings make an even stronger case:

As a group, Internet users are more likely than nonusers to have a robust social world. The use of email seems to encourage deeper social connectedness. The longer users have been online, the more likely it is that they feel that email has improved their ties to their families and friends. Forty percent of Internet veterans—those who have been online for at least three years—say there has been a lot of improvement in their connections with family and friends because of email, compared with just over a quarter of Internet newcomers (those online for six months or less) who report that.

Even more impressive are the Pew findings that

more than those who have no Internet access, Internet users say they have a significant network of helpful relatives and friends. Some 48 percent of Internet users say they can turn to many people for support in a time of need, while just 38 percent of nonusers report they have a large social network. Furthermore, only 8 percent of Internet users indicate they are socially isolated—that is, they say they have no one or hardly anyone they can turn to for support. In contrast, 18 percent of nonusers say they have no one or hardly anyone to turn to.[16]

Finally, a Harris poll found that

> because people are online, they tend to communicate more often with their friends and family. Almost half (48 percent) of all adults who are online at home say they communicate more often with friends and family than they did before they could use email. Only 3 percent say they communicate less.
>
> Perhaps the most interesting finding is that many more people say that they meet and socialize with friends and family more often because of the Internet than do so less often (27 percent v. 9 percent). This debunks the theory that Internet users cut themselves off physically from social interaction.[17]

All said and done, meaningful and reinforcing interactions seem to be quite common in the online world. Under what conditions these suffice to satisfy the first prerequisite for community remains to be established. As I argued in the previous section, the conditions for forming shared cultures are possible to create online, but they are not often provided. Call me moderately optimistic on this account. As I see it, the evidence suggests that if the Internet were to be made more community friendly along the lines discussed in the first section, online communities might be much more common.

CYBERSPACE DEMOCRACY

The same question can be applied to online, offline, and hybrid communities: Can they be democratically governed by drawing on the Internet? For democracy to thrive, at least four prerequisites must be satisfied. Numerous studies show that two key prerequisites, sharing information and voting, are quite feasible on the Internet. The third element, that of deliberation, has been explored much less often but, as I explain below, seems to pose no insurmountable difficulties once Internet designers put their mind to fashioning the software needed for deliberation in cyberspace. The same holds for the fourth element, that of representation.

Much has been made in several writings on the subject, and even more in numerous projects dedicated to the subject, that information can be distributed, stored, retrieved, duplicated, and illustrated with much greater ease and at much lower costs on the Internet than in the offline world. This is undoubtably true. One should not, however, accord too much importance to information sharing as an element of democratic governance. True, it is helpful to provide voters with all the speeches made by politicians, a full catalogue of all the positions they have taken in the past, and every vote they have cast. The same is true of having websites chock full of information about the issues of the day.

However, at the end of the day, voters can cast only one vote per election. For instance, in a presidential election they cannot vote for the environmental policies of a given candidate but against his foreign policy, for his position on choice but against his ideas about health insurance, and so on. Hence, detailed information about these issues and the positions of the candidate are not particularly useful for their decisions as to for whom to vote.

Those who suggest that people's decisions take the form of an index in which they would inform themselves about numerous issues and then vote for the candidate who gets the highest score, do not take into account that, in actuality, decisions typically seem to be made in a lexographic form: two or three considerations (for instance, the state of the economy and whether or not the country is involved in a war) make up for most of the "index" for most voters.

More important, the process is much less information-driven for numerous voters than is quite often assumed. Values, party affiliations, and loyalties and community pressures play a very important role in determining the one choice they can make.

In short, the fabulous information features of the Internet are prodemocratic, but they surely add much less to existing democratic institutions than the more dedicated information enthusiasts presume.[18]

Initially there was great concern that voting on the Internet would lead to large-scale ballot box stuffing, fraud, and other forms of electoral abuse. However, as new encryption techniques have developed and procedures for recognizing e-signatures have been approved, these concerns have subsided. It seems that in the future, with proper procedures in place, e-voting could be made at least as secure as offline voting, which, after all, has never been perfectly authenticated.

The main difficulty in this area lies elsewhere, namely in access. Democracy, of course, requires that all those who have reached a given age and are citizens of a given polity and have not been convicted of a crime will be allowed to vote. At the moment, significant parts of the population, especially the poorer and otherwise disadvantaged, do not have personal computers and hence cannot vote electronically. However, this defect is rapidly being corrected as the cost of computers and other devices that allow access to the Internet are plunging. Providing the rest of the population with a device needed to vote could be easily contemplated.

France long ago provided all citizens with devices resembling personal computers to provide them access to Minitel, France's pre-Internet public electronic system. While Minitel is not used for voting, the distribution of Minitel terminals to private citizens and their placement throughout France in public kiosks demonstrates the possibility of providing widespread access to an electronic network.

Deliberation, an important prerequisite for sound democratic processes, is discussed much less often than information-sharing or voting because of a tendency to view democracy in a simple way, as a process in which people vote and the majority rules. Ross Perot, for instance, proposed that leaders and experts could present Americans with a set of options, and then the people themselves could vote for their preferred one, skipping the deliberative step.[19]

It is, however, widely recognized that if a proposition is put before the voters and they are allowed to immediately click on an icon to register their responses (say in some kind of electronic form of the kind of initiatives many states offer their voters), the result will reflect the worst impulses of the people, their raw emotions, readily wiped up by demagogues.

Democratic polities provide two antidotes to this danger: delay loops and opportunities for interaction among the voters. First, they allow time for voters to examine the issues and discuss them with other community members—in town meetings, over their fences, in bars, and so on—before votes are taken. For e-democracy not to turn demagogic, it will have to provide such delay loops—in other words, time for deliberation—and opportunities for interaction among the voters in between the time a proposition or a slate of candidates is put before the voters and the time the votes are cast.

Delay per se provides no difficulties. There is no reason votes have to follow immediately, or even very closely, after the choices are presented to an electorate.

The second element, interaction, provides more difficulties. As we have seen in the discussion of communities, chat rooms' composition and rules of access and anonymity do not provide sound conditions for meaningful interaction, let alone democratic deliberation. If democracy is to thrive on the Internet, provisions will have to be made to provide for, indeed foster, the kinds of interaction deliberation requires. Deliberation is most fruitful among people who know one another and in small numbered groups with low turnover—the same conditions that nurture communities.

The difficulties here are not inherent in the technology; there seem to be no obvious reasons these conditions could not be readily met online, but so far they have not been—largely, it seems, because they may not be profitable and because of ideological objections to any setting aside of online anonymity.

Democracy works best, as has been well and long established, when the voters do not directly decide which policies they favor (as they do in plebiscites and in initiatives), but instruct their elected representatives as to what their basic preferences are, and then allow them to work out the remaining differences. (The more limiting the mandate the voters provide their representatives, the stricter the instructions, and the more difficulties representatives have in working out the inevitable compromises that democracy entails, as people of different values and interests must find a shared course.) This is, of course, the way parliaments work, as well as state assemblies and most city councils.

The Internet, which has not yet been groomed to serve democratic processes, has no established procedures for representation. However, there are on the face of it no special difficulties in providing for representation. Indeed, decades ago I conducted an experiment on this matter using a much more "primitive" technology than the Internet.

The experiment was conducted with the help of the League of Women Voters at a statewide level. The league's New Jersey chapter was attempting to decide, as it does once a year, which issues deserved priority. We organized the league's members into groups of ten, and they conducted town meetings by means of conference calls. Each group chose its own priorities and selected a representative to take these preferences to the next level for discussion. We then held conference calls with groups of ten *representatives*, who decided among themselves which views and preferences to carry to the third and final level, at which statewide policy decisions were made.

A survey established that the league's members, who participated in the decision and representation process, were highly satisfied with the results. The experiment allowed all the members of the league to participate in the decision-making process, and yet the elected representatives were free, within an area indicated by those who elected them, to work out a league-wide consensus.[20]

There is little reason to doubt that such a multilayered, representative model can be applied to online communities, but can it serve nationwide democracy, in which many millions of individuals are involved? Can there be a representative nationwide democratic process that relies at least in part upon online devices?

I suggest that the answer is in the affirmative, drawing on the magical power of exponential curves: If representatives were layered in the suggested manner, millions of participants could quite readily be included. Suppose that various experts addressed the country on Sunday from 10:00 to 11:00 AM about whether the United States should cut back the military by 50 percent over five years. The conference buzz would start with groups of fourteen citizens, each having an hour to discuss and vote. Each group would elect one representative to participate in conference call discussions with thirteen representatives of other groups. Each group of representatives would in turn elect an individual to speak for them, and so on in a rising pyramid. If this process occurred seven times, by six o'clock in the evening 105 million adults could be reached, which is more than the 91 million who voted in the 1988 presidential election.

The same basic approach could be readily applied to the Internet. Voters could convene in, say, twenty-five-person online town meetings. Their discussion would be much more productive than those of chat rooms because the number of participants would be limited, they would already have some shared attributes (all from the same area?), and they would realize that at the end of a given time period they would have to provide a mandate to their elected representative on the next level of this town hall pyramid. Then the representatives of the separate twenty-five-member groups would be convened and so on.

Participants would soon learn that the views of those groups that provide their representatives with very detailed instructions, leaving them with little room to negotiate, as a rule would more than likely be left out of the final consensus-making process than those that provide their representatives with relatively broad mandates. Moreover, members would realize that if many groups were to provide their representative with narrow and strict instructions, national politics would tend to be confrontational and unproductive.

A major issue is left unaddressed here. Multilayered or representative democracy conducted by the use of the Internet could vary a great deal in terms of two variables. One is the scope of issues submitted to a full court multilevel deliberative process of the kind depicted above. For instance, is the public at large going to be invited to deliberate and instruct its representatives only on a few issues every umpteen years—or much more often? Second, are the representatives chosen in the "lower" levels going to change with each issue, or will they serve set terms? And will any of the modifications suggested in the preceding discussion make virtual democracy more democratic or more populist?

In short, the Internet could not only fully duplicate offline democratic procedures and outcome, but it could improve upon them. It would be much easier online than offline for millions not merely to gain information and to vote, but also to participate in deliberations and in instructing their chosen representatives.

CONCLUSION

This chapter argues that some qualitative accounts and quantitative data suggest that communities can be formed on the Internet. They are much more likely to thrive in clubs in which membership is relatively stable, participants disclose their identity, and the subjects under discussion are significant and encompassing rather than narrow and specialized. Furthermore, it is important to recognize that because people live both on and offline, online communities can reinforce offline ones.

Regarding the use of the Internet for democratic processes for on or offline communities—small or large ones—we agree with those who suggest that information-sharing and voting can be quite readily accommodated. However, I stress the importance of providing for deliberations and representation, the software for which is, as a rule, not available.

All that has been argued so far is that virtual democracy is quite feasible. It remains to be discussed whether or not greater reliance on virtual politics would make the joint on and offline polity more or less democratic than it currently is.

NOTES

1. See Elizabeth Frazer, *The Problems of Communitarian Politics: Unity and Conflict* (Oxford: Oxford University Press, 1999); and Robert Booth Fowler, *The Dance with Community: The Contemporary Debate in American Political Thought* (Lawrence, Kans.: University Press of Kansas, 1991).

2. Amitai Etzioni, *The New Golden Rule* (New York: Basic Books, 1996), 127.

3. Benjamin D. Zablocki, "What Can the Study of Communities Teach Us about Community?" in *Autonomy and Order: A Communitarian Anthology*, ed. Edward Lehman (Lanham, Md.: Rowman & Littlefield, 2000).

4. For more discussion, see Amitai Etzioni and Oren Etzioni, "Face-to-Face and Computer-Mediated Communities: A Comparative Analysis," *Information Society* 15, no. 4 (1999): 241–48. A revised version of the article is included in Amitai Etzioni, *The Monochrome Society* (Princeton, N.J.: Princeton University Press, forthcoming).

5. Pew Center for the People and the Press: Technology and Online Use Survey 1998, November 1998, cited in Pippa Norris, "Who Surfs?," in *Democracy.com: Governance in a Networked World*, ed. Elaine Ciulla Kamarck and Joseph S. Nye Jr. (Hollis, N.H.: Hollis Publishing Company, 1999), 81.

6. Gallup Poll, conducted February 20–21, 2000, reported in David W. Moore, "Americans Say Internet Makes Their Lives Better," Gallup News Service, February 23, 2000. Gallup Organization home page www.gallup.com/index.html.

7. Sherry Turkle, *Life on the Screen: Identity in the Age of the Internet* (New York: Touchstone Books, 1995).

8. For a contrary view, see Jerry Kang, "Cyber-Race," *Harvard Law Review* 113, no. 5 (2000): 1130–208.

9. For a discussion of MediaMOO, see Amy Bruckman and Mitchel Resnick, "The MediaMOO Project: Constructionism and Professional Community," *Convergence* 1 (Spring 1995), available at www.cc.gatech.edu/~asb/papers/convergence.html (accessed January 28, 2004).

10. Howard Rheingold, *The Virtual Community: Homesteading on the Electronic Frontier* (Reading, Mass.: HarperPerennial, 1993), 239.

11. Rob Kaiser, "Internet Has Neighborly Side as Users Build Virtual Communities," *Knight-Ridder Tribune Business News: Chicago Tribune*, December 20, 1999. For a discussion of the digital divide between Blacksburg and a neighboring town, see Marcia Stepanek, "A Small Town Reveals America's Digital Divide: Equality Has Yet to Reach the Net," *Business Week*, November, 4 1999, 188ff.

12. Norman H. Nie and Lutz Erbring, "Internet and Society: A Preliminary Report," *Stanford Institute for the Quantitative Study of Society* (February 17, 2000), available at www.stanford.edu/group/siqss.

13. Press Release, *Stanford Institute for the Qualitative Study of Society*, February 16, 2000, available at www.stanford.edu/group/siqss.

14. *Stanford Institute for the Qualitative Study of Society. New York Times*, February 16, 2000, sec. A, 15.

15. "Survey Shows Widespread Enthusiasm for High Technology," report from the Kaiser Family Foundation, National Public Radio, and Harvard University's Kennedy School of Government, February 29, 2000, available at www.kff.org.

16. "Email: the Isolation Antidote," in *Tracking Online Life: How Women Use the Internet to Cultivate Relationships with Family and Friends*, a Pew Internet Project Report, released May 10, 2000, available at www.pewinternet.org/reports.

17. Humphrey Taylor, *The Harris Poll #17: The Impact of Being Online at Home* (New York: Harris Interactive, March 22, 2000).

18. See Bruce Bimber, "The Internet and Political Transformation: Populism, Community, and Accelerated Pluralism," *Polity* 31, no. 1 (1998): 133–60. Citing Walter Lippmann, Bimber argues that any problems with a democracy are not the result of a lack of information, and that providing citizens with extensive information will not radically change their political behavior. See also David M. Anderson, "The False Assumption about the Internet," *Computers and Society*, March 2000, 8–9. Anderson argues that the Internet can and does do much more than merely provide information.

19. See "Ross Perot, One-Way Wizard," Editorial, *New York Times*, April 24, 1992, sec. A, 34.

20. For more about this experiment, see Amitai Etzioni, "Teledemocracy," *Atlantic* 270, no. 4 (1992): 36–39; and Etzioni, "Minerva: An Electronic Town Hall," *Policy Sciences* 3, no. 4 (1972): 457–74.

13

The Internet and Political Transformation Revisited

Diane Johnson and Bruce Bimber

Over the last decade, efforts to discern the consequences of new information technologies on democratic communities have reached roughly their fourth generation. The first pioneering claims date to the late 1980s and early 1990s, well before the Web had emerged on the political scene. That early work stands out for its far-sightedness in raising questions of fragmentation, the possible decline of representative processes, and the existence of tensions between the dynamics of traditional mass media and those of newer, narrow-cast technologies.[1] By the mid 1990s, a second generation of enormously optimistic work appeared mainly in the popular and technical press, predicting far-reaching improvements in community and democracy because of information technology. Knowing that technologies such as radio and television had profound implications for the structure of political influence and the nature of public life, many boldly asserted that the Internet would have equally strong or even greater implications, but that these would be chiefly beneficial where so many of the effects of broadcast media had been undesirable.[2] That work, which DiMaggio et al. describe well in their review as exhibiting "unjustifiable euphoria," was followed by a round of critiques by scholars, many of whom argued that the Internet would change little or nothing about American politics or that new technologies would instead damage the health of democracy.[3]

Until quite recently, this conversation about information technology and political transformation unfolded in the absence of solid empirical evidence of any real scope. Some case studies were published in the early and mid 1990s, along with a little work reporting quantitative analysis, but the debate advanced largely on theoretical grounds or in some instances on merely the impressions and intuitions of observers. Since about the turn of the century, empirical evidence of greater weight has begun to accumulate into a fourth generation of work. That evidence, along with a more mature theoretical basis for speculations, has led to a much more sophisticated body of ideas and literature.

In an article written in 1997 and published a year later, one of the present authors evaluated the state of thinking and research about the Internet and political change in the United States.[4] That inquiry observed that many of the claims advanced about information technology fell into one of two categories, populistic predictions about technology empowering individual citizens, and ideas about improvements in the state of community and society that could be generally labeled communitarian. Neither of these lines of reasoning had much merit, the argument went back then, in contrast to a more likely direction of change in politics toward ever more fragmented, accelerated, pluralistic democracy.

In this chapter, we revisit that inquiry into the state of thinking and research. We do so in light of new literature and theoretical claims, recent empirical findings reported by scholars, and of course new developments in politics itself. The question motivating the current discussion is as follows: From the perspective of the latest generation of literature, what are the major theoretical features of the debate about information technology and political change in the United States, and what do we know to be true or not true as a matter of fact? Our review leads us to the conclusion that with some new variations, populist and communitarian ideas about technology still cast a very long shadow across the debate despite the absence of much supporting evidence. We remain enormously skeptical about these kinds of predictions regarding new technology. We find that advances in research have largely strengthened the earlier case that use of new technologies in the political system is making democracy ever more pluralistic. We explore briefly the idea of *postbureaucratic group politics* as a way of characterizing these changes.

POPULISM AND INFORMATION TECHNOLOGY

The belief that use of new technologies will restructure political power in a populist direction remains as important as ever in contemporary thought, though recent claims are often more nuanced than the early predictions. This strand of thinking is focused primarily on two issues: the mobilization of citizens into politics, and reduced importance of mediators, such as political parties, the media, and organized interest groups, in citizens' political interactions with one another and with government. Populist expectations about new media resonate with American's long affinity for direct forms of democracy and with concerns about declining political participation and the dysfunctional role of intermediaries in the U.S. political process. Former Clinton pollster and current political commentator Dick Morris illustrates the continued cache of this idea: "Two hundred years ago, Thomas Jefferson had to shelve his vision of a direct democracy. . . . Through the technology of the Internet, we have overcome the logistics that defeated Jefferson. Again we can move in the direction his vision would have led—toward direct democracy."[5]

Morris's and others' enthusiasm follows a long and venerable—if not always correct—tradition of meeting new technologies with expectations that the lot of democracy will be improved by their use. The telegraph was greeted with optimism much like Morris's for the Internet, as was the telephone, radio, and television.[6] One strand of the American civil religion is aversion to state power, and another is belief in "progress," especially of the technological kind. These two strands intertwine in a widespread trust that technological progress brings or perhaps even represents progress in the processes of governance as well.

One important new feature of populist theory of technology is the idea that elites and political intermediaries will grow less important as people are able to go directly to the government for their information and to voice their concerns. Morris, for instance, contends that "All across our society, the Internet is eliminating intermediaries," and Richard Huggins notes that the Internet is "a direct channel of contact between leaders and led."[7] Not only will a mass audience be able to follow politics and express its views to government, but it will also be fundamentally less dependent on linkage organizations and group politics. The function of the Net, in this conception, is to facilitate a running national poll of public opinion, with immediate electronic feedback from citizens to government and vice versa.

Technology advocate Howard Rheingold has now argued for nearly a decade in this vein, claiming that online social networks have the potential to circumvent the role of the mass media and reinvigorate citizen involvement in U.S. politics.[8] Similarly Tracy Westen, president of the nonprofit Center for Governmental Studies, acknowledges that while television is still far more important than the Internet in terms of political communication, this "will change, and perhaps more rapidly than we can imagine."[9] As preliminary evidence that the Internet provides the electorate with the ability to make improved decisions, he cites the results of the Democracy Network created by the Center for Governmental Studies in 1996. He claims that this "real world, working laboratory experiment" during five elections has shown that the Net can be used to improve political dialogue between candidates, and between candidates and voters. Online organizations such as Grassroots.com and Vote.com and research centers such as the Pew Internet & American Life project and the Markle Foundation also promote the idea that increasing the availability of political information online will lead to a greater political participation among the U.S. citizenry. The magazine *Wired* frequently runs articles that speak to the emergence of a new electronic age of direct democracy.

Scholarly views of the Net's transforming potential, on the other hand, seem on the whole to have become more subdued in recent years. While sources such as Corrado and Firestone were optimistic in 1996 that the Net might promote "unmediated" communication between citizens and government, decreasing the reliance on elected officials, party organizations, and organized interest groups,[10] the view of Margolis and Resnick four years later was far more sober:

> Although cyberspace has become wildly popular and undergone major technological transformations in recent years, it has not had nearly the effects on society that either its proponents or its detractors predicted. . . . [It] has not become the locus of a new politics that spills out of the computer screen and revitalizes citizenship and democracy. If anything, ordinary politics and commercial activity, in all their complexity and vitality, have invaded and captured cyberspace. Virtual reality has grown to resemble the real world.[11]

But acknowledging that new technology has failed to meet the optimistic early predictions of direct democracy proponents does not mean that scholars have abandoned the idea that the Internet may affect political engagement in ways that are generally populistic.[12] Rather, the current views tend to be more balanced and the arguments more subtle. Joseph S. Nye, for instance, posits that it is possible to imagine both a better and a worse political world as a result of the Internet.[13] In the positive scenario, Nye contends that the new technology makes access to information cheaper and more plentiful, and can make political participation easier (including voting); moreover, the Net may end the hegemony of broadcast television that has undercut parties and made politics so expensive. This is in line with the populist argument. On the other hand, he thinks it is also possible that we may see a "thin democracy in which deliberation has greatly diminished," for instance, in which citizens use set-top boxes on Internet TVs to "engage in frequent plebiscites that will be poorly understood and easily manipulated behind the scenes."[14] Nye concludes, however, that technology alone will not produce either of these changes because so much depends on other political choices; plus, the new information revolution is likely to enhance democracy by increasing choices for some while it hurts others, especially the "have nots." Many of the scholars who discuss the notion of a "digital divide" also focus on the latter issue.

Kenneth L. Hacker provides another example in his conclusion that, under the right circumstances, the Internet could have a positive effect on political engagement in the United States. At the end of an article on the White House Computer-Mediated Communication system (WHCMC), he writes that,

When the digital divides begin to close significantly for all social categories, when the organic and digital domains of political communication and politics work closely together for the common good of all Americans and when political interactivity is part of government communication with its citizens, the new technologies of political communication such as the WHCMC system will be able to contribute to an enhancement of participatory democracy in the United States.[15]

A third example is Scammell's claim that while we have thus far seen mainly "the same old electoral and institutional politics with no evidence of huge new communities or participating citizens," it is possible that we are looking in the wrong places.[16] Her central point is that citizens, as consumers, are "increasingly aware of [their] political power and increasingly willing to use it."[17] Moreover, this is not simply referring to groups of activists, but the "day-to-day activity of increasing millions of ordinary folk whose regular conduct of leisure and consumption has an ever-stronger political edge."[18] The Internet plays a crucial role here because it opens "new worlds" for the citizen-consumer, illustrated by events such as the Seattle demonstration against the World Trade Organization in late 1999.

What does the research evidence say about these possibilities? Few empirical researchers who study the Internet would argue that enough data is available yet to nail down exhaustive tests of various hypotheses associated with these ideas. But evidence is mounting. Surveys examining political participation have consistently shown either a miniscule influence of new media on aggregate levels of political engagement or none at all. Since 1996, the American National Election Studies (ANES) have asked two very simple questions about access to the Internet and use of the Internet for political information during campaign seasons. These data exhibit no relationship between use of new technology and traditional measures of political participation when factors such as education and income are controlled. The ANES measures of Internet use are admittedly very crude, but they clearly do not show support for the populist hypothesis that new media are drawing citizens into political engagement.[19] Neither have other large-scale national studies turned up any clear evidence of that kind. A study conducted by the present authors and Richard Davis of visitors to campaign websites during the 2000 election cycle, for instance, shows that the audiences for campaign websites are comprised not only of citizens with a high likelihood of voting anyway, but also of citizens who for the most part have already made up their minds for whom they will cast their vote.[20]

Evidence from the remarkable primary season of 2003–2004 has not been analyzed as of this writing. The meaning of the Meetups, Moveon efforts, blogs, and Howard Dean story will take some time to discern. Many of the techniques were new, and it may turn out that a secondary effect was to draw in a few people to politics, but there is good reason to hypothesize more of the same from earlier years—that the chief effect of the technology was to connect energetic groups of highly like-minded people with one another and with their preferred candidate. Those connections can be very consequential for launching a primary run, but are not so important in the bigger picture.

Of course many possibilities remain open matters. Forms of political engagement may be changing, not only as technology itself evolves but as new generations of citizens replace the ones for which most survey research was designed. W. Lance Bennett has suggested, for instance, that lifestyle choices increasingly represent overtly political acts. A decision whether to buy clothes from Nike or coffee from Starbucks may, in this view, be no less importantly an act of political engagement than displaying a button or bumper sticker.[21] To the extent this assertion is right, then the tried-and-true survey measures of the ANES may be missing political acts significantly connected to new media and therefore missing some mobilization effects. At the same time, the levels of time and effort that people dedicate to new media vary enormously, as does the breadth of activities with which they are engaged "online." Few surveys have caught up with this rapidly evolving set of behaviors by employing sufficiently rich and varied measures to capture all the possible possibilities for mobilization.

It is likely that better instrumentation employed in research guided by better-developed theory will turn up new relationships between use of information technologies and political engagement; however a good deal of evidence so far suggests that re-engagement of the disaffected is not likely. So far, all the evidence points away from anything like a significant mobilization of previously disengaged people into politics simply because of the availability of new media. As a key element in populist thinking about technology, the proposition that more people are being mobilized into politics because of technological change so far finds little empirical support.

What about the second element of the populist thesis, namely diminished reliance on political elites? The proposition that people's interaction with one another and with government is less highly mediated is far more difficult to test authoritatively than the mobilization thesis. Are interest groups less important now than ten years ago? Certainly no prima facie trend stands out. Our own examination of collective action and policy advocacy suggests that the nature and identity of political groups and organizations may well be changing, but that the presence of intermediaries and political elites is probably not diminishing. That is, the importance to politics of a class of political intermediaries strikes us as no less important than ever, though membership in that class may be undergoing some interesting changes.

The literature on this subject now documents a number of cases of established interests as well as new citizen groups exploiting the capacities of new media to mount collective political efforts.[22] One interesting example is the

Know Your Customer protest in 1999. In this case, the Libertarian Party used the Internet to launch its campaign against the so-called Know Your Customer rules proposed by the Federal Deposit Insurance Corporation (FDIC) and three other federal agencies. According to the agencies, the proposed rules would have standardized and formalized the existing practice of most banks to learn individual customers' banking habits and patterns in an effort to distinguish between legitimate and illegitimate financial transactions. The Libertarian Party interpreted this as a clear violation of Americans' privacy. Lacking the financial resources or membership size to provide much of a direct political threat, party officials decided to use electronic mail and the Web to leverage citizen involvement against the proposed rules during the first months of 1999.

The party launched a website called "DefendYourPrivacy.com" that permitted citizens to file official comments on the proposed rules and send e-mail to their members of Congress. The party then sent a message to its own e-mail list of ten thousand people, asking recipients to visit the new website and pass the message on to other citizens. In the next three weeks, the party brokered about 170,000 messages to the FDIC, which had opted to accept public comments online. In total, the FDIC accumulated more than a quarter of a million public comments regarding Know Your Customer, nearly all opposed. In the face of vehement citizen opposition and the loss of support in both Congress and in the banking industry, the FDIC and its sister agencies withdrew the regulations. Given that citizens traditionally pay scant attention to the relationship between the banking industry and its regulators, the Libertarian Party's ability to generate public comments from more than four times the number of its total dues-paying membership of forty thousand is even more remarkable. To many people, this looked like a populist uprising.

Another example that looked similar to some people was the Million Mom March, which took place on the Capitol Mall in Washington D.C. on Mother's Day 2000. This was the largest demonstration in U.S. history about gun control. The march originated in the efforts of a single person, Donna Dees-Thomases, who decided in August 1999 that gun control was an issue of salience to mothers and resolved to mobilize other mothers in a political effort. Dees-Thomases' first action was to register "Million Mom March" as an Internet domain name; she then obtained a permit for a march on the Capitol Mall. The aim was to persuade Congress to pass what she called "common sense gun laws."

Dees-Thomases recruited volunteers among friends and acquaintances, formed a steering committee, and organized a set of state coordinators who in turn recruited more volunteers. The group built its volunteer base and spread information about its plans through its website, e-mail, and telephone banks. In the end, the Million Mom March became a mainstream political event supported by traditional elites and the media, and starting in February or March of 2000, its evolution is explainable largely in those terms. In its earliest stages, however, low cost communication techniques were a necessary ingredient in the group's formation and rise to media prominence in the absence of a policy organization and even a paid staff. As one participant put it, until February, the organization "existed largely in cyberspace."[23] By the time of the march, organizers claimed its website had received about 5 million visits. Official estimates of the size of the march on the Washington Mall (and in other cities around the country) are not available, but by even the most conservative estimate the rally exceeded a hundred thousand participants. While far short of the eponymous "million," the group was nonetheless a very large-scale political march.

Like the Know Your Customer protest, this event had the appearance of populism: citizens joining a collective effort in the absence of traditional political elites. The two events indeed form some of the most compelling evidence so far available about how political groups are using new media to advocate for political positions.

But more than anti-elite populism or the elimination of intermediaries from politics, these cases reveal something else. They suggest changes in the identity, tactics, and resources of political elites and mobilizers. Much more intriguing than the presently unanswerable question of whether new people were mobilized into politics is the unequivocal fact that the mobilizers and intermediaries responsible for these actions were not traditional ones. Libertarians of course have been around for a long time. But they have never before organized 170,000 Americans to do anything. The technology permitted a peripheral political organization to act like a mainstream mobilizer. In the case of the Million Mom March, what stands out is that the largest gun control rally in the United States—as well as a small counterprotest—was organized almost entirely outside the bounds of the gun control lobby (and the NRA in the latter case). The March effort began in the absence of any formal political organization by exploiting the low transaction costs made possible by technology. That technology permitted a small, poorly funded group of would-be political organizers to attract the attention of the most important political intermediary of all, the mass media, and then build a traditional political structure. Following march day, the Million Mom March eventually merged with the Brady Campaign to Control Gun Violence, formerly Handgun Control, and easily the most important traditional antigun group. This meant two things: a novel, "grassroots" group used technology to overcome initial barriers to collective action, then eventually took on the mantle of a more traditional political elite; and a traditional political interest group adapted its structure to accommodate a populistic new group operating under different premises and ways of framing a political problem. Far more than the growth of populism, this looks more like a change in the character of pluralism. We will return to this point shortly.

COMMUNITY AND INFORMATION TECHNOLOGY

While populist ideas about new media address chiefly matters of the structure of citizen-to-government communication, claims about new media and community confront issues of citizen-to-citizen communication and interaction. Perhaps even more so than in populist thinking about technology, community-oriented claims about what changes technology is likely to bring are bound together with normative conceptions about what constitutes a better society. Proponents of the populist claim are often openly liberal. Teledemocracy, for instance, "emphasizes the potential of new technologies for individual empowerment" by giving individuals direct input into decision-making.[24]

A central feature of contemporary communitarianism, on the other hand, is the familiar critique that liberalism places far too much emphasis on individualism and rights, and far too little emphasis on duty, virtue, and responsibility. Like the populist claim regarding the Internet, the community claim reflects dissatisfaction with the current state of political engagement in the United States. The vast majority of predictions about how technology will enhance community appear rooted in disapproval of the contemporary state of community and society. In his classic work on community and social change in America, historian Thomas Bender wrote that "modern Americans fear that urbanization and modernization have destroyed the community that earlier shaped the lives of men and women. . . . These popular concerns have been abetted, if not actually stimulated, by the writings of historians and sociologists that are laced with references to the 'erosion,' or the 'decline,' or the 'breakup' or the 'eclipse' of community."[25]

Social change is a fact of life, and this type of lamentation for the past is nothing new.

Robert Putnam, chief advocate for the view that recent decades have witnessed an accelerated decline in the quality of community in the United States, in fact contends that the debates about the demise of community have been endemic in the United States for at least two hundred years.[26] In the early 1930s, Emile Durkheim noted that despite the material advances wrought by the division of labor, people continued to long for what they saw as the idle pleasures of a previous era.[27] Durkheim himself saw the restoration of community as vital in the transition from tradition to modernity.

Though technological change is often a contributor to the changes in society that lead to nostalgia over community-lost, a belief that technology can also improve community appears as an undercurrent of social thought. One of the first modern statements of this idea was made in 1939, when George Gallup predicted the possibilities presented by radio technology, the wide distribution of newspapers, and the new survey techniques he had popularized. He envisioned the arrival of a "town meeting on a national scale," where new technology would allow the national polity to act as if it were a community of neighbors discussing problems together.[28] This is not merely a liberal or populistic invocation of technology because of the emphasis on technologically mediated interaction between citizens themselves. A much earlier antecedent comes from 1820–1840, when the rapid growth in the United States postal service established viable mail delivery for the first time. Observers then spoke in sometimes awestruck terms of the creation of a national community because of the new possibilities for communication.[29]

So it has been with the Internet. As the technology expanded into popular usage in the early 1990s, Howard Rheingold made one of the earliest claims, arguing that "community" is created when people interact with one another on the Internet sufficiently long that they develop lasting relationships.[30] Amitai Etzioni argues that new technology enhances community by removing spatial and temporal bounds.[31] He concedes that computer-mediated community is not a perfect substitute for the real thing, and notes that real communities are better than virtual ones at communicating affect, holding participants accountable, and creating strong and intimate bonds.[32] Yet, Etzioni argues, the new technology can contribute to building and sustaining community in other ways. Technology allows the development of community in spite of physical distance, and this facility exceeds what is possible by telephone in at least one way, namely allowing social bonding to occur asynchronously. Moreover, community-building through the Net is not bounded by political borders, identities, or appearance. Net-based community also offers a better "memory effect," because of the presence of written records.[33] Communitarian William Galston is more cautiously optimistic, citing the Net's potential for a "significant impact on American society" if the current shift among young adults toward virtual community-building turns out to be a generational effect as opposed to a life-cycle effect.[34]

Other communitarians are skeptical of the technology-based claim. Michael Sandel argues that while new communication technology such as the Internet does create interdependencies that span geography and political boundaries, this interdependence does not have the essence of community within it. He notes: "Converting networks of communication and interdependence into a public life worth affirming is a moral and political matter, not a technological one."[35] Following Jane Addams's progressive era observations on modernization a century ago, Sandel argues that no amount of technological interaction can itself be sufficient to constitute community.[36] Likewise, Benjamin Barber concedes that although it is possible that new communications technologies will foster democracy and civil society in a "Jeffersonian scenario," it is equally likely that we will see complacency and a projection of current attitudes and trends.[37] A third and far more ominous possibility for Barber is that governments will abuse these technologies vis-à-vis standardization, control, or repression.

An important version of theories of community and technology deals with possibilities for deliberative democracy and the creation of a virtual public sphere. As Lincoln Dahlberg points out, the purpose of dialog in the communitarian conception is to "help discover an already existing common good," while in deliberative democracy its purpose is to help "participants move towards understanding and agreement despite their differences."[38] The public sphere claim stems from the fact that the democratic and deliberative public sphere depends upon "spontaneous and voluntary association,"[39] where the better argument may prevail on the basis of appeals to reason among free and equal deliberators.

The Internet's potential to transform the public sphere has been the subject of an impressive number of popular and academic works in recent years.[40] Although the general notion of a public sphere within the democratic tradition was not uncommon in twentieth-century political writing, the current debate stems largely from the particular conception of Jürgen Habermas.[41] According to Habermas, there are impediments to the achievement of a contemporary public sphere. Two of these are the interests of the state in shaping public dialog to protect its own power, and the corruptive influence of the mass media that fragments society into private-oriented individuals who do not (or cannot) engage in reasoned debate about public issues. Many have noted that the Internet appears promising in light of all these considerations, in part because it lowers the barriers to entry into the public sphere. The Net offers new forms of "spontaneous and voluntary" association, especially through bulletin boards, mailing lists, newsgroups, chat rooms, and the like, and it is comparatively free of centralized control and institutional self-interest on the part of the state and media organizations. One example of this claim is by Internet researchers Michael Hauben and Rhonda Hauben, who enthusiastically observe that computer networks can "revitalize the concept of a democratic 'town meeting' via online communication and discussion."[42] They contend that the existence of thousands of diverse conversations at any time on the Net demonstrates the emergence of a virtual deliberative public sphere. Howard Rheingold makes essentially the same argument.[43]

Here again, however, arguments running in the opposite direction are quite compelling. Steven Schneider's case study of a Usenet newsgroup focused on abortion, for instance, tentatively suggests that a high level of inequality in participation questions the democratic quality of the public sphere. Sinikka Sassi observes that the Internet "is a reason for at least some of the present reconfigurations of the public sphere," while at the same time it "elicits conflicting tendencies such as fragmentation and unification" and redefines the boundaries between the public and the private.[44] Zizi Papacharissi suggests while the Net has created a new public space that facilitates political conversation, it is not yet clear whether this public space will transcend to a public sphere in which citizens are better informed and more willing to engage in political discussion.[45] Along with Sassi, Papacharissi agrees that political discourse often becomes fragmented on the Net.

Postmodernist Mark Poster takes a more forceful position, arguing that a public sphere as conceived by Habermas cannot be facilitated through cyberspace, as it denies the possibility of embodied citizens pursuing consensus vis-à-vis the critique of argument and presentation of validity claims.[46] Wilhelm also has more severe doubts. He argues that the current design and use of communications technologies such as the Net "pose formidable obstacles to achieving a more just and human social order." His argument is based on four "challenges" to democracy. These are the barriers to entry into the digital public sphere, the lack of ability to share universally in the virtual public sphere, the potential undermining of the "methodical pace of democratic decision making," and the distortion and compression of the public right-of-way under the pressure of market forces.[47] Some of the most strident claims, moreover, have a sort of anarchic, overtly antidemocratic character, contending that the Internet has the potential to polarize the citizenry. One example is legal scholar Cass Sunstein, who fears that the Internet encourages like-minded people to seek out those who reinforce their own political views, filter out information with which they do not agree, tailor their own news, and harden their positions into more extreme ones.[48]

The chief problem plaguing questions of community and technology is the level of abstraction in concepts and the paucity of agreed-upon terms. Lack of agreement over the definition of "community" clearly fuels the debate nearly as much as uncertainty about causal questions of the consequences of technology itself. In popular usage, where "community" is attached to race categories and other descriptive adjectives, the term is sometimes little more than a label for a demographic classification that is easily measured but trivial in its implication for questions of social change. Scholars of community occasionally commit the opposite sin by loading so many abstractions into the concept that definitive measurement of the advance or decline of community or public sphere would be all but impossible. Nearly a half-century ago, George A. Hillery Jr. found an astounding ninety-four meanings ascribed to community in the social science literature.[49] As Gallaher and Padfield put it, "community may well be one of the most overly conceptualized areas in the social sciences."[50] Popular sociological definitions until relatively recently tended to focus on territorially based social organizations and social activity. This was challenged in the 1970s by the historian Thomas Bender, who observed that community is better defined as an experience rather than a place,[51] and by numerous sociologists who argued that communities could also consist of physically separated social networks of kin, friends, and others.

Basing his views on the work of theorists such as Ferdinand Tönnies, Max Weber, and Robert Nisbet, Bender's conception of community contains four key structural components: limited membership, shared norms, affective ties, and a sense of mutual obligation. By way of comparison, communitarian theorist Philip Selznick emphasizes a shared history, a sense of common identity, bonds of interdependence and reciprocity, and effective participation in the cultural and social organization of the group.[52] Meanwhile, professor of law and politics Jeffrey Abramson insists that any rigorous use of "community" must include a shared purpose or common good, equality, loyalty, autonomy or self-government, a common space, deliberation, and an appropriate size.[53] Under such definitional variation in "community," we hold out little hope for the resolution of questions about the consequences of technology for its advance.

The strand of thought on community that has steered best between the problems of superficiality and overconceptualization is that dealing with social capital. Although disagreement does exist about what constitutes social capital, a large empirical literature advancing various measurable concepts now exists. This literature typically operationalizes social capital as either a set of attitudes centering on trust in others, a set of behaviors involving involvement in associations or other social activities, or some combination.

Theoretically, attitudinal and behavioral variables offer a comparatively rich landscape where questions of technological change are concerned. For instance, more effective communication and efficient flows of communication may facilitate collective action and enhance possibilities for face-to-face social interaction in physically proximate communities—an observation made by Tocqueville in the 1830s.[54] Online interaction without face-to-face contact may (or may not) build trust, depending on circumstances. Under the social capital rubric, enhanced social interaction or trust because of technology, both of which are measurable propositions, would have direct implications for larger questions of community.

Jean Camp, for example, contends that Internet communities match or exceed traditional geographic communities regarding norms of trust. She believes that, in traditional communities, trust was a social evaluation that often depended on characteristics such as "race, region of origin, physical attractiveness, charisma, and other completely meaningless information."[55] In her view, trust will become more formal with the growth of online communities, based on a rational evaluation of the other's claims, which she sees as a positive development. Several recent empirical studies of the social consequences of the Internet by Katz, Rice, and Aspden, as well as others, suggests that Internet use is associated with increased community and political involvement, and significant and increased online and offline social interaction.[56] A recent study based on survey research by Wellman et al. also finds an association between heavy Internet use and increased participation in politics and voluntary organizations.[57] In our own view, the most important emergent thesis from this literature so far is that Internet use tends to reinforce patterns of sociability; more socially connected people tend to use the Internet more, and the more people use the Internet, the more socially connected they become.

Still, concerns with translating social behaviour into "community" fill the literature. Sherry Turkle fears that new technology detracts from meaningful real communities.[58] Other academics qualify that virtual communities can exist as long as they are developed around existing physically-based communities,[59] or that online social-capital-building behavior may transfer to "community" behavior at some point in the future.[60]

The findings of Shah, Kwak, and Holbert show that differentiating forms of Internet use is crucial to answering questions about social behavior. Using survey data, they find that use of e-mail and certain information Web functions contributes to social capital, while recreational Internet use undermines it.[61] Their study makes clear that simple arguments that lump "Internet use" into one concept are likely to miss important social effects—positive or negative.

We see two cases of technology and community as paradigmatic of what remains to be learned at this point. The first is the Blacksburg Electronic Village (BEV) in Blacksburg, Virginia, which illustrates the distinction made by Blanchard and Horan between physically based virtual communities and geographically dispersed virtual communities of interest.[62] The concept of the BEV came about in early 1991 as a joint effort by Virginia Tech, the Town of Blacksburg, and Bell Atlantic.[63] The BEV officially launched in 1993. The objective was to minimize the so-called digital divide by making the Net available to community residents through education, structures such as listservs, and free high-speed access at various locations. By 2000, four out of five community residents had access to the Internet.[64] In addition to encouraging individual citizens to take advantage of the Internet's resources, the BEV motivated formal and informal local community organizations to do the same, for instance, by participating in e-commerce through an online mall.

Kavanaugh and Patterson find in their survey research that, as expected, increased access to the BEV was associated with the use of the Internet to build social capital by online communication with other community members, increasing with the amount of time they spend online.[65] Their data do not, however, support the expectation that as access to the BEV increased, so would community attachment and involvement. Thus, their findings tentatively confirm Robert Putnam's suggestion that social capital leads to effective online communication, rather than the other way around.[66]

The second example is quite different: those who visit the National Geographic Society's website. The National Geographic Society claims to be the world's largest nonprofit scientific and educational organization.[67] Members receive *National Geographic* magazine, and the website offers favorite stories from the magazine. In addition, the site offers links to today's related news stories, listings of geographically oriented television shows and books, and homework help for kids and tips for people planning trips. It also provides information on grants given by the society, along with other information presumably of interest to people who care about geography.

Between September and November 1998, the society conducted a large-scale online survey of visitors to its website. Using these data, Wellman et al. find that online interaction supplements traditional offline forms of communication without increasing or decreasing it. They also find an association between heavy use of the Net and increased participation in politics and voluntary organizations.[68] Moreover, online and offline participation in voluntary organizations is positively associated. On the other hand, however, the data indicate that heavy Internet use can reduce commitment to community. Ultimately, Wellman and colleagues argue that there is no single Internet effect. Rather, people who use the Net primarily in asocial activities can be turned away from community, organizational, and political development, while those who use new technology for social activities find it a tool for building and maintaining social capital.

The literature on community and technology therefore suggests several conclusions. The first is that matters of community and technology are substantially richer and more complex than populistic thought about mobilization and the decline of democratic intermediaries. Here empirical evidence does exist for consequences of technology, especially in the social capital literature. These consequences so far are modest, but how trends that are just now discernable may play out in the long run is hard to tell. One of the most likely outcomes is that the technologies of information and communication tend to reflect and reinforce trends in community whose origins lie elsewhere.

Knowing the consequences of technology therefore requires knowing deeper inclinations and forces at work in society. The longstanding debate about whether Americans are rugged individualists or are imbued with an inclination to association, as Tocqueville noted, therefore becomes central. Hirsch makes the intriguing observation that community died with the victory of the Federalists and the emergence of a large republic in the late 1700s, and that the nation's growth in size, complexity and heterogeneity have made its rebirth increasingly unlikely.[69] Deeper arguments such as this rooted in sociology and history, whether right or wrong, may tell us as much about the consequences of technology for community as analyses of the technology itself. It is likely that technology does not so much redirect the evolution of community but advance it along its existing paths.

INFORMATION TECHNOLOGY AND PLURALISM

We do not discount entirely the possibility of technology-related change enhancing direct citizen-to-government interaction or especially its proven potential for altering citizen-to-citizen interaction at the level of community. However, we find a much more compelling way to conceptualize the consequences of technology to involve the nature of group-based political pluralism. Many realms of American community and democracy are defined by group-based structures. Groups are central to the nature of political advocacy in the United States and have been for the better part of a century. These tertiary associations, from the American Association of Retired Persons and the Sierra Club to the National Rifle Association and the National Association of Manufacturers, shape public agendas, influence campaigns through their financial clout, mobilize citizens into political action of many kinds, and of course constitute the central bargaining units involved in the creation of public policy.

These are specifically not the kind of associations traditionally understood to be social capital-bearing because they do not involve face-to-face contact among citizens. They are however one of the principal forms of political intermediaries that populist theory predicts are losing influence under the influence of technology. We see the evidence differently. The vast array of groups that goes so far to define the landscape of American democracy is in almost every instance constituted by a formal organization of some kind. American pluralism is not merely a system of groups; it is a system of *organizations* who raise and expend resources in order to mobilize citizens and influence politics.

The literature on technology and organizations shows something that the literatures on political behavior and community do not, at least not in nearly so stark a way: Technology matters. Developments in the technologies of information and communication lead directly to changes in transaction costs for organizations. Changes in transaction costs in turn lead to changes in organizational structure, strategies, and capacities. The long literature on organization theory extending back to Ronald Coase in 1937 and Max Weber well before him has established a key principle.[70] Technological and other conditions that create high transaction costs tend to reward organizations that are structured hierarchically, with well-defined, clear boundaries, vertical integration of command, and highly compartmentalized, linear management of information and communication. On the other hand, technological and other conditions that create lower transaction costs tend to reward organizations structured more horizontally, with more permeable boundaries, more flexible or even ad hoc internal structures, and rich, nonlinear flows of communication and information.

These two forms of organization, the bureaucratic and postbureaucratic, are of course nowhere perfectly realized.[71] Even the most hide-bound, hierarchical government agency likely lacks a few features of an ideal Weberian bureaucracy, just as the most flexible, ad hoc network may exhibit a few elements of hierarchy and vertical integration. Certainly not all organizations in all circumstances respond similarly or to the same degree to incentives or costs associated with information. But as ideal types, they provide a solid theoretical basis for examining the direction of change in organizations as technological innovations unfold connected to information and communication. These theoretical principles have been borne out to various degrees in the empirical literature dealing with one particular class of organizations, the firm. As technological change has advanced, a wide range of business organizations have shifted toward more postbureaucratic structures.[72]

Consequences for the various classes of organization more relevant to democracy and community, such as political groups and interest organizations, have received far less scholarly attention. In the realm of politics and community, shifts toward more postbureaucratic political organization could appear in several ways. One should be more porous boundaries in organizations. As information and communication move more readily in and out of organizations, the importance of maintaining boundaries for the protection of resources and expertise should be diminished. A result should be more collaboration and coalition-formation among groups: a richer, denser, and more complex network of association among organizations with less clear divisions of labor and less formalized exchanges of resources and expertise.

Another possible effect involves the resources required to initiate collective action and participation and to begin the process of organization-building. As communication costs fall rapidly and information-intensive tasks such as identifying citizens with common interests become simpler, barriers to entry into the realm of organizing, advocacy, and engagement are lowered. Where it previously took substantial staff and funding to mobilize a group of citizens, it increasingly will require only facility with information technology, where the marginal cost of mobilizing citizens is quite small. This hardly means that ten people with no budget can accomplish what the AARP or the United Way can, but it means that they have a higher probability of communicating effectively and attracting participation than their counterparts would have fifteen years ago. Money and resources clearly will continue to matter, but the threshold for entry into politics and community organization appears to be falling, and that fact has consequences for the identity of elites and groups active in the public sphere.

A related effect may be changes in the nature of membership and sense of belonging. As transaction costs fall for identifying and communicating with interested citizens, the importance of formalized membership should fall for many kinds of groups. Where groups can readily identify people with various compatible interests and can communicate easily with them, persuading citizens to enroll as members should be somewhat less important. Indeed, aside from their financial importance to groups, one important impetus to the maintenance of membership rolls is to sustain a pool of mobilizeable citizens known to be generally interested in the group's objectives. When identifying and communicating with people who share a group's concerns becomes simple and cheap because of the capacities of technology, part of the impetus toward "membership" goes away. The situation is similar from the perspective of citizens. From the citizen perspective, as it becomes simpler and essentially costless to receive tailored information and to be notified of events and activities or political decisions of interest, one reason to officially "join" an organization is weakened. In other words, who "belongs" to a political or social organization and who does not may grow less important for both the organization and the individual as the environment grows more information-rich and communication-intensive.

Many of the real-world instances of "new" politics that observers cite as cases of newly populistic politics or sometimes even instances of online community actually represent pluralistic, group-centric society and politics characterized by postbureaucratic features such as these. The Million Mom March and the Libertarians' Know Your Customer protest are prime examples from the realm of politics, as are the Blacksburg Electronic Village and the National Geographic Society's online members from the realm of society. Moveon and the early Howard Dean campaign organization in 2003–2004 are other examples. That these might represent important instances of the advance of populistic society or community we consider unlikely or at best open questions needing a good deal more analysis. Whether they represent an advance toward democratic pluralism with postbureaucratic features we view as a good deal clearer.

Conceiving of the influence of technology on politics and community in terms of changing group dynamics is likely to be one of the most promising approaches in the future. Theoretically, links are clear between an evolving environment for communication and changes in the identity, structure, and strategy of groups, and evidence for how those links actually work have begun to accumulate. This evidence suggests that to the extent that group identities, structures, and strategies shift in a less bureaucratic direction, we should expect to see evolution in the larger character of citizen involvement in community and politics. Organizations adapted to an information environment changing in these ways should be expected to behave differently as they go about the process of advocating, mobilizing other political actors, and initiating citizen involvement. They should be more opportunistic as they rapidly exploit unfolding circumstances, and they should be expected to reconfigure themselves to each event. More bureaucratically structured organizations designed for national political mobilization or for national-scale legal advocacy do not readily change strategies. Organizations with more postbureaucratic features would be better situated to engage in local political mobilization efforts around the country one week and national political advocacy the next. An increasingly post-bureaucratic system would likely be characterized by more amorphous, shifting ad hoc group politics and power wielded less often through nego-tiation among well-defined, highly bounded groups.

Of course, many limitations exist on politics conducted in this way. For in-stance, the capacity to sustain public involvement in events and associations over time is crucial to questions of community-building and long-term polit-ical efficacy. The new, flexible, increasingly ad hoc structures present in postbureaucratic group politics appear less durable than those associated with more highly institutionalized organizations. One adage about Congress has it that passing major legislation requires three Congresses—six years. Traditional organizations appear better suited at exerting influence in that kind of long-haul politics than newer, ad hoc groups associated with inten-sive use of technology. And one of the consequences of more routinized, bu-reaucratic group politics is the formation of shared identities and the evolu-tion of trust on the part of individuals with respect to the collective group. It is not at all clear that less bureaucratic groups foster identification and social bonds in the same way. One result might be a thinning of the character of political relationships. Factors such as these tend to exert a braking effect on organizational change, as they make less bureaucratic structures maladaptive for some kinds of functions.

The postbureaucratic model of group politics under the influence of rapidly changing technology is therefore never likely to be realized in full. It delineates a direction of change, a vector for the historical evolution of politics, more than a fully realizable state of affairs that will one day come to fruition. The ques-tion is therefore not *whether* use of new technology is making politics and community postbureaucratic, but in what direction use of the technology is in-fluencing political change. One important direction, the evidence seems to suggest, is toward a diminished correspondence between traditional distribu-tions of resources and institutionalized organizations on the one hand, and on the other the nature and identity of democratic groups. All of this is to say that new technology does not appear revolutionary for politics and community in precisely the ways that so many observers had hoped and expected. Instead, information technology appears to reinforce many sociopolitical behavioral tendencies, especially the long-standing trend in the United States toward in-creasingly fragmented, hyperpluralistic forms of society and politics.

NOTES

This chapter is based on an article published as: Bruce Bimber, "The Internet and Political Transformation: Populism, Community and Accelerated Pluralism," *Polity* 31, no. 1 (Fall 1998): 133–60. For a fuller treatment of some of the themes, also see Bruce Bimber, *Information and American Democracy: Technology in the Evolution of Po-litical Power* (Cambridge, Mass.: Cambridge University Press, 2003).

258   *Diane Johnson and Bruce Bimber*

1. Jeffrey B. Abramson, F. Christopher Arterton, and Gary R. Orren, *The Electronic Commonwealth* (Cambridge, Mass.: Harvard University Press, 1988); W. Russell Neuman, *The Future of the Mass Audience* (Cambridge: Cambridge University Press, 1991).

2. Anthony Corrado and Charles M. Firestone, eds., *Elections in Cyberspace: Toward a New Era in American Politics* (Washington, D.C.: Aspen Institute, 1996); Lawrence K. Grossman, *The Electronic Republic: Reshaping Democracy in America* (New York: Viking, 1995).

3. Paul DiMaggio, Eszter Hargittai, W. Russell Neuman, and John P. Robinson, "Social Implications of the Internet," *Annual Review of Sociology* 27 (2001): 307–36. Critiques include Richard Davis, *The Web of Politics* (London: Oxford University, 1998); Richard Davis and Diana Owen, *New Media in American Politics* (London: Oxford University, 1998); Michael Margolis and David Resnick, *Politics as Usual: The Cyberspace "Revolution"* (Thousand Oaks, Calif.: Sage, 2000).

4. Bruce Bimber, "The Internet and Political Transformation: Populism, Community, and Accelerated Pluralism," *Polity* 31, no. 1 (Fall 1998).

5. Dick Morris, *Vote.com* (Los Angeles: Renaissance Books, 1999), xviii–xix; Richard Huggins, "The Transformation of the Political Audience?," in *New Media and Politics*, ed. Barrie Axford and Richard Huggins (London: Sage Publications, 2001).

6. See e.g.: Lincoln Dahlberg, "Democracy via Cyberspace: Mapping the Rhetorics and Practices of Three Prominent Camps," *New Media and Society* 3, no. 2: 158; Darin Barney, *Prometheus Wired: The Hope for Democracy in the Age of Network Technology* (Chicago: University of Chicago Press, 2000), 20.

7. Morris, *Vote.com*, xix; Richard Huggins, "The Transformation of the Political Audience?" *New Media and Politics*, ed. Barrie Axford and Richard Huggins (London: Sage Publications, 2001).

8. Howard Rheingold, *The Virtual Community: Homesteading on the Electronic Frontier*, rev. ed. (Cambridge, Mass: MIT Press, 2000).

9. Tracy Westen, "Can Technology Save Democracy?," *National Civic Review* 87 (Spring 998): 49.

10. Corrado and Firestone, *Elections in Cyberspace,* 13.

11. Margolis and Resnick, *Politics as Usual.*

12. For an example of an early advocate of the Net's power to facilitate direct democracy, see Christa Daryl Slaton, *Televote: Expanding Citizen Participation in the Quantum Age* (New York: Praeger, 1992).

13. Joseph S. Nye Jr., "Information Technology and Democratic Governance," in *Democracy.com? Governance in a Networked World*, ed. Elaine Ciulla Kamarck and Joseph S. Nye Jr. (Hollis, N.H.: Hollis Publishing, 1999).

14. Nye, "Information Technology and Democratic Governance," 12.

15. Kenneth L. Hacker, "The White House Computer-mediated Communication (CMC) System and Political Interactivity," in *Digital Democracy: Issues of Theory and Practice*, ed. Kenneth L. Hacker and Jan van Dijk (London: Sage Publications, 2000).

16. Margaret Scammell, "The Internet and Civic Engagement: The Age of the Citizen-Consumer," *Political Communication* 17 (2000): 354.

17. Scammell, "Internet and Civic," 352.

18. Scammell, "Internet and Civic," 352..

19. For discussions, see Bruce Bimber, "Information and Civic Engagement in America: The Search for Political Effects of the Internet," *Political Research Quarterly*

54, no. 1: (March, 2001); and Bruce Bimber, *Information and American Democracy: Technology in the Evolution of Political Power* (Cambridge: Cambridge University Press, 2003).

20. Bruce Bimber and Richard Davis, *Campaigning Online: The Internet in U.S. Elections* (New York: Oxford University Press, 2003).

21. W. Lance Bennett, "The UnCivic Culture: Communication, Identity, and the Rise of Lifestyle Politics," *Political Science and Politics* 31, no. 4 (1998): 741–61.

22. See Daniel Bennett and Pam Fielding, *The Net Effect: How Cyberadvocacy Is Changing the Political Landscape* (Merrifield, Va.: e-advocates Press, 1997); Laura Gurak, *Persuasion and Privacy in Cyberspace: The Online Protests over Lotus Marketplace and the Clipper Chip* (New Haven, Conn.: Yale University, 1997); and James A. Thurber and Colton C. Campbell, eds., *Congress and the Internet* (New York: Prentice Hall, 2002). For fuller treatment of the "Know Your Customer" and Million Mom March cases that follow, along with other examples, see Bimber, *Information and American Democracy*.

23. Quoted in Susan Levine, "Fight against Guns Gives Moms a Cause," *Washington Post*, 19 April 2000, B1. Again for a fuller treatment of this case, see Bimber, *Information and American Democracy*.

24. Dahlberg, "Democracy via Cyberspace," 159–60.

25. Thomas Bender, *Community and Social Change in America* (New Brunswick: N.J.: Rutgers University Press, 1978), 3–4.

26. Robert Putnam, *Bowling Alone: The Collapse and Revival of American Community* (New York: Simon and Schuster, 2000), 24.

27. Emile Durkheim, *The Division of Labor in Society*, trans. George Simpson (1933; reprint, New York: Free Press, 1964). See especially book II, chapter 1.

28. In Mark Poster, *The Second Media Age* (Cambridge: Polity Press, 1995).

29. Richard R. John. *Spreading the News: The American Postal System from Franklin to Morse* (Cambridge, Mass.: Harvard University, 1995).

30. Howard Rheingold, "A Slice of Life in My Virtual Community," in *Global Networks*, ed. L. M. Harasim (Cambridge, Mass: MIT Press, 1993), 57–80. A decade later, Rheingold confessed that he has become "more critical" of ideas he once proposed, but the heart of his argument remains the same. See *The Virtual Community: Homesteading on the Electronic Frontier*, rev. ed. (Cambridge, Mass: MIT Press, 2000), 325.

31. Amitai Etzioni and Oren Etzioni, "Communities: Virtual vs. Real," *Science* 277 (18 July 1997): 295. For a more complete version of their argument, see Amitai Etzioni and Oren Etzioni, "Face-to-Face and Computer-Mediated Communities, A Comparative Analysis," *Information Society* 15 (Oct.–Dec. 1999): 241–48.

32. Etzioni and Etzioni, "Communities."

33. Etzioni and Etzioni, "Communities."

34. William A. Galston, "(How) Does the Internet Affect Community? Some Speculation in Search of Evidence," in *Democracy.com? Governance in a Networked World*, ed. Elaine Ciulla Kamarck and Joseph S. Nye Jr. (Hollis, N.H.: Hollis Publishing, 1999).

35. Michael Sandel, *Democracy and Its Discontents* (Cambridge, Mass.: Harvard University Press, 1996).

36. Jane Addams, *Democracy and Social Ethics* (New York: Macmillan, 1907).

37. Benjamin R. Barber, "Three Scenarios for the Future of Technology and Strong Democracy," *Political Science Quarterly* 113 (Winter 1998–1999): 573–89. Note that

this has changed from his earlier work; in *Strong Democracy: Participatory Politics for a New Age* (Berkeley: University of California Press, 1984), for example, Barber was receptive to the inherent possibilities of communication technologies.

38. Dahlberg, "Democracy via Cyberspace," 167.

39. John Louis Lucaites, "Studies in the Public Sphere," *Quarterly Journal of Speech* 8 (1997): 352.

40. For a small sample, see Sinikka Sassi, "The Controversies of the Internet and the Revitalization of Local Political Life," in *Digital Democracy: Issues of Theory and Practice*, ed. Kenneth L. Hacker and Jan van Dijk (London: Sage Publications, 2000); Zizi Papacharissi, "The Virtual Sphere: The Internet as a Public Sphere," *New Media and Society* 4 (2000): 9–27; Peter Dahlgren, "The Public Sphere and the Net: Structure, Space, and Communication," in *Mediated Politics: Communication in the Future of Democracy*, ed. W. Lance Bennett and Robert M. Entman (Cambridge, Mass.: Cambridge University Press, 2001); Mark Poster, "Cyberdemocracy: The Internet and the Public Sphere," in *Virtual Politics: Identity and Community in Cyberspace*, ed. David Holmes (London: Sage Publications, 1997); and Anthony G. Wilhelm, *Democracy in the Digital Age: Challenges to Political Life in Cyberspace* (New York: Routledge, 2000).

41. Jurgen Habermas, *The Structural Transformation of the Public Sphere: An Inquiry into a Category of Bourgeois Society* (Cambridge, Mass.: MIT Press, 1989).

42. Michael Hauben and Ronda Hauben, *Netizens: On the History and Impact of Usenet and the Internet* (Los Alamitos, Calif.: IEEE Computer Society Press, 1997), 244.

43. See Rheingold, *The Virtual Community*.

44. Sassi, "The Controversies of the Internet," 90.

45. Papacharissi, "The Virtual Sphere."

46. Poster, "Cyberdemocracy: The Internet and the Public Sphere," 220.

47. Wilhelm, *Democracy in the Digital Age*, 7.

48. Cass Sunstein, *Republic.com* (Princeton, N.J.: Princeton University Press, 2001).

49. George A. Hillery Jr., "Definitions of Community: Areas of Agreement," *Rural Sociology* 20 (1955): 118.

50. Art Gallaher Jr. and Harland Padfield, eds., *The Dying Community* (Albuquerque: University of New Mexico Press, 1980), 3.

51. Bender, *Community and Social Change*, 6–8. See also Galston's analysis of Bender in "(How) Does the Internet Affect Community?" Good examples of traditional sociological approach to community studies include Roland Warren, *The Community in America* (Chicago: Rand McNally, 1963); and Talcott Parsons, *Structure and Process in Modern Societies* (New York: Free Press, 1960), 250–79.

52. Philip Selznick, "The Communitarian Persuasion," in *Communitarianism and Citizenship*, ed. Emilios A. Christodoulidis (Aldershot, United Kingdom: Ashgate, 1998), 20.

53. Jeffrey Abramson, "The Internet and Community," *The Emerging Internet: The 1998 Report of the Institute of Information Studies* (Washington, D.C.: The Aspen Institute, 1998). Available at www.aspeninst.org/ publications1/bookstore_communications_emerging_community.html (accessed June 30, 2002).

54. Alexis de Tocqueville, *Democracy in America*, vol. 2 (1840; rpt., New York: Vintage Books, 1945).

55. L. Jean Camp, "Community Considered," in *Democracy.com? Governance in a Networked World*, ed. Elaine Ciulla Kamarck and Joseph S. Nye Jr. (Hollis, N.H.: Hollis Publishing, 1999), 66.

56. James E. Katz, Ronald E. Rice, and Philip Aspden, "The Internet, 1995–2000: Access, Civic Involvement, and Social Interaction," *American Behavioral Scientist* 45 (Nov. 2001): 405–19. Also see James E. Katz and Ronald E. Rice, *Social Consequences of Internet Use: Access, Involvement, and Interaction* (Cambridge: MIT Press, 2002) and UCLA Center for Communication Policy, "The UCLA Internet Report: Surveying the Digital Future, Year Three," February 2003, available at www.ccp.ucla.edu (accessed September 1, 2003).

57. Barry Wellman, Anabel Quan Hasse, James Witte, and Keith Hampton, "Does the Internet Increase, Decrease, or Supplement Social Capital? Social Networks, Participation, and Community Commitment," *American Behavioral Scientist* 45 (November 2001): 436–55.

58. Sherry Turkle, "Virtuality and its Discontents," *American Prospect* 24 (Winter 1996): 50–57.

59. See Anita Blanchard and Tom Horan, "Virtual Communities and Social Capital," *Social Science Computing Review* 16 (Fall 1998): 293–307.

60. See Andrea L. Kavanaugh and Scott J. Patterson, "The Impact of Community Computer Networks on Social Capital and Community Involvement," *American Behavioral Scientist* 45 (November 2001): 469–509.

61. Dhavan V. Shah, Nojin Kwak, and R. Lance Holbert, "'Connecting' and 'Disconnecting' with Civic Life: Patterns of Internet Use and the Production of Social Capital," *Political Communication* 18 (2001): 141–62.

62. Blanchard and Horan, "Virtual Communities," 295.

63. For information on the history and development of the BEV, see www.bev.net.

64. Kavanaugh and Patterson, "The Impact of Community Computer Networks," 497.

65. Kavanaugh and Patterson, "The Impact of Community Computer Networks."

66. Putnam, *Bowling Alone.*

67. See the society's website at www.nationalgeographic.com.

68. Wellman et al., "Does the Internet."

69. H. N. Hirsch, "The Threnody of Liberalism: Constitutional Liberty and the Renewal of Community" *Political Theory* 14 (August 1986): 423–49.

70. R. H. Coase, "The Nature of the Firm," *Economica* 6, no. 4 (1937): 423–35; O. E. Williamson, *Markets and Hierarchies* (New York: Free Press, 1975). Also see Frederick W. Taylor, *The Principles of Scientific Management* (1911; rpt., New York: W.W. Norton, 1967).

71. For an excellent discussion of postbureaucratic organization, see Charles Heckscher and Anne Donnellon, eds., *The Post-Bureaucratic Organization: New Perspectives on Organizational Change* (Thousand Oaks, Calif.: Sage Publications, 1994).

72. Thomas W. Malone, Joanne Yates, and Robert I. Benjamin, "Electronic Markets and Electronic Hierarchies," *Communications of the ACM* 30, no. 6 (1987): 484–97; Heckscher and Donnellon, *The Post-Bureaucratic Organization*; Michael Best, *The New Competition: Institutions of Industrial Restructuring* (Cambridge, Mass.: Harvard University, 1990); Walter W. Powell, "Neither Market nor Hierarchy: Network Forms of Organization," *Research in Organizational Behavior* 12 (1990): 295–336; Francis Fukuyama, *The Great Disruption: Human Nature and the Reconstitution of Social Order* (New York: Free Press, 1999).

14

Toward Civic Intelligence: Building a New Sociotechnological Infrastructure

Douglas Schuler

> While what we call intelligence may be distributed in unequal amounts, it is the democratic faith that is sufficiently general so that each individual has something to contribute, and the value of each contribution can be assessed only as it entered into the final pooled intelligence constituted by the contributions of all.
>
> —John Dewey[1]

TECHNOLOGICAL AMBUSH?

In a recent issue of *Wired*, computing pioneer Bill Joy[2] unveiled a trio of apocalyptic scenarios that he believes could play out in the not-too-distant future. These unpleasantries, resulting from unrestrained, unprincipled, and unregulated genetic engineering, nanotechnology, and robotics (GNR), can be added to the list of big nightmares of the twentieth century (such as environmental disasters and nuclear and bacteriological warfare, which may yet plague us). Each of these technologies, according to Joy, could abruptly unleash problems on so vast and unprecedented a scale that any of humankind's responses would be completely overwhelmed. That such a notable "priest" had so seriously challenged the central teachings of the technocratic church was not missed by the U.S. media, as the story was featured on the front page of the *New York Times* and other prominent newspapers.

Ironically, computers are at the forefront of the problems Joy describes; those catastrophes would be inconceivable without them. Computers, in fact, are the only indispensable element in each of three problems. Joy's scenarios center on technological development outstripping humankind's ability to control it. Unfortunately, according to Joy, the "fail safe points" may already be behind us. A variant on Malthusian predictions (much disparaged but impossible to disprove) may be finally bearing the bitter fruit that Malthus foresaw. The planet's burgeoning population and its deteriorating environmental condition, coupled with humankind's propensity toward disagreement and strife, its disregard for nature, and its penchant for exploiting its innermost secrets, may provide an ideal set of preconditions for a sudden and profound technological ambush.

Joy, of course, is not alone in his warnings. Indeed, our era could be characterized as the age of such warnings. Many scientists have documented the monumental changes like global climate change or extinction of the world's fishes that humankind is currently unleashing on the natural environment. In another recent article, scientists concluded that the human-originated changes currently being wrought on the planet have attained the magnitude of a geologic force.[3] Nobody knows the consequences of ignoring these changes. Yet it is a matter of obvious importance to the inhabitants—human and otherwise—of the earth. A cavalier disregard may be catastrophic. Our own ingrained—and institutionalized—habits may be the biggest barrier to intelligent responses to current and future crises.

Anticipating and possibly averting ecological and other nightmares would likely require changes to our ways of thinking and acting; changes that, depending on their scope and severity, are likely to be extremely difficult to enact. People are loath to change patterns developed, cultivated, and rationalized over a lifetime. Humankind, similarly, is unlikely to modify cherished habits to avert problems of the future based on contested evidence of new circumstances, especially ones that may not seem appropriate to their lives.

In Joy's view, human extinction within a generation is possible. Assuming that his predictions (and ones catastrophic if less apocalyptic) are even remotely possible, an obvious task for humankind is to determine what can be done to understand the situation, avert potential disasters, and develop a more sustainable relationship with our social and natural environments. The equally important but less obvious issue is identifying the underlying conditions that would help make even a partial resolution of the problems conceivable. This chapter describes these conditions and how the idea of a "civic intelligence" might play a useful role.

THE WORLD BRAIN AND OTHER UTOPIAN VISIONS

Joy's concerns, and others like him, formerly were found only in science fiction, as it is that genre where technological and social possibilities are most creatively explored. I would like to invoke the memory of H. G. Wells, the English science fiction writer, historian, generalist, and visionary, who did not live to see the Internet or other recent technological achievements. Wells was not just a science fiction writer who integrated technological scenarios with social issues and outcomes; he was also a historian who searched for broad historical patterns: "I dislike isolated events and disconnected details."[4] Wells was also deeply concerned about the human condition and devoted considerable thought to the prospects of enlightened social amelioration. He discussed, for example, in the 1930s a number of collective problems that would become increasingly apparent in the following seventy years or so (including environmental problems and weapons of mass destruction).

Wells believed that there was a "conspicuous ineffectiveness of modern knowledge and . . . trained and studied thought in contemporary affairs." As a collective body, we are failing to address collective problems in spite of immense individual talent and specialized knowledge. In his quest for possible antidotes, he dismisses all types of ideologies and religions as unsuitable. He also rejected rule by "some sort of elite, in which the man of science and the technician will play a dominating part." Bill Joy, of course, would be a member of such a group, even though that group is responsible to some degree as the perpetrator of the challenges that Joy warns about. Wells places his faith in "science" and not "men of science." Science in his view should "enlighten and animate our politics and determine the course of the world." To this end, he asks, "Is there any way of implementing knowledge for ready and universal effect?" His answer is a world encyclopedia that would provide an intellectual backbone for the human race, a "world brain" that "would do just what our scattered and disoriented intellectual organizations of today fall short of doing. It would hold the world together mentally."[5]

Wells placed his faith in the establishment of a world encyclopedia, a single artifact packaged as a series of bound volumes that would apparently be so accurate that people would have little choice but to make the right collective decisions based on diligent study. Unfortunately, very few people could afford to purchase this set of volumes and fewer still would read them in their entirety and absorb the knowledge therein. Nor is the existence of facts tantamount to the existence of "objective" interpretations of the facts or obvious policies or courses of action based on those facts. "Facts" have meaning only when interpreted, and they have power only when they have consequences. Without saying so directly, Wells suggests that society becomes more "intelligent" by making its citizenry more mindful of the facts.

Perhaps the most ambitious project along these lines was the one proposed by the German philosopher Leibniz. Leibniz was an advocate for artificial intelligence some three hundred years before its official inception. Leibniz conceived of an invention that would be a type of artificial patriarch, almost a god. He immodestly proclaimed in 1679 that his "invention uses reason in its entirety and is, in addition, a judge of controversies, an interpreter of notions, a balance of probabilities, a compass which will guide us over the ocean of experiences, an inventory of all things, a table of thoughts, a microscope for scrutinizing present things, a telescope for predicting distant things, a general calculus, and innocent magic, a non-chimerical Cabal, a script which all will read in their own language; and even a language which one will be able to learn in a few weeks, and which will soon be accepted amidst the world." The system had two extremely powerful components: 1) a universal representation system and 2) a universal calculus for ratiocinating over the facts in the system's vast information stores. Leibniz anticipates Joy's concerns but, unlike Joy, appears to be an uncritical promoter at least of the particular manifestation that he envisions. He presupposes that some type of ultrarational system could actually be constructed and that it could— and would—be used for decision making that was best for all; the idea that the system could be somehow subverted or misused was not considered.

History indeed has furnished us with a host of projects that would enlighten us in some near-mechanical fashion. These include Bacon's House of Solomon, Otlet's Office of Documentation, and Palais Mondial. Some years earlier, in 1888, the prominent American pragmatist, John Dewey, also believed that what was wrong with society was a failure of intelligence and information. Dewey, along with support from Franklin Ford, a financial journalist, planned to offer his own version of a "world brain" in the form of a weekly newspaper entitled "Thought News." This ill-fated idea was universally panned, and Dewey and Franklin failed to produce a single issue of the "Thought News."

Schemes such as those advanced by the visionaries above always fall short of their utopian objectives; they usually fail to recognize one or more fundamental barriers that stand in the way. Their projects are often disconnected from social realities. Some of the projects, Wells's world encyclopedia, for example, would depend on the ability to mobilize large numbers of people in the development of some single artifact. On top of that, there is little or no social or cultural desire demonstrated for the product nor evidence that it would be used at all, much less with the utopian results envisioned by the encyclopedia's prime advocate.

What many visionaries fail to notice is that a grand idea, however obvious to the perpetrator as a "solution," must be coherently embedded in a system of existing social forces, institutions, and conceptualizations. While we ultimately will discuss some ideas for a "world brain" that avoids the undoings of the other utopian projects, we will first examine two additional arguments why establishing a "world brain" or other utopian scheme is difficult.

THE "IMPOSSIBILITY" OF DEMOCRACY

The cooperation of the people is likely to be necessary for any required changes in our techniques for addressing the problems that Joy and others have presented. Cooperation that is willingly embraced through noncoercive means is more reliable and more easily sustained. For those reasons, it appears that democracy in one form or another may be necessary. In addition, the potential reach and malleability of the Internet and other new communication technologies further suggests that it may be possible to devise applications, services, and institutions within the evolving world communication network that would support and strengthen these democratic approaches. Communication, certainly, is key to any effective democratic system. Projects along these, while reminiscent of Wells' world brain visions, would need to be more aligned with the preconditions that support conceptual and technological innovation if they are to be used and useful.

Democracy, as nearly everybody knows, is highly flawed in practice: The wrong people can become elected for the wrong reasons and do the wrong things once in office. Candidates can be favored for their tousled hair, their dimpled smile, their lineage, the slogan du jour. Once in power, elected officials may acquiesce to special interests[6] or be undermined through media-induced scandal.[7] Running for office (in the United States) is so costly that only the very rich have any chance of getting elected. (The most recent New York state Senate race cost over one hundred million dollars.) The role of the media, lobbyists, rich patrons, professional public relations campaigns, and dirty tricks further frustrate any attempt to understand or to participate meaningfully in the "democratic process."

The task of collective self-rule—democracy—has been called an impossible task. Indeed, its impossibility can even be "proved" in much the same way that engineers had "proved" that bee flight is impossible. The task of democracy—if it's done remotely well (so the story goes)—is so exacting, so all-encompassing, yet so frustrating and ultimately unpredictable, that it's been called an "impossible" enterprise. Walter Lippman,[8] in particular, was skeptical of the idea of an "omnicompetent" citizen who possesses sufficient knowledge to participate effectively in the political process. Lippman notes that even though civic affairs was his professional avocation, he was unable to monitor the relevant data, initiatives, and ideas that he believed would be minimally necessary for him to sustain competence in this area. To be minimally competent in the area that this chapter addresses, for example, a person should be well-acquainted with democratic theory, world systems, communication technology, political economy, public policy, environmentalism, the state of the world, and many other topics. Each of these areas is characterized by shifting opinions, initiatives, and discourses, in addition to an overabundance of empirical, verifiable data (whose interpretations are then disputed). (Interestingly, as Wells points out, our elected leaders themselves are far from omnicompetent. Their chief skills, campaigning and political maneuvering, are, in large part, responsible for their success, while their competency in other matters may be underdeveloped.)

A similar criticism can, of course, be directed toward any elite body, however humanely and well disposed they are toward governing the rest of the citizenry. But does Lippman's critique render democracy "impossible," or merely the idea of "omnicompetence" and its purported indispensability? I would claim the latter. Reality is unfathomably complex and we are each incapable of "knowing" even one aspect in its totality. But, impossible or not, democracy or some approximation of democracy is not optional. Decisions have to be made. We have no choice but to cultivate systems of governance that can help us constructively engage with our collective concerns. Lippman's critique is valuable, but not to support the conclusions for which it was originally marshaled. Lippman demonstrates the fallibility of basing a system of governance on the idea of omnicompetency. Indeed, any system of governance should assume the impossibility of omnicompetence and the inescapable reality of imperfect competence, while not allowing ourselves to be defeated by it. This means, in software parlance, turning a "bug" into a "feature." It may be, in fact, the impossibility of omnicompetence that makes democracy the only viable choice for a system of governance.

DUMBING DOWN THE CITIZEN

In the early 1970s, Harry Braverman's "Labor and Monopoly Capital"[9] demonstrated how the process of "dumbing down" workers, primarily through severely reducing their on-the-job responsibility, flexibility, and autonomy (often called "de-skilling") increases management control and, hence, profits to the advantage of capital. As we will soon discuss the idea of civic intelligence, we may hypothesize briefly about whether these ideas may also have some applicability outside the workplace. Is it possible that the citizenry is being dumbed-down in similar ways? And, if so, can we run the processes in reverse to undo the damage?

The key to Braverman's analysis is the decomposition of broad workplace responsibilities by management into discrete constituent parts, which are then used to force workers to perform within circumscribed ranges. This process, often done in the name of "efficiency," dramatically lessens the scope and directionality of worker power. How could this process be replicated in realms outside of the workplace? The first responsibility to be jettisoned (as "outside" their primary work responsibility) in the civic sphere under such a redefinition would be the consideration of issues relating to general social implications. Workers and labor unions should focus exclusively on jobs and job security (and not, for instance, on the social consequences of the jobs); artists should explore and express their individual feelings; scientists and researchers should pursue what is fundable within a narrow, specialized niche (computer science, physics, and other "technical" disciplines would expel implications of their subject matters from the curriculum) while measuring success purely in terms of monetary return on investment. Citizens of course would spend much of their nonworking life shopping for items that would maximize their individual comfort and status while keeping the economic machine running at maximum capacity.

This general process removes the "politics" of labor, leisure, and learning; indeed it naturally results in the de-skilling of the citizen. Economists are the pioneers in this process by adapting and advocating the use of an economic calculus as the sole determinant for all of our decisions. This is the ultimate dumbing down; it reduces human aspirations and agency to that of a greedy and unthinking automaton. The media "de-skills" the citizenry in several ways as well, according to a variety of scholars. Castells,[11] for example, shows how the media's fixation with political scandal encourages cynicism and political disengagement on the part of the citizenry. The media often promotes "the spectacle"[10] at the expense of the intellectually taxing. The ill effects of money on the media, politics, and elections also further increase the distance between citizens and public affairs.[12] Furthermore, Robert Putnam shows convincingly that, at least in the United States, the virtually overnight spread of commercial broadcast television was a primary culprit in the steady degradation of American civic life over the last several decades.[13] One can only wonder what effects this new electronic "opiate of the masses" will have as it continues its spread on cultures outside the United States.

The questions as to whether and to what extent citizen "de-skilling" has been orchestrated, and by whom, will not be discussed in depth in this chapter (although the transformation of the United States from a country of citizens to a country of consumers is certainly an appropriate and provocative topic to contemplate in this regard). It is sufficient to say that civic de-skilling is likely to dampen civic intelligence by influencing the content of, and the conditions under which, issues are placed on the public agenda, and by trivializing and polarizing discussion and deliberation on important public matters. Certainly each de-skilling step introduces changes in both institutionalization, the prescribed processes through which actions are advanced and validated, and in conceptualization of what everyday life entails; each step helps erect ordinary and extraordinary barriers to civic intelligence.

WHO—OR WHAT—WILL GOVERN?

If the dire scenarios that Bill Joy describes (or the less dramatic but no less worrisome environmental catastrophes that atmospheric and other scientists warn us about) have even a minuscule chance of occurring, an urgent need to consider ways to avert them arises. As "solutions" to these problems are likely to be protracted and multipronged and involve large segments of the citizenry, a correspondingly urgent need to analyze the preconditions underlying the development and successful implementation of these "solutions" also arises. What "environments"—social and technological—would be hospitable to the satisfactory resolving of these problems? If we could imagine humankind finding better responses to our myriad problems old and new, what circumstances and resources need to be in place and what steps could be taken that would support these new responses? These preconditions and steps we can call "civic intelligence."

What choices face us in the design of this "civic intelligence"? What attributes could it have? One hypothetical expression of "civic intelligence" would be a massively complex computer system that would make intelligent decisions on society's behalf. This option would be a twenty-first century manifestation of Leibniz's dream, a terrifying cybernetic Frankenstein-on-a-chip from the same cupboard of nightmares that Joy opened in his *Wired* article. The limitations of this approach are manifold but are worth briefly mentioning; the impossibility of accurately, adequately, and comprehensively representing infinitely complex situations with discrete computer logic comes to mind, as do the problems surrounding the implementation of the decisions. Would police or other armed organizations receive their instructions from such an "intelligent" system? The problem of the biases and assumptions of the system's creators becoming embodied—forever?—in such a system is also a sobering and disturbing thought. Imagine an International Monetary Fund (IMF) "expert system" free to impose economic "restructuring" on hapless regions according to the arcane theorems of economists!

Other approaches that rely more heavily on intelligence of the nonartificial variety include having a small elite group making the decisions, nobody making decisions (let the "free market" reign, for example), or a system in which citizens play a strong role. Political scientist Robert Dahl suggests that these three systems—dictatorship, anarchy, and democracy as well as "polyarchy," a hybrid of the others—constitute the entire list of possibilities.[14]

Wells suggested that scientists (at least in his day) would sometimes yearn for a society that would apply their (eminently reasonable) principles and clamor for their leadership, and Lippman believed that an elite group should govern because of the impossibility of omnicompetence. What Lippman didn't acknowledge was that omnicompetence is impossible for small groups as well as for individuals. America's "best and brightest," for example, engineered America's tragic war with Vietnam. Regardless of the role of an elite, the non-elite citizenry will necessarily also have a strong role to play. If an elite group, for example, devises solutions or sets of solutions, they'd then have the thankless and potentially impossible job of "convincing" (through rational appeal, propaganda, or force) the rest of us to accept their jeremiads and prescriptions. A democratic approach, on the other hand, would be to enlist the aid of the citizenry at the onset as part of the overall project. The population or at least a large majority may need to "buy in" and adopt—without coercion or deception—ideas and actions that would be unacceptable without suitable participation in the process that developed those ideas and actions.[15] A more radically democratic view (and the one that might ultimately be seen as the obvious choice) is that the often neglected, sometimes dumbed-down citizenry might provide the intelligence, creativity, energy, and leadership that is needed to recognize, formulate, and reconcile the problems that we are faced with.

As we have seen, governance shouldn't be entrusted to an omnicompetent elite or an infallible computer system. Both are impossible to achieve. Nor should governance place its faith in blind luck through the fantasy that the status quo and/or the "free market" will miraculously solve current problems and avert future ones through benign and unanticipated side effects. A democratic system of governance, then, is the only viable alternative and civic intelligence that is strongly democratic—in spite of the problems previously discussed—shows the greatest promise for an effective and equitable system of governance. This approach increases distribution of creativity and attention while, at the same time, reducing concentration of power away from those people with vested interests in maximizing their gain (often short-term) over the gain (often long-term) of the larger population. There is mounting evidence that this democratization is occurring. As Bill McKibben points out, the vast majority of Seattle's anti-WTO protesters were demonstrating on behalf of somebody else, an impossibility according to homo economicis.[16] Keck and Sikkink report that "advocacy networks" "often involved individuals advocating policy changes that cannot be easily linked to a rationalist understanding of their 'interests.'"[17] An effective and equitable system of governance would help promote the creativity of the civic sector, which is, as others remind us,[18] responsible for launching the major social movements of the last century, including the environmental movement, civil rights movement, and the women's movement.

CIVIC INTELLIGENCE AND HUMAN INTELLIGENCE

Civic intelligence, as I propose it, is relatively prosaic: It is humankind's ability to effectively address issues collectively. (The term has nothing to do with the metaphysical musings on "global consciousness," "hyperintelligence," and the like, which some expect to miraculously and spontaneously emerge, ushered in by global communication networks.) Like the intelligence of an individual, civic intelligence is a relative form that can be less or more effective and creative. Thus it can be developed incrementally through human effort, not through sudden inexplicable revolution anticipated by faith or spiritual longing. Civic intelligence extends the notion of social capital[19] to include an agenda, an orientation toward action in addition to one of observation and study. By transcending the individual, civic intelligence adds another level to the idea of intelligence. Civic intelligence is a form of collective intelligence. It is a premise of this chapter that this type of intelligence, probably to a much higher degree than an individual's intelligence, can be improved and made more effective. How people create, share, and act on information is crucial to that.

Intelligence implies an orderly process for assessing situations, considering possible responses, and determining and enacting appropriate actions. It also implies looking into the future insofar as that is possible and making decisions in the present that will help make future situations advantageous at best, tractable at worst. Sometimes, of course, this will require the postponing of expected benefit. Another important element of intelligence is the ability to acknowledge changing circumstances and adapt appropriately. Plans and other templates for action are indispensable; unfortunately they're not infallible.

Intelligence is the latent capability to interpret, respond, and survive. Its reference point is human and the seat of intelligence is the human brain. The human brain is, of course, a remarkable organ, one whose complexity is unmatched in natural or human-made products. The brain stores information in the form of memory and in reflexive and habitual patterns of responses. It takes in information about the environment in a variety of forms—from "low-level" sensory data to highly symbolic and abstract conceptual information. It integrates all of this information, helps to regulate all the systems and functions in its body, and is largely responsible for the body's thoughts and actions. Although the brain (and the nervous system) is the organ where thought and decision occur in the human body, it is certainly not in charge of everything; it can't, for example, decide to deprive the left foot of nutrients. This contrasts with social systems, which are more reconfigurable, at least in theory. The government, for example, can decide to stop funding health care programs or subsidies to weapon developers. It is also important, for communication in the human body and for our analytic purposes, to realize that although the collection of systems that constitute the human body (or, even, the brain) is an integrated whole, the relationships of its subsystems aren't wholly cooperative; there are conflicting needs and requests that can't all be met. Conflict—and the need to resolve conflict—is crucial in both individual and collective intelligences.

Most of these activities of intelligence are below the level of consciousness, and the decisions that the brain makes are generally habitual and definitely not optimum or correct in any sense. ("Correctness" by itself with no implied or explicit criteria is impossible to demonstrate. A "bad" or "incorrect" decision in the short run can arguably lead to a much better result in the longer term. But—similarly—better in terms of what?! And when is the decision evaluated? And how much did a particular decision contribute to a situation?) There is simply too much (or too little) information—information that is misleading or inaccurate—inadequate time for processing information, and underdefined criteria for evaluating decisions to determine whether decisions are "correct." "Muddling through"[20] is not merely an interesting side note but the defining characteristic of any "intelligent" activity. For that reason, this is a core problem that "civic intelligence" (or democracy) must contend with. This fact, however, does little to obviate the critical need to improve humankind's ability to evaluate and improve its collective decisions.

As I am not a brain specialist (nor omnicompetent), I am unable to go into great depths relating brain-oriented intelligence to civic or socially oriented intelligence. It would be interesting to see how far others would go with this analogy and where they believe it fails. Certainly there is a rich vein—too rich to be mined here—of work in this area. My assumption is that the metaphor only goes so far and that a too literal interpretation and "force-fitting" of data into theory (and, perhaps ultimately, into people's consciousness and policy) would be counterproductive. Nevertheless, some additional exploration of issues raised would be useful. One of these issues is the relationships of the individual entities—people, to be less ambiguous—in a "world brain" to each other. Are some of the individual people less important? What if their demise would lead to a better life for everybody else? Should the part be sacrificed for the whole? Also, what degree of autonomy should individuals be granted? Should people be treated as some type of functional unit whose freedom should be curtailed and behavior routinized for some greater good? The fact is that society has embraced many of these decisions already through innumerable mechanisms over the millennium. I argue that relaxing some of these mechanisms, the current restrictions on behavior and roles, and moving away from both "rationalized" and traditional constraints, will actually be more "intelligent" and this reconsideration will help engender a collection of civic information, processes, and attitudes that will help society as a whole deal with its collective problems.

Below I present some preliminary considerations for a new world brain or civic intelligence that is based on and addresses current social and technological realities. Similar to the approach taken by Leibniz, Dewey, and Wells, I am proposing an approach that builds on the development and use of appropriate communication and information systems. Of course humankind's communication and information systems are currently undergoing massive changes at the global level. The civic intelligence challenge is to develop programs, applications, and policies that help shape this juggernaut into useful forms. We need to ask in what ways can connecting a huge and potentially unruly and fractious group of people from a multitude of cultures and life circumstances help society as a whole deal more effectively and equitably with problems and other issues of shared concern.

PATTERNS OF CIVIC INTELLIGENCE

Following the pioneering insights of Christopher Alexander and his colleagues,[21] I propose creating a set of patterns for developing improved civic intelligence. This discussion of patterns is tentative and incomplete, as it is my first attempt at elaborating these ideas; it is not a "general theory" of civic intelligence, but an assortment of ideas that, hopefully, can help undergird such a theory at a later date. There are six basic pattern categories in this proposal for increasing civic intelligence: orientation, organization, engagement, intelligence, products and projects, and resources.

- Orientation describes the purpose, principles, and perspectives that help energize an effective deployment of civic intelligence.
- Organization refers to the structures, methods, and roles by which people engage in civic intelligence.
- Engagement refers to the ways in which civic intelligence is an active force for thought, action, and social change.
- Intelligence refers to the ways that civic intelligence perceives, analyzes, compares, debates, and *learns* over time.
- Products and Projects refers to some of the outcomes, both long-term and incremental, that civic intelligence might produce.
- Resources refers to the types of support that people and institutions engaged in civic intelligence work need.

ORIENTATION

A thriving civic intelligence must stress values that support social and environmental meliorism while acknowledging and respecting the pragmatic opportunities and challenges of specific circumstances. A central idea of a thriving civic intelligence is that an inclusive democratic mobilization and strengthening of the civic sector is necessary for the purposes of addressing social inequities, human suffering, environmental devastation, and other collective concerns, including the social management of technology. Castells describes how the civic sector has been responsible for initiating the major social movements of our era, including civic and human rights, environmentalism, peace, and feminism.[22] In *Activists beyond Borders*, Margaret Keck and Kathryn Sikkink state that networks of activists are "distinguishable" from other players in international, national, regional and local politics "largely by the centrality of principled ideas or values in motivating their formation."[23]

Unlike many previous "utopian" projects that ignored social realities, a realistic approach to cultivating civic intelligence must be more pragmatic by recognizing what factors promote innovation and by developing programs with these in mind. It is also possible to help develop and promote the factors themselves. In *The Evolution of Technology*, George Basalla suggests that three preconditions must be present in order for a technological innovation to succeed:

- Existing models to extend and build on;
- A social environment that values the innovation;
- Intentions, skills, creativity, and dedication of the innovator.[24]

And to these three I would add a fourth:

- Adequate resources for the innovator.

This fourth factor acknowledges the important role of resources for promoting innovation.

Although the innovations we're considering are primarily social and secondarily technological, Basalla's observations are pertinent. A civic intelligence would help promote social innovation by helping ensure that these four preconditions were met. Each of these preconditions should be in place for civic intelligence innovations in all projects, large and small, and one of the objectives of any civic intelligence project should be improving the base of preconditions for future innovation. As a matter of fact, the entire civic intelligence endeavor might be summed up as a way to ensure that these preconditions are continuously improved and strengthened and made to reflect abiding human values. In terms of Basalla's preconditions, a civic intelligence orientation would help foster a social environment that values civic intelligence innovations, motivates the creation and marketing of suitable models, inspires and educates potential innovators, and identifies and distributes resources.

Organization

As the purview and resources of this project are distributed throughout the world, a global civic intelligence project is also distributed all around the world. It needs to be undertaken "everywhere at once" to be successful. Also, as there is no central force or institution with the skills, resources, or authority to direct the effort, the idea of a centrally controlled hierarchical organization is irrelevant. The organizational structure of critical intelligence becomes a medium of people and institutions who communicate with each other and share information. This network is necessarily composed of a wide variety of dissimilar institutions and individuals who cooperate with each other because of similar values and commitments to similar objectives. Neither authoritarian directives nor market transactions could provide the adhesive that would hold this evolving, shifting, growing network together.

This particular type of organization has, of course, unique strengths and weaknesses. As Keck and Sikkink point out in their discussion of advocacy networks, a network's lack of "power" in the traditional senses has made these networks largely invisible to the research community.[25] Yet it is a result of these "weaknesses" that the individuals and organizations constituting the network must employ different strategies and organize themselves differently to get their jobs accomplished. Indeed, "intelligent" use of information and communication has evolved and become a significant feature. The number and effectiveness of what Keck and Sikkink call "transnational advocacy networks" has exploded in recent years. In 1909 there were 176 international organizations according to the Yearbook of International Organizations. By 1996 the number had swelled to over 20,000.[26] The success, also, of the open source or Free Software Movement (GNU, Linux, and the like) demonstrates the feasibility of large, distributed, loosely organized networks oriented toward the development of technologically sophisticated not-for-profit products. The preconditions Basalla mentioned are doubtlessly contributing to this growth: motivated innovators, a somewhat receptive audience, and the resources to develop and maintain the necessary information and communication capabilities all currently exist.

An effective network depends on many factors, and understanding these factors will be key to improving the existing civic intelligence and anticipating and countering any threats to it. Probably the most important pattern to keep in mind is consciousness of the network itself. To a participating individual or organization, this means that they need to be an active, respectful, and intelligent member of the network. They also must know that the network is in some sense alive; it must be sustained as well as used. Although some competition exists between members or nodes in the network(s) or civic intelligence, success in whatever endeavor will depend to some degree on others. This will vary according to the skill, interests, and philosophical outlooks of the individual members. Providing ideas, contact information, references, or other information that other members of the network can use is an important way to contribute to the network. Discussion among network participants helps identify critical issues and resolve internal divisions. The discussion of issues also lays the groundwork for the important transition from a discussion orientation to an action orientation. Projects provide an important focusing mechanism as an "opportunity structure." Finally, the networks should be accessible: important democratic interchanges take place at the "margins of power,"[27] and these marginal political settings should be encouraged to grow and, also, to be integrated with traditional nonmarginal political settings.

Engagement

Engagement is both a tactic and a philosophy. Engagement as a tactic means that the elements of the civic intelligence networks do not shy away from interactions with the organizations, institutions, ideas, or traditions that are contrary to the objectives of the network. These organizations and the like may be promoting or perpetuating human rights abuses or environmental damage. They may also be thwarting civic intelligence efforts by their adherence to exclusion or other types of civic dumbing down. Engagement, of course, assumes many forms. A civic intelligence should, of course, behave intelligently. This means that the nature of the engagement should be based on the precepts of this paper—it should be principled, collective, and pragmatic, for example. But at the same time, engagement is a philosophy and it represents an everyday and natural predisposition toward action; it represents a challenge and an acknowledgment that the status quo, although not likely to be good enough, can be improved. Engagement, ideally, is flexible, nimble, and appropriate for the situation. Timing plays an important role in appropriate engagement. Research and study also have critical roles to play, but they must not be used as a substitute for action, postponing engagement while waiting for "all the facts to come in." (See note 28 for a good antidote to this malady.)

The recent experiences in Seattle of demonstrations against the World Trade Organization in 1999 show that large numbers of people, even in a relatively prosperous city, share strong feelings (often vague and unarticulated) that many trends of today's society are heading in the wrong direction and that many of society's "leaders," both individual and institutional, are not leading adequately; their objectives, modus operandi, and integrity are compromised to dangerous levels. During the week of anti-WTO demonstrations, one representative from a protesting organization stated in a radio interview that "It shouldn't be necessary to break glass" to put issues on the public agenda. A functioning civic intelligence would, ideally, help put shape and meaning to citizen unease with some of the directions of global capital and bring these issues up for public discussion. This would, theoretically, help prevent some of the ruptures, riots, and wars that result from unresolved civic grievances. An effective and fully functioning civic intelligence would make it unnecessary for some people to "break glass" to be heard. The space in which these voices can be heard—and can confront the voices of power—is called, in a broad general sense, the "public sphere" by Jürgen Habermas.[29]

Intelligence

A central conceptual ingredient of this chapter is, of course, that of intelligence. This may be the trickiest aspect of the concept due to the diversity of views on what "intelligence" is. This section will attempt to elucidate in what ways our conceptualization of a "civic intelligence" could be labeled as intelligent and what people can do to develop this capability.

Intelligence implies that a reasonable view of the situation exists (or can be constructed) and that reasonable actions based on this view can be conceived and enacted on a timely basis. Clearly, the creation and dissemination of information and ideas among a large group of people are crucial. Learning is important because the situation changes and experimentation has shown itself to be an effective conceptual tool for active learning. Therefore, some of the key aspects include: 1) multidirectional communication and access to information, 2) discussion, deliberation, and ideating, 3) monitoring, 4) learning, 5) experimenting, 6) adapting, and 7) regulating. As the concept of civic intelligence begins to be more fleshed out, these aspects would be turned into patterns in the sense that Alexander and his colleagues intended.

Let's briefly touch on one aspect of intelligence—monitoring—and some examples of new civic uses. Technology, it turns out, ushers in both challenges and opportunities. We find, for example, that at the same time our technology and economic imperatives are creating vast problems, it is also introducing some provocative new possibilities for our civic intelligence model. One recent innovation, a system employing seven Earth-orbiting satellites, enables us to monitor Earth's vital signs from space.[30] While the system doesn't specify what we, the Earth's inhabitants, will do with the data, it's clear that we wouldn't have a good picture of the state of the Earth without it. This type of surveillance can expose other events to public scrutiny; it was the French "Spot" satellite that first alerted the world to the Chernobyl disasters. Also, unlike previous enterprises, this project makes its data readily and cheaply available to people all over the world. The existence of "emergency response networks"[31] provides excellent examples of provisional networks that can be erected in a relatively short time to meet specific threats to public health or welfare.

Projects and Products

Projects, both campaign and product-oriented, help motivate and channel activity. An extremely wide number of projects are important within the context of cultivating a civic intelligence. There is ample evidence that the "project" is necessary to marshal sufficient force to accomplish the desired goals.[32] One such example is the manifesto or declaration that communication activists have been developing in recent years, often in conjunction with conferences. These collective statements offer a distillation and articulation of their beliefs and objectives, which they hope will then be used to help undergird future projects and products. Recent examples include the People's Communication Charter, the Papallacta Declaration, the Bamako Declaration, and the Seattle Statement. The People's Communication Charter is an initiative of the Third World Network (Penang, Malaysia) and the Center for Communication and Human Rights (Amsterdam, the Netherlands) and was one of the first and most far-reaching of these statements. The charter presents a holistic view of communication and covers a wide variety of important communication issues, including respect and freedom, literacy, protection of journalists, cultural diversity, participation, justice, and consumption. Key to their approach is the idea that people must be vigilant about defending their "communication environment."

Besides seeking ratification from individuals and organizations, one idea has been to launch an "International Tribunal" to hear complaints and evidence related to issues in the charter. The Seattle Statement was developed at CPSR's symposium Shaping the Network Society, an explicit attempt to broaden the conversation on civic uses of new digital network technology. It was then promoted via e-mail, and signatures were harvested electronically and added, sorted by country of origin, to the electronic list on the Web. The impacts of these statements are hard to forecast and identify. Inexpensive global communication via e-mail, is making this easier—at least to those with access. The Seattle Statement was reportedly used within Hungary to instigate discussion and help raise interest in public networking projects.

The Neighborhood Knowledge Los Angeles (NKLA) project as a broad partnership between academia and the community is a good example of a holistic approach to civic intelligence.[33] One aspect of NKLA is its "early warning system" in which housing conditions in Los Angeles are monitored. In 1995, for example, census figures showed that 107,900 apartments were infested with rats and 131,700 had no working toilets. (Of course we must multiply this figure by several orders of magnitude to get a realistic feel for the actual scope of this worldwide.) NKLA has been compiling "early warning" information of this sort (including, for example, tax delinquencies, building code violations, unpaid utility bills, etc.) onto their website, which is then used by community organizations to devise solutions—including policy work and engagement with government—to their problems. NKLA, along with countless other communities, is engaging in mapping community assets to help community members find out about useful resources—often unnoticed and underutilized in their own midst.

Good projects combine important ideas into a compelling form that people can readily understand and become involved with, and that result in desired change. Two recent innovative projects from Seattle show promise for meeting those criteria. The first project, Sustainable Seattle, is a project that identifies and defines measures or "indicators" that, measured over time, will reveal whether or not Seattle is becoming more or less "sustainable." The project was a citizen initiative, not instigated by the government or by business. Moreover, the civic sector set the agenda—sustainability—not any number of other possible choices that business, government, or even other civic sector organizations may have devised. The set of indicators, discussed and disseminated, now can be used as an ongoing foundation for civic intelligence, developing programs and policies for promoting sustainability. Noting how the values of the indicators are related to each other can also reveal hidden connections and suggest innovate programs. Incidentally, the presence of the indicators on the Web has helped and will continue to help similar projects around the world. The Sustainable Penang project, for example, was launched after activists in Penang saw Sustainable Seattle's indicators on the Seattle Community Network.[34]

Another civic intelligence project was also recently launched. The "Technology Healthy City" project with financial support from the City of Seattle is intended to take a series of information and communication technology (ICT) "snapshots" over time to assess the impact of technology on the region. The project thus far has been citizen-led: One of the explicit caveats was to devise indicators that were designed for the civic sector's benefit. As ICT is widely acknowledged as having major effects on the psychic as well as physical aspects of the region, it will be interesting to see what role, if any, this project can assume in ongoing assessment and actions related to the use and effects of ICT in the region.

Resources

Adequate resources, including time, money, physical facilities, communication capabilities, and focused initiatives for people and institutions, are necessary but not sufficient for effective civic intelligence. Although it would be difficult to measure the magnitude of the need for these resources, the overall project can't wait until all the "necessary" resources are at hand before starting. At the same time, helping ensure that adequate resources do exist is critical for the project.

CHALLENGES

Positive change is not impossible, although all major social and environmental changes, such as the abolishment of slavery in the United States, probably appeared impossible at the onset of the struggle. It also needs to be pointed out that positive change is not inevitable either; there is no inexorable trend that we can rely on to save us. Slavery is gone, but new forms of quasi-legal servitude that would be considered slavery by any other name are becoming increasingly common. Similarly, the practice of torture, however antiquated it may seem, is also still pervasive throughout the developing—and developed—world. [35] The propensity toward evil as a result of individual or institutional intent will always haunt us. History is ruled by ebbs and flows of immeasurable complexity. At the same time, people are the major architects of change—both good and bad.

The biggest challenge of course is to accomplish anything at all that leaves the social or environmental situation in a better state than it was before. Many efforts viewed from the advantage of hindsight seemed doomed at the onset; history, it was said, was "against them." Yet in some cases, history surprised us and the "impossible" was accomplished. The campaign to abolish slavery in the United States took over a century to accomplish its aim. Yet, even now, its tragic legacy persists, providing grounds for future social movements. When social or environmental ills exist, it is society's responsibility to address those problems despite bad odds. Unless the area of amelioration is uniquely immune, focusing on the task to be accomplished is more likely to obtain results than wishful thinking, the "free market," historical "inevitability," or just a run of good luck. We can only move forward by principled action based on what we expect and where we want to go from where we are. An effective civic intelligence links individual efforts with other individual events into networks that can accomplish greater goals than results generated through individual efforts. If these networks become powerful enough to help bring about broad-based positive changes in the world, then more effective civic intelligence can be said to exist.

As in the case of the movement to abolish American slavery, the "advocacy networks" that Keck and Sikkink examined can emerge, accomplish (or not accomplish) their objective, and then apparently wither away. In many cases the skills honed in one campaign are put to use in the next. For example, there is substantial evidence that the woman's suffrage movement in the United States was aided greatly by campaigners, ideas, and techniques acquired during the antislavery campaign. While individual campaigns may still pass through these life cycle phases, the spectacular rise in the number of transnational nongovernment organizations and advocacy networks suggests that a new era of heightened civic intelligence has arrived.

The question then arises in relation to responses of institutions outside the network. If this type of civic intelligence becomes more prevalent and powerful, it would likely become specifically targeted by those people and institutions that are threatened by it. If, at some point in the future, these new types of civic intelligence become sufficiently powerful (and it appears to be already happening in some cases), they will come into conflict with other existing institutions, network based or not, that perceive themselves as threatened. Indeed, if they didn't come into conflict it would be either very peculiar or strong evidence that the networks themselves presented no threat to the status quo through either their impotence or their adoption of less threatening objectives. In any event, it is not the case that strong institutions are powerless in the face of heightened civic intelligence. There is no reason to presume that they are intrinsically incapable of counterattack.

Although gazing into a crystal ball is an inexact science, it seems clear that countertactics could be employed. As information and communication are key to civic intelligence, the key to neutralizing the effects of an active, engaged, and effective civic intelligence would be found there. Many of these tactics have, of course, already been used. In the 1960s, for example, the United States government developed the secret COINTELPRO program based largely on disinformation and character assassination to disrupt and discredit the Black Liberation Movement and the Antiwar Movement. U.S. corporations sometimes create "Astro-turf" front organizations based on economic incentives that mimic public interest organizations that have no economic stake in the issue. Thus, the Farmers for Fairness funded an extensive soft-money media campaign against a politician working for environmental controls on hog manure disposal in North Carolina. And *The Wall Street Journal* reported that Microsoft and other companies have employed people to monitor Usenet news groups for unfavorable comments about their products and post (from a neutral, noncompany address) comments to counter the negative claims. This "info warfare" makes it much more difficult, of course, for the average citizen to obtain the information needed to participate meaningfully in addressing societal issues.

TOO LITTLE, TOO LATE?

Unfortunately, humankind's problems may be so profound, and our ability to respond so divided, unmotivated, and feeble, that attempts to deal with them are doomed to failure. "Grand schemes" such as Wells's World Encyclopedia, Dewey's Thought News, Kochen's WISE, and Jungk's Everyman Project, have periodically sprouted up, attracted a modest following, and then faded away, apparently without a trace.[36] The proponents are likely to be dismissed as cranks by the media and by the conventional wisdom of the era; their schemes are generally utopian, overly ambitious, and, ultimately, unrealistic.

What can we do to ensure that our civic intelligence project is not dismissed as yet another crank scheme? There are two possible strategies. The first is avoid risk by lowering the expectations, goals, and rhetoric. We can dispense with the idea that we are historical actors who are capable of leaving a positive mark on the world. We can become thoughtful observers and theoreticians, for example. We can decide to forgo the idea of social and environmental amelioration, of civic intelligence, and retreat into academicism—or cynicism. The second approach is to ground our enterprise into the context and realities of our era and devise a program that suits the demands of our

lives and our livelihoods, but is based on values and social needs. It is probably possible to shape one's perspective incrementally to make one's work
more consciously supportive of a civic intelligence if that transformation is pri-
oritized. Research—be it academic study or "street level" information-gather-
ing and assessment—can play a critical role and a wide variety of academic
disciplines have important roles to play.[37] Research can and should be a tool
that continually is brought to bear on the shifting, evolving realities of life.

Academics, stereotypically, are noted for their lack of emotional engagement. This is the purported product of rationalism: a cold, calculated, dis-
passionate assessment or mere reportage of data. But unless designed for entertainment alone (if that is even possible), any text, academic or
nonacademic, will have implications for use. Use, of course, may bring with
it a challenge on the world as it exists, a potential for altering the present
course or shoring up the status quo. If the change is deemed important and
the process through which the change could take place is plausible, hope is
not unthinkable. Despair, on the other hand, exists when positive change is
inconceivable, the future, presumably advancing toward a precipice, appears unalterable.

This project builds on the notions of networked groups of people and institutions that are working both within their own communities and outside
and across traditional boundaries using new communication and information technologies where necessary and appropriate. The novelty of this plan
lies with the focus on the civic sector as a force capable of consciously and
pragmatically constructing more intelligent capabilities. Beyond that I have
identified some tentative patterns that, if pursued, will help cultivate that intelligence. This chapter is not intended to provide a blueprint for the future.
It's only intended to identify and attempt to pull together a number of reasonable suggestions based on the need for a renewed and stronger sense of
civic intelligence. Critique may be easier to generate than action plans; it is
also easier to digest as it asks for very little in the way of action, except, perhaps, for righteous indignation. Action plans also are necessarily based less
on evidence and are inescapably proscriptive. Thus academics (whose written and spoken outputs have been circumscribed in various ways) are likely
to eschew them. I hoped to integrate critique and activism in this chapter.

Most people prefer a just social world that offers opportunities for a meaningful life to all people. An environment that was safe and free of toxins and
capable of providing sustenance and enjoyment now and for generations to
come would likewise be among their preferences. Yet it is tacitly assumed
that these goals are too utopian and that they can never happen, or, paradoxically, that they're the natural consequence of capitalist, neoliberalist development, and all society has to do is stay the course. It is acknowledged,
of course, that arriving at this inevitable destination will take generations and
some people (*poor* people, presumably) will necessarily have to suffer as

part of this "natural" process. It is the central contention of this chapter that it is possible to harbor meliorist beliefs—and even act on them—without being a crank. The opposite of this view would be difficult to embrace: That we are so dumbed down that we cannot contemplate any improvements to our own civic intelligence.

> When it becomes a program, hopelessness paralyzes us, immobilizes us. We succumb to fatalism, and then it becomes impossible to muster the strength we absolutely need for a fierce struggle that will re-create the world.
>
> —Paulo Freire[38]

NOTES

1. John Dewey, "The Democratic Form" (address before the National Educational Association, February 22, 1937) in *Intelligence in the Modern World: John Dewey's Philosophy*, ed. J. Batner (New York: Random House, 1939).

2. Bill Joy, "The Future Doesn't Need Us," *Wired* (April 2000), available at www.wired.com/wired/archive/8.04/joy_pr.html (accessed October 10, 2003).

3. Tom Karl and Kevin Trenberth, "The Human Impact on Climate," *Scientific American* (December 1999): 100–105.

4. H. G. Wells, *World Brain* (Freeport, N.Y.: Books for Libraries Press, 1971).

5. Wells, *World Brain*.

6. William Greider, *Who Will Tell the People?* (New York: Simon and Schuster, 1993).

7. Manuel Castells, *End of Millennium, The Information Age: Economy, Society, and Culture*, volume 3 (Oxford: Blackwell, 1998).

8. Walter Lippman, *The Phantom Public* (New York: Harcourt, Brace and Company, 1925).

9. Harry Braverman, *Labor and Monopoly Capitalism* (New York: Monthly Review Press, 1998).

10. Manuel Castells, *The Power of Identity, The Information Age: Economy, Society, and Culture*, volume 2 (Oxford: Blackwell, 1997).

11. Marjorie Garber, Jann Matlock, and Rebecca Walkowitz, eds. *Media Spectacles* (New York: Routledge, 1993).

12. Douglas Schuler, "Part of the Solution? Computer Professionals and the Next Culture of Democracy," *Communications of the ACM* (January 2001): 52–57.

13. Robert Putnam, "The Strange Disappearance of Civic America," *American Prospect* 7, no. 24 (December 1, 1996): 34–48.

14. Robert Dahl, *Democracy and Its Critics* (New Haven, Conn.: Yale University Press, 1989).

15. Carole Pateman, *Participation and Democratic Theory* (Cambridge: Cambridge University Press, 1970).

16. Bill McKibben, "Muggles in the Ozone," *Mother Jones* (March/April 2000): 13.

17. Margaret Keck and Kathryn Sikkink, *Activists beyond Borders: Advocacy Networks in International Politics* (Ithaca, N.Y.: Cornell University Press, 1998).

18. Castells, *Power of Identity.*

19. Robert Putnam, *Bowling Alone* (New York: Simon and Schuster, 2000).

20. C. Lindblom, and D. Cohen *Usable Knowledge: Social Science and Social Problem Solving* (New Haven, Conn.: Yale University Press, 1979).

21. C. Alexander, S. Ishikawa, and M. Silverstein, *A Pattern Language: Towns, Building, Construction* (New York: Oxford, 1977).

22. Castells, *End of Millennium.*

23. Keck and Sikkink. *Activists beyond Borders.*

24. George Basalla, *The Evolution of Technology* (Cambridge: Cambridge University Press. 1988).

25. Keck and Sikkink, *Activists beyond Borders.*

26. Curtis Runyan, "Action on the Frontlines," *Worldwatch* (November/December 1999): 12–21.

27. Jonathan Barker, *Street-Level Democracy: Political Settings at the Margins of Global Power* (West Hartford, Conn.: Kumarian Press, 1999).

28. Carolyn Raffensperger, "Defining Good Science: A New Approach to the Environment and Public Health," in *Doing Community Based Research*, ed. Danny Murphy, Madeleine Scammell, and Richard Sclove (Amherst, Mass.: Loka Institute, 1997).

29. Jürgen Habermas, *The Structural Transformation of the Public Sphere: An Inquiry into a Category of Bourgeois Society* (Cambridge, Mass.: Polity, 1989).

30. M. King, and D. Herring, "Monitoring Earth's Vital Signs," *Scientific American* (April 2000): 72–77.

31. Larry Roeder, "The Global Disaster Information Network" *ASIS Bulletin* (October/November, 1999), available at www.asis.org/Bulletin/Oct-99/roeder.html (accessed February 3, 2004).

32. Keck and Sikkink, *Activists beyond Borders.*

33. Neighborhood Knowledge Los Angeles, available at nkla.sppsr.ucla.edu/index .cfm (accessed February 3, 2004).

34. Douglas Schuler, *New Community Networks: Wired for Change* (Reading, Mass.: Addison-Wesley, 1996).

35. Harold Pinter, "Cruel, Inhuman, Degrading," *New Internationalist* (September 2000): 16; John Conroy, "Up for It," *New Internationalist* (September 2000): 20–21.

36. Wells, *World Brain*; Alan Ryan, *John Dewey and the High Tide of American Liberalism* (New York: W.W. Norton & Company, 1995); Manfred Kochen, ed., *Information for Action: From Knowledge to Wisdom* (San Diego: Academic Press, 1975); Robert Jungk, *The Everyman Project: Resources for a Humane Future* (New York: Liveright, 1977).

37. Douglas Schuler, "Community Computer Networks: A Critical Opportunity for Collaboration among Democratic Technology Researchers and Practitioners," in *Technology and Democracy: User Involvement in Information Technology*, ed. David Hakken and Knut Haukelid (Oslo: Center for Technology and Culture, University of Oslo, 1997), 53–71.

38. Paolo Freire, *Pedagogy of Hope: Reliving Pedagogy of the Oppressed* (New York: Continuum, 1992).

Index

Contributors

Philip E. Agre is associate professor of information studies at UCLA. He is the author of several articles on social aspects of computing, and author, coauthor, or editor of books including *Computation and Human Experience* (Cambridge, 1997), *Technology and Privacy: The New Landscape* (MIT, 1997), and *Re-inventing Technology, Re-discovering Community* (Ablex, 1997).

Maria Bakardjieva is assistant professor in the faculty of communication and culture at the University of Calgary. She is the author of several published articles on social and cultural aspects of information technology, including articles in *Media, Culture, and Society, New Media and Society, The Information Society*, and *Journal of Ethics and Information Technology*. She is coeditor of *How Canadians Communicate* (University of Calgary Press, 2003), and her book *Making Sense of the Internet in Everyday Life* is forthcoming from Sage.

Darin Barney is assistant professor of communication at McGill University and 2002 Hixon/Riggs Visiting Professor of Science, Technology, and Society at Harvey Mudd College. He is the author of *Prometheus Wired: The Hope for Democracy in the Age of Network Technology* (Chicago, 2000) and *The Network Society* (Polity, 2004).

Bruce Bimber is associate professor of political science and communication and director of the Center for Information Technology and Society at the University of California at Santa Barbara. His books include *Information and American Democracy: Technology in the Evolution of Political Power*

(Cambridge, 2003) and *Campaigning Online: The Internet in American Politics* (with Richard Davis, Oxford, 2003).

Albert Borgmann is Regents Professor of Philosophy at the University of Montana. He is the author of *Technology and the Character of Contemporary Life* (Chicago, 1984), *Crossing the Postmodern Divide* (Chicago, 1992), *Holding On to Reality: The Nature of Information at the Turn of the Millennium* (Chicago, 1999), and *Power Failure: Christianity in the Culture of Technology* (Brazos, 2003).

Hubert Dreyfus is professor of philosophy in the graduate school at the University of California at Berkeley. He is the author of *What Computers Still Can't Do: A Critique of Artificial Reason* (MIT, 1992), *Being-in-the-World: A Commentary on Heidegger's Being and Time* (MIT, 1991), *Heidegger and Foucault on the Ordering of Things* (California, 2000), and *On the Internet* (Routledge, 2001).

Amitai Etzioni is university professor at George Washington University. His books include *The Monochrome Society* (Princeton University Press, 2001), *Next: The Road to the Good Society* (Basic Books, 2001), and *The Limits of Privacy* (Basic Books, 1999). A former president of the American Sociological Association, he has also served as a senior advisor to the White House.

Andrew Feenberg is Canada Research Chair in the Philosophy of Technology at Simon Fraser University. He is the author of *Critical Theory of Technology* (Oxford, 1991), *Alternative Modernity* (California, 1995), *Questioning Technology* (Routledge, 1999), *Transforming Technology* (Oxford, 2002), and *When Poetry Ruled the Streets* (SUNY, 2001).

Tetsuji Iseda received his PhD in philosophy from University of Maryland in 2001, and now serves as associate professor in the graduate school of information science at Nagoya University, Japan. He is the author of *Gijikagaku to Kagaku no Tetsugaku* (Philosophy of Science and Pseudoscience), (Nagoya University Press, 2002).

Diane Johnson recently completed her PhD in political science at the University of California, Santa Barbara, and is currently a visiting assistant professor at Boise State University. She is working on a book-length project that analyzes the effects of globalization, including the introduction of new media, on press-government relations in Latin America.

Richard Kahn is a PhD student in the social sciences and comparative education division of the graduate school of education, UCLA. He has a chapter forthcoming (with Douglas Kellner) on Internet subcultures in *The Post-Subcultures Reader*, and has written the entry on "Internet and Cyberculture" for the *Ency-*

clopedia of Social Theory. His website is http://getvegan.com, which contains his top-ranked critical ecology blog, Vegan Blog: The (Eco)Logical Weblog.

Douglas Kellner is George Kneller Chair in the Philosophy of Education at UCLA. He is the author of many books on culture, politics, and society, including *Television and the Crisis of Democracy* (Westview, 1990), *Grand Theft 2000: Media Spectacle and the Theft of an Election* (Rowman & Littlefield, 2001), and *The Postmodern Adventure: Science, Technology, and Cultural Studies at the Third Millennium* (Guilford, 2001).

Yumiko Nara obtained a PhD from Nara Women's University in 1996 and is an associate professor at the University of the Air in Chiba City, Japan. She is the coauthor of *Life in Japan: Reflection on Fifty Years of Change and Future Prospects* (Kenpakusya, 2000) and *Exploring New Frontiers on Artificial Intelligence* (Springer Verlag, 2002).

Mark Poster is Chair of the Department of Film and Media Studies at the University of California at Irvine and a member of the history department. He is the author of *What's the Matter with the Internet: A Critical Theory of Cyberspace* (Minnesota, 2001), *The Second Media Age* (Polity, 1995), and *The Mode of Information* (Chicago, 1990).

Douglas Schuler is a faculty member at The Evergreen State College, former chair of Computer Professionals for Social Responsibility, and a founding member of the Seattle Community Network. He is the project director of CPSR's "Public Sphere Project." He is the author or editor of several books, including *New Community Networks: Wired for Change* (ACM/Addison-Wesley, 1996), *Shaping the Network Society: The New Role of Civil Society in Cyberspace* (MIT, 2004), and *Community Practice in the Network Society: Local Action/Global Interaction* (Routledge, 2004).

Leslie Regan Shade is associate professor of communication studies at Concordia University. She is the author or editor of several books, including *Gender and Community in the Social Construction of the Internet* (Peter Lang, 2002), *E-Commerce vs. E-Commons: Communications in the Public Interest* (Canadian Center for Policy Alternatives, 2001), and *Civic Discourse and Cultural Politics in Canada: A Cacophony of Voices* (Ablex, 2002).

Sherry Turkle is Abby Rockefeller Mauzé Professor in the program in science, technology, and society at MIT and director of MIT's Initiative on Technology and Self. She is the author of *Psychoanalytic Politics: Jacques Lacan and Freud's French Revolution* (Guilford Press, 1992), *The Second Self: Computers and the Human Spirit* (Simon and Schuster, 1984), and *Life on the Screen: Identity in the Age of the Internet* (Simon and Schuster, 1995).